PRIMAL LOVE

*

OTHER BOOKS BY DOUGLAS M. GILLETTE

King, Warrior, Magician, Lover: Rediscovering the Archetypes of the Mature Masculine

The King Within: Accessing the King in the Male Psyche

The Warrior Within: Accessing the Knight in the Male Psyche

The Magician Within: Accessing the Shaman in the Male Psyche

The Lover Within: Accessing the Lover in the Male Psyche (Coauthored with Robert Moore)

PRIMAL LOVE

Reclaiming Our Instincts for Lasting Passion

DOUGLAS M. GILLETTE,
M.A., M.DIV.

ST. MARTIN'S PRESS
NEW YORK

LIBRARY OF CONGRESS CATALOGING-IN-PUBLICATION DATA

Gillette, Douglas.
    Primal love: reclaiming love with passion / Douglas Gillette;
foreword by John Bradshaw; preface by Harville Hendrix.
        p.   cm.
    ISBN 0-312-11776-0
    1. Man-woman relationships.   2. Love.   3. Intimacy (Psychology)
I. Title.
HQ801.G447   1995
306.7—dc20
                                                      94–42387
                                                      CIP

First Edition: February 1995

10 9 8 7 6 5 4 3 2 1

For all the courageous men and women
who will not give up their hopes for joy and fulfillment
in each other's arms

CONTENTS

✷

FOREWORD

❋

DOUGLAS GILLETTE has been a pioneer in the awakening of "deep democracy." His past books have made a significant impact on changing the polarized patriarchal power structure that causes so much violence in our world.

His new book *Primal Love* is the state of the art in evolutionary psychology. I absolutely devoured this book, and I know you will too. Once again Doug is offering us balance. The balance between a polarized spiritualism that tells us all is love, and a materialism which tells us to get all we can and "the easy ones twice."

This book offers us an evolutionary genogram and asks us, like the great family systems thinker Murray Bowen, and the great "soul" man Thomas Moore, to know, love, and make peace with the family of our animality.

Especially fascinating is Gillette's summaries of the "hot issues" we have inherited from our primate patterns. They need to be understood just as deeply as the "hot issues" from our families of origin.

I have often said (in jest), show me a happy person, and I'll show you someone who is not in a relationship. Part of the problem in relationships is an unrealistic expectation rooted in an overspiritualized notion of love. We go into our love lives without any biological moorings and try to sustain fierce and passionate sex as disincarnated spirits. No wonder it does not work for the majority of marriages.

I'm sent literally hundreds of manuscripts a year, many of them on relationships. This is the best book on relationshps I have seen in twenty years.

—JOHN BRADSHAW

PREFACE

✳

WHY AND HOW are men and women attracted to each other? What is the real basis of their bond? How should they conduct their relationships? What roles should each take, and why? And what causes so much conflict between them? These questions about the origins, motives, and goals of our intimate partnerships open up the landscape of one of life's greatest mysteries— human love. From the beginning of recorded time, the joyful and pain-fraught alliance between the genders has been the subject of reflection by wise and articulate men and women.

The first answers, given in various creation myths, usually depict our intimate relationships as having a divine origin. In early philosophical speculation, for example that of Plato, men and women are believed to have originally constituted a single entity, an androgynous being of such beauty and power that the gods, in fear and envy, split them into separate sexes and sent them off in opposite directions. Their yearning for each other was their attempt to restore their primal unity. In the folk traditions descended from Greek mythology, attraction between the sexes was the result of Cupid's capricious arrow, and our disenchantment with each other was the wearing off of the divine elixir.

The struggle to understand love—and the loss of it—has now been joined and elaborated by psychology, cultural anthropology, and evolutionary biology. These modern sciences have given a decidedly earthly and historical tone to this enterprise. From the perspective of depth psychology, attraction to a particular kind of person is an unconscious and childlike attempt to reconnect with our early caregivers. Its purpose is to restore the original family setting, either because it is familiar to us, or in order to correct our parents' mismanagement of our earliest emotional development—through our would-be adult relationships. From this perspective, our disenchantment and conflict with each other arise because two "regressive," and thus incompetent, infantile persons fail to meet each other's childhood needs.

From the perspective of anthropology and evolutionary biology, the relationship between the sexes, and the motives both for their bonding and their conflict, tend to be unconscious knee-jerk responses to the "survival directive." At this level, all sexual organisms strive to mate with the most genetically fit members of the opposite gender in order to achieve their own "practical immortality" through the genetic superiority and the long-term survival of their offspring. According to some scientists this is innately true of our human partnerships; personal fulfillment and all other aspects of our lives together—economic, emotional, and social—are secondary. Nature values these functions only to the degree that they serve this primal impulse.

In this volume, Douglas Gillette contributes a brilliant and illuminating chapter to this saga by adding the insights of evolutionary biology and the study of primate behavior to clinical and depth psychology and cultural anthropology. From his perspective, grasping the intricacies of contemporary human male/female interactions requires tracing their origins to the mating rituals, role designations, and parenting patterns, not only of our prehuman hominid ancestors but also of our closest primate cousins. He divides human history into three ages which he calls "jungle time," "savanna time," and "civilization." Because of changing ecological contexts—the receding jungle, the appearance of grasslands, the emergence of villages, and, finally, civilization—each age required certain patterns of bonding and protection, role assignments, and parenting procedures in order to ensure the survival of our children. The adaptive patterns demanded by these ecological changes, in part because of the sheer duration of geological time, produced genetic mutations that were passed down to succeeding generations. The living museum in which many of the rudiments of these changes are apparent and available for study is the world of our closest primate relatives.

Close scrutiny of the variety of patterns in primate male/female interactions provides the imagination with a vivid and instructive picture of the prehistoric relationship between the sexes and offers clues to the complexity and mystery of our contemporary partnerships. This perspective pushes the explanation of mate selection, bonding, adultery, serial marriages, jealousy, divorce, and sex roles beyond depth psychology to our prehuman past and the vicissitudes of survival. While he does not negate the psychological view that much adult behavior in intimate relationships is a repetition of unresolved childhood issues, Gillette is convinced—and he makes a compelling case for his point of view—that marital therapy and all relationship counseling, must be informed additionally by this evolutionary, historical perspective if it is to be comprehensive and effective. I agree.

Adding the insights of evolutionary biology and primate behavior to his understanding of psychology and cultural anthropology, the author has written a clear, compelling story of the history of male/female interactions. This landmark study illumines the mystery of why modern men and women have so much difficulty making their relationships work. Part of the mystery is that most of who we are and the reasons we do what we do in our relationships can be attributed to events which took place before we were born.

All therapists will be helped by this book to see their clients in a broader, more luminous perspective, and since the book is written in clear, simple English, all couples will have access to this powerfully healing material. Integrating Douglas Gillette's insights into their relationship lives will help couples erode the complex mysteries surrounding their partnerships, evoke more empathic self and other understanding, and empower them to take responsibility for their relationships at a deeper, more primal, and paradoxically more *human* level.

—HARVILLE HENDRIX, PH.D.
Author

ACKNOWLEDGMENTS

※

FIRST, I want to express my deep appreciation to Gladys Rios for her careful reading of the manuscript and for her constant support and inspiration throughout the conception, organization, and writing of *Primal Love*. I want to express similar appreciation to Steve Wilson. Both spent many selfless hours giving me their feedback and encouragement. I also want to thank my counselees—individuals, couples, and groups—whose life situations and courage have given me so much to think about and challenged me to see more deeply into the instinctual dynamics we are all struggling with, however unconsciously.

I am deeply indebted to Dr. Harville Hendrix and John Bradshaw for their ongoing support for my work in general and this project in particular. They have both contributed very generous endorsements of *Primal Love*. I also wish to thank John Gray for his enthusiastic support, reflected in part in the glowing affirmation he's allowed me to quote on the jacket. My thanks as well to the primatologist Frans De Waal who spent many hours carefully reviewing the manuscript to be sure my reporting of the results of primate studies was accurate. I'm happy to say the book passed this important test with flying colors. I wish also to express my appreciation to Dr. William Wolf, a professional psychological test designer, who helped me fine-tune some of the self-evaluation exercises. And my thanks to Doug Chamberlain who did a lot of the legwork for some of my research.

In addition, I want to thank my agent, Candice Fuhrman, who worked above and beyond the call of duty to help me shape the manuscript, and whose unwavering faith in this project got me through some difficult moments.

My first editor at St. Martin's Press, Jared Kieling, one of the best editors I have worked with, was accessible, enthusiastic, committed, and enormously helpful in birthing the final version of the manuscript. His questions and criticisms allowed me to clarify a number of points and fill in the blanks where readers might need more information in order to follow my arguments. I also want to thank my second editor, Jennifer Weis, for her central role in marshaling the resources—personal, artistic, and financial—of St. Martin's Press for the promotion of this book. Jennifer guided the painstaking process by which a manuscript becomes a published book. I also want to express my appreciation to Ensley Eikenburg, Todd Keithly and Tina Lee for all their liaison work.

Finally, I am indebted to the researchers and theorists from many fields who have labored so tirelessly to advance our understanding of the many complex issues I've been able to bring together in this book. Some of the people whose work I've relied on most heavily are: Harville Hendrix, John Bradshaw, John Gray, Theodor Reik, Anthony Storr, Anthony Stevens, Alice Miller, and Kalman Glantz and John Pearce—psychologists, analysts, and therapists; Jane Goodall, Frans De Waal, and Desmond Morris—primatologists; Robert Ardrey and Adrian Desmond—ethologists; Helen Fisher, Robin Fox, and Donald Symons—anthropologists; E. O. Wilson—sociobiologist; Paul MacLean—brain researcher; Robert Pool and Anne Moir and David Jessel—synthesizers and popularizers of brain structure and hormonal research into the differences between the sexes.

All these people and many more have my deepest admiration and my profound gratitude.

Introduction:
A Journey of Discovery

✳

The Human Animal

WE HUMAN BEINGS are profoundly mysterious, and we are so in our essence. We are the most complex structures in the universe that we know of, a confusing and painful wedding of animal and angel, of our primordial origins and our spiritual aspirations. Our many-layered depths and heights are never so thrilling and at the same time so agonizing, so transformative and so tragic, as in our most intimate relationships. For those relationships we give our best efforts, realize our most powerful longings and potentials, and sacrifice our own well-being—even our lives. We call the feelings such relationships arouse in us "love."

We are, indeed, complicated, and each one of us is unique. But our complexity, when looked at closely, resolves itself into a definite set of patterns. Even our uniqueness as individuals reveals universal, underlying structures and dynamics that bind us all together in a common experience of love.

It is these patterns that define and drive our intimate relationships. These patterns are not one thing for one person and something entirely different for another. They are constant. They cross the boundaries of cultures and of distant times and places.

How well we learn the inner maps these patterns make, and work with them creatively and even joyfully, determines whether we succeed or fail in our relationships. If long-lasting, enjoyable love is what we want, then it behooves us to get clear about the underlying structures and dynamics that give a universal form to our relationships, to accept the reality of them, and to learn to work *with* them instead of trying to deny their power in our lives.

Psychologists have seen many of these patterns, and ascribed most of them to our childhood experiences. That's certainly part of the truth, and psychology's current focus on rediscovering the inner child has been very helpful for both individuals and couples. Our childhoods do give the final stamp of individuality to the underlying dynamics we all share. But there has been a missing piece to the relationship puzzle without which some psychologists have tended to overpathologize our "issues" in intimate relationships.

They couldn't have done otherwise because it's only been in the last thirty years that we've finally had the tools to understand ourselves on this deepest level, after centuries of ephemeral ecstasy and needless suffering. Those tools, which can revolutionize our approach to the problems of intimacy, have been supplied from what must seem to many like unlikely sources—the sciences of evolutionary biology, anthropology, brain and hormonal research, and primate ethology.

What we now know more clearly than ever before is that we are—thoroughly and completely—*primates*. There is not a single human behavior that is unique to us, or that is not at least prefigured in the other species of our animal family. We are deluxe-model apes. But we are still apes. And no more so than in our love lives.

There is a lot of prejudice against such a startling fact. It seems to deny us our uniqueness as a species with "free will." But then, as poets, philosophers, and psychologists have been telling us all along—and as we know from experience, when we're honest with ourselves—where love is concerned, genuine free will is in short supply.

Denying our natures and shaming the animal within ourselves and our mates is not merely unhelpful. In the end, it ruins our chances for realistic success in our relationships. What we shame and deny does not go away. Instead, it finds ways of sabotaging our happiness. If we can see our underlying animal motives and accept them—in ourselves and in our mates—then we really *are* free to be all of who and what we are. Shamed instincts become compulsions. Freed instincts become a source of life and joy. And life and joy is what we all hoped our intimate relationships would bring us.

Our Primate Patterns

By piecing together three decades of research, we now know that, as personally painful as many of our experiences in love are, they are universal givens of our primate natures. For example, the tendency for many men to marry women who remind them too much of their mothers and then to feel terrifyingly vulnerable to the "power" of their mates, the tendency for both men and women to replay their childhoods in their love relationships, our inclination toward sexual boredom with our partners and the lure of extramarital dallyings, the different and often conflict-generating ways men and women have of being romantic with each other, codependency, emotional withdrawal, overuse of erotic materials ((both verbal, as in romantic novels, and pictorial, as in photo magazines) as substitutes for fulfilling here-and-now love lives, the three- or four-year barrier beyond which most relationships seem to be more work than pleasure—all these things and more are not products, fundamentally, of our wounded childhoods. Instead, they are aspects of our all-encompassing primate natures.

Even common complaints about each other, such as women's accusation that men withhold their feelings, and men's accusation that women voice whatever emotion they happen to have at the moment, are predictable aspects of our primate patterns. Men tend to keep many of their feelings private because to express them might frighten or hurt women, and, contrary to popular misconceptions, primate males, including human males, are programmed to avoid hurting females at almost any cost to themselves. Women tend to be emotionally expressive in part because they don't have such a biologically inherited program for more cautious interacting with males.

Intimacy for men is not fostered by an unmonitored voicing of feelings. And intimacy for women is not possible without emotional sharing. If we want to be happy with each other, we're first going to have to accept the primate basis for this discrepancy, and then we're both going to have to stretch to meet each other halfway, at least a significant part of the time.

Likewise, as we'll see, we get our tendency to smother each

other from our primate heritage. The boy in every man activates a woman's mother program, which a man may then read as critical and domineering. And the girl in every woman activates a man's father/protector patterns, which a woman may subsequently experience as invasive. This is the foundational level for codependency in our relationships.

All these areas of conflict in our love lives—and in the more general war between the sexes—are ultimately generated by our different reproductive strategies. We love each other, we need each other, but we are frightened by the feeling that the other is marching to the beat of a different drummer, especially in terms of his and her sexuality. Women tend to be more emotionally and sexually withholding early in relationships, finally, because they bear an unequal burden of physical, economic, and emotional danger and responsibility for the consequences of their sexual expression. This drives men crazy. A man feels painfully divided between his drive to nurture one woman and the children he has with her (in order to ensure their best chances for survival), and his equally powerful desire to make the best possible use of his millions of sperm, to give himself multiple options for "practical immortality." Evolutionary biologists call this disturbing pattern a "mixed reproductive strategy." This drives *women* cracy.

Both men and women experience partner variety as an important ingredient in the spice of life, but men somewhat more so than women.[1] All of our other differences—the ways we perceive, feel, and think about things, the ways we behave, and our fundamentally complementary interests and enthusiasms—have evolved to make us more interesting to each other, to attract us to each other, and to give more punch to our reproductive strategies.

These strategies were evolved millions of years ago to meet the requirements of environments very different from the ones we now live in. We may experience such a seemingly cold idea as not having anything to do with the joy and pain we're going through with each other. But I would ask you to suspend your disbelief, at least temporarily, and allow for the possibility that there are deeper forces at work in our love lives than meet the eye.

Our reproductive strategies are wired into us as a three-layered patchwork of conflicting desires. Each layer bears the imprint of a distinct ecological habitat from a distant time in our evolution. But all three of our layered adaptations are still present. Nature never destroys an old system and starts from scratch. Instead, when a different environment demands a changed animal, nature develops new structures and pieces them onto the old ones as best it can.

As we'll see, in the oldest layer is the program for a kind of selective promiscuity on the part of both men and women. This has millions of years of forest-dwelling ape evolution behind it.

In the second layer, we find the beginnings of monogamous commitment to each other. This layer evolved to help us survive in a grasslands environment where meat—and hunting—were the main sources of food, and where there were no trees to climb in order to escape the ever-present predators. This situation threw men and women together in pair-bonded couples in which intense cooperation, if not perfect sexual exclusiveness, became the key to the survival of their children.

The third, most recent layer is the idea of sexually exclusive, lifelong monogamous relationship. This is not a biological program in the full sense of the word, though part of it is: the part that comes out of the childhood needs we have for lifelong emotional security and faithful love (from a fantasy parent). This is the result of our ongoing childlikeness as a species. But the other part of this third layer of our primate patterns has been created by culture, mainly as a result of the rise of agriculture and the religions which have supported this relatively recent lifestyle.

In some ways our cultures are *substitutes* for further biological evolution. They allow us to adapt to radically different environments, environments which include our cultural ideals. They extend, rather than change, our underlying biologically based desires.

The problem is that the two oldest layers of our primate patterns in no way prepare the animal part of us to accept being overridden by either our childhood needs or the monogamy ideal. So we are at war with ourselves and with each other. The best many of us have been able to do is to adopt the mixed reproductive strategy of primary commitment to one person and fooling around on the side, either in a lifelong *non*exclusive monogamous way or in a serial monogamy pattern. Others of us, even more strongly influenced by the third layer of our primate inheritance, have resigned ourselves to shutting down sexually. But avoiding sexuality in our relationships is an invitation to disaster. This disaster arrives either in the form of a prolonged period of listlessness, or in one or both partners eventually being unfaithful. Some few couples actually do achieve a lifetime of happiness—including sexual happiness—with each other. Relationship therapists believe these lucky few constitute about 5 percent of the married population.[2]

Among other things the patchwork solutions that nature has crafted for us often lead to fear and anger toward each other. The fact is that men are terrified of women's anger and women are terrified of men's. Beneath the level of our minor irritations with each other, such as when one of us fails to fulfill our part of the daily responsibilities like taking out the trash or fixing dinner, is the level of gender rage.

This rage is now coming to the surface. Men and women in our culture are shaming each other openly, and with an unprecedented viciousness. Each escalation of women's shaming of men, itself partly a response to men's past shaming of women (and vice versa as far back in the history of civilization as we can imagine) is being met by a reluctant but gradually intensifying male shaming of women.

The message of this book is that it's time to stop shaming each other and to get to the heart of the matter.

Part of the way we can stop shaming each other is to realize that none of the dimensions of our love lives is a matter of either/or. They're always both/and. It's not that *either* we love one person *or* want sexual/emotional variety. We want both. It's not that *either* we feel the joy of idealizing each other when we're in love *or* harbor hidden resentment and hostility toward each other. It's that we feel both sets of emotions. It's not a case of *either* being dependent *or* being independent, of being *either* animal *or* human. It's *both/and*. The both/and perspective brings us awareness of the complexity of our relationship situation, and the grace to accept ourselves and our mates as the wonderful and maddening creatures we both are—to ourselves and each other. And awareness and acceptance are the first steps toward reconciliation with each other and toward getting the fulfilling love we each want.

The three layers of our primate patterns are also responsible for the life-enhancing aspects of our intimate relationships. The joy of falling in love, of sharing emotional and material resources with each other, our deep capacity for enduring bonds, for loyalty and intimacy, our desire to "get it right" with the one who's hurt us or whom we have hurt, our innate sense of fair play, our hunger for reciprocity, our delight in complementary personal and work-related roles, our creativity and spontaneity, our powerful and more or less continuous sexual desires, our enormous stores of empathy and compassion, our altruistic urges, our sense of deep satisfaction in parental love and self-sacrifice—for our flesh-and-blood children and for each other's inner child—all these and other dynamics in our love lives are marks of advanced primate natures just as surely as are our expressive faces, our deft hands, and the hair on our heads.

So, we carry our ancient heritage with all its bewildering and contradictory urges with us, and we cannot shake it off—"free love," serial monogamy, our yearning for a lifetime of emotional security.

The question is: How can we become clear about the hidden agendas of the animals at our cores, accept those animals in ourselves and our partners with love and compassion, and learn—together—to convert what have seemed like insurmountable problems into opportunities for real, and long-lasting, happiness?

A Personal Discovery

I used to begin every new relationship with the hope that *this* was *the* one, that I was finally about to resolve the inner conflict between my monogamous marriage ideals and my desire for other women. And I used to agonize when the in-love stage would start to fade, and, with it, the intensity of my sexual passion for the woman I was with. There seemed to be a barrier of two or three years beyond which I couldn't sustain a happy relationship, or my two marriages.

Within that two- to three-year period I encountered the unresolved childhood issues each of us brought to our relationship. We seemed to bounce each other around, one of us playing the critical parent and the other the "bad" child. Then the roles would reverse. Other seemingly intractable, destructive patterns would emerge. Sooner or later irritations would turn to anger; often our discussions and attempts to get to the bottom of our conflicts went nowhere. We'd think we had an issue resolved, but something would still be going on under the surface. We'd chop off one head of the dragon, but it would keep sprouting new ones. With a couple of women who were willing to work in a psychotherapeutic way with me to get at the underlying issues, I spent the money for couples counseling. But that, too, seemed to go nowhere.

I went to therapists on my own as well. They believed that my painfully repeating experience with women was caused by my childhood wounding, by my "mother issues," by my "unintegrated Anima," or just by a stubborn childishness on my part, a Peter Pan complex perhaps. They were partly right.

But after thousands of dollars for therapy and enormous emotional investment, I finally stopped focusing so narrowly, and I started looking at my friends and my own clients with the dawning perspective that relationships might somehow be set up to fail around the third or fourth year. Everywhere I looked there were men and women in the same painful situation.

I started reading everything I could find about gender relations, about anthropology, about human evolution, brain and hormonal research, our sexual inclinations, and about primate ethology—searching for a lost piece of the puzzle. I got much more than I had bargained for. I'd been interested in these fields since childhood, but it had never occurred to me that their findings might really be important for my understanding myself in intimate relationships. I had always accepted the idea that we are primates, but I thought, probably like most of us, that we had left the majority of our animal background behind us 300,000 years or so ago. I was reluctant to surrender my sense of free will. I wanted to believe I had transcended my animal-likeness and could make my personal life whatever I wanted.

But as I read volume after volume of technical research I became convinced that there was a hidden pattern buried in our

animal past that made and then unmade our modern relationships. Gradually I began to accept the notion that these academic
probings might have something direct to say to me about my
personal joy and pain.

I reluctantly gave up the sense of my own omnipotence and
became much more humble. And as I reflected and studied I
began to have "Ah-hah!" experiences. "So *that's* what this is!"
Strangely, I began to feel a sense of relief. My joys and sufferings
were parts of larger tidal forces that pushed and pulled us all.

I began to apply my still murky insights to some of the issues
my counselees were wrestling with, and I was startled by the fact
that no sooner had they seen the primate patterns operating in
their love lives, and lifted the shame from them, than they felt
lighter and freer. They could now make empowered decisions
about their relationships. I saw couples freed to work creatively
together to make their relationships much happier and more fulfilling. I saw some decide, with real enthusiasm and joy, to start
with each other again from this new appreciation for the animal
in themselves and their mates. And I saw others decide to go
their separate ways, but without the degree of mutual blame and
shaming I had seen before.

I had found a missing key. I began creating exercises for the
many groups of men and women around the country and internationally with whom I worked in weekend and weeklong gender
seminars. I developed what I now call the Ape Embodiment Exercise; the Gender-Empowerment Exercise, in which men verbally affirm women's uniqueness and preciousness, and in which women
do the same for men; and the Womb/Phallus Sound Exercise.

The results were astounding. Relationships were often revital-
ized—sexually and in every other way; couples moved beyond
their tense standoffs with each other; and I myself was brought
to greater clarity about the nature of our primate patterns for
love.

About This Book

I have two purposes in writing this book. The first is to give men
and women a powerful tool of self-knowledge, on a level deeper

than current psychology has been able to explore. The second is to help us learn to work *with* our animal natures, not *against* them, so that we make our relationships yield the happiness they seemed to promise when they were new.

This book is thus about lifting the shaming of our animal natures. It's about learning to bring our human capacities for rational thinking and deep compassion into engagement with the animal at our cores, and at the cores of our mates.

Honoring our primate heritage does not mean giving in to its impulses in a wholesale way that denies our humanness. It means that we must take a more careful and appreciative look at our animal motives, at their positive, life and relationship-affirming aspects as well as at their destructive elements, and work to integrate them into our intimate relationships—if we are to make those relationships what we wanted them to be in the first place. I believe the only way to do this, in the end, is to celebrate and channel our animal exuberance.

This book is divided into three parts. Part 1 takes us on a kind of inner safari that links us to the vast sweep of our evolutionary history, a history each of us brings to our relationships along with the more personal aspects of who we are.

Part 2 explores what's *really* wrong in most relationships. It takes a liberating look at gender-based anger between the sexes and shows how our cultures have shamed our animal natures, with disastrous consequences for us as individuals and for our would-be lifelong partnerships. And it shows how our ongoing childlikeness, which is a defining characteristic of our species, is both a blessing and a source of problems for couples.

Part 3 lays out a practical course of attitudinal changes we can make and actions we can take to revitalize our relationships and transform them into joyful, instinctual, and mutually fulfilling bonds. In order for the insights offered and the courses of action recommended to work to best advantage, both partners need to read this book. If getting that to happen is a problem for you, you are about to find out why, and to learn what you can do about it.

PART ONE

✳

A PASSIONATE HERITAGE

1

DELUXE-MODEL APES

❋

An Extended Family

OUR FAMILY BACKGROUND is exciting. It's made up of bug-eyed tarsiers and ring-tailed lemurs, of fierce dog-faced mandrills and chest-beating giants. All of us—tarsiers, lemurs, Old and New World monkeys, the lesser apes, the great apes, and the deluxe-model ape—*us*—are smart, emotionally resilient, impressionable, creative, and curious about our environments. Some of us become astronomers. Others create new art forms on the forest floor.[1] Some of us are expert nut crackers and termite fishers.[2] We all have stereoscopic vision and thumbs we can use as tools. We all have nails instead of claws. We all love our children (at least as best we know how).

Our different ecological environments and evolutionary histories have developed us both to keep our common family heritage and to adopt very different ways of life. We've developed and had wired into our brains many different ways of organizing our societies and experiencing our romantic and sexual relationships.

A few of our species are naturally monogamous.[3] Some of us prefer harems.[4] Many of us are enthusiastically promiscuous. Some species, including humans, hunger for a variety of approaches. The vast majority of our females come into estrus or "heat" when they're ready to make babies. In one of our species, *Homo sapiens,* the females have curiously evolved to *hide* the signs of their most fertile periods. Most of the females in our extended family have rear-entry vaginas. A few species have frontally tilted vaginas. As a consequence, we can enjoy face-to-face lovemaking.

Most of our family lives in trees. A few of us live on the ground part of the time. And a number of us, like some baboons and most humans, live on the ground all the time—except of course when we're space-shuttling or playing on the moon.

In some of our societies females hold administrative positions.[5] In most, their power comes mainly from emotional forcefulness, "moral-suasion," and the personality "imprinting" of our young.

Some of us, like orangutans, are loners. A few of us organize our societies as matriarchies. Most of us live in patriarchal arrangements of one kind or another. Our loner family members have discovered that food resources are scarce in their neighborhoods, and that going it alone is better than trying to feed a whole tribe. Our matriarchal species live in more or less danger-free environments with plenty of food. Patriarchal species have evolved to help us survive in life-threatening ecological systems.[6] The greater the dangers—especially from predators but also from hostile bands of the same species—the tighter the patriarchal control.[7] From the more easygoing patriarchies of the so-called Barbary apes (really a species of monkey), which share some of their power with females, to the military dictatorships of the savanna-dwelling mandrills, most primate species are headed by what biologists call an "alpha male." But politicians—male and female—flourish in all our primate communities.[8]

In many of our species some division of labor between the sexes has evolved.[9] Our two genders have specialized to one degree or another in various physical and psychological aptitudes and abilities. In almost all of us, females show powerful mothering impulses which are biologically based but which often have to be fine-tuned through teaching. In most, males show great enthusiasm for their protector roles. But these, too, often have to be refined through varying forms of "boot camp." In a few species, including our own, males show a desire to be involved fathers. In most they show much greater interest in career advancement and power politics.

Our closest relatives in this rich, diverse family tree are the great apes—the orangutans, gorillas, chimpanzees, and bonobos (the so-called "pygmy chimpanzees"). And of these by far our *closest* relatives are the chimpanzees and bonobos. Chimpanzees live in modified patriarchies in which everyone has a voice, including the females, in who gets to be alpha male. Bonobos live in modified matriarchies that keep the outer trappings of patriarchy, but in which the real power is in the hands of the females.[10] Our brother and sister species make and use tools, create culture, eat both vegetables and meat, have a working knowledge of medicinal herbs, teach their children, and honor good mothers, alpha males with character, and warriors and hunters, and feel deep bonds of friendship and empathy for each other.[11] They're also *very* sexy. Both chimpanzees and bonobos are inveterately promiscuous, but they also occasionally fall in love.

In *all* the great apes we can see prefigurations of relationship patterns that we ourselves know very well.

Mirror, Mirrror

In Michael Crichton's *Jurassic Park* the distant ancestors of birds—dinosaurs—are resurrected after 70 million years. They're reconstructed by extracting fragments of their DNA from mosquitoes locked in ancient amber and mixing them with frog DNA.

A wonderful thing for anthropologists, psychologists, and anyone trying to understand human beings with subtlety and depth is that we don't have to extract ancient DNA and reactivate it to have *our* ancestors alive again and walking among us. They're already here—the great apes, especially the chimpanzees and bonobos—*especially* the chimpanzees. Technically they're not actually our ancestors. But they're so close to us that researchers comparing our characteristics with theirs—our social structures, our aptitudes and abilities, our psychologies, and our DNA—can draw detailed conclusions about what our common ancestor was almost certainly like.

Pulling together the work of many other primatologists and anthropologists, Michael Ghiglieri has mapped the social and gender-relations similarities and differences between chimpanzees, bonobos, and humans in general terms.[12] The following table is my own adaptation of some of his findings.

SOCIAL CHARACTERISTICS	CHIMPANZEES
Friendships and socializing between females:	Due to common attraction to males
Character of these female bonds:	Generally weak but may include mutual aid and occasional adoption of orphans
Types of social groups:	Many related males: organized into dominance hierarchy which can be characterized as patriarchal; communities closed to outsiders; many females who associate as friends
Mating system; mate sharing:	Many sexual partners and promiscuous mate sharing
Territoriality; defense by males; level of aggression:	Community territory defended by related males; expansion achieved by killing males outside the group
Competition between males for females:	Deadly between communities; occasionally within the home community
Male investment in fatherhood:	Slight, but cases of orphan adoption exist
Difference in male/female size:	Moderate difference; males are 123% the weight of females
Retention of younger males within the group:	Usual (uncommon among the other primates)
Tendency of females to leave the home group:	Common

BONOBOS	US
Due to common attraction to males and perhaps territory	Due to work situations, voluntary organizations, and friendships through marriage
Generally weak but often includes the sharing of vegetable foods (not meat), mutual grooming, and mutual sexual stimulation	Stronger than in the other apes and includes much sharing of resources, but only as long as their nuclear families are not deprived
Many related males; organized into dominance hierarchy which can be characterized as "officially patriarchal"; communities closed to outsiders; many females who associate in their own dominance hierarchy, a hierarchy which, in the end, may be more powerful than the male hierarchy	Many related males; many culturally determined variations of dominance hierarchy systems most of which can be characterized as patriarchies; communities somewhat open to outsiders; many females who generally are not organized into hierarchies as stringent as male hierarchies, and whose status is largely determined by that of their mates
Many sexual partners and promiscuous mate sharing	Many sexual partners and limited promiscuous mate sharing; only marginally effective cultural sanctions in favor of monogamy; a "double standard" which may be ultimately based on different male and female reproductive strategies usually applied
Community territory defended by related and allied males; fighting between male groups defending different territories can be serious but seldom if ever fatal	Community territory defended by related and allied males in extraordinary cooperation for primates and showing signs of intense male bonding; expansion achieved most often (but not exclusively) through lethal warfare
Intense between communities, much less so within the home community	Can be deadly between communities, less so within the home community
Slight, but greater than among chimpanzees; includes food sharing and grooming	Greatest among the apes but generally less than female investment in mothering
Moderate; males are 136% the weight of females	Moderate; males are 120% –130% the weight of females
Usual (uncommon among the other primates)	Usual (uncommon among the other primates)
Seems to be common	Very common

As we can see, our human, chimpanzee, and bonobo ways of organizing our societies and experiencing our relationships are very similar. We know from DNA studies and research into the rate of genetic mutation that bonobos split off from our common chimpanzee-human line about 3 million years ago—*after* we and chimpanzees had split (between 7 and 5.5 million years ago).[13] This means that bonobos developed in a way that may not be as relevant to our understanding of ourselves as chimpanzees are. Still, bonobos may have evolved to exaggerate or emphasize some tendencies already present in our common ancestor.

Interestingly, as we'll see, both bonobos and human beings are "neotenous," or childlike, chimpanzee species, and we share many physical, psychological, and social similarities with each other. This probably means that our similarities existed as potentials in our ancestor of 7 million years ago even though our two species evolved separately, under different environmental pressures, and in a *parallel* way.

An example of this is the more or less equal status of bonobo males and females and our own human potential for developing a similar kind of equality. We almost certainly will never develop the more nearly matriarchal societies that bonobos have because different evolutionary forces were at work in our formative stage on the savannas of East Africa than were at work in the formative stages of bonobos. The savanna environment seems to have further tightened the patriarchal tendencies our common ancestor most likely possessed. And yet it's still true that when given more secure environments we do tend to move away from strict patriarchal systems and toward more bonobo-like social arrangements. This is strong evidence for the idea that while probably somewhat patriarchal our common ancestor also embodied matriarchal social elements.

Primatologists such as Jane Goodall, Frans De Waal, Duane Rumbaugh, and Suehisa Kuroda, anthropologists such as Helen Fisher, Donald Symons, and Robin Fox, ethologists such as John Hurrell Crook, evolutionary biologists such as Ernst Caspari, and sociobiologists such as E. O. Wilson, and many others in these fields, have shown that the similarities between our three species are much more specific than my version of Ghiglieri's table indicates. But by putting Ghiglieri's overview of our general characteristics together, and making allowance for some uncertainty about which characteristics were *dominant* in our common evolutionary past, we can make an educated guess as to what our common ancestor was like—his/her social life and the nature of his/her relationships. That vital, creative, sexy being still lives in the jungle time of our deepest desires. (We'll get a glimpse of this magnificent animal at our human cores in chapter 3.)

Biology is *not* destiny—not quite. Our cultures do a lot to *modify* our instinctual patterns. But no amount of training can *eliminate* them. Our evolutionary heritage is far more evident and powerful in our human lives than we have been led to believe. Its influences are often subtle, especially if we look at them one by one, or from the isolated perspective of a single scientific field. But when we add them up and place the findings of a number of sciences side by side, we witness an amazing convergence of the data as their independent conclusions reinforce each other—not only in terms of the broad outlines but also in terms of the details of our probable evolutionary journey as a species.[14] We begin to see the powerful impact of biology on our lives. This is as true for our love lives as it is for every other aspect of our humanness.

2

BEYOND THERAPY

❋

Our Ecstasy, Our Pain

MAGDA AND CHARLIE were from two very different cultures. She was from Veracruz, Mexico, a city known for its seaside fiesta atmosphere and its sexually active women. Charlie was from a medium-size industrial city in Illinois, known for its Protestant work ethic.

They met at a mutual friend's house in Charlie's hometown when Magda was there on vacation. They were immediately attracted to each other, and after Magda returned to Mexico they started a lively correspondence. They also supported the phone company. Charlie flew down to Veracruz five times in the next six months. One romantic evening, as they were walking along the palm-lined beach, he asked Magda to marry him. She said yes. Six months after that, they were holding their gala reception in the central plaza of Veracruz. Then they were off for what they later described as a "paradisal" honeymoon on the pirate island of Curaçao in the Netherlands Antilles, where they made nonstop love for a week, pausing only to gaze into each other's eyes and share the remaining secrets of their hearts.

But within three years Magda and Charlie were locked in a war of attrition. One of the reasons Magda had married Charlie was to escape what she believed was a tendency of Latin men to be sexually unfaithful. She saw her sensitive gringo as a loyal knight who would rescue her from that heartache. Charlie, though he didn't know it at the time, experienced Magda as a woman about as different from his repressive, domineering, and sexually inhibited mother as he could have imagined.

But in those post-honeymoon years Charlie had come to see too much of his mother in Magda. Now she seemed manipulative, critical, and sexually withholding. And Magda, convinced of Charlie's infidelity, was going through his things whenever he was out of the house, looking for evidence of another woman—motel receipts, mysterious charges on his credit cards, scribbled notes, discrepancies in his schedule. Frightened and enraged by Magda's increasingly frequent grillings, Charlie retreated into his own inner hell of resentment and guilt, withholding from her his feelings, his hopes, and his sorrows. Magda edged toward bitterness, Charlie toward regret. The problem was that they were both right about what the other one was doing to undermine their relationship. Magda *was* being oppressive and domineering, and Charlie *was* being unfaithful.

In the next two years, in spite of the best efforts of their therapist, Magda and Charlie settled into lives of quiet desperation and bitter disappointment with each other. Beneath the level of their painful standoff, though, their love for each other was still very much alive. They just couldn't get to it anymore. And in spite of the fact that they came from two cultures seemingly worlds apart, they each encountered in the other the very behaviors from their own cultures they had hoped to escape.

Magda and Charlie, many of us may have noticed, are not alone. Over 50 percent of marriages in our society now end in divorce—some, perhaps, too hurried after only superficial brushes with relationship issues, others *way* overdue.[1] Eighty-seven percent of those who stay together are significantly unhappy. Many of these couples are pursuing what the relationship specialist Harville Hendrix calls "parallel marriages."[2] At least 30 percent of our marriages are platonic, the end stage of once fully romantic partnerships.[3] Over 70 percent of married men admit to having affairs, around 50 percent of married women.[4] Up to 30 percent of all babies born in hospitals are not the husband's.[5] Men and women become sexually bored with each other anywhere from a few months to several years after their first joyful encounters.[6] Equally devastating, they become locked in verbal, emotional, and often physical battles for dignity and self-expression, and finally turn away from each other with feelings of emptiness, hostility, and despair.

In fact, the currency of our suffering is *universal*. It is not confined to any particular culture.[7] It is a bittersweet plague on *all* our houses. All human beings everywhere, and in all historical epochs, have known the pain of love's great disillusionments.

In therapy, Magda and Charlie shamed each other mercilessly for betraying each other's most cherished hopes. And, reaching beyond the personal level, Charlie would say things like, "That's what *all* women want—to trap you!" And Magda would say things like, "All men are liars!"

At the time I worked with Magda and Charlie, I was still using standard psychological interpretations of their situation. I was just beginning to do cross-cultural anthropology and primate research. Unfortunately, not all stories are success stories.

Shamed to the Core

We live in a culture of shame and denial about a lot of things, but especially about our animal natures. Perhaps most cultures are at the same impasse. Freud believed that *all* civilizations are based on repressed sexuality which then finds release in creative activities, such as building skyscrapers, weaving blankets, or sending men to the moon. Most recently, anthropologists and evolutionary biologists have proposed that the human part of our brains—our neocortexes—evolved mainly to inhibit us from expressing our sexual and aggressive desires directly.[8]

All of this is probably true. The catch is that shame and denial don't work. In the end, what we try to pretend is not a part of us will not agree to be, as Freud called it, "sublimated" and redirected into civilization building. It looks for chances to get what it wants—directly. The more we repress our animal cores, the more restless they become, until they finally erupt in frustration-driven violence and beyond-the-bounds sexuality—their last desperate measures for securing self-affirmation.[9]

More and more psychologists are now seeing shame as the central problem in our psychological and even our spiritual woundedness. Some are now calling it the "master emotion," and naming it as the true source of most of our conflicts and neuroses.[10] They have identified the target of this primal shaming as the inner child, and they have devised therapies for healing this child, reparenting him or her, and comforting, championing, and channeling his or her energies. All of this has been extremely helpful. At the same time, it has become clear to me that the inner child, in himself or herself, is not the ultimate target of our shaming.

Over a period of time I began to ask myself what exactly *is* it about the child that we try so hard to destroy? It's certainly not its cuddly cuteness or its sweet-tempered dependency. It's not its smiles and cooings. All these things are socially acceptable, and tend to affirm our own importance as adults and evoke our feelings of love. These aspects of children are not threatening to us.

No. What we target in our families, in our religions, and in our societies as a whole are two things—the child's sexuality and his or her aggressive self-affirmation. It frightens us to be in the presence of a being who shamelessly seeks pleasure, the gratification of its desires, the unrestrained expression of its anger, and which seems to believe that life is for play and enjoyment. What really scares us is that this exuberant, shameless child reminds us of our own failed attempts at fulfillment, our own desperation, and our own abandoned hopes. Our disillusionment is hardest to face when we encounter someone who doesn't agree with our despair, who still has faith in the goodness and responsiveness of life. And that someone is what every child is.

It dawned on me that these childlike qualities of unashamed sexuality and aggressive self-affirmation were characteristics of our nearest animal relatives—the other primates. While they too have to learn to conform to the behavioral standards of their communities, the other primates remain much freer than most of us to go after what they want. I wondered if this was the reason why so many people feel scornful of apes and monkeys even while being amused by them. Is the target of our derision their freer expression of desires which are *ours* too, but which we've been shamed into viewing as unacceptable?

Many of the great psychologists—from Freud to Theodor Reik, from Erik Erikson to Norman O. Brown—have come close to making the connection between the child and the animal explicit. But they've stopped short of identifying our shamed inner core as our primate ancestor, still thriving in our deepest brains, souls, and bodies. Part of the reason they've paused at the threshold of this realization, I am convinced, is that to say in so many words that our civilization is built at the expense of an inner animal which cannot be completely tamed is to call the whole civilization project into question—something few of us are prepared to do. A second, related reason is that each of the great psychologists, like the cultures of which they were a part, insisted on the primacy of human free will. If we're not really as free as we think we are, what becomes of our moralities? The third reason most psychologists have fallen short of identifying the ultimate target of our shaming is the simplest. They didn't have the knowledge we now have about the other primates or about our genetic links to them.

Now that we are getting far more perspective on our primate ways of feeling, thinking, and behaving, we are in a position to *truly* heal ourselves.

Beyond Therapy

Much of Magda and Charlie's misery becomes understandable as innate patterns of primate relationship behavior. Had there been awareness of these patterns and careful stewarding of their primate heritage, Magda and Charlie might have been able to get through the rocky period and each give the gift of lasting love in the ways the other needed it. For example, if they had been able to realize that Magda's sexual suspiciousness and jealousy were natural and healthy—up to a point—it could have taken some of the sting out of these things for Charlie and some of the compulsive force out of them for Magda. Sexual suspiciousness and jealousy are nature's way of safeguarding a couple's pair-bond long enough to get their children off to a solid start.[11]

Likewise, we can't activate a woman's natural "mother program" without also bringing some of her critical, controlling behavior with it. What often feels to men like a woman's attempt to shame and dominate them is, at least at the foundational level, her natural "moralistic aggression" which all primate mothers have.[12] It's their instinct for disciplining and teaching their children (including a man's inner child!) to fit into the community.

Many primate mothers push their sons in particular so that when the time comes they can compete for alpha male status. Part of Magda's manipulativeness can be seen as an example of a female primate trying to gain emotional and economic security, and feeling shamed by her failure to achieve it. Though Magda was unaware of this, and although she and Charlie didn't have any children, the hidden goal of a woman's grasping is to ensure the survival of her real or even her *potential* offspring.[13] In this sense, Charlie was right: all women *do* have an instinctual tendency to be entrapping—no matter what their culture.

Charlie's fear and rage at Magda's invasiveness was part of a predictable primate pattern: the tendency for males—even those who have achieved king-of-the-hill status—to feel irrationally vulnerable to the power of their "mothers." It also reflected the primate male need to *not* be dominated by the females of the community. In order to maintain a sense of empowered male identity, a state of mind absolutely essential for a male's reproductive success, including high-enough testosterone levels and firm erections, a primate male cannot feel belittled or put down by females.[14] If he does, he will, like Charlie, feel both impotent and rageful.

Charlie's tendency to desire other women, as painful and threatening to Magda as it was, was not primarily the result of his childhood wounding at the hands of a sexually cold mother. Nor did it come from any conscious intention on his part to hurt Magda. Rather, it was mainly an expression of Charlie's mixed reproductive strategy.[15] In this sense, Magda was right: men do tend to be sexual liars—no matter what culture they have been raised in.

Traditional psychology can help couples deal with exaggerations of these patterns, and in the process help them manage their biological inheritance better. But, from my perspective, it is enormously helpful to realize that these "symptoms," at normal levels of intensity, are really expressions of biological and emotional strategies which nature has evolved to enhance the survival of our species. At this level, nature doesn't care about our individual egos, and it uses our falling in and out of love as a tool for achieving its goals. Certainly, and unlike the other apes, we can make more out of nature's proddings than this. But not without getting clear about the primate patterns we're dealing with in ourselves and our partners—and *unshaming* them.

Some traditional marriage counseling still focuses on superficial negotiating, such as who's going to make the bed in the morning and who's going to take the kids to school, and so on. Other, much more thoughtful approaches, most notably John Gray's, focus on the differences between men and women and practical steps we can take to better meet each other's relationship needs. Still other approaches focus on how our inner children interact in our relationships. The wisest, most sophisticated of these inner child relationship therapies is Harville Hendrix's Imago Therapy, in which the process of healing our inner children by healing our relationships (and vice versa) has been taken to its logical and most fruitful conclusion: Hendrix maintains that healing our inner children is what our relationships are *for.*

I believe that this is a vital psychological goal, certainly of modern relationships, and Hendrix's pioneering work has opened up opportunities for truly deep healing that were unavailable to us before. At the same time, I believe it's vital to keep *nature's* intentions clearly in mind as well. From the biological perspective, healing our inner children in our relationships is a way of furthering nature's goal for us. It's a "proximate mechanism," a set of feelings and behaviors that *seem* to be ends in themselves, but are really ways in which we, as individuals and as a species, pursue our ultimate goal of successful reproduction.[16]

Many of our current psychologies are being guided—misguided really—by two assumptions. The first is that all that's really wrong with us in our love lives is our damaged childhoods. And the second is that men and women are essentially the same.

I agree that childhood wounds *are* major contributors to the unsatisfying condition of most of our intimate relationships, and we need to take responsibility for healing them ourselves (because no one else will) if we are to have even a chance of making our relationships what we need them to be. But instead of seeing 100 percent of the problem there, I'd assign about 50 percent to unresolved childhood traumas, at least for most of us.

To the second point: we've gone from old-style Freudian therapies that basically saw women as imperfect men and tried to re-
make them in the male image (a project our culture is still toying
with) to many "new age" therapies that seem to be trying to turn
men into *women*. These therapies assume that the female model
for intimate relationship is the healthy one, and that our marriages will work if men become more sensitive, more vulnerable,
more willing to share their feelings—more like women. I agree
with this too—up to a point; each gender can benefit by integrating *some* of the life experiences of the other. But some women (as
well as men) may have exaggerated, even pathological, "intimacy" needs, and there may be good reasons why some men
(and women) don't share their real feelings.

The emphasis on *inner child* as culprit comes out of our growing realization that children, in virtually all our families, are bru-
talized to some degree, at least psychologically. The emphasis on
man as culprit comes out of a new sexist ideology which excuses
women from responsibility for the emotional and physical devas-
tation between the genders, and which denigrates men for their
higher levels of testosterone. But testosterone has its virtues in
our relationships, as in other things, and estrogen isn't always on
the side of sweetness and light.

In addition, our society has a century-old fascination with the
machine, with the industrial model of interchangeable parts.
Ironically, some of the people promoting the superiority of the
female way are, apparently unconsciously, teaching women to be
as much like men as their natures will allow. Not only is this
hopelessly confused; it is enormously destructive. This ideology
is pitting the genders against each other in ways unknown
through all our millions of years of primate and human evolutionary history.

The demand that we pretend to be interchangeable in our
ways of perceiving, feeling, thinking, and behaving is maddening
and disorienting. Instead of complementarity in aspects of our
temperaments and our work, which is what we have evolved for,
the direct competition—including moral—between men and
women, driven by the mistaken idea that we are not only equal
but *the same,* is polarizing us. Women trying to be quasimales

are frustrated, and men trying to be quasifemales are frustrated. The sex lives and romantic relationships of both are suffering. We've lost the key to the wonderful "chemistry" that is the essence of relationship love. The result is that we are experiencing almost intolerable strains on our gender identities and deepening the tragedy of our ages-long mutual shaming. Both men and women are now expected to be "men" at work and "women" at home, a feat all but the most pliable of us fail to pull off. And for good reason—we're not made for it.

If a woman can't be more like a man, she's considered defective. If a man can't be more like a woman, he's considered a menace to the planet. Perhaps, though, societies that wander too far from nature self-destruct. In the end, that may be a good thing, but in the meantime we have a lot of needless suffering to endure.

A couple once came to me expressing two radically different perspectives on what was wrong in their relationship. That in itself isn't unusual, of course. What struck me was the simplicity of their perspectives and the neat way they fell into the two psychological camps I call Old Freudian and New Age.

She complained that he always wanted her to dress up—nylons, skirt, and high heels. She said, "A woman has to look sexy to *get* a man. But once she's got him, he's supposed to love her for her soul. It shouldn't matter how she looks."

He complained that she always wanted him to give her more attention, as he had in their first few months together. He said, "All that sensitivity and closeness stuff is great *in the beginning*. But once you're married, other things become more important. Reality sets in. There are bills to be paid."

The fact is, they were both *completely* wrong about relationship reality, at least from the point of view of our primate programs.

Conventional therapies might try to negotiate a compromise between them and leave it at that. Freudian therapy might try to get the woman to look at her supposed insecurity about her appearance or her presumed repressed sexual desires. And New Age therapy might push the man to examine his neurotic "fear of intimacy." These approaches may each contain part of the truth, and each might be able to help this couple to some extent.

But consider their situation from a primate perspective, the unfulfilled animal needs each was trying to get the other to meet. Those needs divide along gender-characteristic lines. And each of them has a long and noble evolutionary history behind it. Put simply, the perspective of New Age therapies is an expression of predictably primate female needs—the need for relatedness, for connectedness on a soul level, and the need for emotional and, ultimately, physical security. Not looking sexy can be a woman's way of testing the loyalty of the man. "Is he going to stick around and be faithful long enough so that I can get Junior off my hip and take up foraging for roots and tubers and dodging predators myself again?" On the East African savannas from which we are all descended, a woman with an infant at the breast was radically dependent upon the emotional loyalty of one primary male, and the key to her survival was a constant state of heart-to-heart connectedness.

My male client's basically Freudian point of view is an expression of predictably primate male needs—the need for some degree of emotional detachment, for concentrating on protecting and providing ("There are bills to be paid!"). On those same East African savannas, a man felt the pressure that a dependent female and her children placed on him. His mind and heart had to be clear so that he could successfully focus his energies on repulsing predators and bagging game.

In addition, partly because of this hunter program, men are wired to be visually oriented, and much of men's sexual enjoyment is based on what they *see*.[17] It's important to a man's animal soul that the woman he's with look as young and healthy as she can. That means that she's a good bet for his reproductive success.[18] It's also important that she look sexy. Not only does that arouse him; it also raises his standing in the hierarchy of other males and increases his chances of eventually winning alpha male status.[19]

It may be the late twentieth century, but our bodies and brains and our animal souls don't know it.

* * *

Patricia and Gary came to see me about their increasing sense of alienation from each other. They were both intelligent and well educated. She was a supervising nurse in the labor and delivery department of a major hospital, and he was a graduate of the Art Institute of Chicago. They said they loved each other very much. But Patricia was feeling a smoldering resentment toward Gary, and Gary admitted that he was having outbursts of uncontrollable rage.

When I asked Patricia why she was feeling resentful, she said, "I'm tired of being the man in this relationship! Gary hasn't had a job for six months. He does a lot of things around the house. He washes the dishes, he washes the clothes, he cooks, and he's always there when I come home to give me a backrub. And I really appreciate him for all those things. But, just once, I'd like to be taken out to dinner and not have to pay!"

She looked at Gary with a combination of apology, fear, and anger. "I need a man who's dependable, someone I can feel secure—financially secure—with. Gary, you're just starting out, and I know it's hard to get a job in art." She paused. "But damn it! I need you to get it together!"

Gary threw up his hands; he looked frustrated and helpless. He turned to me and said, "I thought we're all supposed to be liberated now." He looked back at Patricia. "We talked about all this. We used to laugh at all those stupid people still caught in the old stereotypes."

Patricia was icy. She said, "I'm not laughing now."

It's a bitter pill after thirty years of liberation, but the fact is, a part of the primate program of every woman wants an alpha male, a man who has been able to get far enough up the male ladder of success to provide her with the physical, financial, and emotional security she needs in order to feel that she has options. And options, whatever else they may *seem* to mean, translate ultimately into producing children and giving those children the best chance for their own eventual reproductive success.[20]

We can teach our neocortexes any set of cultural ideals we want. But we ignore our instinctual depths at a price few of us wish to pay. The problem with many of our popular therapies is that marriage, at the *instinctual* level, has never been for in-depth counseling, men and women are fundamentally different, and the inner child is not the *ultimate* target of our shaming.

If we want to be happy in our relationships and if we want them to last far beyond the natural three- or four-year barrier on which so many come apart, then we *do* need to get to work on our individual childhood issues. As a part of that process, we also need to challenge many of the shaming messages we've internalized about ourselves and each other from our churches, our schools, our peers, and the media. But I believe it's time for our theologians, our philosophers, our sociologists, and our psychologists to realize that their fields of study and practice are based on—not divorced from—the perceptions, feelings, ways of thinking, and modes of behavior of thoroughly primate minds.[21] In a very real way they are all branches of primatology.[22]

When our primate heritage is lifted up into the full light of our human consciousness, in a therapeutic setting that includes and enriches the insights of our traditional therapies, then we can have realistic success in our relationships, and in other areas of our lives as well.

The therapy that is beyond therapy is not for fitting ashamed apes into neurotic civilizations. It is for unshaming, celebrating, comforting, and channeling the animal within.

3

How We Got This Way: The Three Layers of Our Primate Patterns

❋

The "Wise" Chimpanzee

IN HIGH SCHOOL BIOLOGY we learned that plants and animals are classified into kingdoms, phyla, classes, orders, families, genuses, and species. The man responsible for this modern way of thinking about the different forms of life on this planet was the eighteenth-century Swedish botanist, Carolus Linnaeus. Linnaeus was proceeding very well with his classification scheme until he came to us. Then he hit a roadblock, and, as he later confessed, he copped out.[1]

Even with the limited knowledge available in the eighteenth century in the fields of anthropology and primate studies, the problem for Linnaeus was that he could find no scientifically justifiable reason for giving us our own separate genus. It seemed clear to him that we and the chimpanzee shared so many physical characteristics that either we had to consider ourselves a species of chimpanzee or we had to accept chimpanzees as human beings. Linnaeus believed that he either had to classify us as *Pan sapiens*—"the wise chimpanzee"—or he had to classify chimpanzees as *Homo troglodytes*—"the earthy human." His problem was that if he told the truth he would face certain persecution from a Church, which had not long before burned innovative thinkers at the stake.

Two hundred years later, we know that our similarities with chimpanzees are greater than even Linnaeus imagined. Genetic studies tell us, for example, that chimpanzees and bonobos have 98.3 percent the same genetic material as we do, and that most of the remaining 1.7 percent is "junk," genes that have no function.[2] That's a closer correspondence than exists between certain individuals within the same species of fish.[3] In fact, chimpanzees and bonobos are more closely related to us than they are to gorillas, their next closest relatives. And it is now thought that bonobos, with their long legs, flat faces, and neatly parted hair, closely resemble our common chimplike ancestor of about 7 million (some scholars say 5.5) years ago.[4]

But our likeness to chimpanzees and bonobos is far more than physical. We used to believe that we human beings were unique creatures, nearly completely separated from the rest of the natural world by our mental prowess and our God-given souls, which bestowed upon us the celestial qualities of love and compassion. But after thirty years of studying chimpanzees and bonobos in the wild and in zoos we now know that they are profoundly political animals, that they make and use tools, create cultures, pass on their knowledge of medicinal herbs, make art, grieve over dead loved ones, engage in warfare, adopt orphans, hug, kiss, and have very humanlike self-awareness.[5] In fact, our psychological differences—the ways we perceive, feel, think, and behave—are matters of *degree,* not *kind.* While we have far more capacity for empathy and for strategic thinking than they do because of the evolution of our neocortexes, every one of our human characteristics is at least *prefigured* in our nearest animal relatives, including the universal patternings of our love lives.

How well we know and work with this animal heritage that still forms the core of who and what we are determines whether or not we will have success in our personal lives. Our animal heritage is divided into three distinct layers, each of which was wired into us at a specific time in our evolutionary past.

Jungle Time

I've based the following sketches of the stages of our evolution on the best research now available. These sketches of our prehistory come from a twofold process of reading backwards in time from what we see in human beings today, and forward in time from fossil data and the evidence of the "living fossils," the chimpanzees and bonobos.

By comparing our rapidly advancing understanding of chim-

panzee and bonobo behavior with data on modern hunter-gatherer peoples and more general anthropological findings, as well
as with the wealth of cross-cultural studies now available on the
similarities and differences between our genders, and with the informed speculations of paleontologists, physical anthropologists,
and evolutionary biologists, we are able to see the emergence of
a coherent picture of our most likely physical, social, and psychological evolutionary journey. While there are fascinating debates about some of the fine points, the majority of scientists
from these different fields are mostly in agreement. The main
source of controversy is about the probable *causes* of certain
trends in our evolution—not about the *facts*.

You'll see that I've concluded each section with a list of "Hot
Issues" that tend to be destructive to our relationships, and
which I'm convinced come out of the three layers of our primate
patterns.

I've included extensive chapter notes at the back of the book
for readers who want to learn more about the intricacies of the
current debates. And for readers who *really* want to enter the scientific labyrinth, there's always the bibliography.

With these things in mind, let's begin our brief safari through
the history of our species—and our love lives.

Our jungle time was what geologists and paleontologists call the
Miocene period in the earth's history. It lasted from about 22
million years ago to 5.5 million years ago. The setting for our
jungle time was the rainforests of East Africa and parts of Asia,
including what is now India. Our jungle time was our ape time.
The oldest layer of our primate patterns was wired into us then,
when we went by such names as *Proconsul, Kenyapithecus,* and
Ramapithecus. We were already remarkable primates. We seem
to have spent a large part of our time on the ground,[6] and our
canine teeth were growing smaller, perhaps an indication that we
were already making and using tools and weapons and that
males were fighting less and cooperating more in order to form
stable societies.[7]

Somewhere around the time we were becoming *Ramapithecus*
we diverged from our gorilla-bound relatives. For the most part

we ate fruits, nuts, and berries.[8] Occasionally we would get "meat hunger," and the males would hunt monkeys, bush pigs, and other small animals, and then share the meat with females, especially those females who were in heat.[9]

Our societies were probably organized around loose, informal associations of female friends and tighter, more rigid male hierarchies in which the supreme prize was alpha male status.[10] Though this changed later, in the early days of our jungle time, younger males would often be driven out of the community to fend for themselves, to join other bands, or to form tribes of their own,[11] and young females would often wander off in search of less familiar males, perhaps responding to an ancient version of the lure of the stranger.[12]

Intimacy between members of the same sex was common, but inter-gender closeness was rare except between mothers and sons[13] or during the brief periods of consortship in which a single male and female would gaze into each other's eyes, hold hands, and walk off into a secluded part of the forest together for up to several weeks at a time.[14] We were sexy even then, often making love several times a day—for food, for fun, to ease group tensions, and, of course, to create more of us.[15] *Selective promiscuity* (in which the most desirable sexual partners were sought after, but with no thought of ongoing "commitment") was the rule. A female in heat would mate with just about any male, but what she was really after was the alpha and his immediate supporters, who, because of their achievements in status and power, seemed like good bets for the genetic superiority of her potential children.[16]

The alpha male would try to get as close to a monopoly on the estrus females as he could, thereby assuring that a substantial proportion of the next generation would carry his genes.[17] He would, however, reward his male followers with opportunities to copulate with his temporary "wives."[18] His henchmen would support him, in part, to win this opportunity to gain their own practical immortality.

Because food in the forest world was abundant and there for the picking, and because predators could easily be eluded by scampering up the ever-present trees, males and females were all economically self-sufficient.[19] Both males and females "worked" and earned their own livings. The larger and more powerful males physically attacked females mostly by accident, for example, if one of the females happened to get in a male's way when he was in the midst of battle frenzy.[20] Occasionally, males demanded sex, and consortships, with reluctant females; and after some resistance, the females would usually comply.[21] But perhaps more often, the sexually receptive females would advertise their desire by thrusting their estrus-swollen buttocks in the air, by shoving their genitals in a male's face, or even by grabbing his penis and initiating fellatio.[22]

What females almost certainly looked for in males was courage, fierceness, and aggressiveness (but not too much), the ability to obtain and hold status and provide leadership, intelligence—especially as it related to political astuteness and the ability to build coalitions that took the wishes of the female population into account—and selflessness in defense of the community.[23] In addition, females probably looked for tender qualities like male willingness to play with the children and adopt orphans.[24] Females may also have valued so-called paedomorphic, or childlike, qualities in males such as male vulnerability to the "moral suasion" of females, especially their mothers, male willingness to kiss, to caress and be caressed, and male compliance with the female desire for face-to-face sex which, over several million years, was becoming more and more prevalent as a result of the females' increasingly common frontally tilted vagina.[25]

Females also wanted their mates to be strong and healthy as well as show signs of age and maturity such as whitening beards.[26] They also probably selected males more and more for larger penis size.[27] As their vaginas moved around to a frontal entry position females may have found it more difficult to experience orgasm.[28] The washboard surface of their vagina's frontal wall, which had contributed to orgasms in the past when rear entry had stimulated it directly, was now of little use if male penises remained small and thin. The answer was penises that could fill the vagina and make contact with the washboard again and, even more importantly, massage the originally secondary source of female orgasm, the clitoris.

What males probably looked for in females was estrus and fertility, health and youth, temperaments that were provocatively yielding and generally friendly and nonthreatening, evidence of good mothering skills (which usually led to greater female status in the community), fierceness in defense of offspring, and some childlike qualities such as roundness and softness, higher voices, and somewhat compliant natures.[29] Breasts became more and more important to males as face-to-face lovemaking became increasingly common because they provided the same visual stimulus for male sexual excitement as buttocks had before.[30] Permanently enlarged breasts also helped to mask the females' true position in their fertility cycles by mimicking pregnancy. This made females "unattractive" to other males, and thereby helped cement the newly emerging pair-bonds between one female and one male.[31] But because the enlarged breasts reminded males of estrus-swollen buttocks, eventually this strategy, like so many others, failed to ensure sexually exclusive monogamous relationships.

Jungle Time Hot Issues

Among the hot issues that come out of our jungle time and that still create tensions between us in our love relationships today are:

• **Promiscuity**—This is part of the sex drives of both men and women. It generally is a somewhat more powerful—and less selective—drive for men than women, although there are exceptions.[32] Promiscuity, as we'll see, is one of our reproductive strategies, the one most prominent in our jungle time. It causes us untold personal suffering today—not because it's bad in and of itself—but because it runs headlong into the reproductive strategies that evolved in our savanna time and the civilization period—namely, serial monogamy and, later, the lifelong monogamy ideal.

• **Recreational Sex**—While the ultimate goal of sex is reproduction, nature has made it serve other purposes as well, purposes which can be termed "proximate mechanisms." For example, among chimpanzees and especially bonobos, sexual pleasure is a strategy for reducing group tensions and cementing emotional bonds between many different individuals. We know that recreational sex rather than sex for procreation only has been an important factor in our evolution for two main reasons. The first is that today we are one of the sexiest animals around. Men think about sex almost continuously,[33] and women are at least potentially receptive most of the time.[34] The second is that we see just such recreational sex among a number of our primate relatives, again especially among the "living fossils"—bonobos. Sex for recreation wouldn't be a problem in itself for most of us. But when it is linked, as it frequently is, with our yen for promiscuity, it is powerfully destructive to our would-be monogamous relationships.

• **Extreme Male Competitiveness and Emotional Isolation**—In our jungle time, males were fiercely competitive, and, except for occasional friendships, emotionally isolated from each other.[35] Their competitiveness came out of the hierarchal structure of male society in which the most powerful and socially adept were able to get the most females and thereby assure their reproductive success. Though not an infallible indicator, the size of male canine teeth is often used to judge the intensity of inter-male competition in primate species.[36] The larger the canines, the greater the rivalry. When we see the canines diminishing in size over a period of time usually one of two things is at work—either the animal's diet is changing from meat to fruits and vegetables or the level of inter-male fighting is dropping.[37] We know that our jungle-time ancestor, like the modern chimpanzee, was primarily, though not exclusively, a vegetarian;[38] so the probable cause for the reduction in the size of the canines which we observe both in the fossil record and in modern human males is more likely an indication of greater and greater male cooperation. But a third factor may be considered as well. Reduction in the canines may also be a symptom of our increasing reliance on weapons.[39] In any case, it is almost certain that jungle time males were fiercely competitive and that the kind of male cooperation that later became a hallmark of our species (compared to other great apes) reached its peak during the relatively rare episodes of hunting.[40] As a legacy from our jungle time, human males to this day have a strong tendency to distrust each other and to fight with each other for status, wealth, and ultimately for females and their own genetic survival. Today, this deprives men of the emotional support they need from other men for their professional success and for their relationships with women.[41]

• **Women's Economic Self-Sufficiency**—In our jungle time, females and males were both economically self-sufficient. We can surmise this from the fact that modern chimpanzees and bonobos show this social arrangement. Theirs is largely a gatherer society in which the predominant foods are abundant. In the jungle time layer of our primate patterns males and females as individuals pretty much go their separate ways, though there is mutual gender dependency on the community level—the females rearing the children and the males defending the territory, among other things. Today, our rising divorce rates are largely the product of women's growing economic self-sufficiency.[42] They are a testimony to the fact that economic dependency on the part of women has been one of the forces that has buttressed our pairbonds. In the absence of this dependency (as we'll see, a product of our savanna time), our society is restructuring itself in a way that closely resembles, and, indeed, is an expression of, our primate jungle time patterns.[43] In some of the following chapters we'll explore some problems that women's growing economic— and seemingly emotional—"liberation" runs into when it comes up against the two other layers of our primate heritage.

• **Single-Parent Families**—This too is a jungle time pattern, and is closely related to women's economic self-sufficiency, which gives them this option. It is a jungle time pattern in that it harks back to those distant days, still present within us, in which males did not share much in the raising of the children, and were probably unaware which children were actually theirs.[44] Primate males in general show far less "paternal investment" than females show "maternal investment." Studies show that, though greatly modified in human males, this underlying apelike pattern continues to exist among us. As we know, single-parent families are almost always made up of a woman and her children. And they are often structured so that the father is excluded as much as possible, perhaps vilified, and often viewed largely as a source of additional income ("meat"). This furthers the decline in men's interest in ongoing paternal investment[45] and fosters problems of gender identity on the part of the children.[46] Recent studies have also shown that fatherless families tend to produce children who are underachievers in school[47] and who have a greater tendency to become involved in violent behavior.[48]

• **Intense Mother-Child Bonding**—The primary jungle time primate social unit among almost all species is the mother-child bond.[49] This fits with the patterns of the hot issues above. The problem for our relationships today is that we also have inherited the advanced primate patterns for pair-bonding and paternal investment. Therefore, the tendency on the part of many young mothers—inherited from our jungle time—to isolate themselves emotionally from their mates and make their primary source of intimacy their children[50] violates the pair-bond instincts. It causes the woman to forgo the very male emotional support she's inherited from our savanna time to need, causes the man to feel excluded and used (as a mere source of income), and ends up misusing the children—inappropriately—as substitute pair-bond partners.

• **Mutual Gender Isolation**—Based on our observations of chimpanzees and most of the other primate species, we can conclude that our jungle time ancestors showed relative male/female isolation.[51] Females tended to bond with females and males tended to bond with males—and in very different types of groupings. Today, as we move toward a more jungle time–like society, we in fact see greater and greater mutual gender isolation. The problem is that this runs counter, once again, to our savanna time and even our civilization inheritance, as we'll see. A further destructive aspect of this hot issue may also be that women often associate with women and men with men primarily to air grievances about the other sex.

Savanna Time

Our savanna time spanned the geological ages known as the Pliocene (5.5 million years ago to 1.7 million years ago) and the Pleistocene (1.7 million years ago to the present) up to the invention of agriculture about 10,000 years ago. It saw rapid and dramatic changes in our environment, and, as a result, powerful changes in us. Our savanna time added the second layer to our primate patterns. We started out with the label *Australopithecus ramidus* (4.4 million years ago), became *Homo habilis* (2.3 million years ago), and then *Homo erectus* (1.7 million years ago). By around 400,000 years ago we had become *Homo sapiens,* and around 200,000 years ago we emerged as fully modern humans.

What happened? Our environment initially got a lot drier. As it did, the forests of East Africa shrank rapidly. Some protochimpanzees stayed in the trees and retreated with the dwindling jungles. They became the modern chimpanzees and bonobos. Some of the protochimpanzees got stranded on the vast new grasslands. They became the australopithecines, who eventually became us.

As the trees withdrew we gradually adapted to earthbound lives. But we learned to "fly." Our legs lengthened, our hips changed, our feet became flat pads for launching our now powerful strides, and we walked and ran upright.[52] Our teeth were changing too. As early as *Australopithecus* our grinding molars were reducing in size, probably an indication that our diet was shifting from fruits and vegetables to meat.[53] Until the invention of fire about 300,000 years ago, which enabled us to cook the toxins out of our vegetables, many of the grassland plants were poison to us.[54] The most obvious and plentiful, if dangerous, source of food on the savannas was other animals. In the early days we may have scavenged from the kills of the large social carnivores.[55] But our old chimpanzee hunting skills came in handy. We refined our weapons and became predators ourselves.

The new environment radically restructured our society, as it did our love relationships. Already somewhat territorial in the jungle, we now developed a typical carnivore's sense of a home base and of an "invincible center" that housed the females and young and which we would defend to the death.[56] Males were now forced to cooperate on a much more intense and regular basis.[57] They were forced to set their differences aside and learn to control their competitive urges so that they could repel the predators who, in a mostly treeless landscape, now had the upper hand, and so that they could successfully hunt large game animals. The male hierarchy, with its alpha male and his loyal enforcers, became the key to group survival.[58] In these and other ways our societies combined features of our old jungle-dwelling ape communities and the tighter, more authoritarian *and* more cooperative societies of wolves and wild dogs.[59]

Our relationships, too, underwent powerful changes, changes that would make them truer bonds of intimacy. The consortships from our jungle days (the predecessors of our own experiences of falling in love) grew into longer-term pair-bonds between one male and one female.[60] Evolutionary biologists and anthropologists have proposed a number of theories to explain this development, and have traced what appear to be converging forces in our environment that pushed us in this direction. For example, one way that males could cooperate more intensely with each other was to divide up the females, assigning one or several— depending on the status of the male—to each.[61] Such an arrangement became increasingly critical as evolving females gradually lost the obvious signs of their estrus, or "heat."[62] Now, males couldn't tell which females were fertile or when. The solution was to "own one" and make love with her on a regular basis. Sooner or later, she would become pregnant.

Another part of the impetus for the monogamy scenario was the dawning realization on the part of both males and females that somehow sex led to children.[63] Most animals act *as if* they know this, but even chimpanzee and bonobo males don't seem to be able to distinguish their own offspring from those of other males. Among other primates, males will sometimes kill all the infants of other males and then monopolize the females who come into estrus as a result.[64]

The awareness of fatherhood got a boost from yet another source. In the jungle, males had always done the hunting.[65] But they had hunted only occasionally, and the game was small. They would then distribute scraps of meat to others. There was never enough to satisfy actual *hunger;* meat was a delicacy.[66] But on the savanna meat had to *satisfy* hunger and provide most of the group's nutritional needs.[67] That meant that each male was kept very busy trying to supply relatively large quantities of meat to the females and young. Practically speaking, it didn't take these ancient scavenger/hunters long to realize that no matter how hard they worked they could only come up with enough meat for *one* female and her (his?) children.[68] It now became vital to a male's genetic survival that the meat he was supplying at so much cost and physical risk to himself contribute to *his* genetic survival—not to another's.

Because of these and other factors the monogamy bargain was sealed. Males became dependent on females to take care of their children, to make a home in the territory's center, and to cook the meals.[69] And the females became dependent on males for most of the food and, ultimately, for life itself.[70] While the proximate mechanisms increasingly felt like love, the ultimate goal of this division of labor and complementary partnership was the good of the children and the ensuring of the couple's own "practical immortality."[71]

Perhaps not surprisingly this several-million-year-long experiment in human pair-bonding, with its life-and-death consequences—not only for individual males and females, but, more importantly, for their reproductive success—got wired into our brains, so much so that modern brain researchers have found substantial differences in the brain structures of men and women.[72] These anatomical differences result in very different male and female ways of perceiving, feeling, thinking, and behaving as well as differences in some of our natural interests and abilities as groups. (There are always individual exceptions, and both genders show the signs of primate flexibility.)

The bargain between one male and one female for the survival of their children demanded sexual loyalty on both their parts, something neither of them was fully prepared to accept.[73] Because of their biologies and their wiring for greater physical and emotional commitment to their offspring, women were probably somewhat more amenable than men to this arrangement.[74] But both males and females, still moved by the ancient call of our jungle days, almost certainly sneaked off into the bushes occasionally with someone new.[75] Still, as a result of the dangerous grassland environment and its economic necessities, both genders pushed the other in the direction of monogamous commitment. Sexual jealousy was invented by nature to help us stay to-gether.[76] With it came the beginnings of guilt. And the nuclear family was born.

There was only one problem with this new reproductive strat-egy: Relationships were programmed to fail somewhere in the third or fourth year, right at the time when the child, the product of the first in-love stage, was weaned, got down off his mother's hip, and began foraging for himself or herself.[77] The anthropolo-gist Helen Foster calls this savanna time legacy—which modern people—continue to live out—the "four-year-itch" syndrome. Around the fourth year after a pair-bond's exuberant beginnings, perhaps after tears and regrets, either the male or the female, or both, would often go their separate ways in search of a new ge-netic mix. Serial monogamy, bred into us over millions of years, became a rough-and-ready compromise between the reproduc-tive strategies of our jungle time and the demands of the new en-vironment. We could still have multiple partners *and* get our children off to a good start. We could have our cake and eat it too, just not at the same time.

Throughout our savanna time our brains were being dramati-cally restructured, mainly by the growth of our neocortexes, our so-called human brains.[78] Some of this growth spurred the devel-opment of language, a potential in chimpanzees and gorillas, but a tool which became vital to our human survival.[79] Language en-abled us to fine-tune our already well-developed primate com-munication skills, and it enabled us to teach our young more efficiently and with much greater subtlety.

The frontal lobes of our neocortexes were evolving to further our capacities, on the one hand, for future-oriented strategic thinking and rational analysis of things and events in our environ-ment, especially the dangerous ones. This part of our neocortex became our now famous *left brain*. On the other hand, the *right* frontal lobes were growing in order to enhance our capacity for empathy. Because of our gradually lengthening childhoods, our ancestral mothers needed to love us even more than their mothers had loved them. In addition, the growth in feelings of love and empathy helped draw males into a greater sense of brotherhood with each other. And *all* of our relationships benefited—mother-child, male-male, female-female, *father*-child, and most importantly in terms of our intimate relationships, *male-female*.

But there was a price to pay. The neocortex evolved also, we now believe, to put a damper on our more ancient drives for sex and aggression.[80] In order to have a more stable, harmonious, and cooperative society—the prerequisite for survival on the savanna—and to more or less affair-proof our pair-bonds, nature had to get our exuberance under control. It accomplished this by using the power of our developing neocortexes to override our instincts. Shame was born, and, with it, a growing sense of alienation both from our *own* natures and from the world of nature as a whole.[81] It gradually became a matter of "us against the animals"—those animals out there, but also our own inner animal.

Savanna time became tundra time as the earth moved into a series of ice ages which began about 1.7 million years ago. As *Homo erectus,* we first ventured out of our African homeland and spread over large areas of the Old World. Some of us even returned to the forest, but with a new lease on life. It's even thought that we may have passed through a water-dwelling phase when, for a time, we may have become isolated on an island during an extended period of flooding in East Africa.[82]

We continued to evolve and refine *each other* through the characteristics we chose in our mates.[83] Along with the old turn-ons, men looked for sexual loyalty and emotional consistency from women. They also looked for even stronger and more empathic mothering capacities, and greater intelligence. These qualities signaled that females could more effectively care for and teach their children, vital child-rearing ingredients in increasingly complex cultures. Paradoxically, men also stepped up their selection of women with more childlike features.[84] These childlike features—physical and emotional—indicated to the male that his prospective mate would be emotionally bonded to him and reluctant to abandon him. They also meant that she would be motivated to cooperate with him in their life-and-death economic partnership. In addition, since males and females were now thrust into intense one-on-one relationships, a male needed his mate to help him steer clear of his feelings of emotional and physical impotence around his "mother," feelings which such long-term domestic proximity to a single female could too easily evoke.[85] Therefore, males tended to select females who could walk the fine line between competent mothering and "subdominant" partnership.

In addition to the old characteristics that females looked for in males, during our savanna time they too started adding to the list. Among the new items for a woman were her potential mate's sexual loyalty and emotional consistency, and his greater intelligence, including his ability to control his aggressive urges so that he could get along with the other males and perhaps move up the male hierarchy ladder to alpha status itself.[86] If a woman could hitch her wagon to such a rising star, in the new monogamy arrangement especially, she herself and, more importantly, her children could enjoy a more secure future. A male's hunting skills were of more than passing interest in the new world of work role specialization.

Our female ancestors also chose males who showed evidence of a strong interest in nurturing—in nurturing *them* (their lives depended on it), but also in nurturing their children (*their* lives depended on it)—in other words, strong fathering impulses. And last but not least, females needed to see childlike qualities in males.[87] A woman needed to contact and mother a man's inner child because if she could evoke his childlikeness he would feel less threatening to her and she could gain some degree of emotional power over him, an important contributor to her ability to ensure her economic and psychological well-being.[88]

Savanna Time Hot Issues

Among the hot issues in our present relationships that come out of this layer of our primate patterns are:

• **Serial Monogamy**—This term means "one monogamous relationship after another." An extension of our jungle time consortships, our savanna time impetus for serial monogamy is both a joy and a source of misery for us today. It gives us pleasure by affording us the experience of falling in love many times during the course of our lives. But the fact that our relationships continue to be programmed to fail somewhere around the third or fourth year so we can be freed to pursue our next romantic adventure is the leading cause of human heartbreak. (Helen Fisher has shown that it is in the fourth year of marriage that the incidence of divorce is highest—in virtually all cultures.) This serial quality of our love lives is painful for both men and women, but more so for women, who are more often its victims.[89] The monogamy aspect of this arrangement (with its implied sexual exclusivity) is also painful, especially for men, who often must wrestle mightily with their jungle time promiscuous urges even while they're trying to form stable pair-bonds with one woman at a time.[90]

• **Sexual Jealousy**—A normal, healthy kind of mate "territoriality" on the part of both men and women, sexual jealousy is one of nature's attempts to affair-proof our serially monogamous relationships as much as possible. Nature's goal, as in every other aspect of our love lives, is to ensure that our children get off to a good start. Of course, when other issues are involved—childhood emotional wounding, for instance—healthy jealousy can become pathological possessiveness.

• **Shame and Guilt**—These are effective tools—at least in the short term—for controlling our sexual and aggressive behavior in order to help safeguard the nuclear family and stable societies. Even before the savanna time expansion of our neocortexes, shame and guilt had proven to be at least as effective as fear in enforcing conformity to group standards.[91] But it's possible to have too much of a good thing. Shame is responsible for the majority of our psychological suffering.

• **The Economic Subordination of Women**—A legacy of our ancient savanna time environment in which so much that is distinctly human about us—physically and psychologically—was formed, the economic subordination of women is a sword that cuts both ways. It can give some women, at least in some circumstances, the feeling of being loved, valued, and cared for, and it can give them options unavailable to most men.[92] At the same time, women's economic dependency can cause them to feel like helpless victims. It can lead to the disowning of their own aggressive feelings and cause them to express these feelings in passive-aggressive and manipulative ways.[93] It also deprives women of career options that men may have.

• **Intense Pressure on Men to Protect and Provide**—Although this pressure is easing somewhat,[94] for many couples in our more jungle time–like modern world this legacy of our savanna time is still a powerful force in many of our relationships. This, too, is a sword that cuts both ways. On the one hand, men can feel pride in their ability to protect and provide for their families—unless, of course, they are deprived of this opportunity by economic and social factors (such as racism).[95] On the other hand, it can cause men to feel like victims, bred to give their lives in work and war for women and children.[96] Men can feel that women have options they don't—to work or not work, to have children and become housewives, to invest their time and energy in things they enjoy such as volunteering for a variety of community service projects, engaging in artistic expression, or socializing with their friends, and in general to be choosier about how they live their lives.

• **Mutual Dependency**—Under normal conditions, being dependent on each other is healthy and fun. This savanna time inheritance of male-female teamwork can be a source of great pleasure for many couples. But when the pathological neediness that comes from damaged childhoods is present, our healthy dependency can turn into what is now called codependency.[97]

• **Our Ongoing Childlikeness (Neoteny)**—One of the major thrusts of our savanna time evolution seems to have been the gradual development of more and more childlike qualities—physically and psychologically. As we'll see, our ongoing childlikeness is both a blessing and a curse in our intimate relationships. It's probable that nature, *through* us—through the expression of our sexual preferences—caused us to select each other for these childlike characteristics. The problem for modern couples is that child*like*ness can easily become child*ish*ness. Then men and women may act in emotionally immature ways that can destroy their relationship happiness.

Civilization

Around 200,000 years ago our physical evolution more or less came to a standstill, and our cultures took over as the most powerful environmental factors in the shaping of our humanness.[98] With the domestication of fire around 300,000 years ago, vegetables became an important part of our diets again (except for those of us who were living in tundra environments). Perhaps for several million years we had been gathering wild grains. But by about 10,000 years ago we began their systematic cultivation. The agricultural revolution, and everything that followed—including cities, industry, and high tech—accounts for the third layer of our primate patterns.

With the coming of agriculture, our populations exploded and we settled down in crowded urban centers. These urban centers, constructed in true social carnivore fashion with temples, palaces (for the alpha male), and fortresses as re-creations of the "invincible center" arose in Mesopotamia, India, Egypt, China, and the Americas. Our high cultures became civilizations with stratified societies, complex governments, written languages, rapid technological advances on many fronts, and monumental architecture. With the rise of these civilizations what anthropologists call the great religions emerged.

Property ownership had always been a part of human culture. But now *the* property to own was land and the structures we could build on it. Marriage came to serve the primary purpose of creating *heirs* so that a couple's hard labor on *their* plot of ground could be passed on to their children.[99] Property ownership, in other words, became *the* way to assure our genetic survival. In such a cultural environment, men and women could no longer separate after three or four years and simply move on. A woman couldn't take one half of a field with her, and since the man was now heavily invested in his *male* children as the heirs of his wealth, he couldn't wander off in search of genetic novelty either. A man became a husband—a "housebound" man—and a woman became his partner-slave. Both became the indentured servants of the land and wealth they were able to accumulate.

In order to prop up this new method of achieving our practical immortality, the cultural ideal of *sexually exclusive, lifelong* monogamy was invented.[100] Often more honored in the breach, this cultural creation nevertheless also seemed to answer the biological need, a product of our ages-long evolution as a neotenous or childlike species, for lifelong emotional security, with substitute parent figures our spouses.[101]

The religions that emerged in this agricultural context moved in the direction of supporting the lifelong monogamy ideal, especially after 500 B.C.[102] Judaism and Christianity in particular were quick to give their stamp of approval to this arrangement. They sanctioned the new monogamy ideal as the highest expression of human and divine love and they punished our frequent rebellions against this partly unnatural system with threats of hellfire. The result was a neocortex in overdrive. The shaming of the animal at our cores, begun in our savanna time, now greatly intensified, and our natural primate tendency toward neurosis moved into full swing.[103] We and our relationships are still reeling from this "sentimental" brutalization of our primal natures.

Civilization Era Hot Issues

The hot issues that are still with us from this third, partly biological and partly cultural layer of our primate patterns include:

• **Our Sense of Enslavement to Each Other**—Chained to our property as the only way of ensuring our genetic survival, civilization era men and women have often been denied the means to escape relationships that have run their course. Modern couples may still feel themselves entrapped by each other—"for better for worse, for richer for poorer, in sickness and in health, 'til death us do part." Even in our present more jungle time–like culture the biological ingredient in the sexually exclusive lifelong monogamy ideal—our childlikeness/childishness—may keep us in unhappy relationships through constricting feelings of emotional neediness.

• **Work Is Good, Pleasure Is Bad**—It requires far more effort to create and maintain civilization than it does hunter-gatherer cultures.[104] It demands a shift away from our instincts in general, including our instincts for creative play, for emotional investment in interpersonal relationships, and for bodily pleasures of all kinds. To accomplish this shift from pleasure to much more intensive work our civilizations have used one of the most powerful weapons our neocortexes have evolved—shame. Now, in a highly complex urban environment, we must work harder and faster in order to try to accumulate enough property and wealth to give our children a good chance for survival. In the process, we turn away from pleasure as the major source of our life's meaning and delay *real* gratification—often forever. The consequences for our relationships of this alienation from our instincts include the loss of time and energy for deep emotional sharing and joyful lovemaking.[105]

• **The Shaming of Our Sexuality**—At the top of civilization's pleasure hit list is our sexuality.[106] From my perspective, Freud was right: civilization is largely the product of shamed—and then "sublimated" or redirected—sexual energy. But shaming our sexuality is one of the major causes of unhappy relationships. And our increasingly profound alienation from nature is having the many destructive effects we are now beginning to see on a global basis.

• **Sex Is Only for Procreation**—Even if sex as an expression of animal pleasure is demonized, it is still "useful" to civilization: it continues the species. But the violence done to our animal cores—the true source of joyful relationships—is enormous. And in spite of the recent trend toward reviving our jungle (and savanna) time ways of loving, our civilization era religions continue to encourage in many of us the neurotic ideals of virginity and an ascetic, workaholic lifestyle.[107]

• **The Spiritualizing of Our Relationships**—As we reject our animal needs for sexual expression and aggressive self-affirmation—two of the most important sources of relationship joy—and move our relationships toward merely platonic partnerships in which we imagine that the most noble form of love is "caritas," we set the stage for such destructive dynamics as:

  • **Sexual Malaise**—in which we turn away from our partners as sources of animal pleasure;

  • **Rage**—in which our pentup unhappiness is expressed in verbal, emotional, and even physical violence toward each other;[108] and

  • **Erotic Substitution for Joyful Relationships**—in which our sexual and aggressive desires show up as visual or verbal fantasies in our books, magazines, movies, advertising, gossip, and titillating media stories about sex and violence.[109]

Forward to the Past

We are now undergoing yet another primate pattern-based relationship revolution. Two factors are combining to challenge the civilization era layer of our evolutionary heritage.[110] First, our modern urban societies have removed most of us from the land and many of us from the ownership of *any* significant property. In addition, we now have lenient and effective laws for enabling men and women to divorce, divide their mostly paper wealth, and continue to share, although lopsidedly in most cases, the raising of their children. Secondly, because of contraception and women's entry in large numbers into the workforce, women are now economically much more self-sufficient.

The current relationship trends do not signal our movement to a fourth level of primate evolution. Instead, they represent a massive retreat from the culturally created lifelong monogamy ideal to the two older genetically based layers of our primate patterns. As divorce rates soar and extramarital affairs become available to the masses (especially the masses of women now in the workforce), our intimate relationships must again deal with the ancient realities of the promiscuity of our jungle time and the serial monogamy patterns of our savanna time. Sexually transmitted diseases, especially AIDS, are now applying the brakes to this retreat to our primal roots. But even AIDS can't change the nature of those roots, and, in the end, either by using sufficient precautions or by finding a cure, we will continue to go forward to the past.

The two oldest layers of our primate patterns were always at work within us, even at the height of our civilization era moralities. But there is now no *economic* basis for continuing our lifelong monogamy ways, and there is only our childlike need for perfect, ongoing emotional security on the *biological* level to keep us wishing for the now partially eclipsed monogamy ideal. As we'll see, there *are* ways for us to share lifelong love with one person. But without environmental and strong enough genetic support, no amount of *shaming* can work permanently to keep us from being what we really are. From my perspective, not even the healing of each other's inner child as a major relationship goal is going to stem the tide.

If we want to extend our relationships into lifelong partnerships, we're going to have to come at the problem from a different angle.

Hot Issues of This Transitional Time

• **Confusion about the Purpose of Our Relationships**—Caught between the competing drives of the mixed reproductive strategies from the two oldest layers of our primate patterns, our civilization era lifelong monogamy ideals, and our most recent psychological theories, many of us feel completely lost about the purpose of our relationships. From my perspective, many couples seem mesmerized by one or more of the proximate mechanisms nature created to serve its ultimate goal of successful reproduction. Dealing effectively with the proximate mechanism of our wounded inner child, for example, *is* certainly what our relationships can help us do. But to become lost in the project of healing our inner child in a relationship context may be yet another sign of the degree of our alienation from nature. Keeping the biological function of marriage and longterm relationship in mind, and seeing our other relationship goals from this perspective can help keep us grounded in reality, connected with our own primal natures, and reduce our confusion.

• **Gender Polarization**—As women seek to free themselves from aspects of the civilization era and even the savanna period and return to our jungle time—a healthy pursuit up to a point— a minority is moving in the direction of a pathological hatred of men and of male-female sexuality.[111] Men, reluctant to attack women at the same level of intensity, are nonetheless beginning to respond by escalating the conflict.[112] If present trends continue, it's difficult to see how men and women could fulfill their powerful, instinctual primate patterns for heterosexual love and pair-bonding.

• **What Happens to Our Children?**—In our jungle and savanna times, "fatherless" children of single-parent families were still immersed in tightly knit tribal units of twenty-five to fifty adults.[113] These children continued to have three absolutely vital ingredients, along with mother's love, for achieving their own healthy gender identities. They had *community,* and they had

powerful *role models* within those communities for both maleness and femaleness, along with a wealth of *nurturing personal
interactions* with mature members of both genders. Many of our
children have none of these things.

Where Do We Go From Here?

So, here we are, a confused and confusing species. We send our
inevitably mixed messages to each other and then try to figure
out who we (and that other person we love so much) really *are*.
Shot through with ambivalence, we engage in elaborate courtship dances with each other—approaching, then distancing, then
approaching again. We seek to feel 100 percent secure that the
wished-for partner is *the one* when, at least on the level of our
two oldest primate layers, there's no such thing. We supposedly
have trouble with intimacy. But who wouldn't, given our evolutionary history of patchwork solutions to life-or-death problems
in changing environments? Indeed, we and our relationships
seem to be real messes.

There *is* good news, however. It is my experience that by
knowing what we're made of, by understanding something of
how it happened, by accepting our complexity, and by working
with rather than *against* it we *can* make a world of realistic relationship happiness *for* ourselves and *with* our chosen partners.

Let me suggest that you go back and look again at the Hot Issues
pages of each of this chapter's major sections with an eye to becoming clearer about some of the largely destructive dynamics in
your present relationship—where they really come from and
how they got into your love life. Let what you discover sink in.
Encourage your partner to do the same. These are not *excuses*
for you or your partner to continue hurting each other. Rather,
they are *explanations* for behavior on both your parts which you
may have misunderstood. You may *really* love each other but
may not be meeting some of each other's instinctual needs, needs
which to a significant degree may be coming out of your primate
patterns.

If this is the case, there is much hope for your relationship.

4

REAL TIME:
THE PAST IN OUR RELATIONSHIP PRESENT

✳

Making Sense Out of Chaos

"I'M SO CONFUSED," Tammy said in exasperation. "Ed and I were so happy, so excited about each other when we started out. It seemed like we could handle our problems then. Now it's like the problems never got resolved. I guess we did *handle* them, but somehow we never got to the bottom of them. Where does love go anyway?" She looked defeated.

Ed mumbled wearily, "I'm not even sure anymore what the problems *are*. I've read about the inner child and we've tried some therapy together. But we still don't *get* anywhere. This isn't how I wanted to live. I'm tired."

He *looked* tired.

Often when couples come to me for help it's very late in the game. They've usually lost most of their goodwill and enthusiasm for each other and their relationships. Now they aren't motivated enough to make the changes they need to make in order to stay together happily. Often they've reached a stage of sexual malaise, and one or both of them is already having an affair. At this point the road to repairing and refurbishing their relationships is very difficult. Giving new life to faltering relationships is *always* difficult, but without goodwill and enthusiasm it's almost impossible.

When I was a pastor in a Christian church I was often asked to perform marriages for hopeful young couples. Most of them had no idea what they were in for. I would warn them that my experience and research told me they had anywhere from six months to two years or so to work out the *major* problems between them, because after the courtship and in-love stages of their relationships had passed their motivation to really *solve* their problems would most likely decline.[1] Of course, our optimism and denial being what they are, most of these couples didn't believe me. Many of them limped back into my office several years later in the throes of pain and confusion. What had gone wrong? How could this have happened to *us?* We had had such a unique love, immune from the problems of others. The beaten and desperate look in their eyes always moved me deeply, and I would help them search for a way to turn disillusionment back into joy. In those days, before I realized the importance of our biological heritage, I had limited success. Now, when I can get them to suspend their disbelief about the vital part our primate patterns play in our love lives, I can help tortured couples (and individual men and women) relax and become much more creative about resolving their relationship problems.

These problems are almost always the result of a painful combination of childhood traumas *and* confusing messages from the layers of our primate patterns. They are often identifiable by the "hot issues" that arise from these three layers. Sometimes all the hot issues in a relationship come from one layer. More often a mixture of issues from all three disrupts a couple's life together. With my awareness of the importance of our childhood experiences *and* our animal natures, I can now help women and men untangle this complicated emotional mix so that they can work creatively with their primate patterns for happier and more fulfilling long-term relationships.

David and Marlene: Jungle Time

As difficult as it may be to actually *feel* the connection at first, our jungle time is powerfully present in our lives today. It directly affects our daily-life attempts to find and keep the love we want. The destructive side of the hot issues that come out of this ancient layer impacts us in painful ways. Of course our pain feels personal—and it is. But what is really going on is *im*personal nature looking out for the good of our species.

For example, our relationship-disrupting desire for selective promiscuity as well as the more positive experience of sex as pleasurable and fun for its own sake, are legacies of those jungle days in which we were sexual several times a day—and with different partners. In our jungle time, sex held our societies together. It literally "connected" us to each other, eased tensions, especially when we were squabbling over food, and made us feel more friendly toward each other. Of course, it also made more of us, and our promiscuity assured a varied mix of our group's genes, an essential part of a species' adaptability to changing environments.

Our own culturally exaggerated male competitiveness and isolation is another inheritance from our jungle time. Those ancient male rivalries still haunt men's interactions with each other today. While there were sometimes genuine male friendships in the forest, the usual social pattern was for males to form only temporary coalitions in order to get and keep power. This was in contrast to the ongoing friendships among less power-oriented females. Then as now, males were taught to keep a stiff upper lip and to endure hardship and danger without a whimper.[2] This biologically based and culturally reinforced male tendency to limit feeling in order to compete, provide, and protect is a deep source of much of the grief and loneliness so many men feel today. If we don't challenge it and grow beyond it, men will be left feeling extremely vulnerable to the emotional power of women, as well as profoundly alienated from those aspects of their personalities that have nothing to do with providing, protecting, or competing.[3]

In the jungle all the females were "liberated." They were all economically self-sufficient and gathered their own fruits and vegetables. Females *as a group*—not as members of pair-bonded couples—were dependent on males *as a group* for protection from predators and other bands of protohumans. The only food that females were dependent on males for was meat, which in our jungle time was relatively unimportant.[4] This meant that females felt no compelling urge to bond with particular males, at least not for prolonged periods of time. Even when females did temporarily bond with alpha males, their "relationships" generally lasted only through their periods of estrus. Today, as individual women achieve economic freedom from their male partners and rush to reclaim this most ancient part of their primate heritage, they often run into conflict with the instincts of many males and even other females that are based on our *savanna* time, when females *were* economically dependent on males.

In our jungle time, neither females nor males were aware of fatherhood, and there was no need for individual males to become emotionally involved with *individual* females and their children, or vice versa.[5] So the most powerful bonds were between mothers and their children, and all our families were "single-parent." Males operated mainly on the periphery of the tribal territory, both physically and psychologically, and took little part in the social interactions between females and young.[6] In our modern social situation we see a huge resurgence of single-parent families, intensive mother-child bonding (often referred to as "inappropriate cross-generational bonding"), and the marginalizing of fathers—all factors which damage or destroy our chances for lasting happiness as couples.

The inheritance of our jungle time had direct and emotionally devastating consequences for David. I facilitate two men's support/therapy groups, which meet weekly in my office. When I interviewed David for membership, he told me a story of emotional betrayal and abandonment by his wife, Marlene. He also revealed his deep feelings of isolation from other men, and his anger about that even more primary betrayal.

He and Marlene had been married five years, and what at first had been a loving partnership had drifted into mutual fault-finding and recrimination. As their fighting got worse David found that his sexual interest in Marlene evaporated, and Marlene, for her part, became cold and withdrawn. But on one of those rare occasions when things did click Marlene had become pregnant. There had been complications with her pregnancy, and Marlene had had to quit her job and spend a couple of months in the hospital. Trying to be the dutiful husband and father-to-be, David had visited her every day. But he told me he'd always gotten a sinking feeling when he'd entered the room and found his wife cool and uncommunicative. After her initial rebuff, as he reported it, she would start grilling him about things in general and about money issues in particular. They would both end up in tears, she crying silently in her bed, and he in the parking lot, head bent over the steering wheel of the car.

After the baby came—a daughter whom they named Isabel—Marlene instantly became the devoted mother. David told me that in those first months after Isabel's birth, Marlene had pushed him even further away. He had come to feel cut off from his own family. That was hard enough to bear. But he really loved his daughter and it devastated him that he was being pushed out of *her* life as well. He came to feel, as he put it, like a "walking wallet." His function seemed to be to provide for a family he could not be a part of. Marlene poured out her feelings to little Isabel in long, often tearful soliloquies, and Isabel became her main reason for living.

David felt isolated and lonely. He also felt put down as a man and sexually frustrated. He had tried to talk to a couple of male friends about his situation, but they had basically "run for the hills." He also turned to three of his female friends. But he found no real support or understanding from them, either. Two of them strongly encouraged him to leave his wife. But they had ulterior motives; they wanted a shot at a relationship with him. The third was moralistic and judgmental.

At an office Christmas party, drunk and miserable, he'd made a pass at one of his female colleagues, and she, also drunk and miserable, had taken him up on it. They'd gotten a motel room, and David had come home at three o'clock in the morning. Marlene had spotted the makeup on his shirt.

Six months of hell followed in which David and Marlene fought daily, angrily accusing each other of betraying their marriage. It was at this point that David asked me about becoming a member of one of my men's groups.

Over the next year and a half in the group David found what he had been looking for all his life in terms of male friendship and nonjudgmental support. He also encountered some gentle yet firm challenging from the other men about some of his attitudes toward his wife. The powerful therapeutic effect that being challenged and supported by caring men had on David was dramatic. He'd felt in an emotional vise with Marlene, and while he'd stood up for himself as best he could, he had tended to feel intimidated by her anger. That was because, without male community, he'd tended to see life, relationships, and himself through *women's* eyes. Now, he was learning to see things through the eyes of *men*. His gender identity firmed up and from this newfound strength he was able to feel less shamed by Marlene's coldness and anger. He was also able to love her more and show her more patience on the one hand and strength on the other.

Finally the day came when he asked *her* to make some changes in her attitudes and behavior. And, in spite of her objections, he insisted on spending more time with Isabel. Once Marlene got the idea that he was serious she called her former boss, got her old job back, rented a studio apartment, took Isabel, and left him. When David didn't come crawling back within the next three months she filed for divorce.

Now, although he has liberal visitation rights, David says that Marlene makes it very difficult for him to see three-year-old Isabel. Sometimes she's not there when he arrives to pick her up. Sometimes Marlene claims Isabel is sick when, David says, it's obvious she's simply been confined to her room. And if he's ever late bringing her back Marlene threatens to restrict his visitation privileges. He feels betrayed again and further marginalized, and from the things Isabel occasionally says and the sometimes critical and hostile way she acts toward him he can tell that Marlene is filling Isabel with her *own* disappointment and frustration about him. At least David now has a supportive community of other men. But of course even that doesn't erase the pain he feels about the loss of his family.

David's story is necessarily one-sided. I never had the opportunity to hear Marlene's version. But judging by what David said about her it is easy to see that she too was in a lot of pain. And no doubt childhood issues on *both* their parts contributed to the destruction of their relationship. Perhaps Marlene's parents had been distant and unaffectionate. Perhaps her mother had harbored feelings of resentment against her father. Perhaps her father had been a "walking wallet." From what David revealed in the group it was clear that *his* mother had been extremely critical and shaming and often cold and withdrawn like Marlene, and his father had been physically and emotionally absent most of the time.

But viewed from the perspective of our evolutionary heritage, what David and Marlene went through together didn't come only from the personal level of family idiosyncrasies. Instead, I believe we can see the clash between two layers of their primate patterns. Marlene, no doubt through the filter of her childhood experiences, was angrily reclaiming her jungle time and raising many of the hot issues that come from it. And David, through the filter of his childhood experiences, showed a hurt and bewildered clinging to the patterns of his savanna time, the time when the nuclear family as we know it had first come into being.

Natasha, Frank, and Richard and Carla: Savanna Time

Nature invented serial monogamy to help our children survive on the dangerous savannas, and sexual jealousy to keep us together long enough to get them weaned.[7] Sexual shame and guilt were the enforcers. Because hunting was the most important way for our ancestors to get vital proteins and since males were the hunters, women became economically dependent on men to a very large extent.[8] Of course, men became dependent on women too, because women did most of the gathering of vegetable food and they were the ones who maintained the "invincible center" of the hearth fire and raised the children. The fact is, as men and women became more and more economically *inter*dependent in the new nuclear family arrangements, they became increasingly indispensable to each other as individuals. Men felt intense pressure to be the primary providers and protectors. And women felt much more vulnerable and anxious about their economic futures and those of their children. Their differing work roles were already present to some extent in the jungle. But in the harsh savanna environment they became magnified.

In addition, for reasons which we'll look at later, our ancestors became more and more childlike in certain ways. Our childlike inventiveness and creativity have always improved our chances for survival and given us amazing capacities to adapt to new environments. But our childlikeness also accounts for our child*ish*ness and our tendency to become, as psychologists now call it, codependent.

Natasha

Natasha had returned after about a year for more counseling. "Another relationship down the drain!" she cried. "What's *wrong* with me? I can't get my relationships to last more than a year or two. Then either the jerk I'm with or I—usually *I*—lose interest. I suppose you're going to tell me I'm afraid of intimacy."

"No," I said, "I don't think it has anything to do with fear of intimacy." She looked at me warily. I said, "Based on what I know about you I'd say you were, at least at one level, serially monogamous—by nature. I think most, if not *all* of us are. In every relationship you've told me about, you show tremendous capacity for intimacy. You share your thoughts and feelings, and you accept the man's. You work hard to define yourself as an individual and, at the same time, to be close to your partner."

"Yes, I *do*, don't I?" she said.

"Well, I'm not going to tell you you're immature, either. I think you have some issues you need to work on. You already know that—like maybe going for men who satisfy your need for excitement but who can't give you the kind of security at least part of you wants. But I don't think the capacity to stay with a relationship that is fundamentally disappointing, as many people do, is mature, either. Also, you're a complex and multifaceted woman, and you're naturally looking for a man who can resonate with you, at least well enough, on many levels. Until you find a man like that, I think your pattern of serial monogamy will continue. When you do find such a man it will probably ease off on its own. If not, there's still nothing *wrong* with you for going from one man to another if you're not basically satisfied."

I continued, "There no doubt *are* people—both men and women—who are under the power of a 'Peter Pan Complex' or whatever. But in my view, there are people who are addicted to the ' 'Til Death Us Do Part Complex' too. I think maturity is, to paraphrase Joseph Campbell, following your bliss. I don't mean that casually. I mean allowing yourself to feel your real feelings—your real joys *and* disappointments—evaluating them carefully, and then acting in your own interest. And your own interest can include self-sacrifice, for example, for your children or your mate. But not out of any kind of masochism or guilt or feeling that if you don't you're selfish or defective in some way."

"You mean it's okay to get tired of a relationship that I'm not satisfied with on some basic level?" she asked, somewhat amazed.

"Absolutely," I responded. "In my view, it's not only okay—it's the most responsible thing you can do. And it's completely natural."

"You don't think I'm being a perfectionist?"

"We'll keep an eye on it," I said. "But up to this point, I don't think so. In fact, I think you're so worried about being a perfectionist that you tend to *over*commit, even when the signs are all there that you're not going to get enough of your needs met."

"So I can stop feeling ashamed of my 'serial monogamy' pattern?"

"Yes. It sounds like a paradox, I know. It *is* a paradox. But if you can stop feeling ashamed of what is a part of a natural, biological program within you, you've taken the first realistic step toward extending your relationship past the limits of the serial monogamy pattern."

Frank

By his own admission Frank was insanely jealous. He said that when he and his girlfriend were at a party, she'd get into animated conversations with other men, and on the way home they would argue. Once, their argument led to a physical fight on the street in front of frightened onlookers. Finally, Frank had fallen to his knees on the sidewalk, crying and pleading, "Please! I can't help it! I can't control myself! I can't!"

They patched things up for a while. Then one day they had a scene in a restaurant. Their waiter had come up to them, smiled, and said, "Hi!" Frank's girlfriend had responded in kind. Frank had instantly become cold and withdrawn. He'd then become hypercritical of the food and everything his girlfriend did at the table—slurping her soup, dropping her napkin and asking the waiter for another. She'd finally asked Frank what was wrong with him *now*. And, he confessed in therapy, "I started in on her about wanting to go to bed with the waiter. I said, 'Why don't you just tell him you want to jump him, and I'll catch a taxi and leave you two to get it on?'" That incident, Frank told me, was the last straw. Not many days later his relationship was over, destroyed by his jealousy.

I worked with Frank for two years in counseling. What emerged was a picture of a childhood in which he'd always been the low man on the totem pole in his famiy. As the youngest in the family he'd always felt like all he'd ever gotten were the leftovers—of attention, of love, and even of material things. He'd never gotten a new bike, for example, and most of his clothes had been hand-me-downs. Even his junior high school sweetheart had been a castoff from his older brother. Frank claimed that even after she'd started to go out with him she'd shown in a hundred little ways that she was really still interested in his brother.

What I saw in Frank was a man whose shaming childhood wounds had exaggerated our natural primate tendency, inherited from our savanna time, to be possessive of our partners, and sexually jealous.

Frank said that in the early 1970s when the hippie movement was still in flower he'd lived in a commune where jealousy was taboo and free love was the rule. He said he'd really tried not to feel possessive and jealous when women he was attracted to went to bed with other men. When he did feel jealous, he'd beat up on himself for it, feeling guilty and ashamed.

In one of our early sessions I said to him, "You know, an exaggeration in one direction often breeds its opposite. I think the pain of exaggerated jealousy can call forth a radical *denial* of our *natural* tendency to be possessive of each other—in other words, free love. But the solution, in my opinion, is not to deny the power of our jealousy, but rather to accept that it is normal and innate up to a point. So, what we're going to do in your therapy is two things. We're going to work together to help you *accept* your jealousy as a natural part of your being a human male; and you'll learn to stop shaming yourself about it. And second, we're going to work to help you consolidate a stronger sense of your own masculine strength and self-worth—to get beyond your original family situation in which you really weren't allowed to have anything of your own."

I continued, "From everything you've told me it's clear that you've been damaged in your sense of self-worth, and that's resulted in your natural territoriality going off the scale. We just need to make a few adjustments to turn the volume down. That's all."

I could see the weight of a lifetime of shame beginning to drop from his shoulders.

Richard and Carla

Richard and Carla had met at the office of a prominent Chicago-area commercial real estate company. He was a high-powered salesman and she was an executive secretary. After six months of dating they decided to get married. Their agreement was that she would quit her job, they'd have a child, and they'd buy the kind of house in the suburbs they'd both always dreamed of. And that's what they did. They bought an amazing house on a huge property in an expensive northwest suburb where the average appraisal ran around a million dollars. Carla saw Richard as her white knight who had rescued her from a childhood of poverty and a work life that had felt to her like high-paid slavery. Soon they had little Jeremy, and their fantasy was complete.

But about the time Jeremy reached his ninth birthday the bottom dropped out of the commercial real estate market. For two years nothing moved. Richard had several big deals pending, but they just wouldn't come through. Soon they were living on his draw. But they were still behind in their mortgage payments and other bills.

Richard's sister and mother saw his and Carla's life unraveling, and helped them with money when they could. But the money they could offer was a drop in the bucket compared to their bills. Gradually Richard became demoralized, and though he started to look for another job, his efforts were half-hearted. The great protector-provider was crumbling. Carla was terrified.

She could see her dream of never working again and of being taken care of financially for the rest of her life shattering. She became angry with Richard, blaming him for not living up to his part of their marriage bargain. She railed at him for not listening to her when she'd warned him the year before that all indications were commercial real estate was not going to recover, not in this century. Rather than rising to the occasion and summoning his will and courage Richard sank further into his emotional paralysis.

When Richard's sister cautiously suggested to Carla that maybe she ought to think about getting a job to help out with the expenses, she said, "I worked for fifteen years! I'm not going to work again. I've paid my dues!" Richard's sister responded, "Richard's worked for fifteen years too, and he doesn't have the luxury of quitting!" Carla reacted by disinviting Richard's family for Christmas and by accusing them of not loving Jeremy. Richard's sister snapped back, "You're in danger of losing your house and going bankrupt, you won't help bail, and the ship is sinking—how much do *you* care about Jeremy? It seems to me that *you're* more important than your husband and even your son!"

Soon after this conversation Carla's attacks on Richard, and now his whole family, grew in intensity. Paranoia entered the picture—"You're all trying to destroy my dreams, dreams I've worked hard for, and dreams I have a right to!" Veiled threats and criticism became temper tantrums and pouting that sometimes lasted for days.

Richard felt increasingly guilty and ashamed for, as he put it, "not providing for my family the way a *real* man would," and his will and courage waned even more. Neither he nor Carla could adapt to their new situation. Exasperated, Richard's sister and mother finally stopped lending them money to support their clearly irrational course of *in*action. Richard's sister suggested to him that he was "enabling" Carla's petulance and her reign of emotional terror, and that, in fact, he'd become "codependent." Richard smiled weakly and said, "Well, there's nothing I can do about it." Carla's family criticized her for marrying, as they said, "such a wimp."

Eventually the ship sank.

*   *   *

Certainly, childhood wounds contributed greatly to Richard and Carla's inability to cope with the threat to their lifestyle. Richard's father had been hypercritical of him; nothing he did had ever been good enough. Richard had learned to protect himself from his "failures" by shutting down. Shamed for her storybook dreams from the time she was a little girl, Carla's anger was, in part, her attempt to protect herself from feeling that her family had been right about dreams not coming true.

But I believe their dysfunctional reaction to their financial crisis—at a more fundamental level—follows the lines of our savanna time primate patterns as well. Carla *needed* her powerful hunter and Richard *needed* his nurturing and supportive tender-of-the-hearthfire. They each needed the other to play these savanna time roles so badly that when they both failed to fulfill their ancient programs—because of their childhood wounding— neither of them could move forward. Neither could step out of their scripts. In addition, "civilization" had overloaded their grasslands wiring. Million-dollar houses were far more costly to keep up with than wildebeest herds.

George and Marva: Civilization

The hot issues of our agriculturally based industrial civilization showed up in George and Marva's life of low-level, chronic misery. They fervently believed in the main credos of this civilization—'til death us do part; work is good, pleasure is bad; sex is shameful, so save it for the "sacred act" of procreation. And they responded to these beliefs as many of us do to one degree or another—with fits of moralistic rage, sexual malaise, a "spiritualizing" of their marriage, sexual unfaithfulness, and overuse of erotic materials.

George and Marva were fully involved members of my church. They were both on the church council, and he was the leader of the youth group. I always thought that George was a little "squirrely" and that beneath her plump, friendly exterior, Marva was on the "bitchy" side. I didn't realize how right I was until a year or so into my pastorate when they came to me to "help them find Jesus again" in their marriage.

They had claimed from the first day I met them—in fact they'd made a point of it—that Jesus was the third person in their marriage and that in a spiritual sense he accompanied them everywhere, even into the bedroom. I wondered how this worked in terms of their sex life. But I let it go. For a couple so intimately connected with the God of love they did a lot of carping at each other. I told them I thought I could help them find God again in their marriage, but that that would involve their doing some real soul-searching and being absolutely honest about their real feelings and what was really going on in their relationship. When they resisted complete honesty, which was often, I reminded them that, as the Bible says, "the truth will set you free."

Over a period of time George gradually revealed that he felt trapped in his marriage. Marva lifted the veil of her superficial amiability and complained bitterly that George spent less and less time with her and that he seldom had the energy to make love to her. They both insisted, though, that they had a very spiritual marriage. When I asked them probing questions—for example, Did they ever see each completely naked? Did they ever look at themselves in a full-length mirror?—they winced. Once, George launched into a tirade against the morals of the teenagers in the youth group.

I found out that Marva had a huge collection of romance novels. When I asked her what she felt when she read them, she looked angry and defensive, and said, "Nothing!" But when I caught her in an unguarded moment she snapped, "Well, they're better than what I have with George!" George looked like he'd been hit by a truck.

Several months into our counseling work, a fourteen-year-old girl from the church came into my office with a predictable story. I knew she was the main baby-sitter for George and Marva's three-year-old son. She told me that the last Friday night George had made a pass at her. I asked her what she meant. She said, "Well, Mrs. Cameron had gone upstairs to get ready for bed, I guess. And he came over to me with a funny look on his face. Then he reached under the couch and took out one of the *Playboys* he kept there. I knew they were there—I found them once when I was looking for one of Chris's toys. He showed me some of the pictures and told me he'd like to see me posing like that. I backed away and said, 'Please Mr. Cameron, I don't like this.' He got really angry and said, 'Come on. I'm taking you home right now!'"

"And that was the end of it?" I asked.

"Yes," she said. "But I don't want to go back there. I don't want to baby-sit for them anymore."

I said, "Well, that's probably a good idea. Are you okay?"

"Yes, of course. I wasn't born yesterday. I just thought you should know."

I thanked her, asked her to let me know if she felt upset about the incident in the future and wanted to talk about it, and determined to schedule an individual session with George.

When I brought up the subject, George turned bright red, hung his head, and started sobbing. "I'm so ashamed!" he wailed. Now, the *real* work of helping George and Marva unearth their feelings about themselves and their marriage had begun.

The suppressed and repressed desires of the two older layers of our primate patterns—our jungle time and our savanna time—*will* find ways to express themselves and sabotage our civilization era's most "noble" attempts at denial. George's jungle time sexual desires and Marva's savanna time romantic pair-bonding instincts powerfully challenged their civilization era spiritual ideals. Of course, this was destructive for the kind of marriage they were trying to have. But it also carried a tremendous healing potential. Including these older layers of their animal selves in their marriage could open up George and Marva to a far more complete and much more satisfying relationship.

Good News

Not surprisingly, most of the couples I work with are in deep trouble, and our primate patterns are showing up in destructive ways. I look at most of my friends and they're living lives I wouldn't want, either.

But there is a positive side to most of the hot issues we've inherited from our primate past. The very things that hurt us also give us life and joy. For example, from our jungle time our enthusiasm for promiscuity and recreational sex brings us sexual joy and spontaneity, and variety makes our lives interesting. Male competitiveness can be invigorating. Women's economic self-sufficiency restores a lost side of femininity and gives women options they haven't had for a long time. Mother-child bonding and even single-parent families at their best provide children with their primary experiences of being loved and wanted.

From our savanna time our tendency toward serial monogamy, reinforced by sexual jealousy and feelings of shame and guilt, give us the experiences of falling in love, courtship, and in-depth exploration of ourselves and other people. They also give men the joy of fatherhood. Even the economic subordination of women gives them a set of options largely denied to men, and the pressure on men to protect and provide gives them a kind of pride that few women know. Our mutual dependency gives us affectionate and deep bonds with each other and the satisfying feeling of working together as a team. And our ongoing child-likeness is the source of our playfulness, our curiosity, and our creativity. Without these things our lives would be dull exercises in survival.

As for civilization, I'm afraid I have to agree with Freud that, for the most part, it tends to make most of us at least a little neurotic. But even here work has its own rewards, erotic materials of various kinds can help us feel alive when other things fail, and "spiritualized" relationships evoke powerful emotions of friendship and loyalty—of caritas love, as the ancient Greeks called it. In addition, our civilizations have enhanced our sense of morality and law, given us a certain freedom, even as individuals, by enforcing agreed-upon mores, and provided us with the bright vision of lifelong love for one another.

Our primate natures can be our allies if we learn to work *with* them—even our jungle and savanna time patterns. But we have to be able to *see* them at work in our relationships in order to harness their tremendous power for helping us grow and unfold as individuals and as couples. The following exercise is designed to help us take a first step toward seeing the primate patterns in our present relationships.

Hot Issues in Your Relationship:
A Self-Evaluation

This exercise is set up to help you evaluate the *disrupting* influences of the primate patterns in your relationship. Some of the questions are only for women, others only for men; most are for both. The results are intended to be qualitative and relative; there's no way to give absolute weight to the scores. What the exercise *can* do is determine how strongly you (and your partner) are being influenced by each of the three layers of your primate patterns, and what effect they are probably having on your relationship.

If you are in a relationship now, and you both want to do this self-evaluation—which I would encourage—you may not want to score yourselves on the following pages. Most likely you will want to do this exercise separately—and privately. So you will need to take out separate sheets of paper, copy the subject headings on the left side of the paper, and number the questions that apply to you as a man or woman. Copy the numbers as they appear. (Don't number consecutively, because not all the numbers will apply to you.) You don't have to copy the questions. Then, from left to right at the top of the page opposite the subject headings write "Strongly Disagree (-2)," "Disagree (-1)," "Uncertain (0)," "Agree (+1)," and "Strongly Agree (+2)." In other words, copy the format in this book.

Place an "X" beside the question number in the column you feel best describes your behavior and feelings—"Strongly Disagree," "Disagree," and so on. Some of the questions are statements of feelings and some are descriptions of behavior. The fact is, we're not always in touch with our feelings; and our behavior reveals unconscious feelings, often feelings we don't like to admit.

Needless to say, this exercise requires absolute honesty if it's going to tell you what you need to know. If you're not currently in a relationship you can score yourself in terms of your last or your most emotionally significant relationship as you remember it. If you *are* in a relationship, and you've each done this exercise, you may or may not choose to share your scores with each other. That will depend a lot on what condition you think your relationship is in.

Jungle Time	-2	-1	0	+1	+2
Promiscuity 1. I have had many sexual partners 2. I have had promiscuous fantasies					
Recreational Sex 3. I enjoy sex for its own sake, with or without feelings of love					
Male Competitiveness and Isolation 4. As a male, I feel cut off from deep friendships with other men, friendships in which I could share my real situation and my real feelings					
Women's Self-Sufficiency 5. As a woman, I am financially independent of my partner 6. As a woman, I believe financial independence enhances my relationship 7. As a man, I believe my partner's independence enhances our relationship					
Mother-Child Bonding 8. As a mother, I experience my child(ren) as more emotionally vital to me than my partner 9. As a father, I feel my partner devalues our relationship in favor of our child(ren)					
Single-Parent Families 10. As a single mother, I am comfortable raising my child(ren) without a husband 11. As a single mother, I view my child(ren)'s father(s) primarily as a source of income					

Strongly Disagree (-2)   Disagree (-1)   Uncertain (0)
Agree (+1)   Strongly Agree (+2)

JUNGLE TIME	-2	-1	0	+1	+2
12. As a separated or divorced father, I feel quite *comfortable* living separately from my previous family					
13. As a separated or divorced father, I *resent* being perceived by my previous family as a "walking wallet"					

SAVANNA TIME	-2	-1	0	+1	+2
Serial Monogamy 1. The relationship pattern in my life is that of serial monogamy					
2. If I felt emotionally and/or financially free to do it, I would want to have a series of relationships throughout my life					
Sexual Jealousy 3. I feel intense sexual and relationship jealousy toward my partner					
Shame and Guilt 4. I feel guilty and ashamed of my feelings and actions toward my partner, especially my aggressive feelings and actions and my sexual desire for others					
Economic Subordination of Women 5. As a woman, I am financially dependent on my partner					
6. As a woman, I feel *content* with this arrangement most of the time					

Strongly Disagree (-2)   Disagree (-1)   Uncertain (0)
Agree (+1)   Strongly Agree (+2)

Savanna Time	-2	-1	0	+1	+2
Intense Pressure on Men to Protect and Provide					
7. As a man, I feel intense *pressure* to protect and provide for my partner (and our children)					
8. As a man, I feel *content* with being the primary (or sole) protector and provider					
Mutual Dependency					
9. I feel that I couldn't live without my partner					
10. My partner and I are dependent on each other emotionally and in terms of maintaining a home					
Childlikeness					
11. I enjoy my partner taking care of me; for example, cooking, bringing me my coffee, buying me things					
12. I am childish in expressing my feelings and desires, often demanding my own way and going into a "snit" when I don't get it					

Civilization	-2	-1	0	+1	+2
Feelings of Enslavement					
1. I have felt trapped in my relationship, and cut off from exploring other relationships					
Work Is Good; Pleasure Is Bad					
2. I work hard and find little time or energy for pleasure					

Strongly Disagree (-2)   Disagree (-1)   Uncertain (0)
Agree (+1)   Strongly Agree (+2)

CIVILIZATION	-2	-1	0	+1	+2
Sex Is for Procreation 3. I believe that premarital sex is wrong					
Anger and Rage 4. I feel angry about the sexual practices and morals of others					
Sexual Malaise 5. I feel sexually bored with my partner					
Spiritual (Platonic) Relationships 6. I feel very little sexual desire for my partner, but I feel strong emotional, intellectual, and spiritual companionship with him/her. I feel that this is more important than sex with him/her					
Sexual Unfaithfulness 7. I am being, have been, or would like to be sexually active with others					
Erotic Substitution 8. I use magazines, romance novels, videos, and other erotic materials to enjoy myself sexually/romantically without my partner					

Strongly Disagree (-2)   Disagree (-1)   Uncertain (0)
Agree (+1)   Strongly Agree (+2)

Add up your positive points (+), then your negative points (-) for each section. If the positive points exceed the negative, subtract the negative. If the negative points exceed the positive, subtract the positive. (Zeros don't count.) If your total score is 3 or more *positive* points in a particular section, the destructive potentials in this layer of your primate patterns are impacting your relationship in ways that you need to be aware of. If your total score is 3 or more *negative* points in any one section, the hot issues in this layer of your primate patterns are not a major factor at this time. It's been my experience with couples that these dynamics change over time, partly in response to how well they're getting their needs met at any given stage of their relationship. While this exercise can be a guide for alerting you to potential problems and areas of relative calm and satisfaction (at least for now), in the end you will have to do some serious reflection to determine for yourself where you think the areas of tension are, or are likely to be, in your relationship. Let your "gut feeling" be your ultimate guide.

You might want to summarize your findings below and how you feel about what you've learned, or use separate sheets of paper, or a journal. Often, writing our observations and emotional reactions down helps clarify them. Reading what we've written keeps our insights conscious. For example, you might notice that in spite of strong feelings of disapproval (perhaps of yourself or others) for jungle time–like behavior, you've scored heavily in that section. It could be important for you to record this discrepancy and explore your reactions in detail.

Not only do our primate patterns show up as hot issues in our love lives; they also structure the *forms* our love takes, the *stages* our relationships go through, and the *chemicals* that fuel our passions—and our boredom. It's to these all-embracing influences of our primate past on our relationship present that we now turn.

5

Predictable Passions: The Forms, Stages, and Chemistry of Love

✳

OUR ENGLISH WORD "LOVE" covers a lot of territory. We know it signifies feelings of affection, attachment, bonding, loyalty, compassion, respect, and empathy for others. It may also indicate the presence of passion—emotional and sexual. But we know from experience that we have to put "love" in context—the context of the particular *kind* of relationship we're in. For example, the love of a parent for a child is different from the passion of new lovers, and a child's love for his or her father has a different tone entirely (Well, not entirely!) from the love between marriage partners. And we know that these kinds of love feel different from erotic excitement, or, for that matter, from the love we may feel toward a brother or sister, or a friend.

Not only does love come in different *forms,* in terms of our intimate relationships it comes in *stages* as well. The forms of love and the stages of love in our intimate relationships are closely tied to each other, so that different forms come into play at different stages. Body and brain chemistry both cause and result from the tidal forces we call "love."

But before we look more closely at the relationship between our primate patterns and the forms, stages, and chemistry of romantic love let's do another self-evaluation exercise. Answer the questions below with as much honesty as you can. Then read the chapter. At the end, I'll show you how to score your answers.

Where Am I?: A Self-Evaluation Exercise

This exercise is designed to help you determine which forms of love are the most significant in your relationship right now. It will also help you realize which stage you're probably in. Chances are you already have a good idea, but you may be surprised.

Read the questions and mark Y (Yes) or N (No) in the appropriate box next to the number of the question on the scoring grid on page 80. Don't spend too much time thinking about any question. Read it carefully but go with your "gut feeling."

1. I look at my partner and think, "How handsome/beautiful he/she is," without necessarily feeling sexually aroused.

2. When I'm with my partner, I feel a "chemistry" between us.

3. When I look at my partner, I sometimes feel myself short of breath and tingling all over.

4. I would frequently rather cuddle than make love.

5. A very important thing to me in our relationship is that my partner is a supportive companion for me— through thick and thin.

6. I usually feel good about giving up my own interests and desires for my partner's happiness.

7. I delight in just watching my partner, as if from a distance.

8. I feel that I can't keep my hands off my partner at times.

9. The quality that characterizes our relationship best is a feeling of ecstasy.

10. What I usually want after a hard day's work is to be soothed and comforted.

11. My partner and I frequently have stimulating conversations that often feel more satisfying to me than many other features of our relationship.

12. My partner's happiness is of paramount importance to me.

13. A kind of emotionally detached appreciative evaluation of my partner stands out as an important aspect of my feelings about our relationship.

14. I feel aroused by the smell and taste of my partner, the texture of his/her skin, his/her voice, and many other physical qualities.

15. My relationship is profoundly fulfilling, almost as if it has restored a missing piece of my life.

16. My partner's childlike innocence and spontaneity really tug at my heartstrings.

17. I feel deep appreciation for my partner as a person, and at the same time I seldom feel sexual with him/her.

18. Making my partner happy is one of my most important goals in our relationship.

19. One of the most important aspects of our relationship is to be seen with my partner and to have others see him/her as a real asset to me.

20. I feel that I want to "make babies" with my partner.

21. I like to buy gifts for my partner, write poems for him/her, and listen to love songs.

22. I feel that I could never leave my partner, because he/she really needs me.

23. My partner and I have what I would describe as a spiritual relationship.

24. Selfless giving characterizes our relationship, even when I feel the giving is mostly one way.

25. Although my partner and I seldom "set the night on fire," the pilot light is almost always burning.

26. My partner is very attractive, alluring, and sexually provocative.

27. Our relationship has a mystical, magical quality that is more powerful for me than any of its other attributes.

28. My partner and I sometimes use the affectionate terms "Mom" and "Dad" for each other.

29. The quality that best describes our relationship is that my partner and I are a good team.

30. I feel that by delaying the gratification of my own desires I'm growing in my capacity to love my partner.

SCORING GRID

	1.		2.		3.		4.		5.		6.	
	Y	N	Y	N	Y	N	Y	N	Y	N	Y	N
1			2		3		4		5		6		
7			8		9		10		11		12		
13			14		15		16		17		18		
19			20		21		22		23		24		
25			26		27		28		29		30		
TOTALS:												

Don't skip to the end of the chapter. Please continue reading. I'd like you to become familiar with my thinking about the forms and stages of love before you interpret your scores. That way your scores will mean much more to you.

Chemical Fires

I had just locked my car and was heading across the parking lot toward the drugstore. A woman, probably in her early forties, came my way. I must have had that wide-eyed "Wow!" expression on my face. She looked up, caught herself in midstep and hesitated for a split second. Our eyes met and held each other's for a heartbeat. Then she looked down, smiled what seemed like an appreciative and knowing smile, and we passed each other. But in that moment it felt as if our souls had brushed against each other. The feeling was almost palpable. It was as if we'd each raised a hand and our fingers had touched lightly, with mutual recognition and respect. "Chemistry," as we say, had happened.

I went on into the drugstore feeling pleasantly surprised—stunned actually—by that momentary miracle. I felt affirmed somewhere deep in my male essence, suddenly and unexpectedly refreshed and alive.

What we talk about as chemistry between two people is not just a metaphor. In our mysterious cellular depths where our souls and bodies interact our emotions create chemical reactions, and chemicals shape our feelings and give them their intensity. While scientists still don't know very much about it, enough research has been done to give us clues about how chemistry is related to the *forms* and *stages* of love inherited from our evolutionary past.

The Forms of Love

Philosophers, poets, theologians, and most recently psychologists have tried to define the various forms of love. In the process, for all their good intentions, they've often scrambled each other's terms and definitions.

My own way of understanding the different forms of love separates them into seven main kinds. The first is *aesthetic appreciation*. When we feel this emotion we are experiencing the object of our appreciation in an almost tactile way, drinking in its—or his or her—form, color, texture, sound, taste, and smell; but we're still somewhat emotionally distant. We feel wonder and satisfaction at the beauty we are experiencing, and the chemical fires are beginning to flicker; but they haven't been fanned into the flames of passion yet.

If that happens, they flare into the second form of love—*sexual attraction*. In this form of love, as we all know, the awakening "urge to merge" that is present in aesthetic appreciation grows into all-consuming desire.

The third form of love, *romance,* may or may not then be added to the mix. Romance is the passionate desire to merge *souls.* In romance we unconsciously experience ourselves and our partners as one. In this form of love, as psychologists have said, we mostly project elements of our unknown and unacknowledged depths onto the other person. This includes unfinished business with our parents and other members of our original families, and repressed aspects of our once-whole selves. We often idealize—while at the same time we resist—the other person, and experience our own unactualized qualities as characteristics of our partners.

The other four forms of love—*parent-child, child-parent, friendship* (including brother/sister love), and *caritas* (which I identify with *agape,* selfless giving to others)—may all be present in our fully developed relationships. In fact, elements of *all* the forms of love may be present to some degree or another. But, strange as it may seem at first, it is possible to feel deeply romantic about someone without feeling sexual, or sexual without feeling romantic. It is also possible to feel caritas love for someone we don't like and would never choose as a friend. We can feel a lot of parent-child love for our partners and not feel romance, or even friendship. And so on. This is one of the reasons why "love" is such a confusing set of feelings to sort out. It's one of the reasons we often find it so difficult to understand ourselves in our relationships.

The particular combination the forms of love manifest in our relationships is determined by several factors. Our life experiences tend to turn up the volume on one or more forms of love and turn it down on others. For example, unmet childhood needs for love from our parents may lock us into a pattern of seeking the "perfect parent" in our mates. Or unfulfilled needs for friendship (or brothering or sistering) may cause this form of love to be more important for us than, say, sexual attraction. Our innate temperaments play a part too. For instance, some people are probably more romantic by nature than others, just as some people have a higher sex drive than others.

But all the forms of love are outgrowths of our primate heritage at the foundational level. They are all present at least in rudimentary form not only in the other apes but in many other animals as well. What's more, the *stages* of love which, in part, evoke the different forms of love in our relationships, startlingly re-create for each of us the whole evolutionary history of our human intimacies.

The Stages of Love

As psychologists have seen, our relationships go through predictable stages. Occasionally the order changes—for example, when friendship love, characteristic of the later stages of most relationships, precedes attraction, falling in love, and courtship. But this reversal of the usual order is rare. Usually our relationships begin with *attraction,* pass through an *in-love* stage, go on to *courtship,* then *bonded comfort and conflict,* and finally reach burnout or *boredom.* We would all probably like to avoid the "conflict" part of bonding and find some way to circumvent the "boredom" stage. While these unpleasant aspects of our love lives were invented by nature to ensure genetic variety, it's been my experience that if couples know what they're up against in terms of our primate patterns and the stages of love, and intervene to keep their relationships fresh, vital, and instinctual, they can short-circuit nature's plans and extend their relationships into long-term—and fulfilling—pair-bonds.

The sequence of the stages of love is the result of millions of years of evolution and reflects a growing enrichment of our human experience of intimacy. The stages of love are innate; within flexible limits they progress according to "time-released" patterns within us.

Attraction

When I was a teenager the movie version of *South Pacific* was big. I was fascinated by the story and, of course, the music. One of the songs that moved me was "Some Enchanted Evening." It seemed to resonate with my experience of love, which for me often came unexpectedly and with seemingly life-transforming force. I loved the feeling. I also hated it because it unleashed barely controllable emotions and desires. That initial attraction was without doubt the most powerful feeling I'd experienced up to that point. Whatever else it did for me, it made me feel incredibly alive.

We now know that at least part of that feeling of aliveness at the attraction stage of love comes from the interaction of male and female chemistries. Although our species has a generally poor sense of smell, research has shown that women *are* sensitive to the smell of Exaltolide, a synthetic testosterone-like chemical, especially when they're ovulating.[1] It seems possible that men too can smell the sexual chemicals wafting from women. We also know that, if we can get close enough to each other, men and women are turned on by chemicals secreted by each other's armpits, especially butyric acid (the modern perfume industry notwithstanding).[2] When a man kisses a woman she can actually pick up traces of testosterone in his saliva,[3] and, below the level of consciousness, women swoon for the compound 5-alpha-androstenol in male sweat, a chemical messenger whose job it is to announce "Powerful male present!"[4]

Men's sexual interest is additionally triggered by *visual* cues from women, most of which have ancient roots.[5] Most men respond to a woman's youthful looks (a subliminally noted indication of her capacity to bear children); clear, smooth skin (an indication of her good health); the way she smiles, tosses her hair, and in general carries herself (a signal that she's both tender and fierce—willing and able to be a full partner); and a hundred other visually encoded communications.

Women's initial interest is triggered by visual signals from men too, such as their upper body strength, the "character" evident in their faces and their bearing (signs of their capacity to overcome adversity), and so on.[6] But for women in general, visual signals are less important than they are for men. What's more important for women are the signals communicated by touch.[7] Women can read the nuances of feeling in a man's touch, and from these (along with other cues) intuit the nature of a man's personality and intentions.

Touch, of course, assumes that a man has been able to get

close enough to make physical contact, something a woman will usually permit only after she feels reassured by her initial visual impressions and by conversation.[8] A man's visual orientation and a woman's tactile awareness lead to a difference in the ways men and women must handle their initial attraction to each other. Men's visual emphasis, as we'll see, is almost certainly a legacy of their savanna time, when spotting prey or predator at a distance was essential to survival.[9] Women's tactile sensitivity may come out of their ancient roles as mothers who needed to be able to feel the slightest mood shifts of the children they carried against their bodies throughout much of their first three or four years of life.[10]

Our two genders could certainly learn from each other's ways of negotiating the difficult, often emotionally and sometimes physically dangerous passage through the initial attraction stage. Women could learn to be more skilled "hunters" of potentially good relationships, and take more initiative. And men could learn to be more careful in their assessment of the merely visual cues they receive, and much more sensitive to a woman's personality. But having said this, our modes of approaching each other are biologically grounded. We can learn more flexible behaviors in the initial attraction stage, but we can't turn the underlying male/female patterns upside-down.[11] Men will still be the primary initiative-takers and hunters—the "penetrators"—and women will still be more evaluating and receptive—the "receivers." To the extent that we ignore or disparage this biologically grounded male/female difference, we block our understanding of each other. If we expect the other gender to behave like us or respond the way we do we will be disappointed and confused. As a result, women may experience men as "predators," and men may experience women as willfully withholding in order to gain the upper hand.[12]

The most powerful *forms* of love in the attraction stage are aesthetic appreciation and sexual attraction. With some modifications from our savanna time (for instance, the search for a long-term mate), this stage of love is governed mainly by our jungle time, which can kick in anytime, anyplace—at the bar, museum, workplace, party, classroom, drugstore, or wherever we happen to run into each other. While we can stay attracted to our partners for years, the time frame for this stage—as a stage in itself—is usually from a few minutes to several weeks. Then the next phase of relationship may, or may not, kick in.

In Love

It's three o'clock in the morning, and Renée can't sleep. She looks at the clock, sighs, and tosses and turns some more. Finally, she switches on the light, gets out of bed, and heads for the living room. "What the hell is wrong with me?" she asks herself out loud. Images of Ben flood her mind, the same images that have been torturing her all night—his smile, the lines around his eyes which say, "I love life, but I've been through hell too," the tenderness and strength in his voice, the energy of his hands on her body, the way he handled the confrontation with the mechanic. And she thinks, "I'm really falling for this guy, and I don't *want* to! I'm letting him have power over my feelings!" She runs her fingers through her hair. "How do I know I can trust him?"

"My God," she whispers to herself, "I must be *in love* with him!"

In the in-love stage an intense drama begins between feelings of anxiety and ecstasy, pain and pleasure, old feelings of worthlessness and new feelings of empowerment. We idealize our beloved, and at the same time may feel intense hostility toward him or her. The psychologist Theodor Reik saw that this idealization/hostility dynamic is a struggle between giving away our power in submission to our idealized partner and desperately, even angrily, trying to recover it.[13] We secretly blame him or her for taking our power when we ourselves have unconsciously and compulsively given it to them. Our boundaries are open and our defenses are down. And we may panic when our partner—inevitably—sometimes fails to reciprocate.

We're off center and unconsciously engaged in a fantasy of merging with the other.[14] We find it difficult to keep a clear sense of who we are, where we end and the other person begins. We're deeply irritated by this uncomfortable situation, and like a hooked fish we struggle to break free. But if our in-love feelings are strong enough we feel our beloved reeling us in.

We may get hopelessly confused between our legitimate need for independence and the delicious experience of finally depending on someone else. On an unconscious level, that someone else seems to offer us the bliss of perfect union with the parents we always wished we'd had.[15] We feel the struggle between the powerful bonding process and our need for personal freedom. But if our new relationship is going to move ahead, the feelings of joy and of personal validation and empowerment eventually triumph, and, in the midst of our tears, we step into the passionate paradise only lovers can know.

During this process, what biologists call "female coyness"[16] often comes to the fore. This so-called coyness is a kind of resistance to the male hunting and penetrating strategy. It's not meant to communicate a woman's unavailability. But it *is* meant to convey her capacity to be careful in her selection of a partner. Female reticence is not passivity. Rather, it is the reflection of the biological truth that a woman is investing far more than a man when she falls in love—in a direct, biological, and on-the-line way. Since nature's goal for making us fall in love is to get us to make babies, it pays a woman to be more cautious than a man at this stage. She is the one who will bear the physical consequences of nature's intentions.

Female coyness is already present in the preceding attraction stage. It shows up as a woman's relative lack of responsiveness to visual cues. *She* requires *him* to make the first move and prove to her that he is worthy of coming close enough to really arouse her. This gives her time to make an initial assessment. In the in-love stage, this whole dynamic is amplified. Studies show that men *do* tend to fall in love faster than most women. They also show that women, once they fall in love, tend to become more deeply committed.[17]

Of course, other factors, such as the scarcity of attractive men (who are available), can complicate this scenario and make women much less cautious and prone to move just as fast—in some cases faster—than men.[18] But other things being equal, the underlying biological pattern makes itself felt. Neither a woman's body nor her animal soul realize that birth control can protect her from the biological consequences of throwing her natural caution to the winds. Only the human part of her brain—the neocortex—knows this, and it seems to have a difficult time sharing its information with the rest of who she is.

In terms of the chemistry of the in-love period, we know that in addition to testosterone as a factor in both men and women, adrenaline is at work propelling us into a state of heightened awareness and hypervigilance, and into intense moods of fear, anger, and euphoria.[19] Adrenaline pushes us to *act* in response to what feel like life-enhancing as well as life-threatening situations. It fuels our characteristic fight-or-flight feelings when we're in love. Also, a chemical known as PEA (phenylethylamine), along with norepinephrine and dopamine—all natural amphetamines—produce feelings both of exhilaration and apprehension.[20] These natural amphetamines keep us up all night sharing our deepest feelings and making love with almost boundless energy. They also cause us to toss and turn on those nights when something's gone wrong—or very *right*—between us.

The *forms* of love that usually have the strongest impact on us at this stage are sexual attraction, romance, parent-child, and child-parent love. Also, we begin to feel glimmerings of friendship for each other. As we've noted, *all* the forms of love may be present at every stage to some extent, but some are more characteristic of one or more stages than others.

The layer of our primate patterns that governs our in-love stage is still our jungle time. Our ancient jungle consortships give the basic shape and emotional punch to our powerful feelings. But the complexity of our inner conflicts and our resulting conflicts with *each other* are due mostly to the tensions of the next stage—the courtship stage. This phase overlaps our in-love stage and comes out of our savanna time. The tensions we now start to experience are the result of trying to fit very *independent,* self-sufficient jungle animals into the makeshift pair-bonds of *mutually dependent* savanna-dwelling teams. While for some people the in-love stage may last only a few weeks (the time frame of jungle time courtships), for most of us it runs anywhere from six months to two years, with gradually diminishing force. For a fortunate few, the in-love dimension can be an ongoing part of their partnerships, and last a lifetime.

Courtship

Sherri hadn't heard from Steve in almost two days. She knew something was up. Finally, she called. Now, she's clutching the receiver as if her life depended on it, her heart pounding as she tries to absorb what he's telling her. "Sherri, I haven't called because I've been thinking." A long pause. "We've been seeing each other for two months now, and I know there's a strong connection between us. I know you've been seeing another guy. You've been completely honest about that. But I think the moment has come to decide who it's gonna be—him or me?" Another pause. "You know I'm in love with you. You know enough about me to know what kind of man I am, and I think you know yourself well enough to know if you want to pursue our relationship or not." Sherri draws a deep breath. Steve tells her: "I want an exclusive relationship with you."

Sherri is silent.

"Sherri? Are you there?"

"Yes, I'm here." Silence. "Okay," she almost whispers.

"What?"

"Okay."

"Great!"

"Steve, I love you."

Joy and fear mingle for each of them as they hang up.

Our courtships usually start shortly after we fall in love and extend into the next stage of relationship—bonded comfort and conflict. Many animals, especially the relatively nonpromiscuous ones such as geese and wolves, go through elaborate courtship rituals to convince each other that they would be good ongoing genetic investments.[21] This is true of us as well.

During courtship we strut and preen and put our best foot forward in a kind of prescripted dance with each other. Women try to display the qualities they think men are looking for (See chapter 3, pp. 37, 45–46), and men try to do the same (see chapter 3, pp. 36, 46). We want to convince each other that we're healthy, that we're childlike enough to be vulnerable, but not too child-*ish*, that we're competent in our instinctual gender roles— women *primarily* as mothers and emotional nurturers, men *primarily* as protectors and nurturing providers, and so on. All of this takes place through a hundred subliminal cues no matter what gender norms are current in our cultures.[22]

Much of our courtship behavior is ritualized. While the partic- ular forms these rituals take are strongly influenced by our indi- vidual cultures, the patterns are universal. In every culture men give gifts to the women they are wooing.[23] Their gifts show that they can provide for and are willing to nurture their beloved. Gifts also demonstrate that they hold the woman in high regard and are willing to at least *consider* being sexually loyal. Often women will prepare meals for the men they are courting, signal- ing *their* capacity and willingness to be nurturing in return.[24] In a holdover from our hunter/gatherer days, men will often supply the meat for these ritual meals, and even cook it, while women will supply the vegetables. This is true even in our culture: our intimate candlelight dinners as well as our more gregarious bar- hopping activities often reflect this pattern. Eating together is fre- quently a prelude to lovemaking.

Even our *emotional* rituals—approaching, rejecting, approach- ing again—are part of the mating dance of many species. In humans this pattern not only reflects inner conflicts (about the whole process of trying to pair-bond) which emerged at the in-love stage and which intensify during courtship; it also is un- consciously designed to test our own and the other person's capac- ities for patience, emotional support, and commitment.[25]

At some point in this phase of our relationships we also begin the ritual process of negotiating for the things we want *for* our- selves and *from* the other person.[26] These mostly unconscious negotiations are over a host of things, from the mundane to the most vital issues of self-definition, from what movies we're going to see to what kind of influence our respective families are going to have on our lives as couples.

Backing off, breaking up, seeing other people, and making up are all part of the ritual as we test and retest ourselves and each other. Often a relationship hits a plateau and seems to stall. Usually plateaus are an unconscious call for one or both people to move the relationship to a greater level of trust and commitment.[27] Sometimes, though, they are signs that things are moving too fast, at least for one of the parties.

Female coyness continues to play a role at this point, although men who moved rapidly through the first two relationship stages may now slow things down considerably when faced with the looming prospect of marriage.[28] We may both hold out for more reassurances from the other, more compromises, more signs of each other's capacities for intimacy and continuing loyalty.[29]

Sometimes the struggle for power that began in the in-love stage degenerates into a full-scale war. We begin to withdraw our idealized pictures of the other person as we learn the disappointing truth that they're neither going to be our perfect parents nor even perfect mates.[30] The extent to which we've worked through the unfinished business with our childhoods becomes critical now. If we've done our homework we'll get through the power struggles and be able to reach adult compromises. But if we haven't, the later phase of courtship is likely to see our power struggles intensifying.

In terms of the chemistry involved, we're still floundering in the soup of sex odors, testosterone, adrenaline, and natural amphetamines. The *forms* of love that dominate our courtships are the same ones that prevailed at the in-love stage—though some of them are probably beginning to feel a little tired. Under the best circumstances friendship love is beginning to grow, and selfless caritas is dawning as we reach a deeper understanding of each other as real people in all our genuine splendor and with our equally real deficits.[31]

The savanna layer of our primate patterns first makes its presence fully felt in the courtship stage. The savanna period of our evolutionary history, as we recall, extended our jungle consortships from a few days or weeks to several years and deepened our feelings for each other from mainly sexual infatuation to the full range of our human forms of love. It's clear from studies of chimpanzees and bonobos that they experience the same seven forms of love that we do.[32] But they almost certainly do not experience them all together in their only-temporary trysts. Instead, for them the forms of love seem to be spread out among both amorous and nonamorous social relationships.

The human case was special. It required all the emotional fire-power that nature could muster in order to coerce free individuals, unused to intense inter-gender cooperation, into forming pair-bonds that would last at least three to five years. So evolution arranged for *all* the forms of love, with all their respective emotional impacts, to become focused on this one intimate union.

Overlapping as it does the in-love and bonding stages of love, the courtship phase usually lasts somewhere between six months to a year and a half or so. If we get through the rituals of our mating dance having convinced each other that we'd make a good long-term genetic match, we move into the next stage of our relationship—bonded comfort and conflict.

Bonded Comfort and Conflict

Joe and Kate settle into each other's arms on the couch. They've both had a hard day, but now comes their reward—snuggling. This night in particular they reminisce a little about the stormy courtship that's now behind them. They talk about the baby they want to have sometime in the next year or two. He massages her back, then settles into her lap for the head scratching he loves al-most more than sex. During the course of the evening minor con-flicts emerge, but neither of them is willing to disturb the tranquility of their hard-won marital bliss. Joe thinks to himself, "*This* is what it's all about. And to think I was ever afraid of get-ting married." Kate thinks, "I hope this lasts forever."

Few love songs are written about this stage of our relationships. Most love stories end here too. We don't seem to be interested in what happens after the prince gets the princess (or vice versa, de-pending on your point of view).

Or maybe it's not that we're uninterested. Maybe it's that we naively believe that once the power struggles have been re-solved—or at least put on the back burner for the time being— and the adrenaline and amphetamines have subsided, all will be well, and we can switch to automatic pilot. After the exhilarating but disturbing fireworks of attraction, falling in love, and courtship, many of us "let ourselves go" or even "go to seed."

Indeed, as we become comfortable with each other, and become "old shoes," a different set of chemicals takes over.[33] Researchers believe that PEA and other amphetamine receptors in our nervous systems probably become satiated after a few months of hyperstimulation. As the influence of these chemicals wanes, natural tranquilizers—endorphins—create feelings of comfort and security.

Now we know the other person intimately—at least we *think* we do—her daily habits, the foods he likes, how she's likely to react in typical situations, how far we can count on him in a crisis, and so on. And *we've* been able to "let it all hang out," too. We've reached many compromises, made and gotten some concessions, and seem to be adjusting to each other well. At this point, if not before, we may get married or move in together, and we may have children.

Anthropologists and psychologists call what is happening to us in this phase of our relationships "bonding." Bonding is a strange process with a life of its own.[34] It seems to occur naturally, organically, as if a force field were being set up around the two people. And it happens to us whether or not we like each other very much, whether or not we get along with each other, and whether or not we're even getting our needs met very well in our relationship. About all that seems to be required is that two people spend a lot of time together. Bonding reaches its peak strength about three years into our relationships. By then we've weathered many storms and developed a history together.

Once the bonding process is fully under way we may come to take each other for granted, "go to sleep on each other," or try to live for our children, focusing on this joint project rather than on our relationship. Along with these patterns of bonded *comfort,* though, we may continue our conflicts and power struggles. Yet now, beyond the negotiating phase, we'd rather sweep them under the rug. Couples often unconsciously arrange uneasy truces with each other at this point, and once-open attempts to work things out give way to the semiresignation of chronic carping, nitpicking, habitual criticism, mild sarcasm, and thinly veiled threats. Having discovered that aggressive self-affirmation has failed to get us enough of what we wanted, we resort to "passive-aggressive" behavior, like "forgetting" to do the little things we know the other person likes.

Whether we go to sleep on each other, try to live for our children, or degenerate into low-level complaining, the security that this bonding seems to provide may be an illusion. If we don't find ways to keep our sexual and romantic interest in each other alive, we are asking for trouble. The chances are pretty good that we're about to move into the next, and final, stage of love—boredom.

The *forms* of love that come to the fore in the bonding period are parent-child love, child-parent love, and under the best circumstances friendship and even caritas love. Again, the layer of our primate patterns that is re-created in our relationships at this stage is our savanna time. The bonding process begins during the in-love and courtship stages and lingers into at least the first part of the boredom phase. Although we may be able to prolong the bonding stage, often by having more children (and thereby replicating the weaning time frame for our relationships), the natural duration seems to be about three years.

It's during this stage or at the onset of the next that many couples (and individuals) come to see me. They know they've lost something vital in their relationships, and they don't know how to get it back.

Boredom

Bonding, instead of lulling us into an often false sense of security, should put us on yellow alert. *Boredom* should shift us to red alert. If we're feeling bored with our partner, we are already in the greatest of the many relationship danger zones. We are approaching what Helen Fisher calls the "four-year-itch" barrier, that hidden reef just beneath the waterline on which the vast majority of our relationships founder—whether we stay together or not. This is when many of us develop the "parallel marriages" that Harville Hendrix talks about, become platonic roommates, and perhaps start having affairs.

Familiarity not only breeds contempt; it also breeds disinterest in general and sexual indifference in particular. We may ask ourselves at this point, "There are so many possibilities out there. Did I make the best choice I could have?" Men especially often run into the biologically generated incest taboo at the beginning of the boredom stage because familiarity with a woman may cause a man to experience her as mother- or sister-like. Since the incest taboo against daughters and fathers having sex is somewhat less powerful than that governing sex between sons and mothers,[35] women may not reach the level of sexual boredom that men do, or at least not reach it as fast. And for men still another factor is almost certainly at work in turning sexual attraction into sexual boredom: the so-called Coolidge Effect. We'll look at this in some detail later.

In the boredom stage, even the old conflicts between us no longer hold our interest. We're ready for a new set of problems and challenges. Biologists have discovered that many other animals have a dual need for security on the one hand and for adventure and variety on the other.[36] Probably every organism becomes sated and then feels restless for new experiences. We humans are no exception. Understimulated (as psychologists call it) in the boredom phase of our relationships, we seek new sources of excitement. Recent studies have even shown that when our PEA and other natural amphetamines drop to an understimulating level, we begin to look for ways to raise the concentration of these chemicals in our systems.[37] Evidently, most of us can't stand to lounge in endorphin heaven for very long.

As we've seen, our savanna time arranged for us to go through all the stages of love, including boredom, so that we would do the best we humans can at pair-bonding, having children, and getting them weaned. Then it was time for us to move on to new relationships and new genetic combinations.

But it's as the boredom stage is looming that our mixed biological and cultural creation—civilization—makes a pass at preserving our now shaky partnerships. This third layer of our primate patterns, as we've already noted, tries to answer our need for a lifetime of emotional security—a childlike quality that's been a part of our makeup at least since our savanna time but which has gained in force over the course of our more recent evolution—by creating the lifelong monogamy ideal. The economic nature of our civilized cultures also pushes us in this direction, or did until the recent past. But the research of anthropologists, sociobiologists, and psychologists, as well as our own commonsense experience, forcefully suggests that neither our security needs nor economics are strong enough to counteract our feelings of boredom.[38] We can't pretend for long that we're excited, stimulated, and happy when we're really burned out. Wishing does not raise our PEA levels.

Still, under the best circumstances our boredom phase *can* produce strongly "spiritualized" relationships in which friendship and caritas love can flower into bonds of richness and beauty. This is especially true in our later years, after men's testosterone levels have begun to drop and sex has perhaps become less important to them.[39] (Aesthetic appreciation can always become more prominent again in this stage.) While for many of us in the current divorce climate boredom propels us out of our relationships and on to new love experiences, boredom *can* last a lifetime—if we accept it as the final word in our partnerships.

The Goal

We frequently get bad advice at many points in our relationships—from family, friends, and even therapists—but never more so than in the boredom stage. This advice is often unhelpful because other people are frequently doing worse in *their* relationships than we are in ours. Usually these people are just confused about their own feelings; they're often also in denial about them. Sometimes, though, I suspect a kind of hidden sadism at work in their advice giving. Even those who love us may sometimes unconsciously want to deprive us of the fulfillment of our relationship needs as much as *they* feel deprived of the fulfillment of theirs. For example, a credo in my family when I was growing up went something like this: "Sex doesn't last in marriage anyway, so when it goes, don't worry about it. Other things—like your responsibilities to each other and your children—are the only things that really count."

A similarly dismal view of long-term relationships is sometimes echoed in the counseling profession. Once when I was seeing a therapist during the end stages of a relationship that had been very important to me, he said, "Doug, sex and romance aren't all that meaningful, really. You can't build a life around them. The only kind of love that lasts is agape. Take me, for example. My wife and I have sex about once every six months, and we're very happily married." This particular therapist was in his early sixties, the time when a man's testosterone level is dropping, and other aspects of our relationships probably *are* becoming more important to us.

My own relationship experiences, my work with couples and individuals in or nearing the boredom stage, and my research all indicate to me that something is wrong with this kind of advice, at least for younger couples. The fact is that most people, myself included, do not accept this sadder and not necessarily wiser view of their relationship dreams and hoped-for sexual joy. At least in our youth and middle age, we don't seem to accept the idea that friendship love and caritas—and sexual and romantic boredom—are the final word on love. The goal for most of us, I suspect, is to keep sexual attraction, romance, and the drama of courtship's sharing and self-affirmative negotiating alive throughout the period of bonded comfort and conflict. These forms of love, supplemented by friendship and caritas, can minimize our boredom with our partners and keep our bonds with each other fresh, stimulating, and growing. Interestingly, *vital,* instinctual relationships offer tremendous hope for the healthy psychological growth of our children as well.

A wise man once said, "Pathos is suffering that is not creative." Our love, if it is going to be more than meaningless suffering, must be exciting, stimulating, and inspiring. Continuing to embrace *all* the forms of love can prod us to grow as individuals and as couples, to deepen, and, finally, to achieve a truly wise and loving maturity.

Okay, So Where *Am* I?: Self-Evaluation Exercise Key

Turn back to the scoring grid on page 80. Add the number of Y (Yes) boxes only for each column and write the number in the total box below. Three or more Ys indicate that this *form* of love is very powerful for you in your relationship right now. This is a *high* rating. Two Yeses mean this *form* of love is moderately influencing your relationship—a *medium* rating. And zero to one Yes answer indicates this *form* of love is virtually not present. This is a *low* rating.

You can plot your scores on the table below.

	Number of Yeses		
	High (3–6)	*Medium* (2)	*Low* (0–1)
Column #1 = aesthetic appreciation			
Column #2 = sexual attraction			
Column #3 = romance			
Column #4 = parent-child/child-parent love (these two forms of love usually come as a complementary pattern)			
Column #5 = friendship love			
Column #6 = caritas (or agape)			

To find out which *stage*(s) of love is/are influencing your relationship the most right now, follow this formula: Add the totals for columns 1 and 2 for *initial attraction*; the totals for columns 1, 2, and 3 for *in-love*; 2 and 3 for courtship; 3, 4, 5, and 6 for *bonded comfort and conflict*; and 1, 4, 5, and 6 for *boredom*. You can plot your scores:

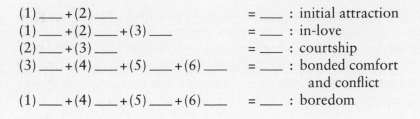

(1) ___ + (2) ___ = ___ : initial attraction
(1) ___ + (2) ___ + (3) ___ = ___ : in-love
(2) ___ + (3) ___ = ___ : courtship
(3) ___ + (4) ___ + (5) ___ + (6) ___ = ___ : bonded comfort
                                                and conflict
(1) ___ + (4) ___ + (5) ___ + (6) ___ = ___ : boredom

If your total for columns 1 and 2 is 5 or more you are experiencing significant elements of initial attraction in your relationship.

If your total for columns 1, 2, and 3 is 7 or more you are experiencing significant elements of the *in-love* stage in your relationship.

If your total for columns 2 and 3 is 5 or more you are experiencing significant elements of the *courtship* stage in your relationship.

If your total for columns 3, 4, 5, and 6 is 10 or more you are experiencing significant elements of the *bonding* stage.

And if your total for columns 1, 4, 5, and 6 is 12 or more you are experiencing significant elements of the *boredom* stage of love.

As we've seen, there are few if any clear-cut divisions between either the forms or the stages of love. Your own scores may reflect the fact that your relationship is in several stages at the same time. Actually, this is the norm. Your scores can highlight some trends in the direction your relationship is headed, but you will have to consult your "gut feelings" as you digest the results of this exercise. The best way to use these results is as a consciousness-raising aid to your own intuitive grasp of your situation.

If you want your relationship to last—happily—it's important to become aware of the forms of love expressing themselves in your relationship and the stage(s) you and your partner are in. And it's vital to act *now* to short-circuit nature's relationship-disrupting plans for you.

If we're going to interrupt the natural cycle of love, though, we have to come to grips with a few more unsettling facts about ourselves and our partners as male and female animals. We have to see more clearly what, along with our individual childhood traumas, is really "wrong" with us. It's to these "unsettling facts" we now turn.

PART TWO

*

WHAT'S "WRONG" WITH US?

6

THE SAME SPECIES—JUST BARELY

❋

Bernie and Janice

JANICE GRIPPED THE STEERING WHEEL. Her knuckles were turning white and tears were already streaming down her cheeks. Bernie's teeth were clenched so tight he could have cracked a filling. It was raining, which made everything worse.

They were on their way home from a party. Their fight had started there. They'd been talking to another couple about a local politician's vote on a controversial issue. Bernie and Janice had found themselves on opposite sides of the fence, as usual. Worse, Bernie and Lydia had agreed, and Janice had found herself siding with Erik.

The *real* issue had nothing to do with politics. It was about their different confrontational styles.

Janice tried to choke back her tears. "Why can't you *agree* with me—in front of our friends—just once?"

Bernie snapped. "Because I *don't* agree with you. You're *wrong* about how this sewer project is going to impact—"

Janice yelled, "Stop it! Stop it! The point isn't whether I'm right or wrong! It's that we *agree,* at least in front of our friends. I just feel terrible when—"

Bernie: "Now *you* stop it! I've had it with your emotionalism!"

Janice: "And *I've* had enough of your damned . . ." she searched for a word . . . "'reasonableness,' as you call it!"

"Well, why can't *you* be more reasonable? Why do you have to *feel* everything as if your life depended on it?"

"And why can't *you feel* anything? Everything for you is a problem to be analyzed! You don't give a *damn* about how *I* feel!"

"Goddammit, that's not true!" Bernie wailed. "Now, I'm *really* getting mad!"

"Shit," Janice said as she broke into full-scale sobs.

"Dammit," Bernie said wearily, throwing up his hands. "You'd better pull over. We can't drive like this. It's too dangerous."

Our Talking Heads

Men and women fight with each other for a lot of reasons. Many of them are personal, but some of them are the result of profound differences in the ways most men and most women perceive, feel, behave, and think about themselves, each other, and the world. While our cultures and our families certainly have an influence on our male and female styles of relating, growing evidence suggests that men and women are *innately* different—and not just in terms of our sex organs and physiques. Our *brains* are different.[1] Different brains make for different psychologies—different souls. Of course there's a lot of overlap between us; we *are* the same species—but just barely.

The gender differences in our brains have evolved over a period of millions of years. Already in chimpanzees we see prefigurations of the same gender differences we experience. Male and female chimpanzees are social in different ways and structure their intra- and intergender relationships differently.[2] Males and females have different aptitudes and interests.[3] We even see differences in work roles. Females spend much more time and energy caring for the young, and males protect the community's boundaries, enforce order within the group, and hunt.

Because of the evolution of our human brains—in particular our neocortexes—we can experience greater flexibility in our gender identities and work roles and closer communication between our sexes. But in other ways, things haven't changed very much in all these millions of years. The reason is that for all our advances in intelligence over the other animals, the particular *kind* of intelligence that nature has evolved in us is still *primate* intelligence.[4] It's not something apart—something abstract or neutral. It's not the same *kind* of intelligence that whales and dolphins have. And if zebras could evolve to our *level* theirs would still be an advanced *zebra* intelligence, complete with zebra herding instincts, zebra kinds of joys, fears, and a zebra horizontal, terrestrial (rather than a primate vertical and arboreal) perspective on things.

Primatologists and animal psychologists have been studying the parallels between our human psychology, perceptions, feelings, behaviors, and even our childhood development, and those of the other primates for several decades now. The correspondences are overwhelming. Even taking into account our human capacity to create cultures far more elaborate than those of our primate relatives, we conform to the general outlines and even many of the particulars of thoroughly primate psychologies, social organizations, and personal relationships.

We know that our cultures and what we are in our *fullest* human expression, including our intimate relationships, are the result of an explosion in the development of our neocortex that began about 500,000 years ago.[5] By 200,000 years ago our brains had reached their present size.[6] But strangely enough, no giant leaps forward in our toolmaking or our art followed.[7] What our new brain apparently *did* do was create complicated "kinship systems," as anthropologists call them.[8] Ultimately, kinship systems are about our personal relationships with each other, especially the mating kind. They're about who marries whom.

But between 60,000 and 30,000 years ago, rapid advances in our tools and weapons, in our personal adornments, in art, and even in our religions began to take place.[9] Many researchers believe that language was the catalyst for this sudden flowering of our technology and spirituality. Some believe that the language centers in our brains were the last things to develop, and that they were just coming on-line at this time.[10] But this idea is controversial. Some physical anthropologists believe they've found evidence for the origin of one of our brain's language centers— known as Wernicke's area—in the latex casts they've made of much *older* ancestral skulls.[11] And one school of linguists believe they are well on the way to reconstructing our original human language, which they call Proto-world.[12] They date it to around 200,000 years ago. One theory suggests that if our language centers really are that old, they evolved mainly to help us keep track of our relationships.[13]

However these fascinating debates resolve themselves, we already have a great deal of knowledge about the more ancient layers of who and what we are. Knowing a little about our multistoried animal brains can help us understand ourselves and our partners better—and why we react so differently to the same situations.

The Three F's, the Three-Storied Brain, and the Layers of Our Primate Patterns

Brain researcher Paul MacLean years ago put forward the theory that our brains are really three brains in one.[14] By now MacLean's theory is almost universally accepted. What he says is that our three brains are embodiments of the three main stages of our overall evolution (as distinguished from our specifically primate and human evolution)—reptile, mammal, and human. By studying reptilian and mammalian brains and behavior and carefully comparing them to human brains and behavior, MacLean has been able to show that our reptile brains, or R-complexes as he calls them, are *truly* reptilian and have remained essentially unchanged for over 100 million years. Our old mammal brains, or limbic systems, with some modifications characteristic of primates in general and our own species in particular, are basically the same brains present in elephants, antelope, and duck-billed platypuses.[15] Our human neocortexes are specialized versions of the more primitive neocortexes of our primate relatives, especially chimpanzees, bonobos, and gorillas.[16]

MacLean's idea is that some of our feelings and behaviors are reptilian, some are generalized mammalian with some species-characteristic qualities, and some are those of advanced apes.

Jurassic Alice

In Michael Crichton's *Jurassic Park* we see reptiles at their worst. Strangely enough, though, as psychologists and social commentators have seen, the cold-hearted monsters of our worst nightmares are within. They live in the deepest and most ancient parts of us, our R-complexes. This core structure bulges upward from our spinal column and constitutes the absolute center of our brain—and our soul. Its contributions to who and what we are are a little chilling. They include our penchant for—and sometimes obsession with—routines and rituals, our possessiveness, our fierce defense of the territory we stake out for ourselves, and our often mixed-up appetites for the three "F's"—feeding, fighting, and "fucking."[17] In the reptile mind, the three "F's" are all aspects of one central reptilian demand: "I want what I want and I'm going to do whatever it takes to get it." Or simply put, "*ME!*"

When we think of it this way we can see that much of our supposedly human behavior really is reptilian. All of our rituals—from our morning routines to our most solemn religious ceremonies—and our jealous, territorial, and possessive behaviors—from our childhood fights over toys to our adult efforts to promote our own self-interest and defend our own psychological integrity and beliefs—are expressions of the prowling *T-Rex* at the base of our brains.[18] Our courtship rituals, the way we have to define and redefine our personal boundaries, and the close affinity we feel for candlelight dinners and sex have the same deep roots. Reptiles strut and preen when they're trying to mate, flashing the message: "Look at me! Aren't I magnificent?" Do we do otherwise?

Schemers, users, leeches, prostitutes (both narrowly and broadly defined), stalkers, serial killers, murderers, rapists, and *all* of us when we show single-minded self-serving patterns in our lives, are "in" our reptile brains. When we're in the reptile we can also get paranoid about what we experience as others' invasiveness. It's certainly true that many men and women are invasive. They see to it that *their* needs are met, often at our expense. But many of us are also hypersensitive about what may be others' innocent attempts to simply get close to us. The reptile at our cores *is* a little on the antisocial side,[19] and many of our so-called personality disorders, it seems to me, can be laid at the doorstep of the R-complex.

"Jurassic Alice" came to me complaining that no one seemed to like her very much, and that even her friends had been deserting her. She was what we call a "high-powered" businesswoman.

She ran her own ad agency. In the past year, though, she'd fallen on hard times. As she told her story about the financial and personal disasters of the past year I read between the lines as best I could. And what I saw was this:

As long as things had been going well at the agency, Alice had been able to keep up the appearance of personal charm and social grace, with a touch of saucy flirtatiousness. She'd been alluring to her clients, especially her male clients, and she'd conveyed the impression of mysterious depths and exciting, mildly dangerous hidden currents. She'd been very strong-willed in her friendships and business dealings, but she'd been able to soften her hard edge with an enticing feminine exterior.

However, as things got worse in her business she'd found herself falling back on inner resources of a perhaps not entirely human nature. Gradually the charming mask had slipped. Her eyes had begun to glitter and her smiles had become a little long in the tooth. She'd begun to snarl when she'd meant to be ingratiating. She'd become, as she herself said, "A lean, mean fighting machine."

Indeed, about all that seemed to be left of her was a calculating predator, ruthless and cunning. She'd forgotten the rules of fair play and integrity, keeping your word, and giving it your best effort, upon which business *and* personal relationships are based. Now, stripped of both clients and friends, the human part of her was withering away.

There was something of the crocodile about her, something clawed and reflexive. I felt the hair on the back of my neck tingling, signaling a warning. She said in genuine confusion but also with barely concealed rage, "I don't get it! I've always been strong, self-motivated, and very ambitious. People have always admired me for that. I'm a self-made woman. That's what everybody wants now, isn't it? So what am I missing here?"

I was silent for a moment. Then I said—carefully—"Maybe your humanity."

Alice was partly right. We *do* admire self-motivated, self-defining, and strong-willed people in our culture. And there *is* a positive side to the reptile at our cores. It does seem that if we can't become self-affirming enough we can't really afford to love others.[20] If we can't draw a line in the sand and say, "This far and no farther!" we are so vulnerable that we can't be giving. We have a tendency to be too easily overrun and overwhelmed by *others'* reptilian agendas. We don't pay enough attention to getting *our* needs met. We become masochistic, self-sacrificial, and self-effacing, turning the other cheek when we ought to be snapping up our dinners with velociraptor glee.

The best psychology (in contrast to some of our self-denying spiritual teachings) is really about freeing the *"ME!"* at our cores.[21] From my perspective, we first have to acknowledge and act on the powerfully self-affirmative impulses of our reptile brains *before* we can free and integrate our primate natures, and before we can be fully human—either as men or as women. The Jewish teacher, Rabbi Hillel, balancing the interests of his reptile and mammal brains, said, "If I am not for myself, who then? And being for myself, what am I? And if not now, when?"[22] He wrote these words of instinctual wisdom two thousand years ago.

Limbic Lorraine

Lorraine had had what she considered to be five major relationships in the last two years. Now, she was an emotional wreck. She was overwhelmed by grief and regret. She told me she was about to end number five and that she was terrified of yet another separation. She just couldn't stand the trauma anymore.

As she shared the details, what emerged was the picture of a woman powerfully addicted to the experience of falling in—and out of—love. She seemed to be a prime candidate for a "histrionic personality disorder" diagnosis. Her life certainly *was* dramatic. But the account of her amorous adventures was so extreme I suspected there was more at work here than a childhood in which she'd probably had to be dramatic in order to get the love and attention she'd needed.

She told me she would meet a man, usually before her current relationship had ended, and would fall instantly in love. She'd feel waves of sexual and romantic attraction, feel "irresistibly drawn" to him, and then spend days in a trancelike state, "drugged," as she put it. She wouldn't be able to eat or sleep.

She'd feel violent emotions at both ends of the spectrum. On the one hand, she'd feel driven to give her life to her new lover. On the other hand, she'd feel wildly resentful of his hold on her. Usually she hadn't spent more than a few hours with him.

Typically she would next "realize" that this man was "The One," end with her previous lover, pack her bags, and appear on the new man's doorstep in a dramatic wee-hours-of-the-morning scene or its equivalent. As the new relationship would move from the attraction, in-love, and courtship stages into the bonding stage—always at lightning speed—the forcefulness of her initial attraction would turn into a hunger to manage and control her partner. Within several months she would become hypercritical of him, from the way he gargled in the morning to the way he handled his business conversations. She would begin her relationship filled with romantic ideas about having children with him and making a "traditional American family," as she called it; but then, when she'd discover that this man wasn't "right" after all, she'd abandon her fantasy with equally violent emotionality. Sometime within the first six months or so she would feel bitterly disappointed. Finally, she would feel bored.

As we've seen, what Lorraine was going through was a more or less normal relationship cycle—but greatly speeded up and with added emotional intensity. I learned that she'd been hyperactive as a child and I thought she might now be suffering from something like PEA starvation. Perhaps she had a chronically low level of natural amphetamines in her brain. In order to get her PEA level up she would throw herself into new emotional adventures. "Limbic Lorraine" was an extreme example, but we *all* do this to some extent. I came to believe that whatever her childhood had been like, Lorraine almost certainly was experiencing a *chemical* feast and famine in her limbic system.

Our limbic systems, or old mammal brains, are the part of us that carries the emotional punch of our instincts.[23] It is in this area of our brains that our powerful feelings of fear, anger, hatred, and love arise. When we fall in love, our limbic systems are flooded with PEA.[24] And later, when we start to feel comfortable with our partners, it is here that our natural endorphins exercise their calming effect.[25] Hyper- or hyposensitivity of neural receptors and over- or underdoses of various chemicals almost certainly account for much of what people like Lorraine are struggling with.[26]

Our limbic systems are genetically wired both for our general mammalian and our species-characteristic primate patterns for mating, parenting, our many forms of personal interactions, and for the structures of our societies—our usual ways of doing business with each other.[27] It is here too that our powerful urges to conform to others' expectations hold sway. Growing upward from and surrounding the R-complex like a collar, the limbic system is almost flawlessly integrated with our reptile brains. Together they form the material basis for our animal souls and give rise to the oldest layer of our primate patterns.

Our limbic systems emerged from our reptile brains somewhere around 70 million years ago.[28] As different species of mammals evolved, including our own, their limbic systems diverged enough to give each species its characteristic aptitudes, feelings, and instincts. Our limbic systems are made up of three subsystems—the amygdaloid complex, the septal-hippocampal complex, and the cingulate complex.

The *amygdaloid complex* carries our feelings of aggression, anger, and aversion ("I like this; I *don't* like that!" "I am this; I am *not* that!").[29] Our aggressive feelings mostly target food and enemies, but we also direct them against each other. In our relationships, as we've seen, we sometimes experience our partner as something to be consumed, eaten, used—and in the worst cases *preyed upon*. All too often, and with some justification, we experience him or her as a hostile *predator* as well. But our anger toward each other also has a positive side. It helps us define ourselves as individuals, maintain our independence, and ask that we get our needs met.[30]

In both men and women our amygdaloid complexes give us the urge to conquer each other. So they're a major source of our relationship power struggles. But an important difference between men and women also almost certainly arises in these structures. Human males, like other primate males, display an amygdaloid-seated enthusiasm for dominance and hierarchy that is fueled by testosterone.[31] Several studies indicate that the testosterone, at much higher levels in most males than in most females, may be acting on different amygdaloid circuitry in the male limbic system.

Our *septal-hippocampal complex* plays several major roles in our primate brains, including acting as the traffic cop for competing emotions.[32] It's also the part of our brains that energizes our sexual drives and, according to some research, receives stimulating input from our hypothalamuses about our sexual preferences—influencing whether we are heterosexual or homosexual.[33]

The *cingulate complex* carries the more sublime side of our "urge to merge." This is where our powerful feelings of love begin.[34] Love in a general sense is a hallmark of mammals.[35] Caring for each other (at least for their children, especially on the part of females), depending on each other, and living in families and communities are typical mammal feelings and behaviors.[36] Our own cingulate complexes embody our specifically primate and human ways of loving, including our aesthetic appreciation of each other, our sexual attraction, romance, parent-child, child-parent love, and our friendship love. Even caritas, though it is deepened and amplified by our neocortexes, may begin in this ancient part of our brains as a kind of self-sacrificial impulse.[37]

The confusion of the three "F's" in our reptile brains carries over into our limbic systems. The amygdaloid complex and the septal-hippocampal complex lie next to each other. When the amygdaloid complex (which gives rise to our feeding and fighting urges) is stimulated, the septal-hippocampal complex (which carries our sexual desires) also becomes activated. Along with creating interesting lovemaking sessions in which we may act as if we can't tell whether our loved one is "food," "the enemy," or the object of our desire, this limbic system arrangement may also account for one reason some couples fight and then make up with wild abandon. Love—and our cingulate complexes—may also get drawn into this volatile mix. But often love, as we usually define it, is a different matter.

Ned's Neurotic Neocortex

Our neocortexes are responsible for our striking appearance—our large, domed skulls and bulging foreheads. We share the older structures of our neocortexes with our jungle time relatives—the chimpanzees, bonobos, and gorillas.[38] But much of it, especially the frontal lobes, was nature's unique invention to help us survive our savanna time.[39] The main by-product of this adaptive device was our humanness.

Our savanna time also partially restructured our limbic systems, giving us the bent for nuclear families and societies that are a cross between those of chimpanzees, bonobos, and wild dogs. But this restructuring of our limbic systems is incomplete. It's a patchwork job, "opportunistic," as biologists call it. Nature seized opportunities to improvise on our existing circuitry as problems for our survival presented themselves. What's more, our greatly expanded neocortexes are largely disconnected from our old mammal and reptile brains.[40] They evolved far too fast to make a smooth neuronal bond with our ancient roots and the animal souls that live through them.

Our neocortexes evolved for two main reasons—to expand and deepen our capacity for empathy and bonding with each other, *and* to enhance our ability to reason, to think strategically, and to imagine the future. Part of what nature was trying to do by increasing these ancestral capacities was help us control our powerful aggressive and sexual urges. Once we had developed weapons, males were far too dangerous to each other to fight physically for females. We needed to learn to compete in more subtle, mental ways. Because of our savanna environment, we needed to curb our sexual appetites enough to form stable, if temporary, male/female pair-bonds. Females needed to develop even closer empathic ties with their children and with the males upon whom they were now dependent. And everyone needed closer emotional bonding with everyone else. We *had* to get along and we *had* to plan ahead—together.

But, ironically, because of our neocortex's lack of connection to the animal it is trying to control, its ability to manage that animal is limited.[41] Now our human brains and animal selves are at odds with each other, and very often the jailer becomes the jailed, as we fall prey to the compulsive acting out of our repressed instincts—*especially* for sex and aggression. As I've noted, shamed instincts often become violent emotions that can overwhelm our more "civilized" egos and cause us to act in ways we'd normally never dream of.

The problem with our neocortex's disconnect from our more ancient brain structures shows up in two related ways—the shaming of the animal and an overemphasis on caritas (and to a lesser extent parent-child, child-parent, and friendship love). Shaming the animal results in conflict-ridden and often poor-quality sex lives, passive-aggressive and sado-masochistic behaviors, and other neurotic symptoms.[42] An overemphasis on caritas love takes the wildness and adventure out of our relationships and may contribute to the drop in our PEA levels.[43]

Often assumed by our spiritual traditions to be the only *true* basis for our relationships,[44] caritas is only *one* of the forms of love. Love is not monolithic. Its *variety* and richness of expression give our relationships their realistic possibilities for long-term happiness. Caritas certainly makes a valuable *contribution* to our love lives, but overemphasizing it usually leads to relationship disaster.

In relationships that have gone dead from the neocortex down, the pressing question is: What are we supposed to *do* with the animal part of us—that energetic, vital, chemically fueled element that gets us into our relationships in the first place? It doesn't go away. It gets angry when it's denied. And it cannot be killed. (This is actually good news because it's our animal nature that is the source of our joy, our spontaneity, and our aliveness.)

The fact is that we can become *trapped* in caritas, the prisoners of our neocortexes, which imagine that, rather than playing their proper role as *modifiers* of our animal passions, they are the end-all and be-all of our human lives. Our neocortexes have even created theologies and moral systems for themselves that bolster this illusion.[45] They may tell themselves they are "little lower than the angels." A misplaced emphasis on caritas love certainly caused "Neurotic Ned" an enormous amount of needless suffering.

Ned and Sheila moved in together around five months after they met on a blind date. They'd been immediately attracted to each other. They'd seen each other almost every day for the next two weeks and fallen head-over-heels in love. More than sexual attraction, Ned said he'd felt a tidal wave of romantic feelings those first couple of weeks. He'd felt he'd met his destiny, and he'd felt complete as a person for the first time in his life. He'd loved Sheila's frank childlikeness and her uninhibited expression of her feelings.

But he'd also noticed, and then dismissed, what he later described as "powerful warning signals." For example, Sheila had been hurt and angry on their first date when he hadn't spent what she considered to be enough money on her. And on their second date, he'd remembered something he'd left in the car at a parking garage. He'd started back for the car when he'd heard Sheila's voice behind him barking in a commanding tone, "*Don't walk away from me! I'm here, you know!*" He'd also noticed early in their relationship that she seemed to need to be the life of the party wherever they went. He thought her laughter was too loud, and her flirtatious manner communicated to all those around her, "Notice me!" These things upset him, but, brushing his own feelings aside, he decided that what he really heard in her bizarre behavior was a call for help.

When they moved in together she immediately filled their bedroom with pictures of herself, as if to say, "I'm here! I'm real!" The longer they lived together, the more he saw her hunger for attention, and he noticed with a combination of alarm and sadness that she interpreted his slightest mood changes as signs of his lack of love for her. Ned tried to reason with her, to cajole her, tease her, ignore her, and fight with her to stop what for him was becoming a nightmarish relationship—all to no avail.

But through it all he couldn't stop himself from loving her. In fact, the little he knew about psychology convinced him (rightly) that she'd had a very painful childhood. He loved the damaged girl in her more and more, and tried harder to give her the security and love she'd been denied. He became selflessly devoted to trying to heal her. At the same time, he gradually began to realize he was trying to fill a bottomless pit, and he began to want out. He tried to end the relationship on several occasions, but each time she would either become the picture of maturity and reasonableness—which encouraged him—or she would go to the other extreme, getting drunk and threatening to commit suicide.

However, as his desperation increased, Ned's selfless love got stronger. Even when he finally gave up his fantasy of satisfying her neediness and filling the void within her, he still felt deeply romantic about her. And even when his romantic feelings finally faded, his caritas love for her grew. From time to time Sheila would really try to get herself together. But she couldn't stick with it. That only made Ned love her more. He experienced her efforts to deal with her inner child as heroic, and her failures evoked even stronger feelings of empathy and compassion on his part.

Ned needed more reptilian "ME!" in his relationship, and more primate alpha male self-affirmation. I worked with him for four years to help him become more "selfish"—more self-serving and more aggressive about getting *his* needs met. And I helped him revalue forms of love other than caritas—especially his sexual desire. Through a whole host of therapeutic techniques, including inner child work, so-called reality therapy, the practices of self-psychology, and imaginal exercises, I finally was able to help him *unshame* his self-protective and self-affirming animal instincts and get them back on-line so that he could act in his own behalf. The day finally came when he said with absolute certainty, "It's either her or me! I'm going to have to kill this relationship *in spite of* my love for her!"

He finally did break free. Now, with a more healthy regard for his *animal* soul, Ned is pursuing several relationships that seem to offer him greater satisfaction of the fuller range of his relationship needs. By his report, one woman in particular is especially welcoming of his newfound animal strength.

Different Brains, Different Needs

In-Depth and Wide-Angle Experiences

Brain research over the past several decades has produced convincing evidence that the brains of men and women are fundamentally different—perhaps at the level of their limbic systems, almost certainly in some of the structures of their neocortexes.[46] Based on past, less-scientific attempts to define gender differences, some people fear the conclusions of this new research. Some women especially fear that this information will be used to "keep them in their place." If there really *are* inherent biological differences between men and women, men may use this knowledge to deny women equality. I understand this fear. Knowledge *can* be a dangerous thing. At the same time, I believe that in the long run we can't afford to turn away from this mounting evidence because it makes us feel uncomfortable. Our relationships especially can benefit enormously from the knowledge such studies are providing, since, among other things, they can help us drop our demands that our partners feel, think, and behave as we do.

We now know that at conception both male and female fetuses have basically "female" brains, and that after the genetically male fetus's testicles have developed (around the sixth week) a bath of testosterone and other "androgens" restructures its brain into a male pattern.[47] This rerouting of neuronal circuits prepares the developing male child to receive its second testosterone bath at the onset of puberty.[48] Then testosterone levels in boys reach twenty times the levels they do in girls.[49] This propels teenage boys into a very different mental, emotional, and sexual universe.

But even before the dramatic changes of puberty, studies show the male and female brains of even young children result in budding differences in their behaviors.[50] Boys in general tend to be more assertive, more single-minded, and more task-oriented, and girls tend to be somewhat more compliant, more interdependent, and more interested in personal relationships. Boys, even at an early age, are more inclined to rank themselves in terms of hierarchies of power, and girls have a tendency to be more interested in compromising and getting along. In general, boys are more interested in *power* and girls in *relating*.

Depending on your point of view, our cultures enhance, or exaggerate, these and other differences between the sexes. But they do not *create* them. They are innate. And these general patterns don't change until later in life (usually in our fifties) when men's testosterone and women's estrogen levels drop. Then our two genders become much more alike—mentally, emotionally, and even physically.[51]

Our different brains make for differences in the way we use language and in the ways we think and feel. Words *shape* the ways we think and feel as much as they *express* them. From tracking blood flows in men's and women's brains, researchers have found that when men speak they use the front and back of their left brains, while women use only the front.[52] These different areas of our brains govern our use of grammar. In terms of vocabulary and word definition, men use their left brains only, while women use their whole brains. The result is that when men speak they tend to do so from a rational, emotionally detached, abstract-thinking mode—as Bernie seemed to do in the example at the beginning of this chapter. Men may often have trouble connecting their speech to their right-brained feelings. Women, on the other hand, often *feel-think* because they're using their left and right brains at the same time. Perhaps Janice (in the same example) was displaying this kind of thinking in her argument with Bernie.

In terms of vision, men tend to use their right brains.[53] Their right brains allow them to grasp whole images and large patterns, but with little attention to detail.[54] For example, they may immediately recognize a complex traffic pattern ahead of them on the road, but not notice the color of the cars or the expressions on the drivers' faces. Women, on the other hand, tend to use both sides of their brains for a somewhat less proficient pattern recognition of the total visual field, but with greater concentration on details.[55] Many women might not be able to "see" the traffic pattern as a whole, but be able to recall details about the individual cars and the people driving them. Men's vision also tends to be more focused on depth-of-field perception and women's more on a wide-angle view of the world around them.[56] Most men are better able to calculate distances to objects in front of them, but theirs is a kind of tunnel vision. Most women are better at noticing peripheral objects and events, but have trouble with depth perception.

Our senses of touch are different too, partly as a result of differences in our nervous systems as a whole and partly because of differences in our brains.[57] Women have much greater tactile sensitivity than men. This leads them to get more out of physical contact than men do. Men tend to be more physically removed, somewhat less sensitive to pain, and perhaps generally more "detached."[58]

Not only do we use the two sides of our brains differently, they're not even connected the same way in men and women. The main connection between the right and left brains is a neuronal bridge called the corpus callosum. In women portions of this structure are generally larger than in men.[59] Scientists don't yet know what effect this may have on the way our brains work. But one theory suggests that this is one reason women's behavior tends to be more holistic and men's more specialized.[60]

Indeed, there is growing evidence that men's brains are more compartmentalized than women's.[61] While many men seem to spend most of their time functioning from their left brains (something encouraged by our technically oriented culture), a significant number of men are primarily right-brained. These are the male artists, poets, and prophets. Left-brain specialization leads to remarkable achievements in rational thought, analysis, planning and abstraction, whereas right-brain specialization leads to equally remarkable achievements in fields that require deep feeling and an intuitive grasp of the big picture. A more balanced use of the two sides of the brain leads to less specialization but more integrated and relational behavior.[62]

Men's and women's testosterone and estrogen levels are a key factor in making all this advanced primate machinery work. Not only does testosterone compartmentalize the male brain in the first weeks of life, it also seems to fuel the detached, rationalistic process in both men and women.[63] In addition, since testosterone is a natural stimulant to our feelings of assertiveness and aggression it gives men a generally greater drive for a certain kind of emotional independence.[64] Estrogen, on the other hand, is a natural tranquilizer and may somewhat dampen most women's assertiveness but empower them to be more *inter*dependent, and verbally and emotionally more effective in relationships.[65]

Different Evolutionary Tracks

When we look back over our long evolutionary history as the deluxe-model ape, we can speculate about why our different brains developed the way they did. They seem to have fitted us for different social and work roles within our primate communities.

As we've seen, our nearest primate relatives live in communities organized around female friendships and male hierarchies. Within these communities there are *some* male friendships and *some* females interested in rank. Males are crafted to compete with each other for dominance—for power and wealth. Power and wealth give a male access to females, and females give him access to "practical immortality."

Primate males protect their communities from predators and other enemies. They also protect their societies from *internal* threats by defending the public order—settling quarrels and disciplining nonconformists. And while in most primate societies, as in most other vertebrate species, males and females are economically self-sufficient, the males usually have the dangerous job of scouting for new food sources. Occasionally they also hunt. These are provider roles.

We know that these male social and work roles are embodied in part in the amygdaloid complex and are fueled by testosterone. Male monkeys who have had their amygdaloid complexes surgically removed and/or had their testosterone cut off lose interest in these tasks. The result is that they immediately fall in rank, *and* in female esteem.[66]

The bodies and brains of primate females are uniquely designed for child-rearing, and usually for a more live-and-let-live approach to interpersonal relationships. Among other things this enables them to share their child-rearing tasks with each other, creating what primatologists call the "auntie" system.[67] Yet when food resources are scarce, they become decidedly *in-tolerant* of each other and fiercely competitive.[68] Among our primate relatives, as with us humans, culture fine-tunes these innate differences in our social and work lives.[69] Both males and females have to be *taught* how to bring their respective biological programs fully on-line in successful and socially acceptable ways.

These contrasts between primate males and females originated with the jungle time wiring of our gender differences. As we've seen, when we were stranded on the savannas these differences in male and female roles were dramatically sharpened. The dangerous savanna world required males to cooperate more closely with each other, to refine their hunting skills, and perhaps even to develop the capacity to wage war in order to protect their communities from other hominid bands. Females had to develop even closer ties with their children and at least some enthusiasm for the newfangled homemaking skills our work specialization demanded.

The savanna environment adapted male bodies for the new emphasis on hunting by evolving male upper-body strength and unique shoulder, elbow, and wrist joints for the forceful and accurate use of long-distance weapons.[70] It also called for the redesign of male brains, especially the expanding neocortex. It makes sense that male vision evolved its emphasis on depth-perception and its straight-ahead focus to help our ancestors spot prey and predator and enable them to calculate the distance and speed of a fleeing antelope or a charging lion.[71] Tactile insensitivity and physical detachment were probably useful in helping men endure the pain and hardships of their new savanna roles. It would even make sense that their neocortexes became compartmentalized for such specialized functions as left-brain strategizing—for the hunt, for warfare, and for tighter and more cooperative social structures.[72] Isolation from right-brain emotional "static" could have been important for the kind of detached, "single-minded" thinking these situations required. And it would make sense that the right brains of these ancestral males, uncluttered by plodding, left-brain logic, could enable them to instantaneously grasp the big picture in these and other dangerous contexts.[73]

It also seems reasonable to suppose that our savanna time further developed female vision, tactile sensitivity, and a holistic approach to relationships. Among other things, an emphasis on peripheral vision could have enabled them to keep track of their children while engaged in other tasks.[74] Their greater tactile sensitivity could have helped them more effectively respond to their children's changing moods and needs through the mother's detection of her child's subtle shifts in posture and body temperature. And feel-thinking brains probably helped them maintain close personal bonds with other females and also with the males on whose "good graces" they and their children depended for survival.[75]

Our Different Ways of Being Intimate

Our different ways of being intimate with each other come out of this primate evolutionary background. The following observations about men and women are mostly self-evident; we see these things all around us. My hope is that in light of the information you now have about our primate origins you'll be able to see them in a different way.

As a result of their savanna time evolution as protectors and providers par excellence modern men often tend to be idea- and work-oriented even in their relationships. They may emphasize what they think of as practical issues—home maintenance, financial concerns, their power and status at work. Women, in their more relational way, may experience these and similar male ways of nurturing as *im*personal and insufficiently connected with *their* emotional concerns. Many men may seem overly "analytical" and a little emotionally detached when they're trying to resolve relationship problems. As a legacy of both their jungle time and savanna time programs not to harm females,[76] most men show extreme reluctance to intentionally hurt women, often going to great lengths to protect them from overt expressions of their anger. As a result, many men report feeling emotionally paralyzed—unable to strike back, even verbally—when they feel that a woman is being verbally, emotionally, or even physically aggressive with them.[77]

As a savanna time development of their protector and provider instincts, men are wired for "fathering" in several ways. For one thing, a woman's vulnerability and tears usually stimulate a man's willingness to put his own needs and welfare on hold in order to help her—"father" her if need be.[78] Chimpanzee alpha males have a strong impulse to care for orphans,[79] and human males show similar desires to extend their protector and provider functions to those less fortunate and powerful than they.[80] Even though many men may not be as responsive to infants as women, they usually become deeply committed to fathering their children soon after the infancy period. They may also nurture *other* people's children, for example, by volunteering their spare time and energy to help facilitate a variety of youth activities and projects.

Coming out of their jungle time and savanna time backgrounds, modern women often place more emphasis on emotional connectedness than men do. They often approach relationship problems from a more integrated feel-thinking perspective and can put their finger on the heart of the matter with impressive intuitive accuracy. They also tend to notice the nuances of personal interactions—tones of voice, half smiles, furrowed brows, and other body language—details men often miss.[81] Neediness and vulnerability in others usually evoke strong "mothering" instincts and behavior—legacies of their jungle time "auntie" systems and their savanna time evolution for increased empathy.

As part of their primate natures, including high testosterone levels, and their jungle time primate patterns for highly sexed, multiple-partner lovemaking, men often feel more urgent about their sexuality than many women do, and give it a higher priority in their relationships.[82] For the same reasons, they also tend to experience their sexual desires as somewhat independent of their emotional relatedness and commitment.[83] From a combination of their single-egg (as opposed to men's many-sperm) biologies, their greater personal risks in reproduction, and their savanna time primate patterns for reliance on one primary male, women usually experience their sexuality in the wider emotional context of personal relationship and bonding.[84]

These and other differing ways of being nurturing and related to each other, our children, and our societies do not mean that one gender is more capable of intimacy than the other. They mean that we have innately different ways of expressing love. It pays us to understand that men and women are *not* carbon copies of each other.

The Different Priorities of Our Relationship Needs

My own research and personal experience have convinced me that the needs of most men and women are somewhat different and have different priorities in their relationships. I believe this marching to different drummers comes out of the different evolutionary backgrounds of our genders, and makes sense only if we see it in this light. Our different priorities of relationship needs (in some cases, different *kinds* of needs as well) are biologically based rather than created by our cultures. Some of our needs come out of our jungle time, others out of our savanna time adaptations, and still others from our civilization era.

The order I'm presenting in the following table is based on the work of Willard Harley[85] and Warren Farrell,[86] as well as on my own survey. While it holds true for large numbers of men and women, our individual temperaments and life experiences *and* how well our present relationships are meeting some of our needs will change the exact order each person ends up with.

WHAT WE NEED FROM OUR RELATIONSHIPS

Men	Women
1. Sexual fulfillment	1. Affection and emotional security
2. An attractive partner	2. Communication, and emotional sharing and honesty
3. Admiration and emotional support	3. Shared core values and beliefs
4. Shared core values and beliefs	4. Financial support

5. Communication, and emotional sharing and honesty	5. Sexual fulfillment
6. Compatible energy levels	6. An attractive partner
7. Domestic support	7. Intellectual and educational compatibility
8. Recreational companionship	8. Compatible energy levels
9. Generosity of spirit in general	9. Recreational companionship
10. Intellectual and educational compatibility	10. Generosity of spirit in general
11. Financial support	11. A good father
12. A good mother	12. Domestic support

These categories break down into numerous subheadings; for instance: cleanliness; details of appearance, including physical type; health; competence at work; home maintenance or cooking abilities; honesty; and so on. Although we may be unaware of it, most of us have pretty detailed desires for our mates in each of these main areas. No matter what we say or talk ourselves into believing, the first six or seven are absolutely nonnegotiable at the deep instinctual level. No matter how much they may seem to reflect *personal* values and preferences, our top six or seven relationship needs are powerful messengers from the deeper layers of our primate patterns and represent to us the particular ways we *must* have those instinctual hungers satisfied. Below the level of our conscious awareness, they tell us whether or not our partner is a good long-term genetic investment. The chances are very good that if our partners are not meeting our overall needs in each of our top six or seven categories, our relationships are headed for serious trouble. Sooner or later we will either give up our dreams for relationship joy or we will start looking for new potential partners.

Now, look again at the relationship needs table and rank your own. Using a separate sheet of paper, follow down the list appropriate to your gender, and number and write out the needs listed, but in the order of importance *you* assign to them. Use a pencil; you may want to change your own answers several times as you work. You may feel unable to decide the priority of various needs. They *all* may seem important. There *is* a certain artificiality in having to make these kinds of choices. But by the end of the process you will have a much clearer idea about how you really feel at the gut level. You will also be better able to gauge how your relationship is doing at this level, and you may have clarified some things you want to ask for from your partner in the future. As always, you will want to be as honest with yourself as you can. You and your partner need to do this exercise separately. Once you're both satisfied with your answers—and only then—you can share your results with each other.

Acceptance of our different brains and hormones and the different instinctual priorities of our relationship needs can lead to creative tensions between us and a new appreciation for each other's gender-characteristic joy and pain. Misunderstanding and shaming each other for our differences can lead to war between the sexes.

7

WAR BETWEEN THE SEXES

❄

Gender Aggression

OUR DIFFERING INSTINCTUAL NATURES are the main source of our problems with each other as men and women. There are two main bones of contention that come out of our male and female primate patterns. The first is our aggressiveness and the different ways we express this basic urge. The second is the *fact* of our sexuality and the different ways we feel it and act on its powerful proddings. These things drive us crazy, especially when we're trying to build intimate relationships. We seem to be living with an animal whose patterns of feelings and actions are *like* ours but also *alien* and confusing.

In the end, our similar-yet-different ways of being self-affirming and sexual are meant to reinforce our different reproductive strategies. They're meant to encourage us to make copies of ourselves. Viewed from the biological perspective, promiscuity, monogamy, adultery, marriage, divorce, falling in love, falling out of love, even our mothers' devotion and our fathers' self-sacrifice, are all proximate mechanisms for fulfilling this primal imperative. But nature's underlying motives almost always work far below the surface of our personal awareness.

Hostility and violence—verbal, emotional, and physical—are extreme forms of the natural aggressiveness of *both* our genders.[1] We don't mean most of our aggressive actions to be hostile or to do real harm to each other. In fact, hostility and violence are usually the *last* resorts of an organism that feels its options for *non*violent self-affirmation have been closed.[2]

As biologists define the term, *aggression* is a living thing's expression of its will to live, of its inherent need to be self-affirming.[3] If we think about it in these terms, aggression isn't a bad thing; in fact, it's essential to the life process—our own, our partner's, our children's, and everyone else's.

All forms of life are innately aggressive in this sense, even plants. Surface appearances notwithstanding, we are all aggressively trying to promote our own well-being and self-interest. It's true that most aggressive actions are confrontational in some way. They are, as psychologists say, *aversive*. But aversive feelings and actions are as important in getting our needs met as loving feelings and actions. However misguided it sometimes is, our aggressive behavior is meant to be powerfully self-affirming—and in ways that are characteristic of our different sexes.

Sociobiologists have identified seven main avenues of aggressive expression in animals, including humans.[4] They are:

1. Aggression in the defense and conquest of territory
2. Aggression in the assertion of dominance and power
3. Sexual aggression
4. Aggression to end the weaning of children
5. Aggression against prey (both narrowly and broadly defined)
6. Aggression against predators (both narrowly and broadly defined)
7. Moralistic and disciplinary aggression

Men and women share most of these avenues of aggressive expression, at least to some extent. (Number four is usually an exception.) But we tend to do so in different ways. For example, we are both aggressively territorial—about each other, our children, our homes, and so on. But men's territorial instincts tend to be more wide-ranging. Good social primates that they are, human males tend to be enthusiastic about defining and defending larger territories like tribes, neighborhoods, ethnic groups, nations, and even abstract philosophical and religious ideas. Ultimately, this male territorial aggressiveness is about guarding and expanding the influence of our genes.

Both men and women are interested in power and dominance—certainly in our intimate relationships, as our power struggles with each other sadly testify. But men are usually much more interested than women in hierarchical ranking and group leadership.[5] Aggressive social structures like corporations and governments are mostly the product of the power interests of men. Both men and women can be aggressive against "prey," including each other. We can both also be aggressive against "predators," again, including each other. But women are seldom hunters or warriors in the same way that men are.

We're both sexually aggressive too. Women can be every bit as forceful and passionate in lovemaking as men, and some women are just as single-minded in their pursuit of sexual partners as their male counterparts. But, due to their evolutionary heritage and their hormonal systems, most men still tend to be more aggressive and "penetrating" than most women. As a rule primate males can only mate with nondominating females, and the sexual "rites of passage" for adolescent males often include their gradually learning to "subdue" all but a few, high-status females.[6] Most males can't even get full erections around dominating or superaggressive females.[7]

Related to this is the fact that for the males of a variety of animal species fear and sexual arousal do *not* go together.[8] On the other hand, females of these same species can and *do* associate mild states of fear, or at least a kind of awe, with sexual arousal.[9] These and related aspects of male/female sexual aggressiveness, I believe, have powerful implications for our relationships. Keeping these things in mind may give us clues about what we can and cannot do in our relationships if we really want to have fulfilling sex lives with each other.

Both our sexes are proficient at moralistic and disciplinary aggression. One purpose of this is to enforce enough conformity to keep our societies running smoothly. Another is to raise our children to be law-abiding and successful citizens. But a third is to try to force members of the other gender to behave the way *we,* as representatives of our sex, want them to. In our relationships we may often use moralistic aggression to try to make our partners accept both our personal *and* our gender-characteristic agendas. As a result, both of us can end up feeling like naughty children. In addition to personal foibles, *he* criticizes *her* for crying at the drop of a hat (her easy "emotionalism"), for her expensive exercise programs, and for taking so much time with her orgasms. Along with his personal idiosyncrasies *she* belittles *him*

for not sharing his feelings more, for being so obviously interested in other women, and for not paying enough attention to
her sexual needs. And so on. They each feel scolded and "re-
gressed" into childlike feelings about themselves by the other.

Gender *Hostility*

As men and women we tend to feel extraordinarily vulnerable to
each other, usually on an unconscious level. Our extreme vulnerability comes out of our deep needs for love, companionship,
and sex. As we've seen, nature created this volatile mix during
our savanna time to make us want to pair-bond. The trouble
with this arrangement is that it leads us to very high expectations
of our partners, anxiety about whether we're going to get these
expectations met, and deep disappointment when they're not.
No matter how we posture, the *fact* of our vulnerability may
often cause us to feel confused and powerless around each other.
We need to be loved—and to make love—the way *our* gender
does. Why can't our partners just *do* these things? Why can't
we get them to understand our needs, and meet them? Hurt
and frustrated because nobody ever told us *how* we're different,
or what we can *realistically* do to live more happily with each
other, we often mistakenly try to reclaim our power and affirm
our needs by getting our partners to conform to *our* gender's way
of doing things. This heats things up between us. Then we may
go from gender *aggression* (healthy gender-characteristic self-affirmation) to gender *hostility* (a not so healthy cutting off our
noses to spite our faces). *He* angrily *demands* that she stop crying—immediately!—that she drop her exercise class, and that she
orgasm when he does. *She* grills him about his feelings, ridicules
him for looking at other women, and becomes sexually withholding.

Gender hostility takes many forms—the anger we may feel
when our partners don't perfectly support us in our feelings, for
instance, in a quarrel with a friend; the anger a man may feel
when his wife excludes him from her bond with their new baby;
the anger a woman may feel when her partner insists she's being
too aggressive in public; our hostility when we feel like sex—or

success—objects for each other, even in our most intimate relationships. In these and many other ways we can feel the primal fires of our long-standing resentments, resentments that come from our ancient uses and misuses of each other as sexes. And, as psychologists say, we "act out" our hostility toward each other in public and private ways. Fighting against feelings of disempowerment and shame when they're not understood and valued and when their instinctual needs are not met, some men resort to violence.[10] And fighting these same feelings—and for the same reasons—some women fall back on manipulation of the men they wanted to love. There *is* a war between the sexes. It isn't funny, in spite of our jokes about it, and it *is* for real. In a hate-filled dance of mutual assured destruction we often end up devastating each other's lives.

Domestic Violence

More than we'd like to admit, domestic violence is often a part of our lives together. We sometimes see it, at least on the verbal level, in our friends' relationships. Occasionally we even see its physical manifestations. We're horrified by stories of domestic violence in the media. It's very painful to admit that similar—though usually less catastrophic—dramas are occurring in our own partnerships.

There's no question that childhood traumas contribute to such intimate warfare, and many disturbing life experiences limit a couple's ability to cope with the tensions between them. Often we've come from homes that were less than happy in which our parents may have seemed constantly at each other's throats, in which a mother or father may have been envious of our joy and self-expression, in which sex was taboo or "dirty," in which a mother's love was smothering and a father's discipline too severe, or in which a host of other more sinister dramas played themselves out. We may also come to our present partnerships with a history of painful past relationships and major career disappointments. All these things and more may make us hypersensitive to the inevitable problems we face in our present situations.

But other factors, factors that come out of our primate patterns, also play a part in domestic violence. These factors are even more foundational and at least as persistent as our *personal* life experiences. These deeper aspects of our relationship lives always arise from the wounds to our instinctual primate selves, which along with damage to or frustration of our sexual impulses, usually exacerbate the vulnerabilities we may have in our gender-characteristic self-images—as men, in our provider-protector identities, and, as women, in our provided-*for* and protec*ted* roles.

For a number of reasons, ultimately biological, masculine identity in particular is a fragile thing.[11] It takes much care and support to maintain, and it is easily threatened. Even though there are instinctual inhibitions against primate males attacking females, many men may come to feel so frustrated and impotent that those inhibitions snap and the full fury of a desperate animal erupts against those they are wired to provide for and protect. Men are *made* to go physical when they feel they or their loved ones are in immediate danger.[12] That's part of their gift to women and children, and the most primal expression of their protector and provider roles. But under extreme conditions in their relationships and/or their work lives, what was intended by nature as a gift to women and children—as well as to group survival—may become a threat to them.

Feeling too much financial responsibility, feeling frightened and impotent about their jobs, perhaps feeling threatened by a partner's flirtatiousness or intimidated by her verbal attacks upon them, some men may go physical at home. Women often can't understand the intensity of the desperation some men may feel about these and other issues. They don't realize the severity of what their partners may be up against in their inner lives—ultimately, the blocked expressions of their jungle and savanna time instincts for aggressive self-affirmation and sexual fulfillment.[13] No one has ever explained to them the different stress reactions of an animal created primarily for hunting and fighting and one made mostly for child-rearing. In addition, it's been my experience that women often underestimate the effect their harsh words and criticisms have on men. Many women seem to have the uncanny ability to manipulate a man's feelings of guilt and inadequacy to the breaking point, a skill almost certainly inherited from ancestral hominid females who learned to use their superior perceptive and verbal talents to cow and corral the males so essential to their survival on the East African grasslands.

Of course, many *men* have no idea what *women* are up against in their inner worlds either. They may not realize the degree to which women may sometimes become overwhelmed by their unmet jungle and savanna time needs, including their needs to be protected and provided for, and the hot issues these may raise (see chapter 3, pp. 37–40, 46–48). For instance, some women may *desperately* need to feel that their partners can be good providers.[14] Their desperation in the face of their mates' financial failures may override a more cool-headed and compassionate assessment of the situation.

Some women may also be anxious, sometimes for good reasons, about a man's ability to fulfill his *protector* role. This may be one reason why some women seem to want to *provoke* physical reactions from their partners—reactions they don't want to get out of hand, however.[15] These women may need to reassure themselves that their partners *can* go physical and that they are capable, like all effective alpha males, of enforcing "order" in their own little tribes, their families, and perhaps in the woman's *inner* life as well. If men and women are unconscious of these dimensions of their primate heritage, their protector/protected, provider/provided-for gender-defining dance may produce results neither of them had imagined or wished for. These primal male and female roles and energies function according to the logic of our *animal* cores, not at the human—or humane—level of consideration for each other's feelings—or even for each other's physical safety. At this level, things are completely *il*logical and potentially dangerous for both partners.

There are many causes of domestic violence, and I don't intend the above discussion to cover the full range. In addition, domestic violence can be, and often is, initiated, not by men but by women. For example, a number of recent studies (summarized by R.L. McNeely and Gloria Robinson-Simpson) show that women are as likely to become physically violent in the *home* setting (the sphere of most women's most intense emotional investment) as men.[16] I once counseled a man whose wife had pulled a gun on him when he'd confronted her about exceeding the limit on their credit cards. "I wouldn't have to charge up the credit cards if you made a decent living!" she exclaimed as she pulled the trigger, wounding him in the arm. He made $45,000 a year, they had no children, and she refused to work. I saw shades of savanna time in overdrive.

According to these same studies, men are also seriously injured more often than women in incidents of domestic violence.[17] This is because women frequently resort to weapons in an effort to balance the size difference between themselves and their partners. Anthropologists and psychologists remind us that beneath the level of our civilized interactions with each other the inner animal is always estimating the danger potential of those bigger and more powerful than it is.[18]

So goes the war between the sexes in our private lives.

Public Violence

Woman has much reason for shame; so much pedantry, superficiality, schoolmarmishness, petty presumption, petty licentiousness and immodesty lies concealed in woman—one only needs to study her behavior with children!—and so far all this was at bottom best repressed by *fear* of man. Woe when "the eternally boring in woman"— she is rich in that!—is permitted to venture forth!
—Friedrich Nietzsche[19]

Man, on a lower plane, is undeveloped woman.
Suffragette slogan.[20]

[These guys are] a bunch of shallow, bald, middle-aged men with character disorders. They don't have the emotional capacity that it takes to qualify as human beings. The one good thing about these white, male, almost extinct mammals is that they're growing old. We get to watch them die!
—A female executive talking about her male colleagues (*Newsweek*, March 19, 1993)[21]

All men are rapists.
—Radical feminist assertion[22]

We're certainly familiar by now with the abuses of so-called patriarchy—men's political, economic, and sexual oppression of women. From denied work opportunities to mass rape, men's public violence against women is a horror story with ancient roots. In the past two or three years, we've also begun to see the ways in which *women* have oppressed *men*.[23] All too often their emotional tyranny has driven men to work themselves to death trying to provide for their families. And women's complicity in warfare, in which young men have been slaughtered by the hundreds of thousands, is a subject all but the bravest have found too frightening to address.[24] "Women and children first!"—the female sense of entitlement to male self-sacrifice—also has ancient evolutionary roots. Even the demand for lifelong, sexually exclusive monogamy can be seen as a form of female moralistic and disciplinary aggression against men, albeit undertaken for compelling evolutionary reasons.[25]

Today, a flurry of false rape charges, false child molestation charges, and false sexual discrimination and harassment accusations show how vicious *both* our genders can be toward one another. The pushing of fear-distorted versions of female agendas, including such proposals as dating contracts, new definitions of rape as a man's *asking* a second time for sex after a woman's initial resistance, and so on, show how far the gender-hostility scales have tipped against men in the last decade. So does the media's regular male bashing, and their blaming of men for so much of what's wrong with the world. More and more, men are guilty until proven innocent.

Even the ideology of androgyny—the idea that men and women are essentially the same—is applied in a way that is hostile to men. From my perspective, what it usually amounts to is: men and women are the same, *except that men are inferior*. Some radical feminists have suggested that because we all start out as essentially "feminine" and it is only after genetically male fetuses are altered by a bath of testosterone that the male pattern comes on-line, men are biological freaks. Few men have had the courage—or have felt entitled—to raise their voices in protest.

Patriarchy or matriarchy—which came first? Did cruel and oppressive men instill hatred of their gender in female victims who became "bad mothers," who *then* produced cruel boys? Or did emasculating and invasive mothers raise angry men who *then* set up patriarchal systems to revenge themselves on the hostile matriarchies of their childhoods?

One theory suggests that along with male jealousy, the patriarchal oppression of women, came out of men's deep need to be as sure as they could that the children they were supporting at so much cost to themselves represented their own genetic survival—not another's.[26] Of course, men could never be completely sure of their paternity (as women *can* be of their maternity). This genetically based male fear exaggerated men's need to control women, to keep them at times under literal lock and key. Savanna time female philandering and the greater need for male-to-male cooperation strengthened our jungle time tendency toward patriarchy. The agricultural period, with its emphasis on personal ownership and genetic survival through inheritance, further intensified this aspect of our gender war.

As fascinating as this and other theories are, from my point of view it's impossible to decide who's more at fault, or to assign historical blame for the ways we have damaged and continue to damage each other. I believe we need to look at the way the whole system of destructive gender relations works and the primate patterns that underly it. We need to get a bird's-eye view of the battlefield and then move to disengage the conflict at this level.

The fact is our two sexes are *deeply* afraid of each other. Our rageful political, economic, legal, and sexual displays are covers for this underlying fear. The expression of anger is a healthy thing, but anger plus *fear* becomes hatred. Rather than trying to right wrongs, what these emotions are *really* after is annihilation of the "enemy." Today in our culture we are certainly venting our ancient resentments. Yet through the haze of our rage, I believe what we're trying to do is tell each other what we've needed and haven't gotten.

Where is all this going? And what is it going to mean for our relationships, and those of our children?

Through the storm of charges and countercharges and our escalating shaming of each other, one thing is clear. We can see it in the core statements of both the woman-haters and the man-haters. At least as much as aggression, the *basic* problem between us is sex.

The Real Reason for the War between the Sexes

According to anthropologists and evolutionary biologists, sex is such a problem because as men and women, we have different—and mixed—reproductive strategies. The fact is, our genes are ruthless. They're completely uncaring about our personal joys and suffering.

Diane and Henry

Diane and Henry sat in my office looking miserable. She was chewing her lip and looking out the window. He was gripping the arms of his chair. I tried unsuccessfully to break the ice. Finally, Diane began sobbing. Henry froze, his eyes on the carpet. Diane wiped her nose.

"I feel so rejected," she said, her voice barely audible. "He doesn't want to even *touch* me anymore. It's been over a year since we've had sex."

She went on to tell how they had made love almost every day in the beginning. She'd been a little inhibited at first, but as she'd come to trust Henry and his love for her, she'd become more and more sexually expressive. Then, just as she was warming up, Henry's interest started dropping. After living together for two years their relationship seemed sexually dead.

After a long pause Henry said, "I don't know what's *wrong* with me. I just don't have any sexual interest in Diane anymore, but I want to jump every woman I see on the street! When I kiss Diane it feels like I'm kissing my *sister*. I feel defective or something—impotent, I guess. But I know I'm *not* impotent because I want to have sex about twenty times a day, just not with Diane! I feel like a failure as a man. I don't get it. I *love* Diane. I just don't want to make love with her." Diane and Henry's relationship had become what at least 30 percent of our relationships become—platonic.

Some therapists might pathologize about Henry's dilemma, perhaps suggesting that he had a problem with intimacy stemming from his childhood experiences. I *did* work with both of them on the level of their childhood wounding. But I found that the main reason their sex life had died had more to do with our primate patterns than it did with their childhoods.

The Coolidge Effect

President and Mrs. Coolidge were visiting a government-run farm. They were taken on separate tours. When she passed the chicken pens Mrs. Coolidge noticed a rooster and hen copulating vigorously. She stopped to watch. Then she asked the foreman if the rooster copulated more than once a day. He said, "Oh, yes, Mrs. Coolidge, dozens of times!" She thought for a minute and said, "Please tell that to the President." Later Mr. Coolidge passed the same chicken pens. He too was fascinated by the rooster's sexual prowess. He asked the foreman the same question, and got the same answer. He scratched his chin, and asked, "Same hen?" "Oh, no, Mr. President," said the foreman, "a different hen every time!" President Coolidge thought for a minute and said, "Tell that to Mrs. Coolidge."[27]

What President and Mrs. Coolidge saw in the chicken pens that day has become known to biologists and animal ethologists as "The Coolidge Effect."[28] It's been observed in many species. For example, a bull enthusiastically copulates with a particular cow around five or ten times. Then he'll completely lose interest. But when a new cow is introduced he'll copulate with *her* with his original level of enthusiasm and for about the same number of times. Afterwards, he's ready for yet another. Interestingly, he never recovers his interest in the first cow. The Coolidge Effect is fine for cattle and other animals, but it's a problem for a promiscuous species trying to form long-term pair-bonds—like *us*.

What the Coolidge Effect describes is the male's need for sexual variety.[29] Variety keeps him sexually active and his testosterone (and probably his PEA) levels up. There's no doubt that the Coolidge Effect plays a powerful—and painful—role in our relationships, no matter what we think we *should* feel and do. It's an important reason men often become sexually bored, and it's a primary factor in their part of the "four-year-itch" drama. As we've seen, our nearest animal relatives, the chimpanzees and bonobos, experience a lot of partner variety. Almost certainly, our chimpanzeelike jungle time ancestors did too. In those days, like the modern chimpanzees and bonobos, we could cycle back and become reinterested in earlier partners because females came into "heat," and that was just as powerful a force in male arousal as partner variety.[30] But with the hiding of estrus in ancestral women we've largely lost this capacity. The result is that we now fall more into the bull's pattern of sexual behavior than into that of our closest relatives.

Women also want partner variety. But a number of important studies have shown that men tend to want *sexual* variety for its own sake, while women tend to want other partners mostly from their desire to find more satisfying *relationships*.[31] Men are hungry for many *sexual* partners. Women are looking for men who seem to be more successful *alpha males*.[32] The consequences for our relationships are devastating. As I've noted before, surveys show that over 70 percent of married men admit to having affairs,[33] as do around 50 percent of married women.[34] And up to 30 percent of the babies born in hospitals are not the husband's. While the current AIDS epidemic seems to have sharply reduced the number of extramarital affairs,[35] I think it's safe to assume that the reported drop in the frequency of illicit trysts is temporary. As soon as a cure—or at least a vaccine—is found I think we can expect our extramarital dallyings to resume these more natural levels. Also, I doubt that AIDS-enforced sexual fidelity is increasing our desire for our partners.

The differing priorities that men and women give to their needs, especially the top six or seven, tell the story. Our different brains, hormonal systems, physical and psychological strengths and weaknesses, and our differing work-related talents have all evolved to reinforce our different reproductive strategies. And our reproductive strategies seem to be organized around the most primal sexual differences of all—those between our sperm and eggs.

Sperm and Egg

A number of scholars, psychiatrist Anthony Storr and anthropologist Donald Symons among them, have suggested that our maleness and femaleness—in their most rudimentary forms—show up in the nature and behavior of our reproductive cells. The roles these cells play in their mating dances with each other somehow resonate with every level of our human being.[36] These and other theorists are not saying that men are *only* spermlike and women are *only* egglike or that we should reduce the complexity and richness of either our gender-characteristic or our individual psychologies to such microscopic terms. But they *are* saying, along with scientists from other fields (physicists especially) that we live in a holographic universe in which the tiniest of particles may contain the complexity of the whole in some mysterious way, and that the whole is a reflection of its simplest origins.[37] Those who study fractals have made similar observations.[38] The implications for the war between the sexes—fundamentally the war between our different and mixed reproductive strategies—is fascinating.

A woman usually produces one egg per month while a man produces billions of sperm. The egg waits for a sperm to penetrate it, while sperm are straight-ahead, aggressive hunters, each of them targeting the same egg. But eggs are not completely passive. They chemically select against defective sperm, and once they've allowed the chosen one into their inner sanctums, they guard against penetration by any other contenders.[39] Sperm must jostle and compete, literally race, for the chance to achieve their individual practical immortality in union with the egg. This scenario seems strangely familiar, because at the macro-level of man and woman a similar dynamic is at work.

At this higher level women usually *are* more reserved than men, at least in the initial attraction stage of love. They're in more of a wait-and-see mode, as we've seen, more careful in their selection of partners. At least at this stage of the mating dance, women, like their eggs, are often "provocatively yielding."

At the same macro-level the sperm's aggressive competition seems to resonate with male competitiveness—for status, for success, for wealth and fame—ultimately, for women. Male hunter/warrior attributes and enthusiasms may also be mirror images of men's hidden sperm wars.

One egg and billions of sperm also result in different potentials for the number of children we can each have. A woman can have perhaps as many as twenty-five children in her lifetime. Potentially, a man can have many thousands. This fact isn't lost on the testosterone-fueled animal. At the most primal level it accounts for men's high ranking of sex among their need priorities and their intense interest in partner variety for its own sake.[40] The provocatively yielding "egg psychology" of most women perhaps knows at the deep cellular level that it has no need for such extravagance.

Most women can't understand men's biological need for variety, and of course it hurts them deeply. It is one of the main causes of their fear of men. And men can't understand why women, especially in the initial attraction and even courtship stages of love, are often so sexually conservative. Men often experience this "egglike" behavior as withholding. It forces them into the initiator-pursuer role, with all the anxiety about possible rejection that comes with it. And it makes it difficult for them to tell when a woman's No really does mean No and when it's just an expression of her "coyness," her need to be persuaded about the man's alpha status.

In the experience of many men, No sometimes means "Not right now." Sometimes it means "Maybe, but I need you to prove yourself." Sometimes it means "Try harder." And sometimes it really *does* mean "No, *not ever!*"[41] The burden of responsibility for deciphering this female coyness code is on the male. He must decide which it is, and his judgment may be clouded by his sexual urgency. This can lead to male resentment.

Because women don't understand our gender differences at this level, either, they sometimes put themselves in emotionally and physically dangerous situations. Some men are only too happy to exploit their naïveté. Both genders inevitably encounter some risks with each other in dating and other potentially sexual situations. Some of those risks are emotional and, in the worst scenarios, physical. A deep sense of shame can be the result if and when things go wrong, especially in our initial encounters.[42]

We can minimize these risks, however, if we understand that we are *not* the same and that our different reproductive strategies really *are* powerful motivators of our behavior. And while we can expect culturally created pressures like morality and mutual respect to play an important role in our interactions, we need to accept the reality that in volatile sexual situations they may not have the final say. Men and women both need to take responsibility for their behaviors in these situations. We can do this only to the extent that we understand, accept, and respect our own and the other person's primate nature.

Our Different Fantasies

Long before George and Marva began to realize that their marriage was in trouble, they both were looking for ways to live out happier versions of love. Though they had no idea this was what they were doing, they both sought affirmation of their reproductive strategies through fantasy, through their own gender-characteristic forms of "pornutopia."

George used his *Playboy*s and other, more sexually explicit magazines to feel sexually alive, to put himself in touch with the imagined *sexual* paradise of our jungle time. And Marva used romance novels to feel romantically (and sexually) alive, and to put herself in touch with the imagined *relationship* utopia of our savanna time. While strongly influenced by our civilization era moral codes, George and Marva were powerfully motivated at the instinctual level by these older layers of our primate patterns. Other couples sometimes live out a different scenario: the man is more driven by his savanna time pair-bonding and fathering instincts, while the woman is more forcefully influenced by her jungle time selective promiscuity program. But, based on numerous surveys, it seems to be true that the usual pattern—at least in our fantasy lives—is for a man to be more impelled by jungle time and a woman by savanna time.[43]

Several lines of research into our different sexual/romantic priorities and fantasies show that most men's *primary* fantasy is of many different sexual partners, most of whom they want little or no emotional connection with.[44] Their *secondary* fantasy is that of finding a woman who will love them unconditionally, be their admiring companion, and take care of them domestically—no matter what sexual liaisons they may make outside their relationship.[45] These primary and secondary fantasies of men show up in the way they usually rank their relationship needs (see chapter 6, pp. 124–125).

On the other hand, *women's* primary fantasy usually is to have a man who will love *them* unconditionally, who will give them the freedom to either work or not work, change jobs when they're unhappy, allow them to choose child-rearing if they want to, and who will be their primary source of personal validation, emotional support, and financial security.[46] Their *secondary* fantasy is either to get sexual excitement and romance from their partners or, failing this, to dabble in extramarital affairs.[47] Like men, women's primary and secondary fantasies show up in the usual ranking of *their* relationship needs.

Nearly all men *try* with varying degrees of success to live out their primary fantasy—by having many girlfriends one after another, by having several at the same time, or by frequenting prostitutes. The reason prostitution is still a "growth industry" in the late twentieth century is that this male need for sexual variety cannot be willed away, no matter what our ethical systems dictate. Most human societies throughout history and in the world today officially allow for multiple wives and wink at prostitution.[48] Usually, those males who live out their primary fantasies best are those who show the strongest signs of alpha male status—wealth and power. Not only can they *afford* more women; but the status and wealth they have achieved powerfully *attract* them.

Most men, though, have to live their lives with a high level of frustration, and even shame, about this part of their primate patterns. They generally can't afford—either financially or emotionally—to live out their primary fantasy. Often the frustration they feel about this leads to the male version of pornutopia. Sometimes it leads to violence. Some men may physically attack their wives because they seem to stand in the way of their actualizing their biologically wired fantasy of multiple sexual partners. Some cases of rape may also come out of this frustration. Contrary to the most popular view of this crime, rape is not a crime of violence; it is a crime of *sexual* violence.[49]

Spurred on by this frustration of their jungle time instincts, some men may even attack other men out of painful feelings of envy. Recently, a major athlete was stabbed outside a New York restaurant. His attacker yelled, "You athletes get all the women!" as he plunged the knife home. I was once on the Geraldo Rivera show with Wilt Chamberlin. Some men both on stage and in the audience attacked Chamberlin verbally out of what seemed to me at the time like barely concealed envy. According to Chamberlin's account, he had been *living out* the primary fantasy most men must put on the back burner their entire lives.

Most women live with a high level of frustration about *their* primary fantasies too. The romance novel market is huge— 40 percent of all paperback sales in the United States. Starved for the fulfillment of their primary *romantic* fantasy, women readers escape into an ideal fictional world in which powerful but benevolent men finally see that *this one woman* is worth sacrificing all for.[50] Although many modern romance novels create strong heroines, the underlying plot is still the same. In seemingly endless variations of the Cinderella theme, the "prince" comes at last, sees a woman's true worth, and provides her with limitless love and options she's wanted but couldn't achieve on her own.[51]

In addition, the bitter, sexist cartoons and male-bashing articles in some women's magazines reveal the frustration of women's primary fantasies in a backhanded way.[52] These articles, for all their breezy style, often show an underlying anger toward men. And usually the more "independence" they advocate for women, the angrier the tone, as if anger and independence go together. Decoded, this connection between women's independence and their anger toward men suggests that women are angry at men for not fulfilling their primary fantasies. According to the authors of these articles, men are to blame for this, and the only appropriate female response under the circumstances is *angry* independence. If these articles weren't really about the frustration of some deep urge I don't think women's independence would have to be angry. It could be joyful—and appreciative of men.

I also think that many false sexual harassment and rape charges may be more about the disappointment and sexual shame some women may feel than they are about anything else. From my perspective, it's time for both men and women to become aware of the primal frustrations that so often fuel our attacks upon each other. It's also time for both of us to acknowledge our fantasies and take responsibility for moving in new ways to make them come true—within the context of our intimate relationships.

Our Mixed Reproductive Strategies

Our primary and secondary fantasies express our *mixed* reproductive strategies, in reverse order for men and women. From our jungle time, as we've seen, both men and women have inherited the primate pattern for selective promiscuity. And from our savanna time, we've inherited the instinct for pair-bonding. Our jungle time impulses are primarily sexual, while our savanna time urges are mostly romantic.

As we've noted, what's happened is that nature has tried to graft a program for monogamy onto a basically promiscuous species. Nature's somewhat botched attempt in this regard often results in a painful *inner* struggle for both sexes. It also makes our interactions with each other worse because it increases our confusion and frustration about our conflicting feelings and those of our partners. At the end of our wits we ask ourselves, as Henry did, "What's *wrong* with me that I want to make love with everyone *except* the woman (or man) I love?!" And we ask our partners, "*Why* aren't I enough for you?" and "*How* could you betray me?"

The clash between our jungle time promiscuous strategy and our savanna time romantic strategy is worse for men than it is for most women because of men's "sperm/testosterone psychology."[53] But this inner split is awful for both sexes. It can leave men with a self-described "physical ache" when they see other women who stimulate them sexually but who are "off limits."[54]

And it can leave many women with the painful question, "Did I marry the most alpha male I could have?"

The civilization level of our primate patterns, with its attempted enforcement of the lifelong, sexually exclusive monogamy ideal, can raise our biologically based inner conflicts to a fever pitch. Marriage has always been mostly about securing sexual rights over each other and building an economic unit together in order to ensure our genetic survival.[55] It has tried to take the edge off our male rivalry for females by at least giving lip service to the idea of men keeping their hands off each other's wives and girlfriends.[56] And it has seemed to offer women life-long emotional and financial security. Both of us have used the marriage ideal to control each other. We've *both* found ways to emotionally—and physically—enslave each other with this civilization-era cultural creation.

But marriage as we know it at the level of our primary fantasies is sometimes a lopsided bargain. It requires men to sacrifice more than women. Because men's primary fantasy is for multiple sexual partners and women's is for long-term emotional and financial security, marriage demands that men give up their primary fantasy in order to fulfill women's.[57] Women sense this of course, and they resent men for *their* resentment. I'm not against lifelong commitment to each other; in fact, quite the opposite. Rather, I believe it pays to face *all* the forces we're contending with as men and women. Compassion and mutual appreciation can grow when we realize that we and our loved ones are struggling with powerful impulses not of our choosing—and experiencing them in similar yet different ways, and with different degrees of urgency. Such an awareness can be an important antidote to the war between the sexes.

What We Can Do

I know these things are painful to hear. They're painful to write about. But I believe all other attempts to explain and come to terms with the war between the sexes are beating around the bush. They're finally exercises in futility. Trying to ignore gender conflicts—as *gender* conflicts—and claiming that our power struggles with each other are *only* about our childhood traumas is worse. It represents ignorance or denial—or both. And ignorance and denial can do a lot of damage to men and women seeking help with their relationships.

If we're going to have *realistic* relationship joy we have to look at the impact on our personal lives of our warring primate patterns for sex and love. We then have a choice. Either we can continue to try to shame our partners into conforming to *our* ways of being intimate, or we can try to make our relationships into mutually affirming partnerships, much greater sources of pleasure than pain. An important way we can make our relationships greater sources of *sexual* and *romantic* pleasure is by honoring our partner's sexual and relationship needs and fantasies and acting as best we can to help each other fulfill them.

Diane and Henry: Another Insight

In the third month of our working together, Diane and Henry had a flash of insight that eventually became powerfully healing for them. About halfway through the session Henry exclaimed angrily, "Remember that time we were making love and you said, 'I don't like this! It's like you're not making love to *me*! It's like it's impersonal—like you're making love with *any* woman!'?"

Diane said, "Yes. That's *exactly* what it was like."

Henry said, "Well, your criticism about the way I make love and all your special needs finally added up. I felt so deflated, so sexually blocked, by that remark!"

Baffled and a little self-righteous, Diane said, "Well that's what making love is. It *is* personal!"

Henry smiled and said, "No, it's not. *Part* of it is, but *part* of it, at least for me—part of my joy—is making love to *Woman* through *a* woman."

Diane snarled. "There it is again! I need you to make love to *me* and *me only*! I can't feel safe, like giving my body to you, if I know you're thinking about other women."

Henry said, "And *I* can't feel safe or like giving my body to *you* if I feel trapped. If making love is about being smothered by a *person* it's like a jail sentence."

Since that session I've reflected in a new way on the sexuality of the many men I've worked with. I've come to the conclusion that men need a balance in their sexual experiences between the personal and the impersonal dimensions—between making love with *one* woman and making love with *all* women, or with "the feminine" in general. Perhaps because so much of a man's sexual pleasure is visual he may experience a woman rather like a work of art, with a kind of aesthetic detachment (often attacked as "objectification"). The color and texture of her skin, the curve of her back, her hair, and a hundred other details of her *body* may excite him in an impersonal, or at least "transpersonal," way. And these things may be as important to his sexual joy as her personal qualities. This fits with what we know about the brain-based male tendency toward detachment, which we've already looked at. It also fits with men's more urgent desire for many different sexual partners with whom they want a minimum of personal connection.[58]

Accepting that women may tend to emphasize the personal dimension of sexual joy, while men may tend to emphasize the impersonal can be healing, whether we can fully understand this difference in our animal makeups or not. Playing with these different ways of being sexual can help satisfy both our savanna time and our jungle time needs and fantasies.

Keeping a Journal of Your Sexual and Romantic Experiences

Most of us are painfully aware of obvious expressions of hostility and shaming in our relationships, such as when *he* harangues *her* for not being more excited about his work, or when *she* criticizes the way *he* dresses for a party. But the more subtle dimensions of our hostility toward each other may elude us. We may not be conscious of our *own* hostile and shaming expressions or be able to quite put our finger on our partner's. Journaling about our painful interactions with each other can help us clarify these things.

Journaling can also make us more aware of our sexual and romantic fantasies—the things we really wish for, the things that really turn us on, and how we feel when we get them—or don't. Dreams, including erotic dreams (such as a delicious dream a male client once had about making love with an Indian woman on a dirty mattress in a Bombay slum), daydreams (when, for example, a woman may spontaneously fantasize about what it would be like to kiss a man she's just met in the elevator), and our aids to "pornutopia" (our magazines, romance novels, and other sexual and romantic materials), the men and women we feel attracted to and *why*—all give us clues about our *real* relationship enthusiasms. Writing these things down—for our eyes only, at least for now—can focus them and help us value them.[59] Before we can work with our partners to make our sexual and romantic fantasies more a part of our actual relationships we first have to know what they are. Only then can we celebrate, comfort, contain, and channel our deepest wishes. We need to approach this journaling exercise without censorship or shame. If feelings of shame come up, we need to write them down too. Professional counseling can help us identify the roots of our shame and work through them to achieve significant healing.

If hostile or violent fantasies surface, this may be a sign that feelings of impotence and inadequacy and/or of unresolved anger toward members of our original families are distorting our current experiences with our partners.[60] They could also mean, of course, that there are major sources of friction *with* our partners. If these kinds of fantasies and feelings predominate I recommend that you seek professional help.

Before we explore the issue of shame itself, and how men and women use this potent force to hurt each other, we need to look at one more conflict-generating factor in our relationships that comes out of our primate patterns—our ongoing child*like*ness and child*ish*ness, both products of our species-characteristic neoteny. It's to the "inner child," seen in this new evolutionary light, that we now turn.

8

CHILDLIKE AND CHILDISH: WHY WE DON'T "ACT OUR AGE"

✳

Our Child*like*ness and Child*ish*ness

HE'S WORRIED ABOUT AN ISSUE in their relationship and he tries to get *her* to talk. She goes into a little-girl pout. He gets desperate. She gives him the silent treatment. He throws a tantrum in the middle of the living room.

Or he won't share *his* feelings about an issue that's driving *her* crazy. She knows he's upset too, but she notices that while he won't address the problem directly his words are filled with innuendos and barely concealed insults. Afraid to confront his "mother," he resorts to sneaky "passive-aggressive" behavior, tactics he learned in his childhood.

Psychologists have come to realize that an important part of our relationship conflicts comes from the clash between our "inner children." Based on the writings of developmental psychologist Alice Miller and others, and popularized by John Bradshaw, "inner child work" has swept the United States in the last decade.[1]

What these psychologists are telling us is that much of our supposedly adult behavior is controlled by the child we all were and which continues to live through us. To some extent all of our inner children were damaged by shame. Shame taught our inner child to repress his or her real feelings—anger, sadness, and fear, as well as joy, spontaneity, and enthusiasm.

What we now need to do, say psychologists, is take responsibility for "reparenting" this damaged part of us. We need to give our inner child the love he or she needed and didn't receive. We need to hear, respect, comfort, affirm, and contain the part of our child that was not heard, respected, comforted, or affirmed as the person he or she really was—and is. This frees us to work in *partnership* with this bundle of energy and powerful feelings who is also the source of our joy, hope, and creativity. It also frees us to live our adult lives in a more mature way. As we've seen, the relationship specialist Harville Hendrix even advocates that as couples we learn to reparent our *partner's* inner child. For him this is the key to happy, fulfilling, long-term relationships.

I agree with these ideas and the therapeutic techniques designed to actualize them. We *do* need to get the childish part of ourselves out of the driver's seat in our lives. The greater the early wounding we experienced, the more difficult our inner child is to manage. But fundamentally the ongoing power of our inner child is not a result of our childhood wounding. At the deepest level, it's a product of our evolution—yet another aspect of our primate patterns. For we are, as evolutionary biologists call it, a "neotenous" or "paedomorphic" primate species. We are a childlike ape.[2]

Our ongoing childlikeness has conferred tremendous evolutionary advantages upon our species. It has promoted our survival by causing us to expand our capacities for curiosity, creativity, spontaneity, and flexibility of feeling, thinking, and behaving—all characteristics of young primates.[3] But along with these survival-enhancing aspects come destructive, child*ish* traits as well. These aspects of our ongoing childlikeness often have disastrous consequences for our relationships. They also give a shaming, vicious tone to our public gender wars. An essential ingredient in both our childlikeness and our childishness is the continuing emotional power of our mothers.

Mark and His Mother

Mark and his mother were very close. From his wife's point of view they were *too* close. He called his mother almost every day and spent an hour on the phone listening to her problems and seeking her emotional support for his own troubles at work and in his marriage. Often their conversations turned into harangues on his mother's part against his wife, Rita, and how "that woman" was raising "my granddaughter," Sonia.

Mark and Rita had been married two years when Rita finally staged a rebellion. One night after listening to Mark talk on the phone for nearly an hour, Rita flew into a rage. She told him she wasn't going to take this kind of treatment, that he had a childish relationship with his mother, and that the time had come to choose between his mother and her.

Soon after this long-overdue fight, Mark and Rita showed up in my office looking for a way to save their marriage.

Rita said she felt violated, that their life was being invaded, and that Mark was treating his mother like his wife. At first Mark was defensive and stood up for his mother and his special relationship with her. But as the session wore on he gradually began admitting that he often felt a kind of "helpless rage" toward his mother. He said he felt powerless to affirm his own or his family's boundaries against her attacks. I got both Mark and Rita to agree to stay together for six months—no matter what—so that Mark could have time to work with some of his mother issues and learn to stand up to what amounted to her toxic shaming.

Slowly and painfully he and I uncovered the causes of his emotional impotence and his childish dependency on his mother. We worked on the *personal* level of his childhood shaming and also on the underlying primate pattern for childish mother-son bonds that affect most of us to some degree or another. After about five months Mark made a major breakthrough.

Toward the end of a session in which I'd been helping him see the universal dimensions of the problem he was up against he suddenly jumped up and started pacing the room excitedly. Then he stopped, walked calmly to his chair, and sat down.

"I get it," he said.

"What do you mean?" I asked.

"What you've been saying is that part of the power of my 'mother issues' is something *all* men have to face. It's a built-in part of our 'primate patterns.' So I don't have anything to be personally ashamed of! I have to take responsibility for overcoming it. But it's a real problem, not something I've imagined. If it's part of my nature, it doesn't make sense for me to shame myself for it."

"Right," I said.

"I feel freed," he said with a sigh of relief. "I don't feel ashamed anymore. I feel like I can *do* something about it now, like take charge of my own life and protect my family."

"Good," I said. "You've taken a step outside the 'mother complex.' I think you *can* do something about it now."

Things came to a head with his mother the next Sunday afternoon when Rita, Sonia, and he were visiting her. His mother made a remark about Rita's "irresponsibility" in letting Sonia suck on the end of a toy rolling pin. Mark let his anger rise to the surface. At the same time he controlled it and channeled it into powerful *action*. As Rita reported in our next joint session, "He was great. He sat there on 'red alert.' Then in a deep voice—like a growl—he said, 'Mother, that's enough! I've listened to you criticize me all my life, and I've put up with your criticisms of Rita for over two years. There aren't going to be any more. I will not—ever—tolerate your criticisms—of me or my family again. If you can stop, great. If you can't, we're leaving, and we're not going to talk for a long time—not until you decide you want a different kind of relationship.'"

Mark went on to say how his mother had flushed with anger and stammered, "How *dare* you talk to me like that after all I've done for you? I've only wanted the best for you. I won't sit still and listen to this insolence."

Mark replied in an even tone, "Mother, there are only two things I want anymore—love and respect. If you can't give me and my family love and respect, our relationship is over."

Mark's mother fled to her bedroom, slamming the door behind her. The whole next week Mark struggled with feelings of guilt, but with Rita's help he kept himself from calling his mother and—inappropriately—apologizing. I encouraged him to wait for *her* to call. Finally she did call, and *she* apologized. Since that astounding conversation, in which the balance of power shifted forever in his relationship with his mother, Mark has been able to consolidate his sense of himself as a *man* fully in charge of *his* side of his marriage. He's also been able to develop a new kind of relationship with his mother. She's now becoming a trusted and valuable friend.

A lot of psychological research and clinical experience has reached the conclusion that our mothers continue to play a very powerful emotional role throughout our lifetimes—with both positive and negative effects on our relationships.[4] This is often true of our actual mothers. But it is *always* true of our internalized mothers, what psychologists call our "mother introjects."[5] The most recent primate studies show that this human characteristic is part of a much larger primate pattern.

Our Ongoing Childlikeness

Neoteny, or paedomorphism, has been a factor in the evolution of other animal species as well as our own.[6] Among our nearest relatives this is especially true of bonobos who have followed a line of development parallel to ours in many ways. Neoteny is the result of a slowed-down maturation process. Because of this slowing down, the adults of a neotenous species continue to show many youthful characteristics throughout their lifetimes. We don't know exactly what forces in our jungle time began this tendency toward arrested development in our species, but, as we've seen, we *do* know that our savanna time pushed us further in this direction. Probably both environmental forces and male and female emotional preferences played a role—what evolutionary biologists call *natural selection* and *sexual selection*.[7] Nature and our ancestral human natures came together to further the process of our growing childlikeness.

The most recent research suggests that an important part of this process was our increasing brain size and, with it, the increasing size of our heads in relationship to the rest of our bodies.[8] More and more we kept a head-to-body ratio characteristic of primate infants. Also, as the size of our brains and heads grew, our ancestral mothers evolved to deliver us at an earlier and earlier stage of development so as to minimize the birthing dangers both to themselves and their babies. Like bonobos, we didn't evolve our childlike qualities all at once. Instead, we acquired them in pieces until we developed the mixture of childlike and adult physical and psychological characteristics we have now.

Our childlike physical characteristics include our flat faces; our large skulls; the expansion of the frontal lobes of our neocortexes (with the resulting loss of the heavy brow ridges of the other apes); our small teeth, including our reduced canines; our long, slender arms and legs; the position of our big toes; our relative hairlessness; the right-angle position of our heads on our spines; and, in women, frontally tilted vaginas.[9] All these are features of fetal or young chimpanzees and bonobos.[10] And the neotenous bonobos, like us, keep many of these characteristics all through their adult lives.

Most fetal mammals have the same right-angle positioning of their skulls on their spines that we do in our adulthood.[11] But just before birth their heads turn upward so that when they begin to walk on all fours they can look straight ahead instead of at the ground. Since we walk upright on two legs it's absolutely essential that our skulls keep their fetal position. If they didn't, we'd have to spend our lives staring at the sky. Our upright posture itself is a neotenous characteristic, according to some scientists.

Similarly, women's frontally tilted vaginas are a feature of mammal embryos.[12] After birth the vagina of most species turns backward so that it runs parallel to the spine. This allows them to have sex in the rear-entry position, the natural position for animals who walk on four legs. Originally carried forward into adulthood by our distant ancestors to make sex in the trees easier,[13] even now that we're ground-dwelling, forward-tilted vaginas make face-to-face lovemaking both possible and desirable. This is true for bonobos as well. For both of us this childlike sexual position has powerful consequences for our relationships because it encourages more *personal* interactions between us.[14] And, in our case, *this* encourages the emotional bonding so vital to a promiscuous species struggling to form long-term relationships.

With the help of larger male penises it also encourages female orgasm, which *further* promotes our attempts to pair-bond.[15] The greater a source of sexual pleasure we can be to each other, the better our chances for stable—and happy—long-term partnerships. Researchers used to believe that female orgasm was mostly a clitoral mimicking of male orgasm.[16] Of course, the penis's orgasm is essential to our reproduction. But it used to be thought that women's orgasms actually worked *against* insemination by pushing the sperm out of the vagina.[17] New studies indicate, though, that women's orgasms actually help keep the sperm *in* the vagina, thus *increasing* the likelihood of pregnancy.[18]

Many biologists and anthropologists think the evidence shows more evolutionary pressures on women than on men to develop neotenous physical characteristics.[19] Women have higher voices than men. (The childlike bonobos of both sexes have higher voices than the more "adult" chimpanzees.) Women have more rounded bodies, smoother complexions, less body hair, and more slender arms than men. And, like juvenile bonobo females, women have lost the obvious signs of estrus and are continuously sexually receptive, although at a less intense level than chimpanzee females during their brief periods of heat.[20]

But our childlikeness doesn't stop with our physical characteristics. Many of our psychological features are also "immature."[21] We show many childlike gestures common to primate youth, especially in our relationships. For example, we suck, lick, nip, and kiss. Our lovemaking, like bonobos', includes french kissing and oral sex. These are echoes of the feeding behaviors of primate infants.[22] We also reach out to each other with our palms upward, we avoid eye contact with the one we're attracted to, and so on. These are remnants of our jungle time gestures of "appeasement," "supplication," and "submission."[23] They're childlike gestures meant to signal our weakness and to ask for help. Our eye-batting and shy looking away are juvenile ape strategies for showing the other—originally a powerful adult—that we're not a threat.[24]

One of the most powerful appeasement gestures for primates is smiling.[25] In chimpanzees smiling is not as fully developed as it is in us. For them it's a nervous grimace designed to show a combination of fear and threat. Parting the lips shows fear, while baring the teeth, especially the canines, sends the message, "I could bite you!"[26] These things are still true for us, as "Jurassic Alice" found to her dismay. But for both bonobos and us smiling has also evolved to show genuine friendliness.[27] It's sometimes even an invitation to play—in more ways than one.

As we've seen, signaling to someone we're attracted to that we're not *too* much of a threat is important, especially in the early stages of our relationships. These and other "immature" gestures show our childlike weakness and vulnerability. And these qualities usually evoke feelings of love and caring from our potential partners.[28]

Sometimes these gestures are heartfelt; at other times they're more like window dressing. Strangely, *pretending* to others that we're weak and vulnerable may help *us* turn down the volume on our feelings of aggression and hostility.[29] And if this happens in just the right way—not too much, not too little—these feelings are partly changed into their opposites. Controlled aggressive feelings may change into feelings of loyalty and devotion, which may lead to bonding and friendship.[30] Theodor Reik showed how this works with the idealization/hostility struggle within us when we fall in love. If our hostility toward our partner can be overcome by idealization feelings, the bonding process goes into full swing. If not, a devastating power struggle develops between us from which our relationships may never recover.

For both bonobos and humans, retaining childlike feelings and behaviors such as our oral expressions, our "appeasement" gestures, and our smiles has led to greater cooperation between members of our communities than we see among chimpanzees.[31] As we've seen, greater cooperation between males and between male and female couples was vital to our survival on the savannas. Our childlike spirit of cooperation was greatly enhanced and refined as the right frontal lobe of our brains expanded.[32] It almost certainly partially restructured our limbic systems as well.[33]

One more powerful childlike characteristic is a hallmark of both our own species and the parallel bonobos—our increased sexuality.[34] For bonobos sex is an everyday, several *times* a day, activity. This prolific lovemaking between males and females, females and females, and occasionally males and males seems to have two main purposes. The first, as we've noted, is to lower group tensions. The second comes from female attempts to get the more powerful males to share their food.[35]

This is a species-characteristic version of the general tendency of many animals to "confuse" the three "F's" which we've already considered. But it's also a childlike behavior that mimics the food begging of primate infants.[36] A female will beg for food and offer to have sex with a male who has the food she wants. He'll mount her, then give her a portion of his food. This exchange of sex for resources sounds hauntingly familiar, and it probably prefigures our own savanna time relationships which still continue in our present-day courtship rituals and even in some of our marriage arrangements. But with a twist. For bonobos, the *male's* payoff comes first; *then* he shares his wealth. For us, even with our present cultural mores, a male will often share at least a *part* of his wealth (dinner, a movie, etc.) *before* he finds out if he'll get his sexual reward. While the fine points of this sex-for-resources or resources-for-sex trade-off may change from culture to culture, our different reproductive strategies, the savanna layer of our primate patterns, our different brains and chemistries, and the different priorities of our relationship needs that result all show that we continue to strike this ancient childlike bargain with each other.

Studies show that men think of sex every few minutes, every day of their lives.[37] Many women too, though usually with less frequency than men, are preoccupied with sex.[38] And our civilizations themselves are testimonies to our powerful sex drives, which have been partly rechanneled into the cultural creations of our "sublimated" libidos.

Our Inner Child Is a Primate Child

When I first started to put inner child psychology together with the evolutionary theory of our neoteny, a startling idea emerged. I knew that we keep many of our childlike traits throughout our adulthoods so that all of us are complex mixtures of the ongoing influence of our inner child and the wisdom, depth, and reason of our maturity. All psychologies talk in some way about the difference between the child and the adult within us. Freud had his "Id" with its exuberant sexuality.[39] Jung had his "Archetype of the Divine Child" with its spiritual hunger.[40] Alfred Adler had his "Will to Power."[41] And so on. Many psychologists since these founding fathers, among them Alice Miller, Karen Horney, Jean Piaget, and Norman O. Brown, have reached similar conclusions.[42] And in most psychological treatment systems this primitive part of us is eventually met by adult psychological structures which we learn to use both to affirm and control this wild creature at our cores.[43] Though stopping short of identifying our inner child with the ancient primate, the different schools of psychology have each *implied* such an identification. I wondered if there might not be a direct and explicit correspondence between the two. Could we see our *specific* adult childlike characteristics in the young of the other apes?

The answer turned out to be a resounding, *Yes.*

For example, a hallmark of human adults is what we can call our "creative play."[44] The arts and sciences, our systems of philosophy and religion, our games, our sports, all our forms of recreation, our thirst for knowledge, adventure, and new horizons, our capacity for new learning and personal growth—our cultures themselves—all can be seen as forms of creative play. New studies of the nature of human genius show that, along with intelligence, a key element is a childlike, creative playfulness.[45] Our fierce hunter and warrior instincts also contribute to the birthing of our cultural creations, but these instincts are usually reshaped by the playful goals of our creativity. When our childlike characteristics can't bend our aggressive impulses to creative ends, these impulses become destructive.

Primate youngsters show this same powerful instinct for creative play, a characteristic which adults tend to lose as they mature.[46] Along with eating and sex, primate young experience creative play as a self-motivating activity whose joy is its own reward.[47] Monkey youngsters have even invented new ways to prepare food—a tremendous cultural advance—only to find, like so many of our own geniuses, that their elders would rather stick to the tried and true.[48]

Bonobo children play organized games together—for example, blindman's buff.[49] They hold a hand over their eyes and grope their way through a self-imposed maze. They also play a kind of patty-cake and never get tired of creating new sounds and making outlandish faces.[50] The famous primatologist Jane Goodall has seen chimpanzee infants creating a kind of protoart. One youngster threw handfuls of sand in the air and watched, fascinated, as the wind caught them and made different patterns of the falling grains.[51] Another traced the outline of a leaf's shadow on the ground.[52] Desmond Morris has sat chimpanzee children at a table with paper, paint, and brushes, and with no instruction they've made paintings that even experts in children's art haven't been able to tell from human paintings.[53]

In many ways, as everyone knows who's ever written a poem or even a term paper, told a joke or a good story, made a speech, or just had a lively conversation, language itself can be a form of creative play. In fact, the very basis of language—giving names to things and describing their relationships to each other—is an exercise in playful imagination. And as the famous linguist Noam Chomsky and others have shown, the capacity for language is something we're born with, a natural characteristic of all children.[54]

We used to think this childlike talent of ours made us unique. Now we know better. An ongoing series of language experiments with young chimpanzees, beginning in the 1960s, has shown that chimpanzee children share an innate ability to learn language with our human young.[55] While their vocal tracts don't allow them to speak many human words, chimpanzees quickly learn to use sign language and various computerized symbol systems. They even teach these languages to each other.

In a fascinating early study of how the development of chimpanzee and human children overlap, Winthrop and Luella Kellogg raised an infant chimpanzee named Gua with their son Donald for nine months.[56] They began their experiment when Gua was seven and a half months and Donald was nine months old. Throughout the experiment the Kelloggs tested both children for I.Q., word comprehension, and physical coordination. Gua consistently outscored Donald for most of the experiment.

Gua was a lot like a human child nearing the "terrible twos." She was more strong-willed than Donald and imposed her chimpanzee "culture" on him, so much so that he began making barking sounds at the sight of an orange. Donald's human language skills fell far behind children of his own age. At this point the Kelloggs stopped the experiment.

But even though he was behind in his development compared

to human children, Donald's neocortex was growing much faster than Gua's. We now know that our neocortexes are mostly undeveloped in infants and very small children.[57] And though our brains are slightly different from chimpanzees before we're born, the infant stage of our development is *almost identical* to that of our closest animal relatives. Donald only began to outpace Gua sometime after his first birthday.

Alice Miller and other developmental psychologists have shown that our first few weeks and months are absolutely critical for the formation of our personalities.[58] We are extremely impressionable and make unconscious decisions in these earliest days about whether or not we are worthwhile, what kind of world this is, and how relationships work. Once these impressions are wired into our brain circuitry and these basic decisions are made, they stick with us the rest of our lives, influencing our behavior, including our relationship behavior, in predictable ways. In other words, in our earliest, formative days the child and the childlike ape are almost identical. Our inner child and the animal at our cores are one.

The Power of Our Mothers

At this crucial formative stage of our lives, our mothers have by far the most powerful influence on our personalities and our decision making.[59] This is true for almost all primates, and it's especially true of chimpanzees and bonobos. All of us learn to relate to each other through this earliest bond with our mothers. Studies have shown that human infants respond more positively, other things being equal, to female rather than male faces and voices for the first six months or so. They seem to know instinctively which parent has their next meal.[60]

Primate infants are also wired for the physical instincts of grasping and sucking—more mother-oriented behaviors.[61] Though our human mothers have lost most of their hair our babies still show these primitive impulses. Mothers often complain about their babies' tearing at their clothes or pulling their hair, and about how powerful those tiny hands are. These physical instincts are strong because they literally meant life or death in our primate past.

They also have psychological importance far into our adult lives. All of our clinging, grasping, sucking, devouring ways of relating to each other come from these early instinctual behaviors.[62] We often "cling" to each other, desperately try to "grasp" the nature of a problem in our relationships, "devour" each other with our love, and so on—all as if our lives depended on it. We often say things like "I'd *die* if you left me!" At the deep level of our childlike primate patterns we really *do* feel we would die without our partners. In this part of us we experience ourselves as needy children and our partners as our mothers.

Primate mothers usually isolate their babies from other members of their communities for the first critical months. This protects them from the unpredictable reactions of others. It also gives mothers the chance to have complete control of the "imprinting" process so determinative for the whole rest of their infants' lives. In this process primate mothers imprint on their children their own ways of experiencing themselves and the world.[63]

In the 1950s Harry Harlow of Wisconsin University did a number of experiments with rhesus monkeys to see which aspects of early mothering were the most powerful in shaping the lives of young primates—physical contact and feelings of love, or food.[64] He took newborn infants and placed them on mechanical "foster mothers." He made some foster mothers of wire mesh with milk bottles but no soft, cloth surfaces, and others with cloth but no milk bottles. He was surprised when he discovered the infants would use the wire/milk bottle mothers only for feeding. As soon as they'd finished they would rush back to the cloth mothers and spend the rest of their time clinging to them. What he found was that while food was, of course, vital to their survival in a real sense, infants needed "love" more. They used the cloth mothers as safe havens when they'd get into trouble playing with other monkeys. If the cloth mothers were removed even for a second the youngsters were panic-stricken.

When Harlow mixed the cloth-mother infants with children who'd been raised by real mothers, he discovered that the cloth-mother infants were socially retarded. When they became adults these orphans could not have fulfilling relationships; they were socially and sexually inept. When the females among them became mothers themselves they were often cruel, rough, or indifferent to their children.

As a control group Harlow also raised a group of female infants without *any* kind of mothering—foster or real. When *they* became mothers they were extremely abusive. They attacked their children and pushed their faces into the wire mesh of their cages. Interestingly, their infants became hyperanxious clingers who wouldn't leave their mothers' sides no matter *how* they were treated.

"Good-Enough" Mothering: Aggressive Self-Affirmation and Joyful Sexuality

Alice Miller, D. W. Winnicott, and other psychologists remind us that mothers don't have to be perfect. They just have to be "good enough," as Winnicott says.[65] They have to be able to strike a balance between showing their love for their children and disciplining them. They need to be able to teach them to balance love and aggressive self-affirmation. This good-enough mothering gives children the resources to get their needs met later in life and to do *their* part in creating fulfilling relationships. Both psychologists and primatologists have shown that when there's a breakdown in good-enough mothering, primates are marked for life with social and sexual problems.

Jane Goodall studied good-enough mothering among chimpanzees at her Gombe Stream research center in East Africa. She discovered that friendly, stable, generous mothers who are both affectionate with their children and firmly disciplining when they need to be raise children who are outgoing and sexually uninhibited. These mothers caress their children, wean them gently but firmly, protect them only when they're in real danger, and share their food with them.

The most famous of these good-enough chimpanzee mothers is Flo. Goodall tells a story about Flo and her daughter Fifi that makes the point. Flo and Fifi were termite fishing at the same mound.[66] Termite fishing is a major pastime for female chimpanzees at certain seasons. A female finds a twig just the right length and thickness, removes the leaves, and shapes it. Then she dips it into a hole. The termites cling, and with one deft movement she pulls the twig out of the hole and licks off the tasty insects.

On this expedition Flo's hole was producing a lot of termites, but Fifi's hole was "dry." Fifi went over to her mother, looked up at her face imploringly, saw a *Yes* in her eyes, and began to fish Flo's hole. Flo waited patiently as Fifi gorged herself. A few times Flo gently tried to push Fifi away as if to say, "Okay, now it's my turn." But Fifi wouldn't budge. Finally, Flo backed away, left the jackpot to her daughter, and moved to another hole.

Because of these and other healthy mother-daughter interactions, Fifi was always relaxed around adults.[67] When she matured she was a popular friend and lover.[68] Because of her mother's fearless enjoyment of male company and an active sex life, Fifi could relate with the big males in a friendly, "provocatively yielding" way.[69]

Psychologists have pointed out for a long time how important the "constitutive glance," or "mirroring," is to our development.[70] Even at our mother's breast we looked up into her face and gazed into her eyes searching for the *Yes* that Fifi so often found in Flo's eyes. "Yes, you're beautiful! Yes, I love you! Yes, your interests are at least as important to me as my own!" This mirroring look of love is what makes us feel good about ourselves and welcomed into the world on the deep level of maternal imprinting. And *this* is what allows us to develop a solid sense of our own worthwhileness—our right to aggressive self-affirmation and joyful sexuality.

"Bad" Mothering: Codependency and Sexual Problems

Goodall also talks about destructive mothering and the damage it can cause to the lives of adult chimpanzees. For example, she tells the story of Passion and her daughter Pom.[71] Passion herself had had a wounded childhood. Unfortunately, as is all too true for us as well, she passed her own wounds on to her daughter. Passion was often cruel and dangerously unpredictable, and she isolated herself from the other chimpanzees, including her daughter. Passion was also a cannibal. She sometimes kidnapped other females' babies and ate them.

When Pom was born, Passion wouldn't help her find her nipple as other chimpanzee mothers do. Pom had to search frantically on her own through Passion's thick chest hair. If Passion wanted to move when Pom was nursing she'd just get up and walk away, leaving Pom to cry as she desperately tried to catch up on her wobbly infant's legs.

By the time Pom was two years old, when normal chimpanzee youngsters are leaving their mother's sides and playing, she was still clinging fiercely to Passion—physically and emotionally. When she did start to play with the other children she kept one hand buried in Passion's fur. Even when Pom finally stopped her physical clinging, if Passion moved even a few yards, Pom would instantly leave her playmates and rush to her mother.

From the beginning, Goodall says, Pom had to literally fight for her life. Her mother's indifference caused what psychologists call "narcissistic deficits"—a deeply wounded, apparently shame-based self-image. These kinds of deficits show up in us as they do in chimpanzees in such things as "separation anxiety" and "codependency." In separation anxiety we are *too* nervous and afraid whenever we have to separate from someone we love, even for brief periods of time. In codependency we learn to pay more attention to another's needs than to our own. We get this way because, like Pom, we learn that we have to keep an anxious eye on our mother's changing moods in order to get at least *some* of our needs met.

In Pom's case her codependency on Passion really did help her survive. When *we* are in a codependent relationship we too feel that our very survival depends on "reading" our partner. What's really motivating us is the terrified, insecure primate child within. We often get so good at reading our partner's mood changes that we come to know his or her feelings before he or she does. The unspoken message we send in our codependent relationships is "*Please* love me. I'll do whatever you want. Just please let me have *some* of what *I* need."[72]

Primate studies like Harlow's and Goodall's have shown that the more abusive a mother is (through neglect or physical attack or both) the more clinging the child—and the "adult child"—becomes, and the more unable he or she is to cut the apron strings.[73] Psychologists, of course, have seen this same pattern in us. Harville Hendrix talks about it as the "fuser/isolator" pattern in our relationships.[74] One of us is, like Passion, an isolator. The

other is like Pom, a fuser. We set up a closed-loop system between each other in which each of us depends on the other to
keep up his or her end of this unhappy bargain. But we get this
way honestly—through childhoods that are painfully similar to
Passion's and Pom's. We don't *choose* this kind of relationship.
Instead, this shame-driven pattern is imprinted within us when
we're too young to reject it.

One of my colleagues tells the story of a chronically abusive
mother and her six-year-old daughter. She says the Department
of Children and Family Services had been called in several times
to give the mother psychological support. The department had
documented a history of the woman's beating her daughter and
burning her with cigarette butts. Finally one night my colleague,
who had had the major role in providing this psychological support, was called to the hospital. The girl had been admitted to
the burn unit with second- and third-degree burns over 70 percent of her body. Her mother had poured gasoline on her and set
her on fire! As my colleague stood over the girl's bed looking
down at her ruined body she heard her calling out, just like Pom,
for the very mother who had burned her.

Often my counselees need to feel their anger toward their mothers for their abuse or neglect. This level of anger is often very
deep and very raw. It's also often just as deeply repressed. Less
taboo than it was, say, twenty years ago, it's still off-limits for
many people.[75] But when we *can* feel our anger toward our
mothers without feeling ashamed of it, the experience can be
powerfully healing. Of course this is true of our anger toward
our fathers and other early caregivers too. But it's been my experience that the core part of our earliest joy and rage is almost always connected with our mothers.

At the same time, I try to get my angry counselees to realize
what flawed, wounded, and magnificent *animals* their mothers
(and fathers) really were—children of nature, as *we* are, struggling in a difficult and often dangerous world. Holding both our
anger toward our mothers and the sobering realization of their
creaturehood together restores a realistic sense of *self*-reliance
and opens the door to reconciliation.[76] It also helps us to stop

using our present relationships as reenactments of our earliest family dramas.

Mothers and Sons

Chimpanzee mothers relate differently to their sons than to their daughters.[77] Researchers believe this is because the developmental tasks of chimpanzee males are different from those of females. In a general sense they're very much like those of human males. A chimpanzee male must gear himself for competition with others of his gender, train to take part in their "border patrols" to protect the tribe's territory, learn to brave dangerous unknown parts of the forest in search of new food sources, gain hunting skills, and establish himself in the male hierarchy.[78] As an adolescent male's testosterone level rises he has to achieve certain make-or-break goals. He must challenge the females in his community one by one and prove his power over them. Then he must take on the other males in order to find his place in the dominance hierarchy.[79]

His ability to do these things depends on the quality of his early relationship with his mother. If his mother was basically nurturing and supportive he can be aggressively self-affirming and sexual. As long as he has a solid background in maternal support he can cut the apron strings when the time comes and bond with the other males. But if his mother was indifferent or actively hostile—in effect, shaming—he continues to stay emotionally tied to her, forever seeking the approval and support he will never get. Like Mark, he's arrested in his masculine development, caught in a childish time warp of unfulfilled needs.

Goodall writes about the rise to power of Fifi's son Freud who was a supremely self-confident male.[80] In the early stages of his fight for adult status, Freud's mother, like many chimpanzee mothers, backed him up in his tests of strength. She sometimes attacked females who resisted his domination, and occasionally she fought other mothers whose sons would not allow Freud his "rightful" place in the male hierarchy. Just like many human mothers, a chimpanzee mother's status and fortunes rise with her son's.

In stark contrast to the Fifi-Freud mother-and-son team,

Goodall reports the sad story of Passion's son Prof.[81] Prof never felt confident enough to leave his mother's side in order to join the other males in their expeditions and "training exercises" in the bush. He was an unreliable border guard, an unenthusiastic hunter, and a poor lover. He clung to his mother until the day she died and then suffered a life-threatening bout of grief.

The special bond between chimpanzee mothers and their sons goes even further in the highly neotenous bonobos. Research suggests this is because a bonobo mother's investment in her son's success yields greater rewards for her in bonobo society than a chimpanzee mother's does in chimpanzee society.[82] Bonobo society is basically matriarchal. But, interestingly, a female's power is still based in part on the status of her *son* in the male dominance hierarchy. Like chimpanzee mothers, bonobo mothers back up their sons in their struggles for power and wealth. But unlike chimpanzees, bonobo mothers contniue to fight for their sons even when they are fully adult.[83]

Even after weaning, juvenile bonobo males—but not females—often "play baby."[84] They rock back and forth when they're upset, whimpering and throwing temper tantrums when their mothers don't immediately respond. They strongly resist any signs of diminishing maternal contact and feel comforted only when their mothers take them in their arms and caress and groom them. Bonobo mothers even continue a childlike pattern of food sharing with their adult sons—but not with their daughters.[85] When a woman marries a man who shows this bonobo-like relationship pattern with his mother, she finds, like Rita, that she's got her work cut out for her.

It could be that neoteny itself not only strengthens the mother-child bond in general but that it also adds intensity to *mother-son* relationships in particular. Bonobo families usually include mothers and their adult sons.[86] Daughters break more easily with their mothers and become independent mating partners. The implications of this mother-son primate pattern—almost certainly a part of our own even *more* neotenous evolutionary background—are fascinating. For even though human males mature enough to set up savanna time nuclear families and pair-bond with women other than their mothers, the truth is they often unconsciously try to re-create the original mother-son dynamic in their adult partnerships.[87] Many men seem to be looking for too much mothering in their love relationships. And this almost always has unhappy consequences for a couple's future.

Looking for Mother: Randy and Darlene

Randy came to see me complaining of a deep depression. He believed it was because he'd married "the wrong woman." He and Darlene had been married for a year and a half, and even before the ceremony Randy had felt Darlene was, as he put it, "too ugly, kind of dumpy, and just not my ideal of a *Playboy* bunny."

In our sessions we discovered that at least part of Randy's depression had started in his childhood, long before he'd met Darlene. It seemed to have its roots in his shaming, instinct-denying family, a family in which *his* joys, *his* enthusiasms, *his* interests, and his sexuality had been put down by his parents and his older brother. At the same time, his depression *did* seem to have something to do with Darlene. Randy believed—rightly—that his anti-joy, anti-sexuality training had played a part in his asking Darlene to marry him. He said she'd never been very attractive to him, that there'd never been much chemistry, but that "everybody" had said, "Oh, that stuff doesn't matter anyway. She'll be a great wife and mother." He'd bought this line. He claimed he'd made "a rational assessment" and decided to downplay his lack of sexual desire for Darlene, hoping it would come along later. He said he loved Darlene very much but that he felt almost constant physical revulsion toward her.

As we worked together over the next several months it became clear that Darlene was psychologically very similar to his mother. Both were prim. Both went to church every Sunday. Both strongly disapproved of alcohol and tobacco. Both were sweet and loving, on the one hand, but critical and moralistic on the other. And both had a strong tendency to "mother" their husbands. Randy hated all of these things—except the sweet and loving part, of course.

One night, at my suggestion, Randy brought teenage pictures of both Darlene and his mother. He laid them out on the coffee table side by side.

"Randy, this is amazing," I said. "They look like the same woman." He looked puzzled. "What do you mean?" he asked. "Can't you see it?" I paused.

After a thoughtful silence, he said, "No, not really."

I said, "We've spent months now discovering the similarities between Darlene's and your mother's personalities and the way you interact with them. But now look at the *physical* similarities."

He still looked puzzled, so by the next session I'd collected a large assortment of photographs of many different women. I laid these out on the table along with Randy's pictures and waited for his reaction. "Oh!" he said. "Now I see what you mean!"

I askd him to choose one or two images of women he felt sexually attracted to. Next, I asked him to choose images he felt he could "love." Then he sat back and compared them. The images he felt sexually attracted to were very different from those he felt he could love. Those he felt he could love looked a *lot* like the images of Darlene and his mother.

Studies of a wide range of animals show that when they become sexually mature they seek to mate with those who remind them powerfully of their parents, brothers, and sisters.[88] Both males and females try to bond with those who remind them especially of their *mothers*. But males have a stronger tendency to do this than females. Since mothers and sons usually look similar, show similar personality traits, and have half their genes in common, researchers have sometimes concluded that mating animals are looking for someone like themselves. That's partly true. But the real push is to find a partner who is both *like* and *unlike* their mothers.

This balancing act is true for us too. Studies show that we tend to marry people from religious, cultural, educational, and racial backgrounds that are similar to our own, and that we specifically look for partners who remind us in a *psychological* way of our mothers, people who have many of their same personality traits.[89]

At the same time, the "like attracts like" principle gets mixed up with the "opposites attract" program. For example, studies with quail have demonstrated that male quail chicks learn the appearance of their mothers and sisters down to the last detail.[90] When they grow up they try to mate with female quail who are very similar to their mothers and sisters—but not *too* similar. If their potential partner reminds them too much of their mothers in particular, the males become impotent. Biologists call this similar-but-not-too-similar pattern the "principle of optimal intermediate similarity."[91] It's apparently based on the genetic intuition that a little inbreeding is a good thing, but that it's dangerous in large doses. It seems to be the force behind the natural incest taboo that is almost universal among animal species.[92] Interestingly, in many animal societies, including our own, this natural incest taboo is stronger against mothers and sons mating than against fathers and daughters.[93]

The struggle of both men and women—but men more so—to find that narrow range of physical and psychological characteristics in our partners that will give us just enough of "mother" but not too much—is maddeningly complicated, and has powerful consequences. Because of the incest taboo against sons mating with their mothers, if a man marries a woman who reminds him too much of his mother, he, like the unhappy quail, is likely to find his sexual interest in her evaporating.

"Familiarity breeds contempt," we say. But worse than that it can breed sexual indifference, even revulsion. When a man tries to have a long-term relationship with a woman who is too much like his mother he often discovers the power of the incest taboo—which intensifies the Coolidge Effect, the four-year-itch syndrome, and the boredom stage of his relationship. Even if he starts out with a woman who is *not* too similar to his mother he may eventually *experience* her that way—against his own will and common sense.[94] His one-time passionate lover may come to *feel* like his mother.

Much to the horror of many women, men in many cultures, past and present, have a strong tendency to experience a split feminine image.[95] This split internal image comes out of their struggle to find a woman who falls into the range of "optimal intermediate similarity." Most women don't fit this scenario, so men tend to experience them either primarily as "mother" or as "lover." In its more shamed and toxic form this split shows up as the famous "madonna/whore" syndrome. If a man marries his "mother" he will eventually find it impossible to make love with her. But his sex drive doesn't disappear because of this inconvenience. In fact, the "mother/lover" split may actually be one of nature's tools for getting us to act on our mixed reproductive strategies.[96] If a man opts for the "lover" side of the equation in his marriage he will often not be able to bond enough *emotionally* with his partner, and he'll start looking for "mother" in other women.

Felicia

Although it doesn't have the same powerful sexual consequences for women, a similar search for "mother"—and to a somewhat lesser extent "father"—is going on for them as well. This search for the original parents has fewer sexual consequences for women for two reasons. First, they're the same sex as their mothers and so don't encounter the most powerful form of the incest taboo. Second, the incest taboo they *do* encounter— against sex with "father"—is, as we've noted, less compelling than the mother-son taboo. Still, the search for "mother" can be devastating for women too.

Felicia had been the youngest of five sisters. Her father had been, as she put it, "an alcoholic dreamer." He'd never been there for her to give her masculine guidance and nurturing. Her mother, herself from a large family, had lost interest in raising children by the time Felicia came along. So she left her to her other daughters to raise while she spent days at a time out of the house visiting her own sisters.

Felicia got rough treatment from her older sisters, and she felt a deep, unsatisfied hunger for her mother's love and attention. Habitually shamed and put down by her sisters, made to do most of the housework, at other times left to her own devices, Felicia remembers her childhood as one continuous ache for her mother's love and her father's affirmation, *and* resentment against her sisters.

Her adult relationships all showed the same pattern, although the individual men seemed very different. Sooner or later Felicia would experience every one of them as either cold and distant—withholding and emotionally absent—like her mother and father—or cruel and abusive like her sisters. Even if the man she was with wasn't really like either of these unpleasant extremes, according to Felicia she would sooner or later push him into *acting out* one or both of these roles.

We worked for three years with the father and sister issues. But we concentrated mostly on her feelings of deep longing for and anger toward her absent mother. Eventually, Felicia became aware of her desperate search for her mother in the guise of her many different partners. She came to recognize how she maneuvered men into acting like her mother and how fragile and exaggerated her need for "mirroring" from them was. She finally recognized how she often punished her partners for not reflecting her own moods perfectly or reading her mind and anticipating her needs. Like the "adult primate child" she was, she clung to her emotionally abusive "mother" for dear life, reenacting her drama of rejection over and over again, each time hoping that *this* time her "mother" would love her, her "father" would support her, and her "sisters" would be good to her.

She finally came to realize that what she'd been doing in all her adult relationships had been trying to get the love she'd been denied while at the same time setting herself up for the pain of rejection. Her search for "mother" had been an excruciating instance of destructive maternal imprinting and its resulting repetition compulsion.

Mark's case with Rita was different. It was a typically male variation on the looking-for-mother theme. As we've seen, Mark's mother wasn't just an internalized image. His *actual* mother continued to have a powerful influence on his life and in his marriage. Mark had married Rita as the "other woman"—the lover side of the mother/lover split. But now that Mark's external mother has lost her power over him it will be interesting to see how he begins to experience Rita. If he can't experience her enough in the "optimal intermediate similarity" range he may begin to transfer his mother issues onto his marriage, *or* he may start the unconscious search for "mother" in other women. In either case the danger is that he'll turn away from his marriage and be tempted to have an affair. But my most recent contact with Mark suggests that he is successfully negotiating this tricky passage into a new relationship life.

Randy, perhaps further down the road than Mark in this respect, has already run headlong into the mother-son primate pattern in his relationship with Darlene. This childlike and childish gravitational pull toward "mother" for both men and women is one more biologically based roadblock to our relationship happiness and one more aspect of the war between the sexes.

Working Through Our Childishness

Both of us are often childish in our search for "mother" and in our emotional reactions when we can't get "her" to love us the way we need to be loved. I've found that men and women usually have a difficult time trying to understand each other's gender-characteristic brand of childishness about mother issues. Women generally have no idea how vulnerable men are to the shaming power of their mothers, especially their internalized mothers. They can't understand why their own mothering behavior can cause men to go off the deep end. It pays a woman to take this male vulnerability seriously, whether she fully understands it or not.

This male weakness is made worse when a man hasn't had a strong yet nurturing father to show him how to make the difficult transition from his childish mother-dependency to mature manhood.[97] Without such guidance from older males, many men spend much of their lives in fear of women. Men often react to what they experience as the overwhelming power of women either by blustering and bullying or by withdrawing emotionally. Neither of these strategies works, and both reveal the terror and shame many men feel (and few will admit, even to themselves) in trying to cope with women's own aggressive self-affirmation.

Women like Felicia who haven't had strong nurturing fathers often have no idea how to relate realistically to men.[98] They often feel unaffirmed and shamed in their femininity. As a result they may show a combination of angry disdain and childish dependency toward men. They can't understand why men behave so differently, and they often distrust them as protectors and providers. Confused by the conflict between their savanna time expectations and their distrust, these women may exaggerate their demands that their partners meet their needs *or* they may turn their backs on men in angry "independence."

The total effect of such gender-identity confusion can make our relationship problems seem hopeless. In my opinion they really *are* hopeless as long as we stay tied to these basically prepubescent levels of gender development. Our inner child, male or female, *cannot* solve our relationship problems—first, because he or she *is* a child and emotionally immature, and second, because prepubescent children, by definition, have not achieved their full gender indentities. For that they need their bath of hormones and a lot of guidance from older men and women.

The hope for our relationships is that we can develop strong enough adult male and female personalities to overcome our childhood wounds and our childish confusion—both products of early shaming. Psychologists have discovered a number of effective techniques for helping us reparent our inner child. John Bradshaw is probably the most well known among them. He has shown an enormous talent for synthesizing and focusing the work of many theorists and practioners into workable strategies for reparenting ourselves.

As already noted, Harville Hendrix has developed the most comprehensive, in-depth relationship therapy yet to emerge. Focusing on what we can do to reparent our partner's inner child, his Imago Therapy has strong connections to brain structure research, evolutionary biology, anthropology, and mate selection studies.

Hendrix's Imago is basically the imprinted *image* of our earliest caregivers. For Hendrix our Imago is a mixture of all the personality traits—positive and negative—we experienced in these people.

In harmony with mate selection studies, Hendrix believes that we fall in love and get into serious relationships with partners who remind us of these imprinters, people who fit our individual Imagos. But he goes beyond mate selection studies by claiming that what we *actually* seek in a mate, contrary to what we *think* we're looking for, are the ways in which their *negative* or *sham-*

ing traits match those of our parents. This part of his theory is very much in line with the evidence from the psychological and primate studies we've already looked at, which shows that primate children are driven to bond most powerfully not with good-enough mothers but rather with abusive and indifferent ones.

As harmful as our primate childishness is to our relationships, it also *benefits* them in a surprising way. According to Hendrix's theory, our inner child makes us fall in love with a partner who at least *seems* to be like the parents who hurt us. This theory fits very well with primatologist Frans de Waal's study of reconciliation among chimpanzees.

After years of research De Waal realized that chimpanzees must reconcile *with the one who's hurt them* or *whom they have hurt.*[99] Others who weren't direct participants in the conflict won't do. They may offer their support and reassurance, but in the end only the wounded parties can make up. And, according to De Waal, they are *driven* to do it—not by other members of the community—but by their own inner need to reconcile. The former combatants *need* to make peace with each other.

Often we too feel this powerful need to make up after a fight. We too need to restore the empathic bond between us. It's a sad commentary on the depth of our alienation from our own animal natures that very often our human pride stands in the way of doing this. That's when our relationships *really* become wars of attrition in which *both* of us are losers. But the need to reconcile with the one who's hurt us is much more far-reaching than making up after a fight. In fact, it often unconsciously—and compulsively—guides our relationship decisions and patterns throughout the whole course of our lives.

This amazing need to "make it right" specifically with the one who has hurt us is most powerful when that person is our "mother." In my view, this primal mandate for reconciliation with our first abuser—with all the codependent dynamics that accompany it—is what *really* fuels our search for the "bad mother" (and to a lesser extent "father") in our relationships. Both men and women bring this instinctual need for healing to their would-be adult partnerships, as Hendrix points out, in hopes that our present partners will really *see* us, have compassion for our vulnerabilities, and affirm our beauty and worth-whileness, and thereby heal our wounds. The often observed phenomenon of people not being able to fall in love with those who are genuinely able to give them the love they need and want and, instead, becoming enchanted with those who abuse them in the same ways their mothers did is explained by this primate pattern. As with the chimpanzees, others not directly involved in our wounding, who offer their support and succor simply will not do. We seem to need someone our inner child recognizes as a match for his or her early abusers in order to accomplish the healing the child seeks. So far as the inner child is concerned, this means that, in our present relationships as they are often constituted, we each need the other to *unshame* us.

One problem with this program for healing is that *because* our partners may be so similar to our wounding mothers (and our families of origin in general), they are likely to have the same inability these early caregivers had to celebrate and affirm us in the ways we needed—and still need. In this sense, the inner child is not competent to choose for us the kind of mate with whom we have a realistic chance of making a truly fulfilling life. In my experience, Hendrix's system works if—and *only* if—*both* people in the relationship are committed to the kind of personal growth he outlines. It may be that the *real* goal of "inner child work"—both within and outside of the relationship context—is finally to give up the whole idea of getting the love we want from people who are so similar to our parents. And even if we were *able* to get this love from a transformed partner, it seems likely that our now freed *adult* desires might very well lead us in completely new directions in terms of partner preferences.

In the absence of such freedom, however, we have a strong tendency to *stay attached* to our partners for however long it takes us to heal our wounds.[100] Our unfinished business with our childhoods, then, actually contributes to our ability to stay with our difficult human pair-bonds. Our ongoing childlikeness and childishness and our need to finally get good-enough mothering help keep us in our relationships—for good and for bad—long beyond the point at which our initial attractions and even our original bonding with each other have faded.

In a strange way, this seems to actually enhance our *species'* goal of reproducing ourselves and giving our children the best possible start in life by helping us create "stable" homes. But for us as *individuals* this part of nature's plan is not necessarily a good thing. It *certainly* isn't if our relationships show no sign of producing the reparenting we need—in spite of our best efforts. But still, what *would* our present relationships look like if we *could* unshame our own and our partner's wounded primate child?

Imprint/Partner Exercise

Mate selection studies have shown that many unconscious factors go into our feelings of initial attraction and bonding with each other. Many of these factors are physical. Others involve aspects of our personalities that we haven't acknowledged or taken responsibility for. Still others involve cultural elements such as our ethnic backgrounds, educational levels, interests, values, and so on.

The following exercise, adapted from Harville Hendrix's "Imago Workup" and his "Partner Profile,"[101] is designed to help us begin to realize how our original imprints, or Imagos, may—or may not—correspond to personality traits we think we experience in our partners.

You'll need to do this exercise alone. However, under the right circumstances, probably in a therapeutic setting, you and your partner may want to share what you've learned from it about yourselves and each other.

Part A: My Imprint

On a blank sheet of paper, draw two large concentric circles and divide them in half horizontally. Label the upper half (above the dividing line) "Positive Traits and Behaviors" and the lower half (below the dividing line) "Destructive Traits and Behaviors." (See illustration below.)

Reserve segments of the outer circle—both above and below—for labeling the relationship to you of various people in your early family—for example, "Father," "Brother" (Ben), "Sister" (Mary), "Uncle George," "Aunt Martha," and so on. Label the inner circle "Mother." You will write their titles and names down twice, once above the horizontal line (for their positive traits) and again below the horizontal line (for their negative characteristics).

Next, beside the name (or title) of each of the people you've listed (and in the appropriate circle), write all the positive traits and behaviors you remember about them in the area above the horizontal line, and all the destructive traits and behaviors you remember in the area below the line. You can summarize these attributes with simple labels such as "kind," "nurturing," "cold," "jealous," etc.

On another sheet of paper write in more detail what you mean by these labels—what you remember specifically about each of

POSITIVE TRAITS & BEHAVIORS

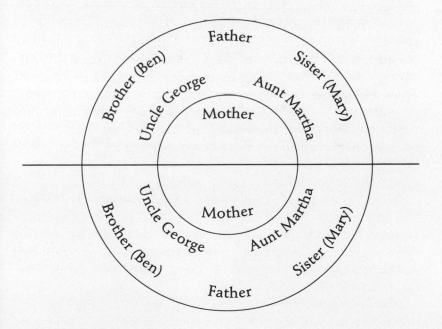

DESTRUCTIVE TRAITS & BEHAVIORS

these people from your childhood—and how you felt about yourself in response to these qualities in them. For example, "Aunt Martha always seemed angry with me. She seemed like she didn't want to be bothered with me. I felt guilty for even being alive when I was around her."

Now on the chart circle the positive and destructive traits that seem to have affected you most strongly, the ones that seem the most powerful or influential to you.

Part B: My Partner

Next, draw similar concentric circles with a horizontal line, but label the inner circle "Core Traits and Behaviors" and the outer circle "Less Important Traits and Behaviors." Again, the upper half will be for "Positive Traits and Behviors" and the lower half for "Destructive Traits and Behaviors." These circles will be used to describe how you perceive your partner in relationship to yourself.

Now, in the space above the horizontal line in the inner circle labeled "Core Traits and Behaviors" list all the positive, empowering traits and behaviors of your partner that affect you most strongly. In the space below the horizontal line, labeled "Core Traits and Behaviors," list your partner's most emotionally powerful negative characteristics. Follow this same procedure for the positive and negative traits and behaviors of your partner that seem less important. Write these down in the areas labeled "Less Important Traits and Behaviors" both above and below the horizontal line (positive above, negative below).

Again, on a separate sheet of paper write in more detail what you mean by your labels in terms of the way you experience your partner and how you feel about yourself in response to these qualities. Then go back to the chart and circle the positive and destructive traits and behaviors which have the most powerful emotional impact on you.

Now, compare everything you've written in the Imprint section with what you've written in the Partner section, paying special attention to the things you circled in each.

On another piece of paper write out and complete the sentences on the following page:

POSITIVE TRAITS & BEHAVIORS

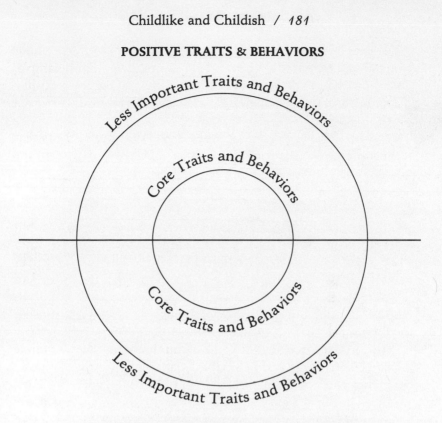

DESTRUCTIVE TRAITS & BEHAVIORS

1. The positive things I receive from my partner are:

_____,
_____,
_____,
_____.

They are similar to:_____,
_____,
_____,
_____,
which I received from my mother;

————————————————,
————————————————,
————————————————,
————————————————,
which I received from my father;

————————————————,
————————————————,
————————————————,
————————————————,
which I received from my brother(s);

————————————————,
————————————————,
————————————————,
————————————————,
which I received from my sister(s);

————————————————,
————————————————,
————————————————,
————————————————,
which I received from (others);

————————————————,
————————————————,
————————————————,
————————————————.

2. The destructive things I receive from my partner are:

_____,

_____,

_____,

_____.

They are similar to: _____,

_____,

_____,

_____,

which I received from my mother;

_____,

_____,

_____,

_____,

which I received from my father;

_____,

_____,

_____,

_____,

which I received from my brother(s);

_____,

_____,

_____,

_____,

which I received from my sister(s);

—————————————————————————,
—————————————————————————,
—————————————————————————,
—————————————————————————,

which I received from (others)

—————————————————————————,
—————————————————————————,
—————————————————————————,
—————————————————————————.

This exercise can give you a good idea how your imprint and your partner may or may not match up on a psychological level—at least in *your experience* of your partner. Often, the more unconscious your relationship has been the closer the match, especially in terms of the destructive (shaming) qualities.[102]

Unfortunately, many of us don't accomplish the mutual healing of our childhood wounds that Harville Hendrix and others have called for. Instead, we use the most deadly weapon of all in our power struggles with each other—the weapon of personal and gender-based shame. It's to this source of our relationship unhappiness that we now turn.

9

SHAME: OUR ULTIMATE WEAPON

✳

What *Is* Shame?

SHAME IS THE ULTIMATE personal and interpersonal disaster. Shame is toxic. It's soul-killing. It destroys our joy, turns us away from our enthusiasms, cripples our ability to affirm ourselves, and alienates us from our instinctual depths. It makes us feel unloved, unwanted, and helpless. It leaves us feeling exposed, disempowered, and paralyzed. It's the origin of envy. It makes everything else we may be feeling in a particular situation—fear, sorrow, guilt, grief—worse.[1]

In our relationships, shame takes the natural tensions between us and turns them into catastrophies. Both a cause and a product of our childishness, shame is the ultimate weapon in the war between the sexes. Shame motivates the emotional destruction we visit upon each other in public and private, no matter how we may sugar-coat it with ingratiating smiles or sophisticated intellectual arguments.

But what *is* it really?

In their books and articles, in their lectures and TV appearances, a growing number of psychologists are talking about their individual understandings of shame. Most of them agree that shame is aimed at who we *are* rather than the things we *do*.[2] It goes after our essence. We can fix most of the things we *do* that hurt others or that are socially unacceptable, but shame makes us feel helpless and impotent; we can't fix fundamentally "bad" *selves*.

Michael Lewis, in his book *Shame: The Exposed Self,* perhaps the most thorough and insightful study of shame ever written, claims that shame is always the result of feeling the indifference or hostility of others. It is the sensation of being exposed to a critical gaze.[3] He says we feel shame when we're alone because we *internalize* the hostile gaze of others—and turn it against *ourselves*.

Our shame reaction to the hostile gaze—the "evil eye"—has ancient roots. When more powerful individuals in primate communities stare at those lower in the pecking order they are signaling their imminent attack.[4] They're saying, in effect, "Avert your gaze and accept your inferior status—immediately—or I will *kill* you!" The lower-ranking individual cringes, looks away, and perhaps makes his or her exit. These are the same physical signs of shame feelings that human beings display too.[5] Shame is our ultimate weapon because its hidden message is "I will kill you if you don't do what I want." While in the human part of our brains we may know that things aren't this dire, the animal at our cores "reads" the shame-generating behaviors of others as expressions of impending doom.

In a milder form, shame has socially useful purposes.[6] Though most psychologists don't say so directly, they seem to agree that the beneficial purpose of shame is to help us contain and channel our aggressive and sexual impulses, to "dampen our excessive arousal,"[7] as they put it.

It seems to me that the *ultimate* goal of *all* our shaming is our sexuality. On its way to this "ground zero," shame attacks our aggressive self-affirmation because in the end all the ways we are agressively self-affirming are preparations for our ultimate "crime."[8] Sex, or more accurately men's and women's different and mixed reproductive strategies, is the one thing about us that is too hot to handle. Whatever else is "bad" about us, our sexual desires are the worst. According to some spiritual leaders our sexual impulses are even "mortal sins," which can condemn us to an eternity of torment administered by a "Just Say No" God.

As awful as the public face of our shame-based gender wars is, when it strikes us where we live—in the relationships we had so much hope for, in the homes we worked so hard to make together, in the lives we wanted so badly to share—shame is the single most destructive force we can know.

I think the effects of shaming our gender essence are far worse than merely "dampening" our "excessive arousal." After working with hundreds of counselees trying to help them get free of their shame I've come to believe that the murderous message of shame is like a hot potato. We want to drop our own fear of death in another's lap and make *them* carry it. We try to escape our own shame-deaths by "killing" someone else—even those we love.

This shame "game" is a powerful soul-killing force in the lives of most of the couples I work with. Interestingly, it often follows the lines of our primate patterns. Men shame women for their "coy" withholding. Women shame men for their wanting "only one thing." As couples, we shame each other for all the "hot issues" that make our lives miserable, issues that all come out of the clashing levels of our primate patterns.

Fight, flight, or play dead; these are every animal's responses to what it perceives to be mortal dangers.[9] We try all these strategies in our relationships. We lie low and batten down the hatches, hoping the shame storm will blow over. But it always comes back. We try to flee. But we all too often flee into loneliness and bitterness, and we *still* have to face ourselves—and the internalized messages of shame (what some psychologists call the "inner persecutor").[10] And we fight. The ultimate goal of our fighting, at least so far as our gender wars are concerned, is to "disappear" the other person, to *remove* the threat—if we can't get our primal needs met. Nagging, blowups, and domestic violence—these are instances of our impulse to fight when we feel threatened. Infidelity, divorce, and desertion are some of our attempts to flee. Platonic marriages, the "silent treatment," and emotional withdrawal—these are ways we try to play dead.

Many of us *think*—neurotically—that we'd rather feel better about ourselves by making the other person feel worse than face and deal with the real reasons for our feelings of shame. But, as psychologists have known for a long time, neurosis is always *false* suffering.[11] Ultimately, it's *worse* than dealing with the *real* pain. Until we deal with the real cause of the pain we feel in our relationships—shame—we'll keep suffering falsely and needlessly.

The Evolution of Shame: Moralistic Aggression

The way that shame comes into our lives is through our moralistic aggression.[12] And the purpose of our moralistic aggression is to enforce *our* will, to make others conform to *our* agendas. Interestingly, as studies of fanaticism have shown, the ferocity of our demands reveals the intensity of our own self-shaming (originally, the internalized shaming we received from others).[13] Tortures and executions throughout the centuries have been designed to shame their victims. They've been engineered to invade and mutilate people's bodies, to violate them physically in the most horrific ways. They've also been made to invade and mutilate people's *souls*. This is also true of the psychological torture we all too often put each other through in our relationships. The message is, "If you don't conform to my will and my agenda (and my 'values' and 'beliefs') I will kill you—psychologically or physically, or both."

Our moralistic aggression against each other as individuals and as sexes has a long history. We can see it to some extent in nonprimate species.[14] But it's a *very* powerful force in the lives of our nearest relatives. Primate mothers moralistically aggress against (discipline) their children in order to make them conform to the community's standards of behavior. Ranking chimpanzee and bonobo females may even aggress against fully adult males.[15] As psychologists and animal ethologists have shown, the most effective way to enforce conformity and discipline, at least in the short run, is through shame.

Alpha males discipline all other community members—except their mothers—in order to keep expressions of aggression and sexuality under control. Alphas don't allow lengthy squabbles or too much rough-housing, and they almost never tolerate violence. They single out sexual infidelity for some of their strongest "moralistic" reactions.[16] For example, if another male is caught trying to mate with one of the alpha's temporary "wives" or if a female is caught sneaking off voluntarily with a lower-status male, the alpha rushes at the offenders fists flying, hair standing on end, and canine teeth bared. The culprits are certainly afraid, but they also act as if they're ashamed. They lower their eyes and heads, grimace nervously, whimper or scream, and make submissive gestures.[17] Research has shown that after this kind of sexual shaming a defeated male's testosterone level plummets, almost certainly *deepening* his feelings of shame.

So, even in our jungle time we knew the sting of shame. In our savanna time, shame became an even more powerful aspect of our lives as we had to try even harder to control our aggression and our sexual exuberance. Males and females both inevitably felt shamed by each other for the childlike dependency they were both forced to accept as part of their pair-bond agreements. As we've seen, that agreement was struck because environmental forces and our evolving neoteny threw us into each other's not completely welcoming arms.

It was also in our savanna time that the shaming power of our mothers was carried over into our relationships.[18] This left both males and females vulnerable to each other's emotional manipulation. Because of the wired-in mother issues that males tend to have it's likely that ancestral men felt their partners' shaming more forcefully than ancestral women did. Perhaps ancestral women realized this on an unconscious level, and used their "mother-power" to shame their mates into something resembling sexual fidelity. Males almost certainly shamed females for *their* indiscretions as well.

We've already seen that our neocortexes grew to help us survive on the dangerous grasslands. Robin Fox and other evolutionary biologists and primatologists believe the main reason for this rapid growth of our neocortexes was to curb our sexual desires. And the main tool in this life-and-death battle for control was our moralistic aggression.

Older males needed to shame younger males' sexual desires in order to keep the choicest females for themselves.[19] Aggressive self-affirmation had to be shamed because sooner or later it always led to aggressive *sexual* affirmation. Males and females both evolved neocortexes that could readily *internalize* this shaming by their superiors in order to keep from being killed outright or driven out of their communities onto the unprotected plains where predators would finish them off.[20] Thus, shame and the threat of death go together.

With the rise of the world's monotheistic religions our neocortex's shaming strategies received the full sanction of a God who dealt in death on a regular basis. He cast us into "the outer darkness where there is a wailing and a gnashing of teeth"[21] for violating *his* prerogatives. According to Freud's interpretation of the Judeo-Christian myths, this aggressive and jealous God was the ancient alpha male tyrant come back to haunt our imaginations.[22] By controlling our neocortexes (our "consciences") he could keep us ashamed of our aggressive and sexual desires while indulging his own.[23] From my point of view, all too often our fallible spiritual leaders have used both gods and goddesses to try to kill the animal within us. And, predictably, they've failed to kill the animal in themselves.

Much of Freud's psychotherapeutic system is about *un*shaming our sexual instincts. Much of Alfred Adler's is about unshaming our aggressive drives. And Jung wrote, "Together the patient and I address the two-million-year-old man that is in all of us. In the last analysis, most of our difficulties come from losing contact with our instincts, with the age-old unforgotten wisdom stored up in us."[24]

In my opinion, the goal of our "last analysis"—our ultimate psychological treatment—is *re*connecting with our shamed instincts and the wisdom of the animal at our cores. Abetted by nature-alienated religions, our neocortexes have done their shaming job too well. Originally crafted to keep us *in* our relationships, they now often make our lives together so miserable with their moralistic, shame-based mandates that we feel we have to get *out* in order to be who we *really* are.

Shaming the Child Is Shaming the Animal

This shaming of who we really are begins early, in our first six months, when our mothers imprint us with their own self-images. If they turn away from us, feel disgust for us, or attack us directly, we immediately take their feelings about us into ourselves and make them part of our own self-images.[25] It's even worse for us, of course, if we become victims of our parents' *physical* abuse. Like Harlow's monkeys we'll have our adult lives tragically distorted by these early forms of shaming.

One of my counselees, a woman who battles intense fear and shame every day of her life, believes she has a *fetal* memory of the time her mother tried to abort her with a coat hanger. In fact, when she was six years old her mother told her that she *had* tried to end the pregnancy. To this day my counselee has a morbid fascination with death and the persistent feeling that she's going to "disappear" whenever her partner doesn't mirror her well enough. Another counselee says he has a memory of being in his crib, crying for his mother. His father came into the room, smacked him, and yelled at him to stop being a "cry baby." His father hit him so hard he had to be rushed to the hospital to get stitches in his head.

Shaming continues as we get older. Marvin remembers standing at the top of a slide in the park trying to work up the courage to take the plunge. Feeling "stark terror," as he put it, he started to cry. He remembers his mother taunting him. "Boys don't cry! I'm afraid I've got a coward for a son!" Another counselee remembers that his father routinely attacked him with sarcasm whenever he showed feelings of wonder and curiosity.

Most of us can remember our parents shaming us for our feelings of anger, sadness, frustration, and aggressiveness. Sometimes we're shamed for the very anger our parents have already instilled in us *through* shaming. One of my counselees remembers being told, "Joseph, someday your anger is going to get you in trouble." That message was scary—and shaming. But where did his anger come from? Today he knows enough about his childhood to realize that it came from early incidents in which he was made to feel "dirty" and unworthy of his parents' love.

Some of us can even remember being shamed for our enthusiasms, our excitement, our creativity, and our dreams and aspirations. "Settle down or go to your room!" is a favorite. "What do you *mean* you want to be an astronaut? You can't even do your math tables. I think you'd better stick to something you can handle."

Our schools often come down hardest on boys in the early

192 / What's "Wrong" with Us?

years. Boys in general *are* more rambunctious than girls. They frequently have a harder time sitting still through those long hours of enforced tedium. They yearn to be physically—and aggressively—active. Later, in high school and college, even today, young women can become the targets of unofficial shaming. They're sometimes still given the catch-22 message that they're intellectually inferior to young men but that, even so, they ought to want to be doctors and lawyers rather than "mere" wives and mothers. So to one degree or another many of us are shamed for the aggressive affirmation of our emotions and the creative play that, as we've seen, are hallmarks of all primate children.

We're also shamed for our sexuality, the *ultimate* target of all childhood shaming. Most of us have "played doctor" and lived in mortal fear lest we be discovered by the adults. We "knew" it was "nasty." And many children are still shamed for masturbating, for enjoying the natural pleasures of self-arousal.

Alex tells a story about his early sexual shaming. He was in kindergarten. The kids were napping after their cookies and milk. He happened to be lying with his head facing a little girl's rump. He noticed a hole in her shorts. He looked closer and saw she wasn't wearing panties. He says he was "consumed by the desire to see her butt." She seemed to be fast asleep, so—very carefully—using only his fingertips, he tore the hole open a little wider. She stirred slightly but didn't wake up. He made the hole a little bigger. Finally, he made a huge rip in her shorts, and there was her naked behind in full view. "It was fantastic!" he said. "I felt really excited and powerful!"

After naptime the little girl and the teacher discovered Alex's pant-ripping activities. The teacher hauled him up in front of the class and berated him—not for ruining the little girl's shorts, nor even for violating her personal "space"—but for his "filthy, depraved" ways. He remembers the word "depraved," though he had no idea what it meant at the time. And he remembers that he felt, as he said, "a black cloud descend over me, like I'd just been given a death sentence, like, for enjoying myself I was now the lowest form of life imaginable."

I remember the time in early elementary school when one of my classmates, Jennifer, always a free-spirited girl, finally got the business end of our teacher's moralistic aggression. In those days girls wore dresses, and Jennifer was always "flashing" the boys. She also liked to sit with her legs open in our reading circle. Our teacher had been after her for months to cross her legs at the knees and keep her dress down. "That's what ladies do," she'd said. But Jennifer refused. Finally one day our teacher had had enough. She jumped up from her chair, charged Jennifer, grabbed her legs, and forced them into the "ladylike" position. Then she launched into a tirade about Jennifer's "dirty, tomboy" habits. She called her a "hussy," which I later learned was a rough synonym for "whore." Jennifer was never quite the same after that. She avoided eye contact with us boys. She abandoned her coquettish smile, and she always, *always* sat in our reading circle with her legs crossed at the knees. Later, in junior high school, she became one of the early teen-pregnancy statistics.

Once when I was about seven I was in my bedroom drawing pictures of what I imagined naked women to look like. My grandmother came in unexpectedly, and I couldn't hide my drawings fast enough. She stood over me like an avenging goddess and demanded to see what I'd been drawing. I had no choice. I had to show her. Days of isolation followed in which I was given the silent treatment by my entire family. I felt I'd done something really horrible, like I'd stumbled into a terrible, forbidden precinct. I felt like a pariah, unworthy of my family's love—or maybe even of life.

Very young primates freely experiment with sex.[26] They grapple with each other, mock-copulate, and eagerly play at fellatio. Contrary to what guardians of puritanical ideals would like us to believe, there *is* such a thing as childhood sexuality. (Freud was right about that.) But unlike other primate children, we are made to feel ashamed of ours. Sexual revolutions notwithstanding, after these early shame attacks many of us never fully recover the full range of our sexual joy.

As young primates, the aggressive self-affirmation of our honest feelings, our vitality, our curiosity, our enthusiasm, and our sexuality bear the brunt of these and other massive shame assaults. Our elders try to make us conform to their own shame-based ways of feeling and behaving. They try to "dampen our excessive arousal." They have to try to crush in us what was crushed in them, because if they can't, they have to face the pain of their own shame directly. And to face *that* pain is to face the inconsolable, grieving, rageful, and violated animal in themselves. Bringing the animal part of us back into our lives—in an honest, direct way—takes courage. It stands opposed to nearly everything we've been taught. And it awakens our deepest primate fears of isolation and death.

Broken Self-Images

The assaults of shame against what psychologists call our "true selves"[27] fragment our original personalities. These original personalities are undeveloped, of course. They're "primitive," as psychologists say. But they *are* whole. They include the full range of our feelings and abilities, and they express all the aspects of our aggression and sexuality.

Bit by bit our families, our schools, our religions, and even our peers chip away at us so that in the end we can show only a small part of who we really are. In the process of fragmenting from these hammer blows we can become hopelessly confused about who we are or what we want for our lives. We may fall under the spell of what Freud called the "superego"—society's rules, norms, and expectations. Of course these rules, norms, and expectations are necessary in order to have societies at all. But things get out of hand.

The lost fragments of ourselves don't go away, no matter how hard we may try to ignore them in the interests of social conformity. Instead, they set up subpersonalities within us that work to sabotage our socially acceptable selves and express their own powerful needs and agendas. Different schools of psychology call these lost fragments neuroses, complexes, shadows, and multiple personalities. Harville Hendrix calls them our lost and disowned selves.[28]

Projection

When we fall in love—along with our chemical interactions, our looking-for-mother programs, and other factors—we're also falling in love with the lost and disowned parts of ourselves, which we're projecting onto our partners.[29] Unable to experience them as part of *us,* we experience them as traits in our partners. We thus use our relationships to feel whole again. And indeed, we *do* feel whole, at least in the in-love stage. Many of our love songs celebrate this wonderful feeling.

Unfortunately, when we pass into the bonding stage this feeling usually wilts, and shame—the reason these parts of us got lost and disowned in the first place—resurfaces with a vengeance. We often start shaming our partners for the very qualities we were so happy with just a few short weeks or months before. Most of us have no idea that these shamed qualities really *are our own,* even if our partners possess them too.

Fortunately, our true, child/animal self neither dies nor gives up its struggle to be a part of our lives. It drives us, against our wills if need be, to grow, to stretch, and to reinclude these lost fragments in our fractured self-image.[30]

Sooner or later all my counselees ask the question, "What's really *wrong* with me?" And I answer (though in a variety of ways), "You've been shamed in your aggressive self-affirmation and in your sexuality. That's it. Period. Now the task is to get *un*shamed."

Gender Shaming

The Girls, the Boys, and the Bar

Elly and Sandra stop at a bar on their way home from work Friday afternoon. They haven't been there fifteen minutes when the first guy "hits" on them. They tell him they're not interested. A few minutes later another buys them a drink. They cold-shoulder him. When a third tries to start a conversation, they politely excuse themselves and move to the outdoor café section. "Men are such jerks!" Elly exclaims.

In another corner of the bar, Stewart, Bill, and Jonathan trade stories about their sexual conquests. They eye every woman in the place, dismissing most, exchanging lewd comments about a few, and desperately struggle not to look at the *most* beautiful. Finally, they find the choicest target in this "target-rich environment," as they put it. Stewart and Bill dare Jonathan to approach her. "I can't go up to *her*!" he protests. "I look like a schmuck next to her. Anyway, I don't do that one-liner routine very well. Women can see right through me. They know I'm checking out their cup size. They don't give me a chance to find out if I'm interested in anything else."

Stewart says, "Yeah. They're all a bunch of castrating bitches."

As we've seen, men and women are marching to different drummers in many respects. This leads to misunderstandings, which can turn into shaming comments and behaviors. Though the focus of our shaming may shift somewhat in the later stages of our relationships, it continues to show up in gender-characteristic ways. It often comes out something like this:

He shames *her* for her supposd:	*She* shames *him* for his supposed:
Sexual inhibitedness and/or withholding	Sexual disinterest in her
Sexual/romantic interest in other men	Sexual interest in other women
Hyperemotionalism	Hyperrationalism
"Bitchiness" and aggression	Lack of masculine strength and decisiveness
Lack of admiration and emotional or domestic support	Lack of sensitivity and emotional support
Materialism	Poor earning potential
Sweetness and naïveté	"Machismo"

In other words, we shame each other for not meeting each other's primate-patterned relationship needs. We do this, in part, because *we* feel shamed when our needs are not being met. We feel ignored or undervalued: If our partners valued us enough, they would naturally do everything possible to fulfill our needs. Our childhood feelings of maternal or paternal neglect can certainly play a part in these perhaps oversensitive feelings. But on the deeper instinctual level what's going on within us is the "shaming" (through neglect) of our primate patterns.

Usually, when the needs that come out of these ancient structures go unfulfilled to any significant degree or for any length of time the wounded animal launches a shaming counterattack. Perhaps feeling ashamed *of* her sexual inhibitedness *and by* her partner's interest in other women, a woman attacks her mate for his "lack of sensitivity" to her feelings, for his "inability to make a commitment" (his "lack of masculine strength and decisiveness,") or even his "poor earning potential."

Feeling ashamed of precisely these things himself, a man may counterattack by shaming the woman for her supposed "hyper-emotionalism," her "'bitchiness' and aggression," or her "sexual inhibitedness." She may counter again by attacking his "macho" attitude, to which *he* may respond by ridiculing her apparent "sweetness and naïveté."

While we go after each other's aggressive self-affirmation in many different ways, what we're really trying to control is our partner's animal sexuality. We're afraid that if our partner starts feeling strong in other ways he or she will feel empowered to live out his or her different and mixed reproductive strategies. And we instinctively know how threatening that would be to our hopes for emotional security.

We shame *ourselves* sexually too—partly for the same reason. In the end, we may end up hiding our sexual desire for our partners *from* our partners. *She* has to sleep in her T-shirt and panties—though she knows he'd rather she sleep in the nude—because she feels too naked, unprotected (from what?), and too inhibited. And *he*'s "too tired" by ten o'clock to make the seductive efforts he knows she wants. They both had plenty of energy earlier in the evening when *she* made the moves.

Public Shaming

Sexual shaming drives our public gender wars as well as our private conflicts. We can see the frustration of aspects of our primate sexual patterns in the statements of the woman-haters and man-haters.

We recall that Nietzsche wrote, "Woman has much reason for *shame;* so much . . . petty *licentiousness and immodesty* . . . and so far all of this was repressed by *fear* of man." (Emphasis added.) It seems to me that Nietzsche was expressing—with vicious anger—his frustrated savanna time need to control women's sexuality which, as we've seen, may ultimately come from male fears about paternity.

We can see one woman's version of instinct frustration in the hate-filled statement of the female executive. She said her male colleagues were "a bunch of shallow, *bald, middle-aged men . . . who . . . don't have the emotional capacity that it takes to qualify as human beings.* The one good thing about these white, male, *almost-extinct mammals* is that they're growing old. *We get to watch them die.*" (Emphasis added.) From my point of view, whatever else this woman is saying about herself and her relationships, she's expressing her frustrated savanna time need for nurturing and virile male protectors and providers, though she'd probably be the last one to admit it. Since these nonnurturing, nonvirile would-be alphas have failed her, she wants them dead.

It's interesting that in order to "kill" them in her imagination she first has to make them subhuman. As the suffragette slogan says, "Man, *on a lower plane,* is *undeveloped* woman." (Emphasis added.) The "All men are rapists" slur also makes men seem animallike. Nietzsche's slander of women makes them seem both animallike and childlike.

Whenever we make our fellow human beings subhuman we are already edging them toward "extinction." We're pushing them out of our communities. If they're not one of us, it's time to cast them out onto the savanna where the lions can make short work of them. Shunning racist propaganda campaigns, concentration camps—death. First comes the public shaming of that which really *is* subhuman about us (and often gloriously so)—about *all* of us. Then comes death—shame's ultimate goal.

Shame and Violence

Many people believe shame is the only thing that keeps us from running wild in the streets, murdering and copulating at will. And, as we've noted, there's some truth in this. But as psychologists who study shame have seen, shame often goes way too far. When it makes us feel unworthy, defective in our essence, disempowered, unvalued, unappreciated, cut off, and with no realistic way to express our aggressive self-affirmation and sexual desires, we will sooner or later resort to violence—verbal, emotional, or physical.[31] This is true of our domestic battles and our public male- and female-bashing. Those who are the victims of shaming respond with desperation and rage. They feel their lives depend on it.

Strong, centered, self-confident men and women who are secure in their own identities, including their gender-indentities, don't have to shame others. It takes a lot to threaten them. They don't have to "kill" their partners before their partners "kill" them. They don't have to wish the other sex dead in order to feel alive themselves.

A Case of Mistaken Identity

We've already seen some of the reasons why we shame our partners and ourselves. We're afraid of and shamed by our partner's emotional or economic power over us and the dependency needs our pair-bonded primate patterns have imposed. We're afraid our partners will betray our relationships, that they—or is it we?—will be sexually and romantically unfaithful. Men may be afraid of and shamed by the possibility that the children they're raising aren't theirs. Both men and women feel frightened and ashamed when they feel their jungle and savanna time needs are not being met (see chapter 6, pp. 124–125). Men especially may feel frightened by and ashamed of their emotional vulnerability to "mother." Our child*like*ness and our child*ish*ness, plus the evolutionary background of our ancient societal organizations with their demands for conformity—or else!—can make both of us vulnerable to the fear of being abandoned, a fear that we feel at the primate level as the threat of death.

There are other reasons we fear and shame each other and ourselves. As we've seen, we may feel intimidated by some of our partner's personal qualities, many of which may be our own disowned characteristics. We may also feel intimidated and so shamed by our different gender-characteristic aptitudes and abilities.[32] Women may feel *innately* fearful of and shamed by men's greater physical size and strength. Men may feel afraid of and shamed by women's generally greater language skills—their talent for saying what they feel, especially during arguments.[33] In the end, these and other gender-based sources of our feelings of inferiority and shame are products of our different reproductive strategies. Sex, shame, death—all too often we lump them together in our experience of ourselves and each other.

But there's another reason we fear and shame each other—mistaken identity. As we recall, we project onto others, especially our partners, the patterns we are afraid of and can't face about ourselves. If it's true that the ultimate target of our shaming is the animal within *us*, then the ultimate and most irresponsible form of projection is making our partners carry our shamed animal for us. As we've seen, we make them carry our mother, father, brother, and sister projections We also make them carry the lost and disowned parts of our inner child. But even more disturbing to me, we make them carry our own primal passions. And then we shame them for it. This may include their expressions of exuberance, joy, anger, aggressiveness, despair, sorrow, insecurity, fear, creativity, and a host of other deluxe-model ape attributes. But especially it includes their sexuality. Since we can't accept our own animal self-interest and sexuality, we make our partners the victims of our unconscious self-shaming. Of course, we get this way honestly. But once we know what we're up to it's our responsibility to stop it.

The strange thing about projection is that it's about mistaken identity. It's probably understandable, even if it isn't either helpful or moral, to shame our partners for *their* primate patterns. But it's *absolutely* immoral to shame them for our own. Then we're just using them as a dumping ground for our rejection of our own core selves.

Frank, we may recall, was insanely jealous. He alienated one after another of his girlfriends by his outbursts of jealous rage. An innocent exchange of pleasantries in a restaurant between his girlfriend and a waiter set him off. At first, when I suggested to Frank that, along with his hand-me-down childhood experiences, part of the reason for his extreme jealousy might be that he was projecting his own promiscuous urges onto his girlfriends, he would hit the ceiling. When this happens in therapy it's usually a clue that I've touched a really sore spot.

As we worked together it became more and more clear to me that part of my getting Frank to accept his primate patterns for jealousy would be helping him come to terms with his promiscuous fantasies. It took a while, but he finally agreed to keep a journal of his sexual dreams and fantasies. He made copies of his entries and we went over them together. Gradually he had to admit the truth of what his own unconscious was telling him.

I suggested to him that whenever he felt a jealousy attack coming on, he take a five-minute time-out. During that time-out he needed to remind himself that whatever had triggered the attack had less to do with his partner than it did with him. He would need to distance himself from his feelings and realize that impersonal forces were manipulating him.

For a long time, he couldn't interrupt his feelings this way. But the day finally came when he beamed at me and said, "You know, it works! If something happens and I get that powerful jealousy kick, if I can back off and cool down I can usually see that my girlfriend hasn't done anything to warrant my reaction. And I can say to myself, 'Yeah, well, I guess I'd like to make love with about half the women I see.' I feel okay about that now. The important thing for me is that neither she nor I act on these urges. What's that saying? 'Work up an appetite outside, but eat at home.'"

Frank turned out to be a success story.

On the public level, the classic case of men projecting their shamed sexual desires onto women is the Adam and Eve story. In a common interpretation of this story, as we recall, Adam blames Eve for his awakened sexuality. This theme shows up again and again in our "sacred" writings.

The Ultimate Death

All these causes of our fears and shame are rooted in one last fear. In the end the death we fear when we feel ashamed is not our own *personal* death. It's the death of our genes, the end of our genetic survival, being cut off from our practical immortality.[34] Most of us don't experience shaming or even our fear of death at this level, of course. But sometimes we get glimmers.

This seems to be true for a friend of mine. Niobe is forty-five years old. She's never been married and never had children. She's recently seen her boutique business fail after twenty years of hard work. Now she says she feels deeply ashamed of her "selfish life," as she puts it. An only child, she says she's suddenly afraid her family line will die out. She wants children—desperately—*now*.

A Proposal

Ask yourself these questions:

1. Your partner is attacking you verbally. You feel like responding in kind. Given the intensity of your partner's attack, might it be okay if your partner felt afraid of you—just a little?
2. Your partner is making you late for an important engagement. You want to lash out in the worst way. Might humiliating your partner be justified—just this once?

3. Your partner sometimes seems sexually insatiable. You feel aroused, but also somehow disgusted. Do you sometimes feel it might be nice to let your partner take the lion's share of responsibility for your sex life together?

4. Your partner's independent actions sometimes seem frightening, as if they might threaten the security of your relationship, though you have no real reason to think they might. Do you ever find yourself wanting to monitor your partner's time?

5. You receive shaming messages from those around you—at home, at work, when you visit your family, sometimes even when you're with friends, but you feel unable to speak up in your own defense. Do you sometimes feel it would take too much effort to do so, or perhaps threaten the security of your relationships?

If you answered Yes to any of these questions your relationship is probably in need of significant *un*shaming.

Self-Evaluation Exercise: Exposing Your Shame Feelings

Shame wears many faces. We can even feel ashamed of feeling ashamed. Our shame feelings may be so hidden, such an ingrained part of us, that we experience them as "normal" or "right." An exercise to expose all the ways we've been shamed would fill a book longer than this one. But the following exercises will help you and your partner uncover the major targets of the kind of shame feelings that *many* people have. You or your partner may react to some of the questions with indignation. "Well *of course* I feel this way. It's only natural." But from my perspective, just because something is *usual* doesn't necessarily make it *natural*. It certainly doesn't make it *healthy* either for you or your relationship.

Answer the following questions with Yes or No.

| | Yes | No |

1. Do you avoid looking at yourself naked in a full-length mirror?

2. Do you need to have the lights off when you make love?

3. Do you feel self-conscious about any of your body odors?

4. Do you feel humiliated easily in either public or private situations?

5. Do you feel guilty when loved ones become the focal point of your anger?

6. Do the sexual and aggressive behaviors of your partner often irritate or disgust you?

7. When your partner takes the sexual initiative do you sometimes feel put off, perhaps even violated in some way, even when you're feeling sexually aroused?

8. Do you sometimes feel inadequate in situations in which you've already demonstrated competence?

9. Do you ever feel like "disappearing"?

10. Do you feel anger when children insist on their own way?

11. Do you feel that your partner is the "bad one" in your relationship?

12. Do you make disparaging remarks about your partner's body from time to time?

13. Do you make critical comments about your body occasionally?

14. Do you feel envy easily?

15. Women: Do you sometimes feel you're not quite adequate as a woman—not "strong" enough perhaps, or not "feminine" enough?

16. Men: Do you sometimes feel you're not quite adequate as a man—not "manly" enough, or perhaps not a competent enough lover?

	Yes	No

17. When you think about the God of your particular religious upbringing, do you sometimes have a vague sense of guilt or "sinfulness"?

18. Do you feel rageful on a fairly regular basis?

19. Do you feel anger or disgust when hearing of a child who's masturbating or in some other way seeking physical pleasure?

20. When your boss, your mother, your father, or some other authority figure provokes your anger, does this emotion generate feeings of guilt?

21. Do you tend to think of bodily secretions and odors associated with sex as messy and unpleasant?

22. Do you tend to feel that the other gender is the main source of relationship problems?

23. Do you feel that masturbation is self-indulgent or in some other way wrong?

24. Do you feel uncomfortable when you think of your children as sexual beings?

25. Do you basically feel the other gender is responsible for most of the problems in the world?

26. Do you feel oral sex is degrading or in some way dirty?

27. Do you ever think of other ethnic groups as more animallike?

28. Do you feel guilty when experiencing aggressive fantasies?

29. Do you feel guilty when experiencing sexual fantasies?

30. Do you tend to feel that the expression of strong emotion is "uncouth"?

206 / What's "Wrong" with Us?

If you answered Yes to five or more of these questions, shame is probably a major factor in your life. And if it's a major factor in *your* life, it's also a force in your relationship. It's absolutely certain that if you feel ashamed you're projecting at least *some* of your shame onto your partner. If this is the case for you, it's probably time to face your and your partner's shame and begin to work through it.

Again, I recommend that you and your partner keep separate journals in which you record, among other things, your memories of early shaming incidents. If you have trouble remembering specific events you might find it helpful to begin your "sources of shame" work with such sentences as:

Whenever I expressed my sexuality I was _____

Whenever I expressed my exuberance or anger I was _____

I was told that oral sex is _____

Try to recall specific events and even specific messages you received from parents, brothers and sisters, teachers, Sunday School, your peers, and others. An essential part of any unshaming process is pinpointing the sources of your bad feelings about yourself and making them conscious. Once you realize that they're "alien" messages and not an innate part of who you are you have taken the first step toward freedom.

In the face of all the evolutionary forces ranged against us, including our childish penchant for shaming ourselves and each other, we keep trying to make our pair-bonds last. We keep hoping that *this* time we can love and be loved forever. We keep believing that *this* relationship will be the one we can grow and deepen with. *This* is the one that will bring us a lifetime of joy and fulfillment.

At times the goal seems impossible to reach. But there *are* forces on our side. Surely we are wired to keep trying "to love and to cherish from this day forward, 'til death us do part." *And*

there are things we can do—concrete steps we can take—
to make our dreams of lifelong love much more likely to come
true. A lifetime of *realistic* romance, the kind of romance that's
based on awareness, acceptance, and even celebration of our
primate patterns, is a promising possibility for most of our relationships.

PART THREE

*

MAKING OUR
RELATIONSHIPS LAST

10

RECLAIMING OUR PRIMAL ROOTS

❋

Recovering Our Wildness

An Embodiment Exercise

ONE OF THE MOST PROVOCATIVE and potentially healing things I do in my workshops is what I call the Ape Embodiment Exercise. In this exercise I lead men and women in a series of physical and vocal activities designed to get them out of their heads and into their animal bodies and souls. I divide the men and women into two same-gender groups, have them pair up, and form two circles at opposite ends of the room. I then take them through a regimen of various primate behaviors—gazing into each other's eyes, grimacing, smiling, "grooming" each other, begging, playing, confronting, making up, and so on. I also ask them to make nonverbal animal sounds to go along with their movements— whining, growling, barking, and what primatologists call pant-hooting. At each step I have them share their emotional reactions to these prehuman exchanges. This encourages them to integrate their humanness, and its capacity to reflect and analyze, with their animal selves.

Then I ask for volunteers from both the women's and men's circles to go through the exercise with a partner from the other gender. I ask for volunteers because as alarming as aspects of the exercise can be when we're doing them with our own gender, they can be even more unsettling when we do them with the opposite sex.

The emotional reactions are powerful and uncensored. Once they get past their initial embarrassment about their "undignified" behavior, the participants express how uncomfortable they feel staring into each other's eyes, and they talk about how their "killer instincts" come up in the confrontational scenario. The begging part of the exercise often awakens painful feelings of powerlessness, deprivation, and shaming rejection. Frequently, the "withholding" partner says he or she felt an almost irresistible urge to give in to the begging partner's demands. People are often deeply shaken by the raw nature of their feelings. But these primal emotions are going on under the surface of our more civilized interactions *all the time,* and they have important implications for what's *really* taking place in our relationships.

For me the most fascinating part of the inter-gender exercise is the confrontation scenario. When a man and a woman must confront each other without using language—only glares, snarls, growls, screeches, and arm-flailing—an amazing thing often happens. One strong, independent woman put it like this: "I was aware when we were 'fighting' that I felt *good* about letting him 'overpower' me. I mean, it wasn't like abuse or domestic violence or anything. I abhor violence. I showed my own strength and fierceness so he'd know *I* was 'dangerous' too. But it felt good to defer to him in the end. And all of a sudden I felt a lot of sexual energy between us." Her male partner said he'd felt it too.

Another woman said, "Whew! What a relief! I don't have to be like a man. I don't have to fight to be more powerful the way men do. I have my own kind of power." And a usually timid man said, "For the first time in my life I felt my animal power with a woman. I didn't really want to hurt my partner, only to 'prove my manhood' or something. That's a very weird feeling for me. At first I couldn't get into it. But when I did, I felt alive—and really sexual." His female partner said enthusiastically, "I've known Craig for years and I've never felt so much energy from him, or my *own* energy when I'm around him. It's hard to put into words, but when he showed his masculine power I felt like a woman." Another male participant said, "My partner's combination of what I would call fierceness and deference really turned me on. It's like this was not about confrontation but about sex."

When we connect with our primal roots and allow them to express themselves most of us automatically connect with the primal roots of our *gender* as well. There's something wonderfully vital, life-giving, and healing about reaching this level of interaction with each other as men and women. We seem to need to test each other's maleness and femaleness in order to open up more fully to our *own* gender energies. When this happens we *both* feel powerful and free. We reclaim our gender-characteristic forms of assertiveness, sexuality, and love for each other. As many participants have said, "confronting" each other as male and female *animals* can release feelings of gratitude and affection toward the opposite sex.

A Tempered Fierceness

We live in the frigid 1990s on the surface of things. And yet as men and women retreat into the woods to reclaim their wildness as "new warriors" and as "women who run with the wolves," *and* as the divorce rate soars—mainly an expression of women's economic self-sufficiency and growing "fierceness"[1]—it strikes me that things are not as sterile as they may seem. The sexual revolution is far from dead. I suspect there may even be a link between our ostensible cutback in extramarital affairs and the rising divorce statistics. Serial monogamy has become the least scary way for men to live out their desire for a variety of sexual partners, and for independent women to continue their search for more fully developed alpha males.

It's clear to me that part of what the women's movement is about—no matter what an anti-sex, perhaps puritanical minority may say—is women recovering the wildness of their ancient reproductive strategies, strategies that when more openly expressed free them enough from "nice girl" clichés to aggressively pursue their real ambitions and their sexual desires.

It's also clear to me that part of what the men's movement is about is men recovering *their* wildness, and feeling free enough from the "nice boy" syndrome to aggressively express *their* real ambitions and *their* sexual desires.

A central part of both movements, for men and women who go this route, is their recovery of pre-Judeo-Christian nature spirituality. It's no accident that women's exploration of "Goddess religion" and men's reclaiming of "Earth God" spirituality are coinciding with the growing concern about ecology. But in saving the "wilderness," we must also move to save our *own* wildness. Assuring the survival of the animals "out there" requires that we first assure the survival of the animal within ourselves.

* * *

As I said in chapter 3, it seems to me we are rushing at breakneck speed to recover our jungle time roots. We're doing it unevenly of course. Many of us are snagged in our civilization-era moralities, and the AIDS epidemic plays into the hands of the moralistic religious right. It also incites woman-haters and man-haters to further emotional violence, since they can now realistically view the opposite sex as the death-bearing enemy. Yet, in time, the witch hunts will subside and we'll continue our quest to recover our authentic sexuality, and with renewed enthusiasm.

Wild, strong women and men living in closer harmony with their primate cores is a wonderful prospect for our human future. I'm concerned that we learn to be strong and wild without doing it at the other gender's expense—or at the expense of the relationships that we want to last.

In my counseling practice and workshops I encourage men and women to reclaim their jungle time wildness. At the same time, I help them stay connected to their savanna time pair-bonding urges and their neoteny-based childhood needs for long-term emotional security. As we've seen, we are a jerryrigged ape—too complicated for our own good. Simple solutions to relationship problems don't work. We can't deny any part of ourselves and expect to be happy. Realistic love requires that we make a conscious effort to meet *all* our needs and those of our partners—not perfectly—but well enough.

Our romantic commitments to each other are not a part of our jungle time instincts. And our promiscuous sexual impulses are not a central part of our savanna time patterns. If we were *only* promiscuous—like chimpanzees and bonobos—things would be much easier. And if we were a true pair-bonding species in which individuals mated happily for life—like wild geese—our love lives wouldn't require couples counseling, or books about how to make our relationships work.

As we've seen, the problem is, we're *both*. Our hunger for sexually exclusive love is just as strong as our hunger for sexual variety (when we view couples as single reproductive systems). Most women tip the scales in favor of exclusive love, while most men tend to weigh in a little more on the promiscuous side—with a lot of individual temperamental variation in between. Our neotenous childhood needs for lifelong emotional security shove us in the direction of monogamous commitment, but not powerfully enough to eliminate our desire for sex with other partners or for more *alpha* alpha males.

Our very complexity has made us an enormously successful species. There are almost 5 billion of us now. And our dazzling civilizations really *are* testimonies to our capacity to rechannel our sexual energies creatively. But the very strengths of our different and mixed reproductive strategies, including our highly aggressive and sexual natures, also cause us a level of emotional pain no other species that we know of endures.

Women, no matter how liberated, are not going to get over either their jungle time need for selective promiscuity (playing the alpha male field) or their savanna-generated and civilization era-enhanced needs for emotional and financial security (ultimately, so they can provide nurturing environments for their children). And men, no matter how sensitive they become as lovers, husbands, and fathers, are not going to get over their jungle time need for sexual variety or their savanna time/civilization era needs for domestic support, admiration for their work, and reassurance about their paternity.

Reclaiming Our Gender Essence
The Sound of Sex

Often in my workshops I have the participants do what I call the Womb/Phallus Sound Exercise. It requires that they be in the right frame of mind. But when they are, the results are astounding. I separate the women and men and have them sit on opposite sides of the room. They make themselves comfortable on the floor and face each other across the intervening space. I dim the lights and a twilight atmosphere descends. I take them through relaxation techniques. I suggest that they clear their minds. Then I lead them downward into their bodies—and into their unconsciouses. I take them down through their shoulders, chests, backs, down through their diaphragms, and into their pelvic regions. I let them feel the grounded, centered sensation of settling into their reproductive essences.

Then I ask the men to make "the phallus sound," to let their deep male instincts speak in a nonverbal way. Amazingly, they don't have to be told what this means or how "maleness" sounds. One by one they begin. An eerie, primal rumbling fills the room. It grows as more men add their voices. It's like music, but from a time and place within them far older than melody. It seems to express tenderness, power, pain, fierceness, exuberance, sweetness, and thrusting arousal. The feelings weave in and out, creating a crescendoing, almost symphonic chorus of resonant male voices. Finally the sound tapers to a soft, pulsing vibration that hangs in the charged atmosphere and then gradually falls silent. The silence is alive with soulful animal energy.

Then I turn to the women and ask them to make "the womb sound." There's a sighing, breathy tone. Then a lyrical female voice begins singing in a mysterious, ethereal way. More women add their voices. Tenderness, power, longing, pain, fierceness, exuberance, sweetness, and arousal. Their crescendoing music seems charged with shameless passion and energetic receptivity. The rich timbre of warm female tones rises to a climax and then gradually tapers off, leaving a feeling of moonlit seas and silvered shores. This silence is alive with soulful *female* animal energy.

I let the powerful feelings sink in. The participants, as they tell me later, are often profoundly moved by how primitive and yet how human they've become—all in the same moment. They're deeply touched by the power of the energies they've given and received as men and women. Something primal has awakened within them.

Usually after these workshops I receive a number of phone calls from excited couples telling me that after months—in one case over a year—of not having had sex with each other they went home from the workshop and made passionate love. One woman said, "I really felt steamy and sultry—hot—like an animal. It was great! I'd always been taught that 'nice girls' didn't have these feelings, much less *act* on them." A middle-aged man told me, "I'd been turned off to my wife after six years of fighting about one thing or another. I just wasn't sexually interested in her anymore. And then during the womb/phallus sound when I sat with the men and felt reinforced by all that male energy, I saw my wife as a woman—as a primate female, as you would say, with her own animal sexuality. It was a revelation. I saw her sitting there with the other women, supported by all that primal female energy, and—Wow! Was I turned on! It's like our original attraction to each other come flooding back and all our 'head fights' didn't mean anything anymore."

I'm reminded of something the British psychiatrist Anthony Storr wrote. It's stuck with me over the years:

> For the majority of the human race, self-esteem is chiefly rooted in sexuality. A confident belief in one's own masculinity and femininity is a fundamental part of human identity. . . . The devices by which men and women conceal from themselves and compensate for a sense of failure as a sexual being are . . . manifold. . . . We cannot escape our physical natures; and a proper pride in oneself as a human being is rooted in the body through which love is given and taken.[2]

John Bradshaw puts it succinctly: "Sexuality is the core of human selfhood. Our sex is not something we have or do, it is who we are."[3]

Whatever we do with our personal idiosyncracies, a firm identity on the level of the primate male or female within us is essential to the health and well-being of our relationships. Whatever a woman or a man does for a living, whatever their push and pull with each other over the little things, in the "bedroom"—the central physical and psychological ground of their meeting—they must be able to call forth in themselves and in each other these primal masculine and feminine energies. We can tolerate our conflicts with each other on the *human* level if our instinctual life together is empowering and life-giving.

The advocates of unisex would like us to believe that there's no such thing as male and female gender essence. I think many of these people are operating out of a genuine concern about past stereotyping of our sexes and caricatures of our gender roles. It's certainly true that stereotypes and caricatures deny our individual uniqueness and try to force us into rigid, often oppressive molds. In my experience gender stereotypes and caricatures usually pick up on real characteristics of our sexes, but then make the mistake of oversimplifying them and demanding that we all conform to too-narrow definitions of maleness and femaleness. I'm opposed to this. Yet I believe the proponents of unisex are ignoring a vast body of evidence from many different fields that contradicts their assumptions. The unisex idea seems to be, in part at least, an expression of good but misguided intentions. In part, though, it may be just one more round in the ongoing war between our sexes.[4]

Claiming there's no such thing as gender essence—at least for the vast majority of us—is hurtful on the public level. It's also damaging and disorienting to many couples in their private lives. Perhaps we "should" be the same. But we're not.

Arlene and Seth

I once worked with a couple who seemed to have things backwards. Arlene seemed to be the "man" in the relationship, while Seth played the "woman's" role. If they had been happy with their emotional role reversal, that would have been fine. But they weren't.

Seth was the sensitive, tender, patient one, consistently nurturing and gentle. He was a poet who expressed wonderfully romantic ideas about relationships in his writing. Arlene was rough, impatient, and aggressive in her dealings with her friends and colleagues. Each seemed to be living out *caricatures* of the opposite sex.

As they talked about what had brought them together, it became clear that Arlene had been drawn to Seth because he reminded her of her gentle, romantic, but ineffectual father, and Seth had been attracted to Arlene because she reminded him of his rough, overbearing mother. But what emerged in our work together was even more interesting. Arlene eventually confessed that she found Seth "kind of feminine." When I suggested to her that perhaps she was projecting her own unacknowledged feminine traits onto him and trying to experience them in this external (and disowning) way, she reacted with outrage. "I can't stand these sweet little things!" she cried. "They act so nicey-nice. They fool a lot of people, especially men. But I can see right through them. Watch out, because they're really killers."

I also suggested to Seth that he might be projecting his dis-owned masculine qualities onto Arlene, making *her* carry his hidden maleness for him. Seth cringed at the idea, but he admitted he'd always felt estranged from other men.

Gradually over the year and a half that our sessions continued Seth became more "manly," more "angular," and more decisive about setting and maintaining his boundaries, and Arlene stretched to include more patience and tenderness in her repertoire of feelings. In spite of all their efforts, however, they finally parted ways. But during some final one-on-one sessions with each of them separately, Arlene told me, "I love Seth, but I guess I need more of a 'man's man.' I need a guy who's tougher than I am so I can feel more like a woman. I never want to be a sweetie-pie, but I *do* want to feel more feminine." And Seth said, "I think Arlene was in my life to help me grow, to help me accept and claim my masculinity. Now, I don't need a woman to carry my masculine feelings for me. I'm never going to be a jock, and I guess that's okay. But I think I'm ready for a 'kinder, gentler woman.'"

After years of trying to help "New Age" couples like Arlene and Seth accept caricatured role reversals they were both unhappy with and "adjust" to what one of my colleagues has referred to as "a totally new chapter in the history of our relationships," I've decided that *both* the traditionalists and the New Age advocates are right—up to a point. Both are expressing part of the truth about how our sexes need to relate. The traditionalists are right in claiming that there *is* such a thing as biologically based male and female gender essence. And the reformers are right in affirming the many different ways men and women—as individuals—have of expressing their male and female energies.

How to Begin Unshaming and Celebrating Your Own and Your Partner's Primate Self

By now you have a lot of knowledge and awareness about your own and your partner's animal nature and how your instinctual patterns, inherited from your evolutionary past, are operating in your present relationship. The rest of this book is a series of practical steps you can take—alone and together—to begin to make your primate patterns work *for* you rather than *against* your love.

I've developed a number of simple techniques and somewhat more complex exercises for doing this. I've adapted some of them from more traditional counseling practices, and I've created others as a result of my day-to-day interaction with bewildered individuals, couples, and groups. In many cases, you can use any one of these processes to accomplish several different goals. I'll suggest some of these alternative uses as we go along. You and your partner may discover some different applications I haven't thought of. The fact is that all of these techniques and exercises support each other, often in unforeseen ways. One way or another, our individual work supports our relationship growth and our relationship growth empowers us as individuals. I encourage both you and your partner to use all the techniques and do all the exercises, and to use them as often as seems helpful, and in the order that works for you.

In my experience, neither personal nor relationship growth happens in a straight line. We run into an issue once and develop some awareness and some capacity to deal with it in a creative way. Then we move on—only to return to it later. But each time we encounter a particular problem we have an opportunity to deepen and enrich our response to it. We have a chance to become more whole and truer to *all* of who and what we are.

It's easy to get discouraged. Don't. Most of us are so alienated from our instinctual roots that we have to go back over the same ground many times in order to solidify a joyful reconnection with them. The process of making your own and your partner's animal natures a life-giving part of your relationship *does* require commitment. You'll need to stick with it if you're going to realize its benefits.

Very often our partners are not as enthusiastic about relationship growth as we are. But our own growth can affect our relationships in powerful ways. It may be that as a result of your own progress you may eventually have to leave your present partner behind. That's a painful possibility. But we each have to ask ourselves what we really want from life. Do we want to continue unsatisfying relationships that have little or no promise or do we want fullness of life for ourselves and those we love? The choice is up to us. It's a lonely choice, but we all make it every day of our lives anyway, whether we know it or not. *I* believe human life is meant to be lived fully. I also believe that by combining the insights and techniques of more orthodox psychologies, especially the Imago Therapy of Harville Hendrix, John Gray's exercises, and John Bradshaw's inner child work, with the "therapy beyond therapy" that I'm proposing, you are giving yourself and your relationship the best chance possible for long-lasting joy and fulfillment.

First Steps

Stop Shaming Yourself and Your Partner

To stop shaming the animal within us does not mean lifting all the controls our savanna time evolution developed to help us form more intensely cooperative societies and intimate pair-bonds. It doesn't mean running wild in the streets and doing whatever we feel like. While some people probably haven't internalized *enough* social shame, the problem for most of us is exactly the opposite. We are far *too* ready to beat up on ourselves—and our partners—for perfectly normal thoughts, feelings, and behavior, especially those that come from our aggressive and sexual impulses. Many people are especially vulnerable to shame feelings when they've shown anger or when they experience sexual fantasies. Sometimes we may even feel ashamed of expressing great energy or enthusiasm. And we've all known feelings of shame when we've committed a social blunder, particularly if it seems to have come out of a state of "excessive arousal."

The simplest technique for dealing with feelings of shame is what I call *intervention*. In intervention we can catch ourselves shaming ourselves and *intervene* to stop it with powerful counter-messages. Whatever the situation, the first part of the intervention message is the same: *"There's nothing to be ashamed of."* The second part addresses the particular circumstance.

Let's say that you've said something potentially inflammatory to your boss. As soon as you calm down, the self-shaming messages start: "How stupid could you be? You've ruined your relationship. You flouted authority again, and this time it'll cost you your job." Stop! *Hear* what you're doing to yourself. Now, *intervene.* Tell yourself—out loud (it's usually more effective): "There's nothing to be ashamed of. I did the best I could under the circumstances. Okay, so I blew it. I'll be more careful next time." Repeat the intervention message until you believe it.

Perhaps you were really excited about something and you tried to share it with your friends. They didn't understand your excitement, and your idea fell flat. A normal human reaction to "unmirrored" enthusiasm is self-shaming; we feel like we've made fools of ourselves. But catch yourself and intervene. Say to yourself, "There's nothing to be ashamed of. So it fell flat? I know my friends love me. And it was still a good idea."

Or maybe you've indulged yourself in terms of some pleasure you usually feel guilty about later. *Many* people shame themselves for pure, animal enjoyment. Intervene and say, "There's nothing to be ashamed of. Life is hard. I'm giving myself something I enjoy. Actually, I feel better now. I feel alive!"

These simple interventions may sound silly, but they do work. They are antidotes to the excessive self-shaming many people indulge in on a daily basis. Remember that our instinctual cores are the sources of our energy, our sensual and sexual enjoyment, our exuberance, our creativity and spontaneity, and our honest feelings. The expression of compassion, honoring regard, and love for this dynamic, life-giving part of ourselves is the most effective way I've found to deal from a position of strength with ourselves, others, and life itself. To stop shaming the animal within is to stop "disasterizing" about things. It's to challenge our fears—our fear of failure, our fear of rejection, our fear of abandonment, and, ultimately, our fear of death.

The Polynesians have a saying that bolsters my own capacity to intervene when I'm feeling defeated, afraid, and ashamed. They say, "You eat life, or life eats you!" True to the animal nature of our savanna time ancestors, I'd rather be a predator than prey.

To stop shaming ourselves is to strengthen our ability to relate to our partners. But we can go a step further; we can refuse to cooperate with our *partner's* self-shaming. Instead of agreeing when he or she is overly self-critical, or worse, adding fuel to the fire with some criticisms of our own, we can intervene. As far as we can, we need to affirm our partner's animal passions. We don't have to agree with his or her interpretation of a particular situation, but we do need to validate his or her feelings—of joy, of sorrow, of hurt, of anger, of hopefulness—whatever. Catch your partner at self-shaming and say something like "I love you. You're a wonderful man/woman. I'm *on* your side and *by* your side, and I support you." Rather than rushing to give advice or render judgment—often unhelpful or even damaging left brain strategies—our first impulse needs to be right brain empathy for our partner's instinctual reactions. Helping him or her think things through more carefully can come later.

EXERCISE #1: ACTIVE IMAGINATION DIALOGUE WITH YOUR PRIMATE SELF

Purpose: This exercise is designed to help you touch base in a deep way with your instinctual self whenever you need to. I'm presenting it here because it's a first step in opening communication with and experiencing appreciation for this wonderful, wild, and powerful part of yourself. The more you can come to appreciate your primate core the easier it will be to stop shaming it.

Comments: Do this exercise by yourself.

1. Find a quiet time and place where you can be by yourself. If you are journaling, take pen in hand and open your journal.

2. Relax and clear your mind. Find the burning issue, the problem you need to work on with your primate self, the thing that's worrying you the most. It could be anything—a delicate subject you need to bring up with your partner, how to handle a friendship in which you feel put down, deciding between two potential relationships, and so on. Take whatever time you need to open yourself to your deep feelings

and honest responses. If you're open to your real feelings and spontaneous responses you're allowing your instincts to speak to you.

3. To dialogue with your animal core, begin by addressing this hidden part of yourself in an inviting way. Write your invitation for it to speak as if you were composing a heartfelt letter to an estranged friend. With the particular problem you have in mind ask this part of you such questions as: Who are you? What do *you* want in this situation? How do *you* feel about . . . (the problem)? Why are you blocking my decision or my wishes with respect to . . . (the problem)? And so on.

4. You may not get an immediate response. The repressed parts of ourselves are often very angry and distrustful. After all, we've probably cooperated with the war of shame waged against them. But continue trying to open communication. You must really *want* to reconcile with your inner primate nature. The animal can feel your sincerity. Remember, our primate selves are driven to "make it right" with the one who's hurt them. "They" need to reconcile as much as "we" do. If nothing comes this time, drop the exercise and try it again later.

5. When you do get a response from your instinctual core, record it as you receive it. Don't censor it or clean it up, don't try to talk your animal self out of his or her feelings, and *don't* shame them. Just let this deep part of you speak. At the same time, don't *rush* toward reconciliation at the cost of your own identity. There may be too much bad blood between you at the moment for a full reunion. But let your inner animal know that you're genuinely open to a constructive dialogue and that while you may not act on *all* of its agenda, you're committed to putting some of its instinctual desires and powerful feelings into practice in your life and in your relationship. Get to know each other and then begin to build bridges of mutual understanding and partnership.

6. You may experience your primate self responding to your invitation in images and emotions rather than words.

While the animal part of us understands much of our human language, as chimpanzees and bonobos do, its vocabulary is limited. What it does understand is the *tone* of your words and your authentic feelings. If your primate self communicates with images and feelings, record these in your journal—again, uncensored. Let him or her present the full range of his or her feelings, including the most aggressive and hostile *and* the most exuberantly sexual, whether they fit your picture of yourself or not.

7. When you feel any particular dialogue session running out of energy, end your communication by reassuring your animal self that you'll be back, and that in the meantime you will be much more open on an ongoing basis to his/her "gut level" input.

Caution: If you encounter *very* hostile reactions or if you feel significantly disturbed as a result of this exercise, consult a therapist familiar with active imagination dialogue who can help you interpret and process the disturbing material. The inner "voices" that communicate with you can be manifestations of all kinds of things—lost fragments of yourself, your internalized parents, brothers and sisters, teachers, even multiple personalities.[5.] In my experience, though, most of the reactions you'll encounter from your unconscious are expressions of your repressed aggression and sexuality, whatever faces they may present.

Active imagination dialogue requires that you develop the ability to sort through the inner presences and distingush between them. Certainly most of us are not multiple personalities in the clinical sense. But we all have other points of view and centers of consciousness within us. I know that if you're not used to doing this kind of inner work the whole idea may seem strange, perhaps even ridiculous. I assure you it *is* strange, but it's far from ridiculous. Many people do achieve significant healing and insight from this process.

For help in learning to sort through and evaluate your inner voices and to further your dialogues you can refer to the books I've listed in the bibliography which contain important information on active imagination dialogue techniques.

Accept, Celebrate, Comfort, and Channel the Animal You and Your Partner Each Are

Accepting, celebrating, comforting, and channeling your animal self and that of your partner is a more complex process than intervening or dialoguing. Certainly elements of acceptance, celebration, comforting, and channeling are present in these activities. But here we want to evoke an even richer experience. Learning to accept our instinctual selves and to act on their agendas involves deepening our connections with them. Again, there are practical things we can do to create this change in our inner—and outer—lives.

Accept Your Own and Your Partner's Primate Self

If you are a woman and you find yourself feeling guilty for "wanting your cake and eating it too"—for example, wanting to stay home and raise your children *and* desiring to advance your career, or wanting to make your relationship work *and* indulging your curiosity about a man you've met who seems to offer you more than your present partner, desiring to be taken care of *and* wanting to be independent, and so on—you need to *accept* that you want *both* sides of these and other emotional equations. Instead of agonizing about the fact that you feel divided, say something to yourself like, "Well, that's how I *am!* I *do* want both. It's part of my primate nature." You might add to this message of self-acceptance, "I'm a complex human being. I got this way honestly, and I have a right to *be* what I am and to want *all* of what I want. It feels wonderful to accept my richness and complexity!" With this new attitude of acceptance you are now freer to act in your own best interest, and to bring more of what you want and need into your life.

You can learn to enthusiastically accept your male partner's animal nature as well. For instance, during a heart-to-heart discussion, rather than feeling frustrated and disgusted by your partner's difficulty in expressing his feelings, you could tell yourself, "Well, he's just being a man. What a struggle he's having! I'm so lucky to have a brain that's wired for easy access to my emotions. The male ape in him is magnificent in other ways, and I admire him for those things."

Needless to say, there are *many* variations of this basic acceptance theme you can use in your daily gender-characteristic interactions.

Celebrate Your Own and Your Partner's Primate Self

Affirm the things that give you pleasure—sensual pleasure and emotional or intellectual pleasure by giving yourself physical and psychological rewards every day. While exercising appropriate caution, forget the "Just Say No" philosophy of life. If you enjoy reading, make time to read. If you enjoy frozen yogurt with chocolate sauce, give yourself this treat. If you enjoy having your back rubbed, ask your partner to do this for you. If you enjoy good cigars, give yourself this pleasure—at least occasionally. If you want to spend the weekend with your partner in a luxury hotel, do it.

Your animal self is the source of your joy and spontaneity and of all your sensual pleasure. His or her curiosity is even the foundation of your intellectual interests. Your primate core wants to touch and be touched. He or she *needs* for you to *live* and enjoy your life, and he/she is hurt, frustrated, and angered to the extent that you try to live your life "sensibly," or worse still, as an ascetic. The ancient Greeks wisely said "All things in moderation." While some people may overindulge their animal desires, many others are far too life-denying. Many of us adhere to the civilization era dictum "Work is good, pleasure is bad." We need to work out healthier and happier compromises between the legitimate concerns of our "sensible" neocortexes—our "human" selves—and our vital animal energies.

You can help your *partner* celebrate his or her animal self by encouraging his/her desire for pleasure too. You probably already know what your partner enjoys. To the extent that you can, affirm those sources of pleasure. "Honey, I know you've wanted to go to the beach for several weeks now. This weekend, let's do it." "How about eating out tonight? I know you've been dying for some Italian food." And so on. All of these things are simple and

obvious, but too often we just don't do them. These little en-
courgements to your own and your partner's animal natures help
turn your relationship into a greater source of pleasure than pain,
into an adventure in living rather than an exercise in denial.

Comfort Your Own and Your Partner's Primate Self

Compassion and empathy are qualities we share with chimpanzees
and bonobos, but, as we've seen, we've evolved to feel these emotions even more fully. Ironically, in most cases our primate selves
have received little compassion or empathy from the human part
of us. In fact, as we've noted, our animal cores have all too often
been the victims of shaming messages from our parents, our peers,
our cultures, and our religions. Most of us have learned to internalize these shaming messages. But what if, instead of *attacking*
our real feelings and desires, we *comforted* the animal within?

Let's say something has happened that causes you to feel anxious, frightened, despairing, frustrated, sad, or angry. You need
to be comforted. Unfortunately, many of us have learned to minimize these feelings of our animal selves, or even deny them completely. "You shouldn't feel that way." "Surely you don't *really*
feel that way." "It doesn't hurt to be hurt." "Keep a stiff upper
lip." These are among the shaming messages many of us have
learned to use as clubs against our real emotions. Rather than
continuing to lie to yourself, feel the power of these feelings. And
feel compassion for yourself. Turn to the hurt animal at your
center and say something like, "It's okay. I'm here. I feel your
feelings. You're absolutely right about what was done to you.
I'm going to protect you, and I'm going to help you get what you
need and want. I'm so glad you're at my center keeping me honest. What would I do without you?"

Of course, the same applies to your *partner*'s inner animal.
What this part of him or her needs when he or she is distressed is
not reasoned arguments, and certainly not support for denying
the reality or power of his/her frightened, sad, or angry feelings.
You need to be able to remove yourself from the turmoil of your
partner's passions far enough to not get caught up in them. You
need to read between the lines of his or her pain and really *see*
and feel empathy for the wounded primate he/she is at this point.

Then you need to comfort this authentic core of his or her personality. "It's okay. I'm here. I'm going to protect you, and I'm going to help you get what you need and want. I'm so glad to be in this relationship with you. What would I do without you?"

Channel *Your Own and Your Partner's Primate Self*

As we've seen, the two fundamental aspects of our primate natures—the ones that have been shamed most consistently—are our aggression and our sexual desires. In the next chapter we'll look in more detail at things we can do to work with these central qualities. Here I want to point out that there are two basic ways we can handle these most primal of our instincts. The first is to *feel* and thereby *accept, celebrate*, and *comfort* them. And the second is to *channel* them into the kinds of actions that will get us more of what we want.

When you feel anger or hostility you need to acknowledge that that's what you're feeling, and accept whatever aggressive fantasies may surface. When you've calmed down a little, you need to formulate a plan for breaking through or going around whatever people, events, or situations aroused your anger in the first place. This is a way your left brain neocortex can cooperate with the primal feelings of your limbic system and R-complex, rather than overriding or repressing them. There are usually good reasons why your animal self feels angry. (Of course, as most schools of psychology caution, our angry reactions are often misdirected. Their real targets may lie in our childhoods.)

Perhaps your partner is habitually late picking you up from work. Often you have to wait half an hour or more. You've tried to tell him or her how upset that makes you. But your angry words seem to have fallen on deaf ears. What can you do? First, feel the full intensity of your anger. Second, let yourself cool down a little, and then try to link your reaction to a childhood situation. Maybe your father was habitually late for your school activities, or perhaps there was a time your mother forgot to pick you up after a party. You had to walk home in the dark, and you were terrified. If you can think of some childhood cause for the level of your present misery it can often take some of the sting and urgency out of it. Of course, there may not *be* any such

childhood background to your present irritation. You may simply—and rightfully—be angered by your partner's apparent lack
of concern for your feelings. Whatever the case may be, channel
your anger into *action*. Take a taxi home, or stop for a bite to eat
with some of your coworkers. Let your partner know that one
way or another you're not going to be left in the lurch.

In terms of your sexual feelings, once again you need to *feel*,
acknowledge, and accept them. You may decide to act on them
with the person who's aroused them—assuming, of course, that
they're willing too (and taking all the precautions necessary to
protect your, and their, health). More likely, if you're in a com-
mited relationship, you'll want to turn those feelings of arousal
into a sense of greater self-confidence and enthusiasm for life.
You may also resolve to engage your partner in more romantic
and sexual interludes. Depending on the present state of your relationship, you *might* want to share your sexual fantasies. Often,
sharing sexual fantasies can be a powerful turn-on for both people.

EXERCISE #2: THROUGH THE LOOKING GLASS

Purpose: The purpose of this exercise is to achieve direct, even "visual," experience of your primate self in order to accept, celebrate,
comfort, and channel this powerful inner reality. Just contacting
your animal core at this level accomplishes all of these things.

Comments: Do this exercise by yourself.

This exercise comes out of a "mirror experience" I had as a
teenager. Since that first experience I've often done this exercise
in order to stay in touch with my animal self. Interestingly, I've
found that my animal self is not a random collection of instincts
and feelings. It's a focused, conscious being with its own identity
and agenda. Some psychologists talk about our unconscious as if
it *were* unconscious. But hypnotherapists have found the reverse
to be true.[6] Our unconscious is actually *very* aware—of *us*. It's
watching us all the time and looking for ways to press its own
agendas in our lives. It's us—our egos—who are unconscious.

At any rate, here's how the exercise works.

1. Find a quiet time when you know you won't be disturbed. Stand in front of a small mirror, one that frames your face and cuts out background distractions.

2. Look into your own eyes. Focus on them. Don't look away.

3. Open up to receive whatever impressions and feelings may begin to emerge. Take as much time as you need.

4. Hold your gaze as the feelings come.

5. Go with them. Let them communicate their primal power to you.

6. Try to "see" the animal consciousness that lies just behind and beneath your human awareness. Try to see the animal eyes that are watching you from your inner depths.

7. Continue to allow your feelings to flow, no matter how unsettling they may be.

8. When you feel it's time for closure, gently break your stare and look away, assuring this part of you that you'll contact him or her again in this way.

9. Record your impressions in your journal. These may include feelings of fear, sorrow, rage, joy, even ecstasy—sheer animal power. They may also include your "human" reactions to these primal emotions. You may have been startled, awed, disgusted, or fascinated.

Once again, I know this and other exercises may seem strange at first. But they do work. And when they do, they speed our personal empowerment and the empowerment of our instinctual lives as couples.

EXERCISE #3: EMPOWERING EACH OTHER AS THE "HUMAN ANIMAL"

Purpose: The purpose of this exercise is to empower yourself and your partner to celebrate, comfort, and channel the many aspects of what it means to be a male or female "human animal."
Comments: Do this exercise together.

I use this mutual empowerment exercise in my workshops. I divide the men and women into two same-sex groups and have each of them repeat after me a kind of ritual formula designed to affirm their male and female energies to each other. Many workshop participants have told me they felt deeply moved by the healing power of the acceptance, and honoring, they received *from* and gave *to* the other gender. It's a sad fact that outside the workshop setting so few men and women "bless" each other in this or similar ways in their "real life" relationships.

Even though this exercise is probably more effective when a number of people are involved, you and your partner can use this formula (or some other of your own creation) to regularly affirm each other. You may want to ritualize the way you do this, perhaps by placing one hand over your partner's heart as you recite. If the man begins, he says to his partner:

> I empower you to be what and who you really are—
> to live with all the fullness of being you desire;
> to get what you need to be happy in this life;
> to actualize your dreams in reality;
> to bring the greatness of your heart,
>   the power of your mind,
>   and the beauty of your body
> fully and shamelessly into this world!
> I honor you for being so powerful and so full of splendor,
>   for being the magnificent animal you are; and for
>   being the sublime spirit you also are.
> I comfort you for the pain you must experience—
>   the pain which I also know, and the pain only your gender
>   can know fully.
> For all your wounds, and for your struggle to triumph
>   over them,
> I admire you!
> Receive my love!

When the man is finished, change places. The woman then repeats the empowering words to him.

I suggest you do this for each other once every other week or so. Of course you may change the words or add whatever words of "blessing" have special meaning for your partner. The only rule is that what you say to each other must convey your empathic acceptance, celebration, and comforting of the other.

Depersonalize What Is Going On between You and Your Partner

It's normal for human beings to react to many of the things people do and say as if they were personal. Destructive or hurtful behavior especially tends to *feel* personal. But, as psychologists have seen, most of what motivates criticism and hostility has little or nothing to do with us as individuals. We now know that many of our patterns of relating to each other are laid down in the first months of life and then reinforced by early childhood experiences. Often when someone attacks "us" we're really just surrogates for the real target of their anger.

What's true on the psychological level is just as true on the level of our primate patterns. Much if not most of our own and our partner's hurtful behavior—no matter how personal it seems, and no matter how hostile—is really about our gender-characteristic needs and their frustration. Most of the time, at this biological level, both of us are stand-ins for our genders. We're "generic" representatives of tidal forces that are driving and shaping our species.

Say, for example, that one way or another *she* keeps bringing up the subject of babies. You go shopping and she gets excited in the toddlers' toy section. You're watching TV and a baby appears selling toilet paper; she goes ga-ga. She keeps trying to talk you into moving to a larger apartment, one that allows pets—and children.

After a while you start feeling hemmed in—pressured to do something you're not sure you want at all. You resent both the pressure and the gnawing sensation that you're about to become a "breeder." This whole thing probably feels intensely personal, like a betrayal of your relationship and a violation of your personhood. Yet, if you reflect more carefully you'll almost certainly discover that the *reason* her baby-making program feels like betrayal of your relationship (as two human *individuals*) and a violation of your *person*hood is that it *is* impersonal. In a real sense it *is* subhuman.[7]

If you can realize that *she's* not trying to hurt you, that she really does love you and want the best for you, and that she's being propelled by ancient primate female longings for home and children—that can take some of the sting out of her impersonal program for you. Paradoxically, this can move you into an even more *personal* connection with her, a feeling of loving acceptance and even celebration of her animal nature. Seeing and embracing the primate female that lives within her throws her human personality into poignant relief. When this happens you can actually cherish her more. You can experience her instinctual behavior as endearing, and feel pride in yourself as a primate male. After all, she thinks of you as an alpha male and wants to realize her practical immortality with *you*.

You can even experience this kind of double vision of your partner in more dire situations—when you're fighting, for example. But whatever the situation, it pays to *de*personalize many of the dynamics going on between you. It's also a more accurate assessment of most relationship problems.

To depersonalize you need to call a time-out, and step out of the scene. Remembering everything you've learned about your own and your partner's biologically based primate patterns and needs, see if you can identify which of them is at work in your partner's behavior. For example, you can say to yourself "This isn't personal. It *feels* personal, but it *isn't*. This is about her savanna time need to pair-bond and make babies. Actually, it's exciting to be in a relationship with such an instinctual woman." Or if, as a woman, you catch *him* staring at another woman, say to yourself "This isn't personal. This is about his jungle time desire to get as many females as he can. It's really exciting to be in a relationship with such an instinctual man." And so on.

I know this may seem far-fetched, but depersonalizing as many of our relationship conflicts as we can is an essential step toward *really* resolving them.

See the Dangers in Your Relationship, and Believe They Are Real

It pays to see the dangers inherent in all our relationships as well as those which may be a threat to our particular partnership because of unresolved childhood issues and unmet instinctual needs—and believe they are real. On both the species level and the level of our individual relationships those dangers usually include the powerful effects of our maternal imprinting and the continuing influence of our internalized mothers, our childish dependency needs, our tendency to re-create our childhood dramas in our present relationships, the Coolidge Effect and the serial monogamy pattern (the four-year-itch syndrome), and the mixed reproductive strategies that encourage men especially to seek sexual variety and women to continue the search for alpha males.

On the common-sense level there are many things each of us can do to minimize the dangers to our love lives such biologically based dynamics pose. We could both probably do considerably better at meeting our partner's primal needs and working through the hot issues in our relationships. If women tend to need men to be healthy, mature, strong yet emotionally sharing, financially solid, fierce yet affectionate, to be able to show their childlike vulnerability but also demonstrate their capacity to overcome their weaknesses, and so on, it would pay men to do the inner work necessary for more fully embodying these and other attractive male characteristics.

And if men need women to be healthy, attractive, sexually provocative yet loyal, strong, fierce yet also yielding and receptive, to have their own independence but be able to admire and support their work, and to show both their childlike vulnerability and a kind of womanly sophistication and maturity, and so on, it pays women to do the inner work necessary to more fully embody these and other attractive *female* characteristics.

Often this kind of danger-reducing personal growth can be accomplished on a fairly superficial level by making mostly minor adjustments in our appearance, our habits, and our daily behavior. A host of self-help books is within easy reach for those who are interested. (John Gray's *Men Are From Mars, Women Are From Venus* is the best; it offers many practical suggestions for making changes in our interactions with each other "where the rubber hits the road.")

Just as often, however, the things we need to do to minimize the dangers to our relationship happiness require a more far-reaching approach. That more far-reaching approach is what *this* book is about.

EXERCISE #4: SHARING THE RESULTS OF YOUR SELF-EVALUATION EXERCISES

Purpose: This exercise is designed to help you summarize and internalize what you've discovered about the primate patterns in your relationship—as a couple.

Comments: Do this exercise together.

1. Go back to each of the self-evaluation exercises you've done and review your results. Look at the Hot Issues in Your Relationship (pp. 71–76), Where am I? (pp. 77–80, 98–99), What We Need from Our Relationships (pp. 125–126), your journal entries for sexual and romantic experiences, the Imprint/Partner Exercise (pp. 178–182), and Exposing Your Shame Feelings (pp. 201–204).

2. Now, summarize your findings, and fill in the blanks below. (Or use a separate sheet of paper or your journal.)

The hot issues in my relationship from my perspective are: _____

_____

The stage of love we seem to be in is: _____

_____

My top seven relationship needs are: _____

_____

My sexual and romantic experiences are mostly: _____

_____

The positive traits I experience in my partner are: _____

_____

The destructive traits I experience in my partner are: _____

_____

I tend to feel ashamed about: _____

_____

3. Next, share your findings with each other. You may be strong enough as a couple to do this on your own. More likely, you will want to do this with a therapist who's willing to work with you in the context of the theory and practice of "evolutionary psychology." The therapist you choose can come from any of the schools of psychology. The important thing is that he or she is familiar with the biologically based patterns in our relationships.

4. However you handle this sharing, be prepared for some sparks to fly. Hurt feelings, defensiveness, and anger are normal expressions of the struggle to become honest with each other. The advantage of a therapeutic setting is that an empathic third party can help you work through your feelings of resistance to the often painful truths about your relationship in an environment of relative emotional safety.

Taking these first steps to contact, stop shaming, accept, celebrate, comfort, and channel our animal selves, to depersonalize our reactions to each other's primate patterns, and to act to minimize the dangers to our love lives usually has an immediate and positive effect on our relationships. While resolving the problems (and potential problems) in our partnerships can take many forms, as I'm suggesting, it ultimately comes down to dealing with our own and each other's similar yet different ways of expressing our aggression and sexuality. Traditional psychologies can often help us deal with these products of our deep psyches quite effectively. But adding the techniques of primate pattern-based strategies and exercises puts us in an even better position to work with our most exciting and painful passions so that we can have the joyful and fulfilling love we want.

11

RECLAIMING OUR AGGRESSION AND SEXUALITY

✳

Courage Is Your Ally

I believe the single most important factor in our growth as human beings is courage. I've seen many counselees and workshop participants come right up to their wounds as individuals and their hot issues as couples, take a peek over the wall at the "monsters" on the other side, and run for their lives. Rather than confronting and reclaiming their animal selves and mobilizing their instinctual resources for making the leap into a new way of life, they turn away from this adventure only to take up their old fear- and shame-based identities again. From my perspective this is nothing short of tragic.

No therapist or workshop leader can *give* you courage. Neither can your partner. What people *can* do is *en*courage each other. We can help each other find and mobilize our own inner strengths.

The animal within us has more than enough courage to carry us through the adventures that lie ahead if we choose fullness of being. But we must form an alliance with its life-giving forces—something most of us have been too ashamed to do. Though in pain from this oppressive shaming, our wild centers will not and cannot die. They are what give us and our relationships joy, passion, and meaning.

As we've noted, the two primary resources our animal selves can provide us with are aggressive self-affirmation and sexual exuberance. Let's take a closer look at what we can do to bring these innate potentials more fully into our lives and into our relationships.

Reclaiming Your Aggression

Our natural aggressiveness is usually suspect. In a real sense we're all competing to out-aggress each other in order to get *our* share of what we imagine to be scarce resources—economic and material, but also emotional and sexual. That we can live in societies at all is due to the development of our powerful, aggression-inhibiting neocortexes, and with them, what we call our "consciences." Under most circumstances, our neocortexes tone down our aggressive impulses. That's a good thing, but, as we've seen, it's a good thing that can go too far. The problem for most people is that they're not aggressive *enough* about affirming their needs. The failure to come to terms with their natural aggressiveness creates intra- and interpersonal conflicts for these people. First, others, including their relationship partners, will most likely push their own agendas at the *expense* of the less assertive person ("Nature abhors a vacuum"). Second, the inadequately self-affirming person will inevitably experience a buildup of resentment and anger, a buildup that can finally result in emotional and even physical violence. It seems that if we can't learn to accept and manage our natural aggression, *it* will manage *us*.

As a result of being inadequately self-affirming, many men and women experience tremendous dissatisfaction in their vocational and avocational lives. Unhappiness in these vital areas of our lives makes our relationship tensions worse. Some of the techniques and exercises we've already looked at can contribute to our being self-affirming in our work and play. For example, Active Imagination Dialogue with Your Primate Self, and Through the Looking Glass can help you become more familiar with how your primate self feels about the way you spend your time and energy, and what *he* or *she* wants to be doing. Techniques for accepting, celebrating, comforting, and channeling your instinctual energy will also open you to your authentic desires. Empowering Each Other as the "Human Animal" includes encouraging words from your partner about actualizing yourself vocationally and avocationally: "I empower you to be what and who you really are—to live with all the fullness of being you desire; to get what you need to be happy in this life; to actualize your dreams in reality." Following are a few more suggestions.

Develop and Express Your Real Interests, and Encourage Your Partner to Do the Same

What are the things that really turn you on, that naturally draw your attention, that are genuinely "re-creational" for you—not the things you may think you *should* be enthusiastic about, but those you really *are?* They can be anything. Sometimes they're simple things like reading books and magazines with a specialized focus, collecting memorabilia or art objects (from kitsch to masterpieces), going to air shows and learning everything you can about the featured planes, building models or crocheting. Sometimes they're more complex pursuits like drawing and painting, doing research in a field that's exciting to you, home-improvement projects, or learning to actually *fly* the planes you admire. These and a hundred other things engage our interest, spark our fascination, and involve us in processes that are their own reward. They evoke, stimulate, and affirm the childlike primate at our cores and satisfy his/her need for creative play.

I suggest you list the things that do this for *your* animal self. But don't *make* the list; allow your natural enthusiasms to guide you. Allow your *real* joy to express itself. Be sensitive to the things on your list that feel the most exciting. *Then, do them.* As far as you can, set aside some time *every day* to engage in the forms of creative play your private self desires. Encourage your partner to do the same.

As Far as Possible, Get into a Work Situation that Expresses More of Who You Really Are and What You Want to Do, and Encourage Your Partner to Do the Same

When we spend most of our waking hours doing meaningless work or even work we hate, we're starving our animal selves. For at least fifty years studies have shown that men (and increasingly women, now that they've entered the workforce in greater numbers) are feeling more and more alienated from their work.[1]

Their work has less and less to do with who they are as individuals, with their own talents and enthusiasms. It also has less and less to do with the natural inclinations that come out of our primate patterns.

Most of the work in both our jungle and savanna times combined mental and physical activities. It also embodied elements of creativity. Making tools and weapons, creating objects of art (for personal adornment and ritual use), gathering, cooking, hunting, and even warfare are all forms of "work" that engaged both males and females in holistic ways. Today, most of us have jobs that force us to compartmentalize and separate our mental and physical beings. And in a technological and industrial society most of our work is anything *but* creative.

In addition, there is far too *much* of it. Studies have shown that some hunter-gatherer and traditional peoples spend only three to five hours a day in actual work.[2] The rest of the time they "play." They socialize, tell stories, take "spirit journeys," and make love. Many of my counselees say they feel the pace of their lives increasing. They feel like they're working harder and faster just to stay afloat. They often look back nostalgically to a time when they got together with their friends more often, when they had time for ball games and picnics, romance, and even good sex with their partners.

Realistically, there's often not much we can do—at least not immediately—to move to more instinctually satisfying work. Yet there *are* people who are in professions and careers that bring them a great deal of satisfaction, that may be better combinations of mental and physical activities, and that may express much more of their capacity for creative play. I suggest you think about ways you might be able to embody more of your interests—as well as your talents—in either your present work or on a different career path. You and your partner could brainstorm together and then strategize about how you could achieve your goals as individuals and as a couple. There's no question that children complicate this already difficult issue. But millions of men and women, even with children, now make several career moves during their lifetimes—not job changes—*career* moves.[3] As frightening as such changes can be, and as difficult financially, in most cases the risks are worth it—in terms of greater personal happiness, *and* in terms of a more instinctually satisfying relationship as well.

So far as time and energy spent at work and consequently not available for socializing, friendships, or even sex is concerned, *when* you can—and *however* you can—cut down on your hours at the office (or other work setting), and plan as a couple how and when you're going to spend more time alone with each other and with your friends. Of course, this could involve scaling back some of your expenditures and rethinking the level of your materialistic desires. But—*do it;* your own happiness and the future of your relationship may depend on it.

Exercise #5: Affirming the Interests of Your Primate Self

Purpose: This exercise is designed to affirm your need for and your right to creative play, both in terms of your vocation and your avocation(s). You can use Active Imagination Dialogue with Your Primate Self, Through the Looking Glass, and your list-making and brainstorming to determine what things need to go into your affirmations.

Comments: Do this exercise separately.

1. Find a time and place to be alone.

2. With five to ten affirmations in mind, gather your courage and say them out loud. Some of the affirmations I use are:

   I am a powerful animal.
   I have a right to enjoy myself.
   I have a right to do work that makes me happy.
   I *am* going to do work that *I* want to do.
   I'm *going* to be creative and playful much more of the time.
   I can make *enough* money doing work I enjoy more.
   I am *free*!

3. Repeat your affirmations until you believe them. Really *feel* them. Let their life-giving power sink in.

4. Find a regular time, every day for a while, to do them. Eventually, as is true for many of these techniques and exercises, you may be able to reinforce your growing capacity to be aggressively self-affirming by simply remembering how you felt when you were doing them.

Reclaim Your Projections

Sometimes it's difficult to know *what* we want to do because we don't know *who* we really *are*. Largely because of early shaming, not only are we out of touch with our primal instincts, we're also disconnected from the particular, unique ways these instincts are trying to express themselves through us—*as us*—as the person we *are* and as the things *we* want and need to do in order to live our lives more fully. Often this lack of self-definition involves us in what psychologists call "merger fantasies"—the feeling that we don't know where we end and the other person, usually our partner, begins.[4] In an unconscious way we may feel our partners are a part of *us* or that we're a part of *them*. Merger fantasies work mainly by *projection*.

As we've seen, we tend to project two basic aspects of our own inner lives onto our partners. The first aspect is what Harville Hendrix calls our Imagos—what I call our Imprints— the internalized qualities of our parents (especially our mothers) and others in our early environments.[5] Our Imprints also involve our childhood *reaction patterns* to this early social setting. The second aspect is our own hidden or unacknowledged qualities— what Hendrix calls our "lost" and our "disowned" selves.[6] We can learn to break the vicious cycle of "repetition compulsion" and withdraw our Imprint projections from our partners, *and* we can learn to "translate" the characteristics of our lost and disowned selves, projected onto our partners, into qualities *we* can finally acknowledge, and some of which we can even enjoy.

Following is a chart I've used with many of my counselees to help them plot the correspondence between their *present reaction patterns* and the *childhood patterns* they're projecting onto them. You can use the chart to break the compulsive power of these old patterns and open up new options for yourself and your relationship.

EXERCISE #6: SEEING THE IMPRINT PATTERNS
AND PLOTTING A NEW COURSE

MY ADULT LIFE: PRESENT REACTION PATTERNS		
Setup: Unconscious patterns	Precipitating Event (action or words)	Reactions/ Feelings

MY CHILDHOOD: PRIMAL REACTION PATTERNS		
Setup: Unconscious patterns	Precipitating Event (action or words)	Reactions/ Feelings

Usual coping strategy	Results	
		Intervention: New Options for Changing My Present Reaction Patterns

Usual coping strategy	Results

Purpose: This exercise is designed to help you break the compulsion to project (what psychologists call "repetition compulsion") childhood patterns—often traumatic ones—onto your present relationship.

Comments: Do this exercise by yourself.

1. Start with the upper row of boxes—the ones labeled MY ADULT LIFE: PRESENT REACTION PATTERN. In the box in the upper left-hand corner record the *setup* for the reaction pattern you're plotting. This almost always is an unconscious attitude on your part. See if you can identify the primary feelings that come out of this unacknowledged pattern. For example, if the reaction pattern you're working on at the moment involves a cycle of jealous outbursts on your part followed by feelings of guilt and recrimination, you might write "Insecurity," or "Inferiority Feelings," "Fear," and so on—whatever you feel most accurately describes your probable underlying emotional trigger.

2. In the next box briefly describe the *precipitating event* that set you off, perhaps a conversation you and your partner have just had. For example, perhaps you caught your partner flirting with another woman at a party. Even though you know he wasn't serious about pursuing her, it was humiliating for you. Feeling frightened and insecure, you yelled at him in front of all your friends. Perhaps he responded by saying something like, "Don't try to control me. I'll do whatever I want to!" You might write: "Caught Jack flirting. I embarrassed him. He told me he'll do whatever he wants."

3. In the box next to this write your *reaction*—the feelings that were triggered in you as a result of the event or words—for example, "Fear," "Rage," "Rejection," "Inadequacy," "Hurt," and so on.

4. Next, describe your *coping strategy*—what you did in response to the precipitating event and the feelings it aroused. You might write, for example, "I berated Jack in front of everyone, and stormed out."

5. In the last box describe the *results* of your reaction; for in-stance, "Jack didn't come home for three days. I don't know where he was, and I'm afraid to ask." (Other situations will involve different kinds of reactions, coping strategies, and results. In another scenario the result might be "My partner cried for hours and withdrew emotionally for a week," "My partner threatened me with divorce," and so on.)

6. Now reflect for a moment about how the *results* of this pattern of *reaction* and *coping* might feed into the *setup* for the next round—for a repeat of the same patterns around the same issue with a similar precipitating event. There's al-most always a direct connection in our repetition compul-sion projections between these two stages of our conflicts—*result* and *setup*.

7. When this connection is clear to you go to the lower row of boxes, labeled MY CHILDHOOD: PRIMAL REACTION PATTERN. *Try to remember a childhood pattern that could underlie your ADULT REACTION PATTERN.* Go through the CHILDHOOD boxes from left to right in the same way you worked through the ADULT boxes. For example, in the scenario we're using here, let's say you suddenly remember how your present pattern feels like an echo of something your father often did, and how you responded. You were anxious for your father's approval. You could hardly wait for him to get home from work so you could show him how well you'd done your homework. You would run to the door when you'd hear him coming so you could be the first one to get his attention. But he'd almost always greet your mother first, and then turn to your sister. You would react with feelings of hurt, rejection, and jealousy. Often, you would throw your papers on the floor, storm off to your room, and slam the door. Some-times your father would scold you, and sometimes he'd just ignore you the whole rest of the evening. He might say things like, "You've got to stop being a baby. You can't always have everything you want *when* you want it,

or the *way* you want it." Although his reaction to your pain and subsequent tantrums may often have been loving and patient, the times when he *did* react with anger deeply affected you.

You might write in the *setup* box "Anxious for my father's approval"; in the *precipitating event* box, "My father would pay more attention to my mother and my sister, just when I was so anxious and needy and thought *this* time he'll really value *me!*"; in the *reaction/feelings* box "I felt hurt, rejected and jealous."; in the *usual coping strategy* box "I threw my papers on the floor and stormed off into my bedroom."; and in the *results* box "He'd sometimes get really angry and yell at me. Even worse, he'd ignore me—abandon me emotionally."

8. Notice how your childhood *results* were often a *setup* for the next cycle of this core drama. Your feelings of emotional abandonment certainly reinforced your anxiety about your father's approval. That's one of the reasons these things are *repetition* compulsions.

9. Next, study your completed chart carefully and notice the parallels between your childhood reaction pattern and your adult reaction pattern. Do you see the "repetition compulsion" element?

10. Now, go to the separate box on the far right of the chart, labeled INTERVENTION: NEW OPTIONS FOR CHANGING MY PRESENT REACTION PATTERN. Write what you want to do to alter the *results* the next time this same pattern comes up. For instance, you may decide to acknowledge your feelings of insecurity, fear, or inferiority—but contain them. To do this you may need to step out of the situation for a few minutes, take a deep breath, and talk to your inner primate child. (See the bibliography for books about ways of working with your inner child.) Then you may decide to return to the situation and try a different coping strategy. You might engage your partner in Active Listening (Exercise #8) and/or firmly—and in as nonhostile a way as you can—tell your partner (Jack, in this case) what

you're feeling and how you intend to deal with these feelings when a similar situation arises in the future. Always use "I" language to describe what your partner can expect from you if he or she continues to behave in a way that is uncomfortable for you. You might tell "Jack" that the next time you catch him flirting you're going to leave quietly—without making a scene—and you're going to go home and put the safety locks on the doors. He can call you in the morning to arrange a meeting to discuss the future of your relationship. Depending on how the conversation goes when you do meet, you can let him know you're going to: (*a*) insist on couples counseling before you agree to resume living together; (*b*) call the other woman and have a heart-to-heart talk with her; (*c*) explain your feelings to his family; (*d*) file for divorce; or (*e*) whatever other course of action seems likely to be effective in removing the source of your pain. Whatever you do, you need to break the cycle of childish reactions on your part and extricate yourself from situations likely to cause them. You need to channel your feelings into effective action, action that gives you a *realistic* chance of getting your needs met.

By seeing the parallels between your childhood reaction patterns and your adult reaction patterns you can see how you're setting yourself up for reexperiencing old traumas, and living those traumas out in your present relationship. That way you break the stranglehold of the "repetition compulsions" that arise from your childhood wounding. You can then act to withdraw your projections, discern what is *realistically* objectionable in the present, and change the results to better satisfy your instinctual needs.

The second kind of projection we make onto our relationships is when we experience in our partners our own disowned qualities—both the qualities we admire and the ones we dislike. In the first category are the repressed talents and abilities which we've been unable to actualize in our own lives. These are elements of our neoteny-based desire for creative play and self-affirmation. In the second category are our repressed instincts for aggression and sexuality per se. Because most of our family's and culture's shaming is reserved for *these* characteristics we often find it *very* painful to experience them fully as a part of ourselves. Then, as we've seen, we frequently make our partners carry them for us. Of course we dislike them as much in our partners as we do in ourselves, and this becomes a major source of conflict in many of our relationships.

EXERCISE #7: TRANSLATING "YOUR PARTNER'S" QUALITIES INTO YOUR OWN

Purpose: The purpose of this exercise is to help you withdraw the projections you may be making onto your partner of: 1) your *own* repressed talents and abilities; and 2) your *own* unacknowledged feelings of aggression and sexual desire.

Comments: Do this exercise by yourself.

TRANSLATION

My Partner's Qualities	My Own Unacknowledged Qualities
(These may actually be your partner's qualities as well as your own; the two are not mutually exclusive.)	
Talents and Abilities I Admire:	My Own Hidden Talents and Abilities:
He can relax and be friendly and open.	I am able to relax and be friendly and open.
He's always reading about things he's interested in.	I feel like pursuing subjects I'm really interested in.
He's really diplomatic in handling people.	I'm really diplomatic in handling people.
Qualities I Dislike:	My Own Shamed Instincts for Aggression and Sexuality:
He's openly angry when someone crosses him.	I'm angry at times too and I need to show it.

He's too interested in other women.	I feel sexually attracted to other men at times.
He really stands up for what he wants in a given situation, sometimes to the point of being obnoxious.	I feel like standing up for what I want in a given situation, even if it seems obnoxious at times.
He's so sexually uninhibited in public, I feel disgusted.	I feel ashamed and inhibited about my sexual desires, but I'd like to feel freer.

1. Copy this chart (with blank spaces where I've given the examples) in your journal. List your partner's qualities as you perceive them—his or her talents and abilities *and* his or her ways of behaving that you dislike—in the left column under the appropriate heading (Talents and Abilities I Admire and Qualities I Dislike). Then do your "translation" in the right-hand column under the appropriate headings (My Own Hidden Talents and Abilities and My Own Shamed Instincts for Aggression and Sexuality). Begin the sentences of your translation with the words "I am" or "I feel."

2. Study your translation. Try to be as honest with yourself as possible. See if you can *feel* the truth of the parallels you've just recorded.

3. Make it a point to observe exactly *how* your partner shows his or her talents and abilities as well as his or her aggression and sexuality. *Learn* his or her ways of expressing these things.

4. Resolve to embody as many of these qualities in your own life as you can, making allowance for your own individual "style."

5. Practice *your* version of these formerly unacknowledged qualities in your daily life.

   Caution: While I'm convinced that many of us need to be more shameless and direct in the expression of our enthusiasms and instinctual urges, it's also true that *some* of us need to learn restraint. If you suspect you're one of these people, I recommend you consult a therapist before you embark on a program of becoming even *more* aggressive than you may already be. All of us—no matter how repressed—need to learn to contain and channel our feelings at times in order to avoid hurting others or even ourselves unnecessarily. Knowing how and when to express our instinctual feelings and how and when to restrain ourselves is something we discover through trial and error. It's an art that takes both subtlety and courage. But it's important to master this art if we want to withdraw our projections from our partners, dissolve the "merger fantasy," and grow in self-definition and self-affirmation.

Learn How to Fight

An essential part of reclaiming our aggression is learning how to fight. By this I mean learning how to assert ourselves and affirm our needs and desires *and* learning how to *hear* our partner's. Thriving, fulfilling, and instinctually joyful relationships are not built at the other person's expense. Rather, they are partnerships between two strong people who are determined to turn their conflicts into win-win arrangements in which *both* get more of their human and primate pattern-based needs met.

An important, time-honored psychological technique for learning how to fight with each other to achieve a win-win scenario is the process known as "Active Listening."[7] Active Listening is far more than simply listening to your partner express his or her feelings, as important as this is. Rather, it requires that you really *concentrate* on what your partner is saying and that you respond by letting him or her know that you *understand* what he/she is communicating, and that you *empathize*. It requires that you *reflect back to your partner* what you've heard him/her say—exactly as your partner has expressed his or her feelings and ideas, with no editing, censoring, or interpretive comments on your part. Active Listening doesn't mean you have to *agree* with your partner's emotional experience—only that you support his or her right to feel the way he/she does. Once you've heard your partner in this way and supported his/her right to whatever feelings have surfaced you can respond with your own. Then your partner *actively listens to you.*

In my own use of Active Listening techniques in helping my counselees "fight" more effectively (and more fairly) with their partners I have added a further dimension to this communication skill. I call this more advanced step "Decoding."

It helps if we can learn to read between the lines of what our partner is saying to hear his or her animal self speaking just below the surface of what he or she *seems* to be saying. Decoding is often difficult; it is an advanced skill. But it can help us zero in on the *real* sources of our conflicts. Fighting about the *real* issues in our relationships opens the door to genuine reconciliation. This kind of heart-felt reconciliation cannot happen if we're stuck in self-deception and shadow-boxing. Once we know what we're really dealing with when we quarrel we can follow our natural inclinations to make up.

Following is an Active Listening exercise with my suggestions for learning how to decode your partner's primate patterns in conflict situations. (Note that many of the previous techniques and exercises key into the Active Listening and Decoding way of giving and receiving each other's aggressive self-affirmation. The self-empowering, self-affirming techniques and exercises bolster our ability to put our own needs forward—shamelessly—and the techniques that stress comforting and *mutual* empowering prepare us for an attitude of empathy toward our partners. Paradoxically, the stronger, more self-affirming *we* become the greater is our capacity to respond to our partners in a positive way.)

EXERCISE #8: ACTIVE LISTENING AND DECODING THE MESSAGES FROM YOUR PARTNER'S PRIMATE SELF

Purpose: The purpose of this exercise is to learn to resolve relationship conflicts in a win-win way by achieving greater awareness, celebration, comforting, and channeling of your own and your partner's primate self.

Comments: Do this exercise together.

1. Suppose your partner—a man—says something to you like "It really makes me angry when you act bored about the things I'm interested in. I mean, I love history. You know that. And I want to talk to you about the stuff I'm reading. But you don't want to hear anything about it."

2. When he's finished speaking you can say something like, "I hear you. You feel angry that I seem bored when you want to talk to me about the things you're reading. I'm sorry you feel that way, Honey."

   First you repeat what your partner has said—not necessarily word for word, but close. In this example, the man used a lot of blaming "you language." His partner changed it to "I language." Next, give your partner an empathic response. In this example, the female listener did this twice— "I hear you." And "I'm sorry you feel that way, Honey." In neither case did she accept her partner's blame or agree that he *should* feel upset by her apparent lack of interest. She simply let him know she heard and understood him and that she could empathize with his pain.

3. If you've understood what your partner has said and given him or her an empathic response your partner will probably say something like, "Yes, that's exactly how I feel!" If you *haven't* understood or been empathic your partner is likely to respond with something like "No, that's *not* what I mean!" He or she may even escalate his/her attack on you—"Why can't you *ever* listen?"

4. But if all goes well your partner may continue speaking by going into more detail about his or her point and perhaps more intense emotional expression. In this case you continue reflecting back to him/her what you hear him/her saying; and you continue empathizing while not accepting blame.

5. If he or she pauses, you may ask a series of clarifying questions. You can also do this if you haven't really understood

his or her first statement. You can say something like "I'm not sure I understand. Do you mean . . . ?"

6. Once things have been clarified and your partner knows you understand his or her point of view and care about his/her feelings it's your turn to speak. Hopefully, you're both working with this Active Listening exercise. If you are, the process of repeating, empathy, and clarification continues, but with a reversal of roles.

There's much more to Active Listening than I've presented here. So again I want to refer you to the bibliography for books that highlight this technique for improving your communication skills.

Active Listening may seem a little artificial at first. When you're first trying it out you may want to practice it in the presence of a therapist trained in its uses. I've found that with just a little practice this format for "fighting" can become a natural part of the ebb and flow of our daily conversations.

Decoding: As a further dimension to Active Listening we can learn to *decode* the messages from our partner's primate self that often express themselves in a cryptic way just under the surface of what he or she is saying. In a sense *all* the major schools of psychology offer decoding programs. We're *often* communicating with each other—or trying to—on multiple levels.

Learning to decode the messages from our partner's primate core in a thorough-going way would fill the pages of a book twice the size of this one. But here I want to point you in the direction of this kind of "cryptography." At the very least, it can raise interesting questions for you about how to more accurately "read" your partner's real motives.

Let's take the example of the couple above. *He says, "It really makes me angry when you act bored about the things I'm interested in. I mean, I love history. You know that. And I want to talk to you about the stuff I'm reading. But you don't want to hear anything about it."*

In terms of traditional psychological interpretations the man in this example is telling the woman that he feels unsupported and "unmirrored" by her. He may even feel a lack of mutuality in their relationship. He *may* be showing what psychologists call "mirror hunger"—an exaggerated need for affirmation from his partner. This could come out of his childhood wounds, perhaps a damaged sense of his own self-worth. We would have to know a lot more about their relationship and their individual life histories to tell which one of them was failing to hold up their end in this situation. But no matter what the reality may be on this level, it's still probably true that at the level of their primate patterns this couple may be failing to satisfy each other's relationship needs.

In terms of the priorities of his relationship needs this man may feel that his partner is failing to *admire and emotionally support him* and that she doesn't share his *core values and beliefs*. In terms of our hot issues, *mutual dependency* (perhaps skewed into codependency), our *ongoing childlikeness* (and child*ish*ness), and even *confusion about the purpose of our relationships* may be at work. As we noted, this man may have unresolved needs for mirroring that could be expressing themselves through codependent and childish demands on his part. He may also believe that his relationship is really *for* intellectual discussions about history. In this case, from my perspective, he's "confused" about the real purpose of his pair-bond. For *her* part, the woman may be consciously or unconsciously withholding her admiration and emotional support, and thereby involving herself in codependent and childish dynamics with her partner. On the other hand, she may *not* share his core values and beliefs.

Beneath the level of the apparent frustration of his relationship needs (perhaps her needs are being frustrated as well), this man may have serious doubts about whether his partner is the best long-term genetic investment he could have made. His savanna time primate self may be trying to communicate something as drastic as, "I feel scared that I've made the wrong choice about who I'm realizing my practical immortality with. Maybe your genes are inferior to mine. Maybe you're not intelligent or empathic enough in your biological makeup. That could mean my children won't have the best chance I could have given them for achieving status and wealth (their own tickets to practical immortality)."

If that *is* what his animal core is saying the situation is much more serious than whether or not this couple shares an interest in history, or even whether or not they are expressing childhood issues about mirror hunger. If you're the woman in this example, it would pay you to *decode* this message and then take whatever steps you need to take in order to meet the relationship needs he's expressing and to reassure him of your "genetic fitness," *or* to free both of you for a more appropriate partnership. I know this may sound cold, but at the level of the nonnegotiable relationship needs that come out of our primate-patterned reproductive strategies, the dynamics between us really *are* impersonal. If you can decode each other's primate-self messages in these and other conflict situations, at least you'll be "fighting" about the *real* issues and giving yourselves the best chance you can for resolving them.

Two More Strategies You Can Use to Reclaim Your Aggression

I want to mention two more strategies that a number of my counselees have used to unshame, celebrate, and channel their natural aggression—assertiveness training and martial arts. At their best, both these processes teach disciplined self-affirmation—the kind that is strong and aggressive but not hostile.

Often our society assumes that women need assertiveness training more than men. But my experience leads me to believe that *both* men and women are frequently far too passive about getting their needs met within their relationships—as well as from life in general—and that both genders can benefit from more self-assertive communication skills.

The martial arts can also increase our ability to be aggressively self-affirming. Because they are physical as well as mental disciplines, they can help us *embody* and express our aggressive impulses rather than repress or split them off as ineffective and neurotic emotions. Anything we can do to reclaim our aggression in a disciplined way strengthens our relationships and increases the likelihood that we can make them fuller and more joyful long-term partnerships.

Reclaiming Your Sexuality

From the combined perspectives of primatology, anthropology, and psychology it's clear that sex is the ultimate target of our shaming. As we've seen, this *is* because we're threatened as men and women by our different and mixed reproductive strategies. Many of the hot issues in our relationships that surface at each of the three levels of our primate patterns arise from the clash between our reproductive strategies—*and* from their frustration.

If our sexuality is the fundamental source of our relationship conflicts it stands to reason that this is the most important aspect of our partnerships for us to come to terms with—if what we want is long-lasting happiness and emotional security with each other. Because nature has arranged for us to become sexually (and romantically) bored with our partners through the mechanisms of the Coolidge Effect, the incest taboo, and the "four-year-itch" syndrome, most of us have to make a *conscious* effort to build this long-term happiness and emotional security into our relationships. We must find a way to integrate our jungle time sexual exuberance with our savanna time romantic pair-bonding hopes. In general terms, we must become greater sources of pleasure—even of ecstasy—to each other than causes of pain and frustration. More pointedly, we *must* unshame our male and female sexualities and accept, celebrate, comfort, and channel them in the context of our partnerships.

Sex Manuals and Therapy

Men and women both need to develop the capacity to cherish, adore, and be open to each other's masculine and feminine energies and each other's bodies as if they were the most beautiful, even awesome, things in the universe. We both need to be secure enough in our own sexual identities and feeling empowered enough in our gender-characteristic instincts to be able to focus on *giving our partner pleasure*. When we mature and deepen as the "human animal" we can come to experience our partner's sexual enjoyment as our own most powerful turn-on.

One way we learn how to give our partners pleasure is by feeling shameless and uninhibited about our own bodies. Only when we know how *we* are aroused do we develop an intuitive feel for how to stimulate our partners. Masturbation is the best way to become familiar with our own sexual responses.[8]

At the same time, it remains true that men and women experience sexual arousal somewhat differently. Different things turn us on to different degrees. This means, among other things, that if we're going to give each other maximum pleasure both men and women need to learn how to *appreciate,* and perhaps even *approximate* the other gender's sexuality. Men, for example, could learn to slow down and more fully enjoy tender yet passionate foreplay, and women could learn to climax more rapidly and so come closer to the usual speed of male orgasm. The fact so much of a man's sexual pleasure comes from visual cues means that it could be in a woman's own self-interest to do what she can to enhance her appearance.

We can also come to view the other sex's general orientation to physical intimacy as at least as delightful as it is disturbing. Men can learn to experience most women's "coyness" as endearing, and instead of feeling shamed and rejected by it, welcome their male roles as "hunters." And women can come to experience male sexual eagerness as flattering rather than degrading of their personhood. We can view the "subhuman" elements in each other as exciting rather than dehumanizing. As we've seen, much of the way we are together in our relationships is *not* personal. For me, this news is energizing. I see the glass as half full rather than half empty in this respect.

Sex manuals abound to help individuals and couples with the intricacies of achieving these goals.[9] If you suspect you may be an especially hard case—that you're overly repressed, that you carry an extraordinary amount of sexual guilt and shame, that you perhaps harbor extreme hostility toward the other gender, or even somewhat paranoid fantasies and suspicions, or if you think you may have been sexually abused in your childhood or adolescence—I recommend that you engage in some form of psychotherapeutic work. This may involve sexual therapy or it may mean a more general approach to personal growth. Healing such deep wounds requires commitment and perseverance, but it can be done. The sooner you start, the sooner you can enjoy an instinctually satisfying relationship.

Fulfilling Each Other's Primary Fantasies

Sex therapy and manuals aside, the *main* way we can make our relationships sexually exciting is to do what we can to fulfill each other's primary fantasies. As we recall, our primary fantasies tend to underlie our different priorities of relationship needs as men and women. Men's primary fantasy usually comes out of their jungle time hunger for a variety of sexual partners, while women's is usually more oriented toward their savanna time desire for romantic commitment.

Since a woman's primary fantasy is generally for a strong but deeply caring alpha male who will devote himself to protecting and providing for her and her children—and this is a sexual turn-on for her—it pays a man to fulfill this role as best he can. This enables a woman to experience him as the primary source of her romantic and sexual pleasure, and minimizes her urge to look for a more alpha alpha. To the degree that other aspects of a relationship are going well enough, a man's ability to approximate this feminine ideal can go a long way toward keeping his relationship fresh, energized, and sexually exciting.

Some of the practical steps a man might take in this respect could include such things as providing the best living he can for his family, continuing the romantic gestures that were part of the courtship stage throughout the later stages of his relationship, listening empathically to his partner's concerns, sharing his own, staying as healthy as he can, demonstrating his capacity to manage his own feelings in a mature way and his ability to "frame" his partner (much as the heroes of romance novels usually provide emotional structure for the heroines, but on a more realistic level, of course), and so on. All of the techniques and exercises we've already looked at as well as those that follow contribute in a direct way to a man's "alphazation." Any time he can shamelessly affirm his jungle and savanna time primate nature in an integrated way he is making himself "irresistible" to his partner.

By the same token, since a man's primary fantasy is for many different sexual partners—and sexual variety is a turn-on for him—it pays a woman to be as sexually provocative for her partner as she can. This enables a man to experience her as the primary source of *his* pleasure, and it minimizes his urge to *act* on his jungle time promiscuous urges. Of course, one woman can't be many. But she *can* be sexually unashamed and uninhibited, eager to be experimental with lovemaking, at least as concerned with her partner's pleasure as her own, and in general "provocatively yielding." This last quality increases male desire—both the "provocative" part and the "yielding" aspect. In addition, if she understands the ways in which her partner's sexual instincts are different from her own and can accept that his desire for other women is a natural part of his maleness (without necessarily sanctioning his acting on it), her chances of helping him stay interested in her—and sexually faithful—increase dramatically. In general I've found that both men and women are so grateful to their partners when their gender-characteristic sexual needs are accepted instead of feared and shamed that their promiscuous urges diminish to the point that they're seldom if ever acted on. To the extent that other aspects of a relationship are going well enough, a woman's ability to approximate the male sexual ideal can go a long way toward keeping her relationship vital, emotionally satisfying, and sexually exciting.

Some of the practical steps a woman might take in this respect could include refraining from escalating relationship conflicts whenever possible, "deferring" to the assertion of his male instincts to "frame" and "penetrate" the relationship dynamics (without, of course, giving up any of *her* aggressive self-affirmation or in any way allowing herself to be abused),[10] being prepared for his expression of feelings—even those that may frighten her,[11] dressing in a sexy way, and so on. Again, all of the techniques and exercises in this book can contribute in a direct way to a woman's growth in her animal instincts for a kind of fierce sweetness.

Interestingly, as Harville Hendrix has pointed out in a different context, the more we act to meet our partner's needs and desires the more we satisfy our own.[12] As we grow to become aware of, accept, celebrate, comfort, and channel our partner's romantic and sexual instincts, we're meeting our own. Other things being equal, when we affirm our partner's gender identity we find ourselves affirming our own. As we've seen, this is the basis of our most powerful sense of self-worth, and, ultimately, the most empowering thing we can do for our relationships.

I realize that proposing these strategies for working *with* rather than *against* our differing reproductive patterns as males and females is not "politically correct," and that it may provoke a frightened and angry reaction from some men and women. Both may feel righteously indignant about being asked to actually *give* their partners, as representatives of the other gender—the one we're supposed to be at war with—what they really want. Men may exclaim: "How can you suggest that I become a 'walking wallet'—a 'success object'—for a spoiled princess?!" And some women may accuse me of asking them to acquiesce to the "degrading" "patriarchal" sexual demands of men.

Let me just say that I'm not proposing anything so drastic or so demeaning of either gender. What I *am* saying is that on the deep level of our primate patterns we can't either of us escape our instinct-based roles—and be happy with ourselves and fulfilled in our relationships. We cannot afford to forget that it *is* our primate selves which give our partnerships their healthy animal glow and thereby encourage them to last.

There are at least three additional strategies we can use for reducing the tension between us around our differing sexualities. Both partners can learn to accept and celebrate the other's forms of erotic materials. Men can come to appreciate romance novels and love stories, and enjoy the fact that in most cases their partners are at least as turned on by these romantic dramas as by explicitly sexual material. Women can come to appreciate erotic movies and magazines, and enjoy the fact that in most cases their partners are more turned on by these pictorial stimulants than they are by romantic stories.

We can also stop feeling so threatened by our partner's occasional flirtatiousness or his or her enjoyment of other men or women. We can even learn to play along. For example, a woman might catch her partner staring at another woman and say something nonshaming and supportive like, "She *is* beautiful, isn't she? I bet you'd like to jump her!" Or a man might see his partner start to glow around another man and say something like "Well, that guy really *does* seem to have a lot going for him!"

A word about more dramatic forms of living out our primate pattern–based romantic and sexual fantasies with our partners. Some couples try to satisfy one or both partners' jungle time promiscuous urges by joining so-called swingers' clubs or by having open marriages. These strategies no doubt work for some people, but they're also risky. Depending on the precautions everyone takes—or doesn't—they could be health risks of course. On the emotional level, while trying to fulfill our jungle time instincts, such programs can run straight into our savanna time impulses. They can open us up to powerful feelings of jealousy—as we've seen, nature's way of trying to safeguard our fragile pair-bonds. They can also encourage us to leave our partners for someone we may meet in this way when we might benefit more from working through our relationship needs and hot issues with our present partners.

If You or Your Partner Has Had an Affair

If you discover your partner has had an affair, try not to panic. Confront him or her and insist on getting to the bottom of the problem together, probably in a couples counseling setting that provides some emotional containment and safety for both of you. Of course, you should insist that both you and your partner be tested for HIV and other sexually transmitted diseases. If your relationship is fulfilling enough for you in other ways, you may decide to stay in it and work to make it better. On the other hand, sometimes affairs are expressions of a relationship's last gasp. They may be the signal we were waiting for to move on.

If *you* have had an affair, the *first* thing to do is be tested for sexually transmitted diseases *before* making love with your partner again. (Of course, you should also have demanded that the potential partner in your affair be tested *before* your first sexual contact.) The second thing to do is sit down with yourself and do some deep reflection. I recommend you do this with a therapist, as long as he or she is not shaming and doesn't assume your "intimacy issues" made you do it. Most of us don't need "pathologizing" at this point, but rather empathy and understanding—shoring up so we don't collapse under the weight of the savanna time guilt feelings that usually surface during or after sexual infidelity. Later, you might very well need to explore areas in which you need to grow. If your infidelity was more than a one-time event, if it truly was—or is—an affair, you need to explore the strong possibility that you're dissatisfied with your primary relationship in some important ways. Most likely, some of your non-negotiable relationship needs are not being met.

Of course, if you find you *are* dissatisfied you have a decision to make. Either you begin the process of asking your partner for changes that will help you get your needs met better—within the context of your relationship—or you begin the process of leaving it. I know this is obvious, but it's been my experience that many people absolutely *refuse* to deal with this decision. They stay in denial about the implications of their affairs, usually because they're afraid—afraid they will be alone, afraid of their partner's anger if they ask him or her to grow, or afraid their partner won't be able to live without them if they leave. You need to muster all the aggressive self-affirmation you can if any of these fears are paralyzing you.

One thing I strongly urge you *not* to do: Do *not* tell your partner about your affair unless the situation demands it. There's no good reason to "confess." In fact, it may be selfish to do this. *You* may feel better, but your partner is almost certain to feel much worse. Confessing to an affair unnecessarily is a mishandling of your guilt, and the chances are very good that you'll do irreparable damage to your primary relationship. If your relationship is worth keeping, simply get to work on improving it. It goes without saying, of course, that if you test positive for a sexually transmitted disease, you *must* tell your partner.

* * *

Following are two exercises designed to help you evoke your powerful animal sexuality. The first is a more focused version of the Through the Looking Glass exercise and the second is a way of breaking the merger fantasy, often a prerequisite, at least in the later stages of our relationships, for maintaining and even enriching our sex lives as couples.

EXERCISE #9: ENVISIONING YOUR SEXUAL POWER

Purpose: The purpose of this exercise is to help you evoke, accept, celebrate, and channel your male or female sexual power.
Comments: Do this exercise alone.

1. Follow the steps for the Through the Looking Glass exercise, Exercise #2 (pp. 228–229). This time, allow your primate self to communicate his or her sexual feelings and desires. Invite him or her to let you feel the exuberance, the hunger, and the joy of his or her sexual fantasies.

2. **Women:** Look into the eyes of the wild female animal within you and open to her sexual feelings—her feelings of longing, of hunger, of tenderness, of fierceness—and to her erotic fantasies. Allow her to express the full range of what she wishes for. Let her show you her determination to enjoy her sexuality, whatever forms it takes.

3. **Men:** Look into the eyes of the wild male animal within *you* and open to his sexual feelings—his feelings of longing, of hunger, of tenderness, of fierceness—and to his erotic fantasies. Allow him to express the full range of what *he* wishes for. Let him show you his determination to enjoy his sexuality, whatever forms it takes.

4. **Men and Women:** As you allow your primate core to communicate with you directly in this way assure her or him that you will listen to and feel her or his sexual agenda more fully from now on, and that you will take her or his sexual passions and fantasies as seriously as you take your other instincts, enthusiasms, and interests. Assure your animal self that you welcome her or him into your life with as

much honor and respect as any other part of you, and that you will listen to the sexual messages she or he sends you through your body—your feelings of pleasure and arousal—as you move through the stages of your relationship(s). (As we've seen, it's only when we block our primate self's sexual expression that she or he forces us to act compulsively and destructively in our love lives.)

5. Close your communication only when you've allowed the full range and power of your animal sexuality to speak to you, felt its energy as life-giving and beautiful, and resolved to live as a more sexual being.

Caution: If feelings of fear, violation, paranoia, or rage surface you've probably contacted your inner animal's reactions to one form or another of gender or sexual abuse. Your "complexes" rather than your primary sexual energy are probably speaking to you. If this is the case, I recommend you see a therapist to help you dismantle your defenses and move toward sexual wholeness.

EXERCISE #10: KEEPING SPACE BETWEEN YOU

Purpose: The purpose of this exercise is to achieve awareness and appreciation of each other's separate gender identities in order to accept, celebrate, and channel your gender-characteristic male and female energies.

Comments: Do this exercise together.

It's been my experience that couples often need a break from each other. We need space between us in order to maintain our own boundaries, dissolve our merger fantasies, and feel drawn to each other sexually. (In a merger fantasy in which you feel "one" with your partner it's difficult if not impossible to feel sexually attracted; there's no one to be attracted *to*!) Unfortunately, many of us don't realize how important this is. We may think there's something wrong with us if we want some time away from each other. Because this need for space runs counter to the romantic ideal of perfect union, we often interpret needing space as a sign that our relationship is no longer working. Since the only space permitted by this ideal is literal separation, we may decide it's time to break up. At the very least our need for distance may propel us into bitter fights that *can* generate some self-definition, and a sense of our own empowered individuality and gender identity. Some couples may fight before they make love for this very reason.[13] Distance *can* spark sexual desire.

As we've seen, familiarity does often breed contempt; and because of the incest taboo, the Coolidge Effect, and the "four-year-itch" syndrome, it also can breed sexual boredom. It's vital to a healthy long-term relationship that we be able to hold onto our separate identities *within* the context of our relationships. There are many ways of doing this. Many of the techniques and exercises already presented are enormously helpful in this respect. To the extent that they empower us as individuals, and as *male* and *female* individuals, they support the creation of a potentially sexually charged space between us.

In addition a powerful technique I've learned to use with couples, one that focuses specifically on this issue of space, is *silence*. Silence for twenty-four hours throws us back on our inner resources as men and women. It temporarily cuts off the nearly constant stream of chatter between our "human" selves, gives us emotional breathing room, and helps us break the merger fantasy with all of its Imprint replays and projections. Having to depend on our inner resources instead of constantly leaning on each other reinforces our legitimate emotional boundaries and our similar but different male and female gender essences. This helps us reexperience the sense of mystery and newness we had about each other at the beginning of our relationships. And *this* helps us feel more powerful—and sexy.

1. As a couple, agree on the day, and the time of day, you're going to begin and end your psychological separation. (If you have children, arrange for someone else to take care of them while you complete this exercise.)

2. During this time do not communicate with words or written messages (except in emergencies of course). You may communicate with preverbal sounds and with facial expres-

sions and gestures, but try to hold even these to a minimum since the purpose of this exercise is to separate you while you're still in each other's presence.

3. Spend a significant part of the time *watching* each other. Notice, as you did in the beginning of your relationship, the things about your partner that turned you on in the first place. See how she moves, how she tosses her hair, how her breasts bob when she walks, the texture of the skin on her thighs, the combination of sweetness and strength that shows in her eyes, and so on. See how the muscles in his shoulders tighten when he works around the house, how he brushes his hair away from his eyes, the flash of his smile, the gentleness and power he shows in his every movement, and so on. See these things afresh and allow yourself to be dazzled by them all over again.

4. After your period of silence is over, come back together with a kiss and whatever other physical expressions you want as a way of *showing* each other how you feel. You may be surprised at the tenderness and passion that well up at this moment of reunion. You may also want to share — verbally—some of the things you loved about watching each other and some of the feelings you had about yourself during your emotional separation.

5. Don't rush back into a merger fantasy and take up where you left off in your "business as usual" with each other. Resolve instead to remind yourself at least once a day from now on that you and your partner are separate male and female animals, and to recall how you felt about yourself and your partner when you were experiencing the space between you. Resolve as well to do this exercise again whenever one or both of you is feeling the need to get some distance.

Instinctual Love Is Romantic

By evoking our unique human empathy and compassion and our amazing reflective and strategizing capacities while at the same time freeing our jungle and savanna time instincts, we can begin to live richer, fuller lives and create energetic, interesting, and passionate partnerships. Once freed from shame, it's incredible what goodwill men and women can have for each other—what vital, aggressively self-affirming and sexy male and female energies we can share.

If you've done the exercises and begun to practice the techniques I've presented, a more joyful and fulfilling partnership is now within reach. Let's see where we are by now in terms of resolving the hot issues in our relationships. Then I want to offer several more strategies that I encourage my counselees and workshop participants to build into their lives to strengthen the connections to their jungle and savanna time primate patterns and to resolve their remaining conflicts.

12

"RESOLVING" OUR HOT ISSUES

❋

As we work to unshame, accept, celebrate, comfort, and channel our own and each other's primate patterns and integrate them with our human capacities for reason and empathy, we are moving *toward* a reasonable "resolution" of the hot issues in our relationships. Because nature jerryrigged the layers of our primate patterns opportunistically in order to adapt us to changing ecological niches, as we've seen, these parts of ourselves are often at odds with each other. Overly complex apes that we are, we can never get *full* resolution of our relationship problems. But we *can* defuse much of their compulsive power over our lives through the processes I've been suggesting in this book. Men and women are *always* going to experience tension between their genders as well as competing urges within themselves. But we can embrace these tensions as creative and exciting stimulants to our love lives rather than painful harbingers of doom.

As you've done the exercises and begun to use the techniques presented, the hot issues in your relationship have probably started to lose some of their punch. Among those you should be feeling some relief from are the ones around your aggression and sexuality, and your feelings of shame about these primal energies. Promiscuity and Recreational Sex from our jungle time— Serial Monogamy; Sexual Jealousy; Shame and Guilt; Mutual Dependency; and Our Ongoing Childlikeness from our savanna time—Our Sense of Mutual Enslavement to Each Other; Work Is Good, Pleasure Is Bad; The Shaming of Our Sexuality; Sex Is Only for Procreation; and the Spiritualizing of Our Relationships, with the resulting problems of Sexual Malaise, Rage, and Erotic Substitution for Joyful Relationships from our civilization era—and Confusion about the Purpose of Our Relationships from our present-day transitional period—*all* of these hot issues should be on the way toward being moderated in your deepening partnership with each other.

Our hot issues play off one another in complex ways, too complex to enumerate here. Some of them stand in *opposition* to each other—like our jungle time Promiscuity urges and our savanna time Serial Monogamy, Sexual Jealousy, and Shame and Guilt dynamics—while others *build upon* each other. Our civilization era Sense of Enslavement to Each Other, for example, is a direct descendant of our savanna time Mutual Dependency and Our Ongoing Childlikeness. The good news is that as we become stronger and more instinctually expressive, the destructive force of these interrelated hot issues begins to subside, allowing us to "outwit" nature to some extent. This enables us to become freer to truly enjoy our relationships and extend them beyond nature's Coolidge Effect and "four-year-itch" syndrome plans for them.

But there still are some hot issues we haven't addressed directly yet. While these hot issues feed into those already mentioned, they form their own somewhat independent networks. They fall into three basic categories. The *first* has to do with our growing hostility toward each other as genders. The hot issues here include Women's Economic Self-Sufficiency, Single-Parent Families, Intense Mother-Child Bonding, and Mutual Gender Isolation—from our jungle time; The Economic Subordination of Women and its corollary, Intense Pressure on Men to Protect and Provide—from our savanna time; and from the transitional period we're now in, Gender Polarization. The *second* category is an issue for men, but one that nonetheless affects their relationships with women—their jungle time Extreme Male Competitiveness and Emotional Isolation. The *third* category is the vitally important present-day question What Happens to Our Children?

Based on my research and on my experience as a therapist, a community organizer, a counselor of predelinquent and delinquent teens, a pastor, a "kibbutznic" in Israel, and a resident of the city of Chicago—and so a firsthand witness to the rising tide of gang activity and youth violence (in the context of our collapsing savanna time and civilization era nuclear families)—I've come up with two basic strategies for defusing all of these three remaining categories of hot issues. The first strategy is about sharing income-earning responsibilities, and the second is about re-creating our human communities.

Sharing Income-Earning Responsibilities

The hot issues of the Economic Subordination of Women and Intense Pressure on Men to Protect and Provide go hand in hand. As we've seen, they have their origin in our savanna time before the domestication of fire, when women were economically dependent on men, and ancestral males had to shoulder the burden of providing most of the food. In our early civilization era (the agricultural period) men and women often worked as a team in the fields, but late-nineteenth-century developments in our industrial economies have tended to re-create the extreme separation of work roles we knew on the savannas.[1]

Intentionally reconnecting with two levels of our primate patterns can help us resolve these hot issues which still plague many couples. Excluding the industrialization process of the last two hundred years, our civilization era primate patterns (as we've seen, partly biological and partly cultural) give us the teamwork model of a more or less equal economic partnership in which men and women do much the same work. Of course, even though they "plow and plant" together, there are still separate gender-characteristic tasks they perform. Most women are simply not as suited as most men for truly heavy labor, and most men are not as suited as most women for jobs that require agile fingers and tactile sensitivity. Also, while it's true that not all women are born to be enthusiastic or good mothers and that some men *are* good fathers, our primate background strongly suggests that most men are not wired for a commitment to fathering as intense as most women's commitment to motherhood.[2] This means it's not likely that the majority of men will *ever* take up domestic responsibilities or infant care with very great excitement. What's more, men shouldn't try to convert the fathering aptitudes they do have into imitations of women's mothering behavior. Likewise, women shouldn't try to turn themselves into pseudofathers.[3]

Nevertheless, our civilization/agricultural era primate patterns can serve as a guide for couples who want to pursue the same profession, collaborate in each other's lines of work, or operate "mom and pop" businesses. In these kinds of economic partnerships we usually see both men and women making roughly equal financial contributions to their relationships.

The other layer of our primate patterns we can draw on for a model of shared economic responsibility is our savanna time—*after* the domestication of fire, when many grassland roots and tubers at last became edible. Women came into their own as equal if not greater economic partners. They could gather vegetable foods with their children strapped to their backs or tagging along. Our work *roles* were different, but our economic contributions were roughly the same.

Using either of these scenarios from our evolutionary background allows modern women to overcome their economic subordination, and it takes some of the pressure off men to be the primary or sole providers. It seems to me that those couples who want to resolve these hot issues (who are not already doing so, as many are today), need to restructure their economic lives according to either the shared-occupation model or along the lines of our late savanna time hunter-gatherer ways. From my perspective, it's a wonderful development that women now have more or less equal access to traditionally male professions, and I can only hope for the day when men will have the same access to traditionally female occupations (including staying at home to raise their children). But even if that day comes, I suspect our innate temperamental differences (as whole, gender-specific populations)—the product of millions of years of evolution in our bodies, brains, and hormonal systems—will result in the majority of men and women sorting themselves into savanna time–like equal but different ways of contributing to the economic well-being of their pair-bonds.[4]

The one pattern that *won't* work is the one that comes from our jungle time. In our jungle time, as we recall, females had complete economic independence—except when it came to meat. The problem with trying to re-create our jungle time economic arrangement is twofold. In the first place, we have an entirely different social system, one that is without meaningful community. This is the legacy of two hundred years of industrialization and urbanization. Nature never imagined our complete economic self-sufficiency as men and women in the context of a nearly total loss of community. The second barrier to reestablishing jungle time economics is that it is no longer *emotionally* possible. We are now wired, however imperfectly, to pair-bond. Our jungle time economies were built on the *emotional self-sufficiency* of both males and females—and a thoroughly promiscuous pattern of male/female interacting. Not only are our modern cultures not set up for such a complete return; our savanna time instincts won't allow it.

Re-Creating Human Community

Communities—in the form of same-sex and mixed-sex support/therapy groups, and as more broadly based social groups—can be enormously effective in helping us resolve our remaining hot issues—Extreme Male Competitiveness and Isolation, Mutual Gender Isolation, Gender Polarization, Women's Economic Self-Sufficiency, Intense Mother-Child Bonding, Single-Parent Families, and What Happens to Our Children?

As we've seen, primate males are almost universally competitive, but our own savanna time male ancestors achieved an unprecedented level of intermale cooperation in order to hunt large game, defend their communities against predators, and reduce the level of male-on-male violence. Our human societies from ancient times to the present have been characterized by a remarkable degree of male bonding and cooperation when compared with all other primate species.[5] Yet, as I've mentioned, it seems to me we are witnessing in our modern industrialized urban societies a regressive return to jungle time–like social conditions in which male competitiveness is reaching devastating proportions. I'm not just talking about the violence of young men in our inner cities; I'm also referring to the economic competition for dwindling resources among men of every social class, and a growing feeling among many of the men I've worked with that they live in terrifying emotional isolation from each other. Add to this the increasing isolation of our nuclear families—and even *their* dissolution. I believe it's possible that, on the whole, human males may *never* have been so isolated from and competitive with one another as they are now.

From my years of experience in the men's movement I've become convinced that vast numbers of men are *starving* for male community and for a level of bonding with other men much deeper than recreational outings and bar-hopping with "the boys." Even though most men have been driven by cultural pressures to repress this hunger, growing numbers of men are joining men's support/therapy groups of many different kinds.

As women seek to find new identities as well as to reaffirm old ones, and as they experiment with aspects of womanhood that have been historically suppressed—their *own* competitiveness, for example—they too could benefit from all-female support/therapy groups.

This is not only true for men and women seeking to enhance their individual lives. Same-sex support/therapy groups can be powerful allies of our *relationships* as well. In traditional societies, for example, men and women had the wisdom to realize that husbands and wives can't carry the weight of all our needs for sharing and intimacy. They also knew that men and women are fundamentally different and that there are forms of intimacy only their own gender can provide. They also seemed to realize that men and women need some psychological space in order to reinforce their own gender identities and be even more appealing to each other.[6] As we've seen, firm gender identities enhance our adult relationships. When we don't have enough emotional space between us we tend to collapse into each other and fall into parent-child/child-parent relationship patterns. We also can fall into a unisex fantasy—a program guaranteed to reduce the sexual energy between us.

Heirs of the female "auntie systems" and the male power coalitions of our primate past, the "secret societies," "long houses," and so on, of our tribal forebears gave each gender the sense of its own specialness and reinforced firm gender identities, as Anthony Storr says, the foundations of male and female self-esteem. By sharing dreams, stories, and gender-characteristic myths these same-sex "support groups" gave men and women an enhanced ability to live empowered lives as couples. Today, same-sex support/therapy groups, through many of the same or similar processes, can enhance our appreciation for the separate, sexually unique, and mysterious person each partner can continue to be to the other throughout the course of their relationship.

I want to raise a caution here, though. The hot issues of Mutual Gender Isolation and Gender Polarization are on the rise in our culture, with potentially devastating consequences for our partnerships. Both genders have legitimate reasons to feel angry with the other; and some of what comes up in same-sex groups *is* our anger for the ways we feel the other sex has oppressed and misused us. I've discovered in working with both men and women in groups that there's often a fine line between our expressions of anger, on the one hand, and gender-caricaturing and male- or female-bashing, on the other. If you join—or form—a same-sex support/therapy group I suggest you monitor the group process carefully, and, with your growing capacity to be aggressively self-affirming, that you speak up if the group turns from the expression of anger to gender-based hatred. A program of gender hatred is not going to help you work through the problems in your relationship.

I've also had experience with intensive mixed-sex therapy and discussion groups—in lecture and seminar form and in weekend workshop formats. I've always found that although gender-based tensions are present, these group settings can be a good way to experience, however fleetingly, something like what our ancient, intimate, mixed-sex savanna communities must have been like.

The hot issues of Intense Mother-Child Bonding and Single-Parent Families (often structured to exclude fathers) can also be worked through in single-sex and mixed-sex groups. These two issues often divide the very men and women who need to be co-operating, even after separation or divorce, in the raising of their children. More and more researchers are coming to believe that fathers are essential to the emotional and intellectual development of both their sons and daughters.[7] Common sense and mounting evidence show that children need an ongoing relationship with both parents in order to achieve firm gender identities and learn how to relate with grace and confidence to the opposite sex.[8]

Helen Fisher and other anthropologists point out that divorce, split families, remarriage, and combined families are natural patterns for our species.[9] An important difference, however, between our savanna time serially monogamous ways and our situation today is that on the grasslands even single parents lived in close-knit communities with both males and females of all ages close by.[10] Our neighbors' campfires were never more than a few feet away. Even after men and women divorced and perhaps remarried, children still related on a daily basis with both their original parents, and there were many other nurturing men and women to hold them, play with them, teach them, and initiate them into group life. In our present social setting separated and divorced men and women of all ages are often terrifyingly isolated—economically, emotionally, and sexually—and our "home alone" and "latchkey" children suffer as a consequence.

We are *social* primates. Our nearest relatives are the highly gregarious, community-living chimpanzees and bonobos. We *need* each other's support, challenge, and nurturing. It seems to me that we *must* find ways to re-create something like the hunter-gatherer bands of twenty-five to one hundred individuals for which our human psyches are bred. There are probably many ways of doing this—from starting our own communities (as some religious groups have tried to do, with varying degrees of success) to deepening and extending some of the voluntary organizations that already exist, such as neighborhood groups, block-club associations, schools, and churches. However we might go about it, I'm convinced that such savanna time–like social arrangements would have a powerful effect on the psychological and physical well-being of our children—and that, from a biological point of view, is what even the deluxe-model ape is finally about. The vital question, What Happens to Our Children? would become a nonissue, and we community-dwelling, pair-bonding male and female primates would have given ourselves the best opportunity possible for ensuring our own "practical immortality" and that of generations to come far into an unforeseeable but unquestionably exciting human future.

AFTERWORD

❋

After uncounted generations in the deafening green of the forest, choosing each other—male and female—for qualities that would someday take us to the moon, exchange our termite sticks for pyramids, and our grimaces for smiles, a tiny band of chimpanzeelike creatures accepted the challenge of the silent savannas enveloping the site of their nativity, stood upright amidst the teeming herds, and touched each other with tenderness. The sons and daughters of alpha males and "great mothers," we formed our unsteady pair-bonds, had our unusual, large-brained babies, and left our footprints in the volcanic mud at Laetoli.

As our minds mushroomed, we looked upon each other more and more with the eyes of love. Our newly invented relationships were often tormented by more ancient instincts which moved us to acts of treachery and betrayal. But still we pushed on to dazzling cities, tools made fabulous by our fantasies, and romantic love. We began trying to make our pair-bonds last a lifetime, in part because in them we seemed to brush up against something more, something that reminded us of a world beyond the forest canopy, the shimmering grasslands, or our dazzling cities.

Now, we have the means to look back on the vast distances we have traveled as our souls have unfolded their tenderness, their fierceness, their capacity for reason, their penchant for self-sacrifice. In the best of our pair-bonds, in moments of ecstasy and in quieter hours of simple companionship, we have intimations of immortality—our practical immortality here, through our children and their children's children as our species moves, a tidal wave of billions now, through time and space—but also of that something more. In those moments perhaps we return to a place deeper than rainforest shadows and brighter than savanna suns, soul-full beings bearing the indelible imprint—forever after—of the passionate primates we've become.

NOTES

✳

Introduction: A Journey of Discovery

1. Bernard Campbell, ed., *Sexual Selection and the Descent of Man, 1871–1971,* index under Polygamy and Polygyny; F. M. Christensen, *Pornography: The Other Side,* 6–7; Jared Diamond, *The Third Chimpanzee: The Evolution and Future of the Human Animal,* 93–94; Helen Fisher, *Anatomy of Love: The Natural History of Monogamy, Adultery, and Divorce,* 66–71; Robert Jay Russell, *The Lemur's Legacy: The Evolution of Power, Sex, and Love,* chap. 4, "Inequality in the Puddle Where Sex Was Born"; Donald Symons, *The Evolution of Human Sexuality,* chap. 7, "The Desire for Sexual Variety"; Edward O. Wilson, *On Human Nature,* 124–126.

2. Harville Hendrix, *Getting the Love You Want: A Guide for Couples,* 68.

1. Deluxe-Model Apes

1. John MacKinnon, *The Ape Within Us,* 90.

2. Jane Goodall, *In the Shadow of Man,* index under Termite Fishing, Toolmaking, Tool-using.

3. Geoffrey H. Bourne, *Primate Odyssey,* 72–73, 258; MacKinnon, chaps. 1 and 2.

4. Bourne, 190; Fisher, *Anatomy of Love,* 126–28; Dian Fossey, *Gorillas in the Mist,* 10–11; MacKinnon, 63, 215–16; Carl Sagan and Ann Druyan, *Shadows of Forgotten Ancestors: A Search for Who We Are,* 321.

5. Bourne, 228; Frances J. White, "Social Organization of Pygmy Chimpanzees," esp. 204, in Paul G. Heltne and Linda A. Marquardt, *Understanding Chimpanzees;* Russell, chap. 7, "Mouse Lemur Mother Love," esp. 113 ff., and chap. 8, "Sex and the Single Lemur," esp. 130ff.

6. Robert Ardrey, *The Hunting Hypothesis: A Personal Conclusion Concerning the Evolutionary Nature of Man,* "The Hunting Hypothesis, Paradise Lost, and the Pliocene Intervention"; Bourne, 178, 184, 190–92, 195, 214, 223; Campbell, 45; Irven Devore, chap. 9, "The Evolution of Human Society," esp. 303–5, in J. F. Eisenberg and Wilton S. Dillon, eds., *Man and Beast: Comparative Social Behavior;* Fisher, *Anatomy of Love,* 197; Wilson, chap. 4, "Emergence," esp. 80–88; Desmond Morris, *The Naked Ape: A Zoologist's Study of the Human Animal,* 179–80—the importance of male cooperation.

7. Ardrey, *The Hunting Hypothesis,* 64–72, 88–95, and *The Social Contract,* 166–73; Bourne, 161, 190–93, 223; Campbell, "Man for All Seasons,"

esp. 45–46, 260–61, in his *Sexual Selection and the Descent of Man;* Morris, *The Naked Ape,* 146–48. An additional factor in the "patriarchizing" of primate societies is the scarcity of food resources. See Brian M. Fagan, *The Journey from Eden: The Peopling of Our World,* chap. 4, "The Savanna Homeland."

8. The primatologist Frans De Waal has shown that chimpanzees are profoundly political. See his *Chimpanzee Politics: Power and Sex Among Apes.* Others have shown that similar political structures and dynamics occur in other primate societies. See, for example, Russell, chap. 8, "Sex and the Single Lemur."

9. Ardrey, *African Genesis: A Personal Investigation into the Animal Origins and Nature of Man,* 134–37; Ardrey, *The Hunting Hypothesis,* 88–92; Ardrey, *The Social Contract,* 166–73; Bourne, 70, 190–92, 195, 242, 408; Fisher, *Anatomy of Love,* 198–99; Goodall, *In the Shadow of Man,* 158, 170, 173ff.; Goodall, *Through a Window: My Thirty Years with the Chimpanzees of Gombe,* 127 and chap. 11, "Sons and Mothers"; Morris, *The Naked Ape,* 22; Wilson, 126ff.

10. Suehisa Kuroda, "Developmental Retardation and Behavioral Characteristics of Pygmy Chimpanzees," esp. 192, and Frances J. White, "Social Organization of Pygmy Chimpanzees," in Heltne and Marquardt.

11. USE TOOLS: Bourne, index under Tools; Goodall, *In the Shadow of Man,* index under Termite Fishing, Toolmaking, and Tool-using; Heltne and Marquardt, index under Tool use; Ramona and Desmond Morris, *Men and Apes,* 246–50; CREATE CULTURE: Ardrey, *The Social Contract,* 129; Heltne and Marquardt, xii, 10; Morris and Morris, 225–27; VEGETABLES AND MEAT: Ardrey, *The Hunting Hypothesis,* "The Pliocene Intervention"; Goodall, *In the Shadow of Man,* index under Hunting Techniques, Predatory Behaviors, Feeding Behavior; Heltne and Marquardt, index under Diet; Morris, *The Naked Ape,* 20; MEDICINAL HERBS: Heltne and Marquardt, Richard W. Wrangham and Jane Goodall, "Chimpanzee Use of Medicinal Herbs"; TEACH THEIR CHILDREN: Frans De Waal, *Peacemaking Among Primates,* 76–78, 257; Goodall, *In the Shadow of Man,* 171; Goodall, *Through a Window,* 33ff., 112, 118, 122; HONOR GOOD MOTHERS: Goodall, *In the Shadow of Man,* chap. 7, "Flo's Sex Life"; Goodall, *Through a Window,* 6, 33, 90; ALPHA MALES WITH CHARACTER: Ardrey, *The Social Contract,* chap. 4, "The Alpha Fish"; De Waal, *Peacemaking Among Primates,* 48–55; Goodall, *In the Shadow of Man,* chap. 10, "The Hierarchy"; Goodall, *Through a Window,* chap. 5, "Figan's Rise," and chap. 6, "Power"; WARRIORS AND HUNTERS: De Waal, *Peacemaking Among Primates,* index under Food-Sharing; Fisher, *Anatomy of Love,* 134–35; Goodall, *In the Shadow of Man,* index under Sharing Food; DEEP BONDS OF FRIENDSHIP: De Waal, *Chimpanzee Politics,* index under Coalitions; Goodall, *In the Shadow of Man,* index under Friendships; Goodall, *Through a Window,* 3, 49, 56–57.

12. Michael P. Ghiglieri, "Hominid Sociobiology and Hominid Social Evolution," 372–73, 374ff., in Heltne and Marquardt,.

13. Diamond, chap. 1, "A Tale of Three Chimps," esp. the graph on 21.

14. This becomes clear when we compare the work of brain researchers such as Paul MacLean and the work of others, as reported, for instance, by Anne Moir and David Jessel, with primatological and anthropological studies (Robert Pool and Helen Fisher's, for example) about the behavioral differences between primate males and females, including humans. It also emerges when we track our different male and female aptitudes and physiques in relationship to theories about the evolution of our work role specializations as men and women. For an example of this convergence, see Helen Fisher's *Anatomy of Love,* chap. 10, "Why Can't a Man Be More Like a Woman?" As anthropologist William Howells reminds us, although there are arguments within the community of scholars about the exact contours of our evolution and some of the causal factors, ". . . each new find carries an ever bigger load of satisfaction and information as it takes its place in the whole landscape of our knowledge. And the highways in this landscape have been found—that is the significant change from the old days." (William Howells, *Getting Here: The Story of Human Evolution,* xiii.)

2. Beyond Therapy

1. It seems clear to me, based on years of counseling and on my own life experience, that if a couple has exhausted all other reasonable alternatives and they are still miserable with each other, they need to separate. Fiftieth anniversaries—in and of themselves—are not badges of triumph.

2. PARALLEL MARRIAGES: Harville Hendrix, *Getting the Love You Want,* 68; 5 percent HAPPY: Hendrix, ibid., 68. Other relationship specialists are slightly more optimistic—for example, Jonathan Kramer and Diane Dunaway, *Why Men Don't Get Enough Sex and Women Don't Get Enough Love,* 9 (19 percent).

3. Some studies suggest that 20 percent of all Americans—married or unmarried—don't want sex at all: Lynn Rosellini, "Sexual Desire," *U.S. News and World Report,* July 6, 1992.

4. Fisher, *Anatomy of Love,* 85–86. The studies cited include an early 1980s survey done by *Cosmopolitan* in which 72 percent of married men and 54 percent of married women reported being sexually unfaithful to their partners. *Marriage and Divorce Today* backed up this finding with the results of its own survey, published June 1, 1987, in which it reported that 70 percent of all Americans admit having engaged in extramarital affairs. More conservative figures were obtained by the more recent University of Chicago survey published in late 1994. See *The University of Chicago Magazine,* October 1994, "Sex by the Numbers."

5. Diamond, 85–86.

6. Diamond, 94; Fisher, *Anatomy of Love,* 87–97; for a somewhat different interpretation, see Symons, index under Coolidge Effect.

7. Fisher, *Anatomy of Love,* chap. 5, "Blueprint for Divorce," esp. 109ff. Also, see index under Four-Year Itch, and United Nations, Statistical Office of.

8. Robin Fox, "Alliance and Constraint: Sexual Selection in the Evolution of Human Kinship Systems," esp. 284ff., in Campbell.

9. Anthony Storr, *Human Destructiveness,* chap. 1, "The Nature of Human Aggression," esp. 10–13, 21.

10. John Bradshaw, *Healing the Shame that Binds You,* vii–ix, chap. 1, "The Many Faces of Shame"; Robert Karen, "Shame," *The Atlantic Monthly,* February 1992; Michael Lewis, *Shame: The Exposed Self,* 2, 11, 23–25, 30–31.

11. Diamond, 96–97; Fisher, *Anatomy of Love,* index under Jealousy; Symons, index under Sexual Jealousy, esp. 112–13, 115, 123, 131–32, 207.

12. MORALISTIC AGGRESSION: Campbell, 285–307; Goodall, In the Shadow of Man, chap. 12, "The Infant," chap. 13, "The Child," chap. 14, "The Adolescent," chap. 18, "Mother and Child"; Goodall, Through a Window, chap. 4, "Mothers and Daughters"' Storr, Human Aggression, 46; Wilson, chap. 5, "Aggression." MEN'S SENSITIVITY TO WOMEN'S AGGRESSION: The literature in this area is extensive, but see, for example, Robert Moore and Douglas Gillette, The King Within: Accessing the King in the Male Psyche, 145, 203, 204–5, 280–81, and relevant notes.

13. Fisher, *Anatomy of Love,* chap. 10, "Why Can't a Man Be More Like a Woman?"; Symons, see note 16 below. Also, see chap. 1, note 9 of the present work.

14. "... mating requires that the female partner be subdominant," in Campbell, 292; Kalman Glantz and John K. Pearce, *Exiles From Eden: Psychotherapy From an Evolutionary Perspective,* 114, 125, 155–59; Goodall, *Through a Window,* chap. 11, "Sons and Mothers," esp. 112, 116–17, for how chimpanzees work this male emotional danger through; Konrad Lorenz, *On Aggression,* 104; Paul MacLean, *The Triune Brain in Evolution: Role in Paleocerebral Functions,* 321–25, 340, 356, 363, 373, 375; Storr, *Human Aggression,* 69, 70ff.

15. Diamond, chap. 4, "The Science of Adultery"; Fisher, *Anatomy of Love,* index under Reproductive Strategies; Glantz and Pearce, chap. 9, "The Reproductive Strategy of the Male"; Symons, 228ff.

16. The more accurate terms are *proximate causation* and *ultimate causation.* See Symons, 7–9, and index under Proximate causal analyses, and Ultimate causal analyses. Also see Robert A. Wallace, *The Genesis Factor,* en toto.

17. Christensen, 3–5; Symons, index under Sexual arousal—by visual stimuli.

18. Symons, 187–91.

19. Robin Fox, "Alliance and Constraint: Sexual Selection in the Evolution of Human Kinship Systems," 308–27, in Campbell. Marriage cements a man's bonds to the older and more powerful males and gives him access to practical immortality. The health, youth, and beauty of his partner signal her reproductive value. Also see Fisher, *Anatomy of Love,* 318, note 15.

20. "Options" for a woman ultimately means bearing and raising children. This powerful desire is wired into human females at the savanna time level of our primate patterns. It does not signify laziness or childishness. It *is* reinforced, however, by the selective pressures on women in their evolutionary past to be childlike in important ways, including a propensity to be economically dependent, as we'll see. See chap. 1, note 9 of the present work.

21. This is one of the implications of all primatological work. Jane Goodall and Frans De Waal have both stressed the continuity between the minds of apes and human beings. For a specialized treatment of this topic, see Adrian Desmond's *The Ape's Reflection,* en toto, and Michael Corballis's *The Lopsided Ape: Evolution of the Generative Mind,* en toto, but especially chap. 1, "Are Humans Unique?"

22. Robin Fox, "Alliance and Constraint: Sexual Selection in the Evolution of Human Kinship Systems," 327, in Campbell.

3. How We Got This Way: The Three Layers of Our Primate Patterns

1. De Waal, *Peacemaking Among Primates,* 171–72.

2. Diamond, 27.

3. Ibid., 28.

4. De Waal, *Peacemaking Among Primates,* 175–76, 181, 227; Heltne and Marquardt, 152, 176, 184, 192.

5. See note 11, chap. 1, the present work. GRIEVE OVER DEAD LOVED ONES: Goodall, *Through a Window,* 196; WARFARE: Goodall, ibid., chap. 10, "War"; ADULT ORPHANS: See note 24, this chapter; HUG, KISS: De Waal, *Peacemaking Among Primates,* 43, 79; Fisher, *Anatomy of Love,* 137; SELF-AWARENESS: Numerous studies have confirmed a very humanlike self-awareness in chimpanzees and gorillas. See, for example, De Waal, *Peacemaking Among Primates,* 83–87.

6. It's important to remember as we proceed through the text and the notes that it is now possible to plausibly reconstruct our probable evolutionary trajectory by combining the extensive data from a number of different fields. Reconstructing our past involves careful detective work. It's often like piecing together an enormously complicated jigsaw puzzle. There *are* those who have written rather uninformed accounts, accounts colored more by their particular gender ideologies than by serious research. The fact is, our evolutionary past is *not* up for grabs: we can't make it anything we wish it to be for the sake of grinding present-day axes. I have tried to be careful and inclusive in offering the evolutionary scenario that many scholars and researchers from many different fields tend to favor. In some cases, I have synthesized what seemed to me to be converging lines of evidence. In most cases, the majority of this synthesizing work has already been done. Some of the fields that are represented in this growing convergence of evidence about our evolutionary past are: primatology (especially the study of the great apes, "living fossils" of our ancient ancestors); physical anthropology; evolutionary biology; the anthropological study of modern hunter-gatherer peoples; the "new anthropology" in general; mate selection studies; sexology; sociobiology; brain and hormonal research; and various schools of psychology. Because of rapid advances in knowledge in these and other fields (including genetics), we now have a vast wealth of information before us. There are still many mysteries to be solved, but we are well on our way to understanding *how* we came to be who and what we are as human societies and as men and women, and *why*. With these things in mind, let's move ahead to reconstruct at least the outlines of our human evolution and the three layers of our primate patterns.

Ardrey, *The Hunting Hypothesis,* 34–35; Richard G. Klein, *The Human Career: Human Biological and Cultural Origins,* 89, 99; D. Tab Rasmussen, *The Origin and Evolution of Humans and Humanness,* 9–15.

7. WEAPONS: Ardrey, *The Hunting Hypothesis,* 35, 45; Fisher, *Anatomy of Love,* 136–37; TEETH: Ardrey, ibid., 41, 45; Fisher, ibid., 136–37; Klein, 99; Rasmussen, 5–8.

8. Fisher, *Anatomy of Love,* 125; William Howells, *Getting Here: The Story of Human Evolution,* 47; Klein, 73ff., 90.

9. Ardrey, *The Hunting Hypothesis,* 93; De Waal, *Peacemaking Among Primates,* index under Food Sharing—among chimpanzees; Fisher, *Anatomy of Love,* 128–29, 134–35; Goodall, *In the Shadow of Man,* index under Hunting Techniques, Sharing Food; Goodall, *Through a Window,* index under Chimpanzees—food: baboons and monkeys hunted; Sagan and Druyan, 286.

10. De Waal, *Peacemaking Among Primates,* 48ff.; Fisher, *Anatomy of Love,* 219–24; Goodall, *In the Shadow of Man,* chap. 10, "The Hierarchy," and chap. 15, "Adult Relationships."

11. This depends on the exact stage of evolution of the society as well as its ecological niche. It may be that there was a time in which our ancestors followed the gorilla-like pattern of male exogamy. At a later stage in our evolution, we almost certainly developed the male-retention patterns of the chimpanzees and bonobos. Whatever tendencies in this direction we exhibited in our jungle time, conditions on the savannas forced us to adopt a male-retention pattern. Fox, "Alliance and Constraint," in Campbell, 307ff. Fox notes on pp. 290, 299 that "uncontrolled" males were driven out of the group; Heltne and Marquardt, 372–76.

12. Fox, ibid., 307ff.; Goodall, *Through a Window,* 198; Heltne and Marquardt, 372–76.

13. Though some chimpanzees and bonobo males and females develop special friendships, especially when the female is in estrus, inter-gender closeness is rare. Most friendships are between members of the same sex. Bonobos do present a picture of more frequent inter-gender affiliation than do common chimpanzees. (See article by Francis J. White, "Social Organization of Pygmy Chimpanzees," esp. 172, in Heltne and Marquardt.) One way of estimating the degree of inter-gender closeness is by studying the size difference between male and female canine teeth. A greater size difference indicates relative "sexual dimorphism," and sexual dimorphism usually suggests intense male competition for females. Intense male competition for females implies that males and females are not living in settled pairs. Pair-bonding among human ancestors would have reduced inter-male competition. This would have tended to reduce the size of male canine teeth, since the canine teeth of primate species—like the tusks of walruses—have developed primarily as weapons in inter-male squabbles for breeding privileges. The evidence from our earliest jungle days is mixed in terms of the sexual dimorphism of canine teeth. However, later savanna stages show a marked reduction in the size of these male teeth (although other evidence indicates that the sexual dimorphism in dentition was reduced through the *enlargement* of female canines). See Rasmussen, 5–9, 22.

14. Fisher, *Anatomy of Love,* 133, 137, 155–56, 330; Goodall, *Through a Window,* 86–90.

15. Campbell, 166–71.

16. While there is this tendency, it is not always the case that females prefer the generally older, more mature, and certainly more powerful alphas and their henchmen. Primate females do a lot of sneaking off with younger, and, to them, more attractive males. Nevertheless, the literature supporting female preference for alphas is extensive. See, for example, De Waal, *Chimpanzee Politics,* 175; Fisher, *Anatomy of Love,* 47; Symons, index under Sexual Attractiveness—in ancestral hominids, political and economic prowess and, sex differences in effects of status on.

17. Fox, op. cit., 290; De Waal, *Chimpanzee Politics,* 167–70; Goodall, *Through a Window,* 54–56.

18. De Waal, *Chimpanzee Politics,* 167–70, 175–79; De Waal, *Peacemaking Among Primates,* 81–83; Goodall, *Through a Window,* 60.

19. Females and males among modern chimpanzees and bonobos are both economically self-sufficient. That is, they do their own gathering of fruits and vegetable matter. Both fish for termites, but the females do much more of this than the males. At the same time, there is a fair amount of food-sharing behavior, which sets the stage for a certain amount of interdependence. In addition, since it is the males who hunt, the females *are* dependent "economically" upon them in the limited sense of meat acquisition. Also, it is the males who scout out new food sources. In this limited sense, too, chimpanzee females are economically dependent on males. (See Fisher, *Anatomy of Love,* 207; Goodall, *Through a Window,* 118.)

20. De Waal, *Peacemaking Among Primates,* 211; Goodall, *In the Shadow of Man,* 153; Goodall, *Through a Window,* 88.

21. Goodall, Through a Window, 86–89.

22. De Waal, *Chimpanzee Politics,* 161; De Waal, *Peacemaking Among Primates,* 204; Dian Fossey, *Gorillas in the Mist,* 88, 188–89; Goodall, *In the Shadow of Man,* 180–82.

23. De Waal, *Chimpanzee Politics,* chap. 2, "Two Power Take-overs," esp. 104–5, 116, 124–26, 137–38, 144; Campbell, 291.

24. Campbell, 165–74, 291; De Waal, *Chimpanzee Politics,* 124–25; Helen Fisher, *The Sex Contract: The Evolution of Human Behavior,* 100; Fossey, 61; Goodall, *In the Shadow of Man,* 230; Goodall, *Through a Window,* 197–98, 202–3; Goodall, lecture at the Chicago Academy of Sciences symposium, "Understanding Chimpanzees: Diversity and Survival," December 11–15, 1991.

25. Fisher, *Anatomy of Love,* 182 and note; Heltne and Marquardt, 164; AN ARBOREAL ORIGIN FOR: MacKinnon, 108; A CHARACTERISTIC OF JUVENILE (NEOTENOUS) BONOBOS: Heltne and Marquardt, 192.

26. Campbell, 248; Fisher, *Anatomy of Love,* 180; MacKinnon, 114; Desmond Morris, *Intimate Behavior,* chap. 2, "Invitations to Sexual Intimacy," esp. 62–63; Symons, index under Physical attractiveness, and 192–94; Wallace, 86.

27. The reason for the extraordinarily large penis of the human male is still a mystery. Why should it have evolved this way? There are two basic theories. The first is that it serves as a method of inter-male aggressive display, and the second is that it contributed to female sexual satisfaction and thereby helped cement our emerging pair-bonds. In this case, it would also have served as female-directed display: "Look at the pleasure I can give you!" The first theory is argued by Jared Diamond (see Diamond, 75–76). It seems to be supported by what primatologists know about the erect penile displays of monkeys whose purpose is to intimidate other males. (See MacLean, 169–71, 214, 233.) The second theory is put forward by Helen Fisher (Fisher, *Anatomy of Love,* 177–78). In my view, there's no reason both could not be true. Often, evolutionarily acquired features are the result of complex convergences of selective forces—both natural and sexual. The argument for the development of large penises in human males for the sake of sexually satisfying females does have the advantage, in my opinion, of keying into another sexual mystery of our species—the difficulty many women have in achieving orgasm. The large penis may be, in part, nature's attempt to solve this problem. See the following note. (Also, see Fisher's commentary on penis length, *Anatomy of Love,* 177–78.)

28. The problems associated with female orgasm and sexual positions present complex evolutionary puzzles. But they are of much more than intellectual interest, for they can easily wreak havoc in a couple's sex life and offer grounds for mutual frustration and blame. A man may feel that his partner is exasperatingly "sexually inhibited" because she has difficulty having orgasms, and a woman may blame her male partner for being "clumsy" and "uncaring" when he tries to bring her to climax. The real problem, from my perspective, whatever its interpersonal dimensions, is fundamentally biological, a product of our evolutionary heritage as males and females. Here, I would like to present the latest thinking about the nature and evolution of female orgasm and the difficulties associated with it for both men and women.

When we come to consider this complex issue in our sexual lives together, several questions arise. These questions are interrelated, and as yet the answers to them are not definitive. I'm going to start from the premise that orgasm in the human female *is* a problem—one that is neither *her* fault nor *his* responsibility. It is not grounds for either gender to shame the other. Rather, looking at the problem as an expression of our male and female primate heritage is grounds for mutual *empathy*. And mutual empathy is the basis for sexual openness and giving.

Simply put, the basis of the problem is that men—and their penises—are made primarily for rear entry intercourse, while women—and their vaginas—are caught between a rear and a frontal-entry design. Evolution has tried to adapt both the woman's anatomy and the man's penis for this profoundly dissatisfying situation.

Given the fact that a variety of studies have consistently shown that large numbers of women have a great deal of difficulty experiencing orgasm (and that some never do), certainly during penetration (Hite, Kinsey, and others; see Elaine Morgan's *The Descent of Woman,* 76), several interrelated questions present themselves. The first is: Is the female orgasm what biologists call an "artifact," that is, a function borrowed in vestigial form from the other gender, and which mimics the vital functioning of a process in that gender? Secondly, does the female orgasm arise from an *anatomical* artifact—namely the clitoris—a cross-gender vestige of the fully functioning penis? Men have nipples that have no biological function under most circumstances. *Women's* nipples are the very source of life for their infants. The clitoris, whatever else it may be, does not have the life-giving function of the male penis, its homologue—which is obviously essential to the reproductive process of our species. Donald Symons, with impressive evidence, argues that both the clitoris and female orgasm are, indeed, artifacts (Symons, chap. 3, "The Female Orgasm: Adaptation or Artifact").

A third question, even more potentially disheartening for women, is: Is female orgasm not only irrelevant to the reproductive process but also a *danger* to it: Is it *dys*functional? Masters and Johnson believe it actually reduces the possibility of insemination by pushing the injected semen out of the vagina (Symons, 92). Helen Fisher, however, claims that new evidence which suggests that female orgasm helps *retain* semen in the vaginal cavity (*The Anatomy of Love,* 183 and note 22). If this were true, female orgasm *would* indeed have a reproductive value. But if female orgasm were *dysfunctional* it would support the idea that it is an artifact.

A fourth question arises in connection with the first three: Is there evidence for female orgasm in nonhuman primates? If there were, it might argue for a reproductive function for *human* female orgasm, and rescue it from artifact, or worse, dysfunctional status. Some primatologists *do* report evidence of female orgasm in nonhuman primates—rhesus monkeys, chacma baboons, stumptail monkeys, and chimpanzees (Fisher, *The Sex Contract,* 33; Herant Katchadourian, ed., *Human Sexuality: A Comparative and Developmental Perspective,* 53ff., Symons, 78–83). But according to some observers, it cannot be *proven* that female "clutching reactions" and other signs of excitement in these animals are, in fact, *orgasms;* they may simply be symptoms of high states of arousal (Symons, 80–82). The only *compelling* evidence for female orgasm in nonhuman primates comes from *captive* individuals which have been exposed to prolonged and direct stimulation of the clitoris or clitoral area. This exposure was either administered experimentally by humans or it was obtained by the animals themselves through uncharacteristically long-duration genital rubbing with other animals, a situation possible only under captive conditions and never seen in the wild (Symons, 82–83). These studies, then, would seem to argue *against* the natural occurrence of female orgasm in nonhuman primates. If it does not occur naturally, it probably has little or no reproductive value. This would once again support the idea that, even if not dysfunctional, primate female orgasm *is* an artifact.

And yet, Helen Fisher and others argue that, even if it seldom, or never, occurs in nonhuman primates, female orgasm *does* occur in humans often enough to suggest that, at least in us, it *does* have reproductive value. According to Fisher, this reproductive value is its encouragement of human pair-bonding (Fisher, *Anatomy of Love,* 183). Female orgasm (whether or not it was *originally* an artifact) evolved in humans as an aid to nature's opportunistic attempt to graft an instinct for couple-formation onto an essentially promiscuous species. It pushed both ancestral males and females in the direction of sexual faithfulness—at least for a long-enough period of time to ensure that their children would be weaned and standing on their own two feet (Fisher, *Anatomy of Love,* 153). This is the essence of the sexual satisfaction theory of large penis size with its implications for female orgasm—mentioned in note 27, above. As Fisher puts it, "Men like women to climax because it reassures them that their partner is gratified and perhaps less inclined to seek sex elsewhere." (Fisher, *Anatomy of Love,* 183.) And, as we'll see, female sexual fidelity was an essential ingredient in the dynamics of the pair-bond experiment of our savanna time ancestors. Fisher goes on, "And for a woman orgasm is a journey, an altered state of consciousness, another reality that escalates to chaos, then elicits feelings of calm, tenderness, and attachment—which tend to cement a relationship with a partner" (ibid., 183).

But even if Fisher is right, we still have the problem of the female orgasm's elusiveness. To grapple with this difficulty we have to ask a fifth question: What is the true site of the neurological trigger for female orgasm? Is it the ventral vaginal wall, as some would have us believe; or is it the clitoris? While some studies indicate that stimulation of the front vaginal wall provides the deepest, most "global" female orgasm (Morgan, 92–93), the majority of current studies report that clitoral stimulation is the central trigger (Morgan, 88). Desmond Morris in *The Naked Ape* supports the clitoral hypothesis (Morris, 74). If the clitoris *is* the main trigger for female orgasm it would explain many women's preference for face-to-face intercourse; the rhythmic thrusting of the male penis and the rubbing of the male pubic bone against the clitoral area provide the most direct stimulation of the clitoris possible during penetration. Indeed, probably related to this situation in women, primatologists report that bonobo females, with their frontally tilted vaginas, prefer front-to-front, or ventro-ventral copulation to rear-entry, dorso-ventral (Heltne and Marquardt, 179). Human females, we recall, also have frontally-tilted vaginas. Bonobo males, however, prefer to penetrate females from behind, presumably because this is how they achieve the greatest visual and genital stimulation (Heltne and Marquardt, 179). This also seems to be true for many human males.

If we assume the correctness of the clitoral theory for human females, we must assume that nonhuman primate females (with the possible exception of bonobos) either do not experience orgasm during copulation (since their clitorises are *not* stimulated by rear-entry penetration) or that, if they *do*, they have a different site for orgasmic stimulation. That different site would almost certainly be the frontal wall of their vaginas, since this is the surface that receives the direct frictional force of the thrusting penis. If we continue to hold to the clitoral theory for humans, in light of this assumption for nonhuman primate females, then it would mean that the center for orgasmic stimulation has changed during the course of our evolution from the ventral vaginal wall to the clitoris.

This is exactly Elaine Morgan's argument. She claims that nonhuman primate females do, indeed, experience orgasm from the rear-entry position through the penis's vigorous contact with the ventral vaginal wall. Morgan claims that vaginal orgasm is, in fact, the ancestral, originally most natural, and still most deeply satisfying orgasm for women (Morgan, 92). But, she says, when the vagina evolved a frontal-entry position in our female ancestors, the hitherto superfluous clitoris (Symons's anatomical artifact) was pressed into service as a secondary—and problematic—source of female orgasm. The advantage that the frontal-entry vagina had—and has—both in bonobos and human beings, is that it *does* make sex a personal experience. (As we'll see, this is a mixed blessing for men, many of whom prefer *less* personal sexual contact.) Hence, it could, as Fisher suggests, powerfully encourage nature's ad hoc pair-bonding efforts, ultimately on behalf of our children. But, even so, the reason the clitoris as the central site for orgasmic stimulation in women is problematic is that it is still difficult to stimulate it sufficiently, at least during intercourse, to cause female orgasm. It's even difficult, as many men and women have found, to get the desired results by oral or manual stimulation. Morgan believes the mechanics just aren't right.

I agree. Either female orgasm is so difficult because it really *is* nonessential for reproduction, consequently does *not* occur in the natural state among nonhuman primates, *is* an artifact, and only became prominent as a part of mating patterns in those species that required more personal relationships between males and females (i.e., bonobos and humans, for somewhat different reasons)—*or* it is a way of attempting to mimic the original, naturally occurring vaginal orgasm, once the vagina had gotten out of sync with the angle of the penis thrust.

The most sensitive area of the male penis is the underside, especially the area just under the penis head. *If* we assume that in our quadrupedal rear-entry past, female as well as male orgasm was the rule rather than the exception, and *if* we assume that the ventral wall, with its washboard surface, was the original site of female orgasmic stimulation, then the most sensitive area of the male penis rubbed against the most sensitive area of the female vagina—and mutual orgasmic satisfaction occurred with some regularity. But the vagina's migration to a frontal-entry position changed this; the *most* sensitive area of the penis then rubbed against the *least* sensitive area of the vagina—the rear wall. In the face-to-face position the *male* could still experience orgasm, though without the aid of the stimulating washboard surface of the female's frontal wall, but the *female* had to rely on the anatomically problematic stimulation of her clitoris. *If* the male, even with the buttock-simulating visual cue of the female's enlarged breasts, still preferred the rear-entry position, he could contact the female's washboard surface, but at the wrong angle. The vagina's frontal wall was now bent forward, while the male penis was turned backward. This left the female at a tremendous disadvantage in terms of sexual satisfaction. Yet this mechanical problem—both for male and female, but worse for the female—must have been of less survival value, less reproductive significance, than nature's attempts to get us to pair-bond through trying to encourage face-to-face copulation with its creation of the frontal-entry vagina. Nature was willing to sacrifice women's sexual satisfaction (and men's to a lesser extent) in the interests of rendering our relationships more personal.

Enter the enlarged penis in the human male. It seems to me that Fisher is right in claiming that an enlarged penis aided in providing ancestral women with greater sexual satisfaction in the front-to-front sexual positions by maximizing the pressure on the clitoral area—something the thin penises of the other apes could never do. But I also think the thicker penis could have evolved to do double duty: its greater width could also have increased the amount of contact with, hence stimulation of, the old site of female orgasm, the washboard surface of the ventral vaginal wall, in the rear-entry position. Perhaps more to the point, the enlarged penis increased the male's pleasure in his frequently preferred rear-entry position (Heltne and Marquardt, 179; Sagan and Druyan, 303–4). Perhaps the enlarged penis was a way of trying to work out a compromise between the old rear-entry position favored by many ancestral males and the new frontal-entry position favored by ancestral females.

Until researchers come up with indisputable proof one way or the other for female orgasm in nonhuman primates, my own opinion is that female orgasm, originally triggered by vigorous penis thrusts to the washboard surface of the ventral vaginal wall in nonhuman and ancestral human primates, was a frequent, if not universal, occurrence. Because of the rotation of the ancestral female vagina to a frontal position—a result both of the paedomorphic direction of our evolution in general (see chapter 8) and its interface with our need to form intimate pair-bonds in order to survive on the savannas—neither the ventral wall of the vagina nor the substitute clitoral region received sufficient stimulation. That loss of stimulation worked *against* the formation of pair-bonds—the very thing nature was attempting to encourage by inventing the frontal-entry vagina. (Actually, nature may have been *resurrecting* rather than *inventing* the frontal-entry vagina, since it is sometimes found in arboreal mammals.) The only way to try to fix this botched and conflicted scenario was to increase male penis size.

It still doesn't work very well in terms of affording mutual and simultaneous sexual satisfaction for both partners. But it *is* better than the alternative. It's also reason enough for men and women to be unshaming of themselves and each other about the mechanical difficulties of their sex lives together.

29. As we'll see, researchers from several different fields, including primatologists, physical anthropologists, evolutionary biologists, and social anthropologists, have come to the conclusion that we are a childlike species of ape—both physically and psychologically. Scientists don't fully understand the causes of our neotenous evolutionary trajectory. But they do know that two major forces played a part, the same two forces that have shaped everything else about us—natural selection and sexual selection. Natural selection has to do with forces in our environment that operate to encourage genetic change over time. Sexual selection has to do with the characteristics that each gender prefers in the other. The "selective breeding" that results from the choices our ancestors made about who they wanted to mate with constitute the sexual selection process.

We can compare the body structures of modern men and women and judge which gender was selected for more physically "immature" qualities. In addition, as we'll see in chapter 8, both men and women selected each other for childlike *psychological* qualities.

See John Hurrell Crook, "Sexual Selection, Dimorphism, and Social Organization in the Primates," esp. 249, 251, 273, in Campbell; Fisher, *Anatomy of Love*, 180; Fisher, *The Sex Contract*, 97; Glantz and Pearce, 106; Morris, *The Naked Ape*, 167.

30. Fisher, *Anatomy of Love*, index under Breasts; Fisher, *The Sex Contract*, 95–96; Morris, *Intimate Behavior*, 42, 52–58; for another explanation, see Rasmussen, 21–22. Rasmussen's idea is that the ancestral human female breast became permanently enlarged in order to simulate lactation, a signal to males other than her partner that she was infertile. Breast enlargement, then, along with silent ovulation (the masking of estrus), could have been an adaptation favoring the development of pair-bonds, since it could have had the effect of discouraging males outside the pair-bond from making sexual advances.

However, the majority of scientists seem to accept Desmond Morris's claim that enlarged female breasts were originally designed by nature (through sexual selection) to mimic buttocks. Buttocks are the primary visual cue for males in most primate species. With the movement of the vagina to a frontal-entry position, large female breasts would have aided face-to-face copulation among our ancestors by giving males buttocklike visual clues.

In my opinion, both factors could have played a part.

31. Rasmussen, 21–22.

32. Diamond, chap. 4, "The Science of Adultery," esp. 93–94; Fisher, *Anatomy of Love,* chap. 4, "Why Adultery?" and chap. 14, "Fickle Passion"; Glantz and Pearce, chap. 7, "The Reproductive Strategy of the Female," and chap. 9, "The Reproductive Strategy of the Male"; Symons, chap. 7, "The Desire for Sexual Variety"; Wallace, chap. 4, "Sexual Selection, Or Aren't Men Splendid?" esp. 77–78.

33. Christensen, 5; Kramer and Dunaway, 7—Men think about sex at least six times an hour.

34. Christensen, 72–73; Fisher, *Anatomy of Love,* 52–53; Heltne and Marquardt, 181—related to juvenile female bonobo sex drive; Symons, chap. 7, "The Desire for Sexual Variety," and chap. 8, "Copulation as a Female Service," and 106, 123, 288ff.

35. De Waal, *Chimpanzee Politics,* 95, chap. 2, "Two Power Take-overs," and chap. 3, "Restless Stability"; De Waal, *Peacemaking Among Primates,* 49–51.

36. Rasmussen, 6–8.

37. Ibid., 6–8; also see notes 7, 13, this chapter.

38. See note 8, this chapter.

39. See note 7, this chapter.

40. Goodall, *In the Shadow of Man,* index under Hunting Techniques; also see notes 6 and 7, chap. 1, the present work.

41. See note 12, chap. 2, the present work.

42. Fisher, *Anatomy of Love,* 107, 295–96.

43. Signs of this include the rise in promiscuous behavior, single-parent families, the economic self-sufficiency of women, and mutual gender isolation—in short, the breakdown of the pair-bonding strategy inherited from our savanna time, as well as the lifelong monogamy ideal from our civilization era. See Fisher, *Anatomy of Love,* 296–311.

44. Campbell, index under parental investment; Robert Trivers, "Parental Investment and Sexual Selection," 60, 141, in Campbell; Diamond, 70–71, 81, 89–90; Fisher, *Anatomy of Love,* 150; Goodall, *In the Shadow of Man,* 185–86; Heltne and Marquardt, 377; Symons, 213, 242.

45. While human fathering instincts are stronger than the fathering instincts of most other primates, compared to women's *mothering* instincts they are weak. See notes 44 and 49, this chapter. Many men report that their interest in investing time and energy in raising their children decreases when they feel pushed away by their mates. Most men's interest in parental investment, at least on an intensive level, seems significantly dependent on the quality of their relationships with their partners. Becoming involved fathers, contrary to their jungle time natures, was a central part of ancestral men's "sex contract with women."

46. Stevens, *Archetypes: A Natural History of the Self,* 121, chap. 4, "Archetypes and Behavior," chap. 9, "On the Frustration of Archetypal Intent," esp. 136–39, chap. 10, "Personal Identity and the Stages of Life," esp. 157ff.; Storr, *Human Aggression,* 69–70. Also see Farai Chideya et al., "Endangered Family," *Newsweek,* August 30, 1993; Irene Fast, *Gender Identity: A Differentiation Model,* 180–83; Nancy Gibbs, "Bringing Up Father," *Time,* June 28, 1993; Michele Ingrassia, "Daughters of Murphy Brown," *Newsweek,* August 2, 1993. Also see note 97, chap. 8, the present work.

47. Farai Chideya, op. cit.

48. Ibid.

49. Campbell, 310; Goodall, *In the Shadow of Man,* 185–87, chap. 4, "Mothers and Daughters," and chap. 11, "Sons and Mothers."

50. This is a painful factor in the lives of many young couples. I've worked with a number of women, and men and women together, who have reported that once the first baby was born the woman withdrew emotionally and sexually from her partner. This seems to be an innate drive to touch base with the foundational primate social bond—that between a mother and her child. (See note 49 above. Also see Russell, for example, 117.) The danger of a woman's allowing this most ancient primate pattern to play itself out in her relationship—with no conscious containment on her part—is that she will alienate her mate and use her children as substitute partners. The first danger arises because she runs straight into her own and her partner's savanna time primate patterns for pair-bonding. The second danger results in what psychologists call "inappropriate cross-generational bonding." Using children as substitute partners can be categorized as a form of child abuse. (See Alice Miller, *The Drama of the Gifted Child.* For an interpretation of this dynamic from a woman's perspective, see Anne Moir and David Jessel, *Brain Sex: The Real Difference Between Men and Women,* 143.)

51. Jungle time males and females, like modern chimpanzees, largely went their separate ways—the females grouped in their "horizontal" friendship and "auntie system" patterns and the males in their hierarchy coalitions, border patrols, and hunting parties. To the extent that our jungle time ancestors may have expressed some traits of the social organization of bonobos (though bonobos are not in our direct line of descent), at some point before our savanna time, males and females may have begun to associate more closely. See notes 9, chap. 1; notes 10, 13, 19, 23, 32, 40, 41, 44, 49, 63, and 65, this chapter. Also see Goodall, *In the Shadow of Man,* 185–87.

52. There are a number of theories that try to account for the development of bipedality in our ancestors. Some researchers believe we were "pre-adapted" for life on the savannas by a bipedal posture as we were emerging from our jungle time. See Howells, 47–51, 71–73; Klein, 181; Rasmussen, 9–15, 18–20.

53. Campbell, 336; Fisher, *Anatomy of Love,* 343—note 48; Klein, 172, 181–82; Rasmussen, 5–6.

54. Ardrey, *The Hunting Hypothesis,* 51–62, esp. 53–57.

55. Ibid., 17–22, 59; Fisher, *Anatomy of Love,* 146–47; Howells, 58, 92–93; Klein, 177, 182.

56. Ardrey, *The Hunting Hypothesis,* 107; Ardrey, *The Territorial Imperative* and other works by Ardrey (see bibliography); Campbell, 248; Fisher, *Anatomy of Love,* 194, 197, 199, 203, 207; Wilson, 107.

57. Ardrey, *The Hunting Hypothesis,* 65–66; Campbell, 307ff.; also see notes 6 and 7, chap. 1, and note 59, below, the present work.

58. See notes 6 and 7, chap. 1, the present work.

59. Ardrey, *The Hunting Hypothesis,* 66, 69, 71, 114; Morris, *The Naked Ape,* 22, 27, 31; Wilson, 84.

60. The American Museum of Natural History, *The First Humans: Human Origins and History to 10,000 B.C.,* 30–31; Fisher, *Anatomy of Love,* index under Consortships, Pair-bonding; Goodall, *Through a Window,* 95–96.

61. Campbell, 308ff.; also see note 17, this chapter.

62. Diamond, 77–84; Fisher, *Anatomy of Love,* 185–87, and as induced by infanticide, 160; Symons, 96–141, 129–41, 127–41, also 100, 106, 107; compared to the masking of ovulation in immature bonobo females—Takayoshi Kano, "Sexual Behavior of Pygmy Chimpanzees," in Heltne and Marquardt, esp. 180–87.

Like male penis size and the difficulties associated with female orgasm, the loss of estrus—or the masking of ovulation—in human females is a mystery. Several theories have been put forward to try to explain it. Jared Diamond summarizes the six major theories in vogue on pp. 79–82 of his *The Third Chimpanzee.* They are worth sketching here.

Theory #1: Concealed ovulation evolved in order to reduce inter-male competition for females on the savannas, where male cooperation became vital to group survival.

Theory #2: Concealed ovulation evolved in order to enhance the pair-bonds between individual men and women; it kept a man guessing about when a woman was fertile, and so kept him tied to her.

Theory #3: Concealed ovulation evolved in order to induce men to supply ancestral females with meat. Since in chimpanzee societies estrus females receive a disproportionate share of meat from hunting males, and since the main source of food on the savannas *was* meat, ancestral females who could hide their ovulation, and thereby keep males guessing about their fertility, could induce their potential benefactors to supply them with meat on a regular basis.

Theory #4: Concealed ovulation preyed on male uncertainty about paternity. It powerfully motivated a single ancestral male to stay close to a single ancestral female. If the male could not tell when his female was fertile, he could never neglect her, which he might be motivated to do if he knew her period of fertility. He might copulate with her—and supply her with meat—*only* when she was ovulating. Since ancestral females depended on ancestral males to supply them with meat, females had to hide their periods of fertility.

Theory #5: Concealed ovulation evolved in order to prevent infanticide on the part of rival males. In some primate societies males kill the offspring of other males in order to induce the females to come into estrus.

Theory #6: Concealed ovulation evolved in order to *reduce* the rate of impregnation.

It seems to me that theories 1–4 dovetail nicely, and probably represent converging environmental and social forces. Theories #5 and #6 seem farfetched and of little survival value to the species. However, it's possible that *all* of these theories are correct, and represent complex interfaces between a host of naturally and sexually selective pressures.

63. In the savanna environment that was encouraging the formation of pair-bonds anyway, (because of the economics of food resources and our growing territoriality,) the dawning realization that sex led to children reinforced ancestral pair-bonding. If a single male could supply enough meat for only a single female and her offspring—which was likely the case—with the realization that sex led to children, it became imperative for a male to know that the children he was provisioning at so much cost and risk to himself were his own. In order to provide as much security for himself as he could—about his own practical immortality—he needed to cement his ties to one female. See Diamond, 70–71, 81, 89; Fisher, *Anatomy of Love,* 167–69; Symons, 242.

64. Heltne and Marquardt, 372–73.

65. Campbell, index under Hunting; Fisher, *Anatomy of Love,* 129, 199, 203, 207; Goodall, *In the Shadow of Man,* index under Hunting Techniques; Sagan and Druyan, 291.

66. Fisher, *Anatomy of Love,* 135; Goodall, *In the Shadow of Man,* index under Sharing Food—meat.

67. Ardrey, *The Hunting Hypothesis,* "The Pliocene Intervention," esp. 51 ff.

68. Fisher, *Anatomy of Love,* 152–53.

69. Fisher, ibid., chap. 10, "Why Can't a Man Be More Like a Woman?" and 154–56, 158; Fisher, *The Sex Contract,* chapter titled "The Sex Contract."

70. Fisher, *Anatomy of Love,* 149–50, 153, 156–57; also see notes 6 and 7, chap. 1, the present work, and notes 53, 54, 65, 67, and 68, this chapter.

71. Campbell, 48; Fisher, *Anatomy of Love*, chap. 10, "Why Can't a Man Be More Like a Woman?" 199, 237; Noel Korn and Fred Thompson, eds., *Human Evolution: Readings in Physical Anthropology*, 72; MacKinnon, 212. Sagan and Druyan, 370; Symons, index under Division of Labor; also see note 9, chap. 1, the present work, and notes 44, 51, 58, 65, 72, this chapter. Also see Wilson, en toto but esp. 126 ff; and Wallace, en toto.

72. Fisher, *Anatomy of Love*, chap. 10, "Why Can't a Man Be More Like a Woman?" chap. 16, "Future Sex: Forward to the Past"; Moir and Jessel, en toto, but esp. chap. 7, "Hearts and Minds"; Sally Springer and Georg Deutsch, *Left Brain, Right Brain*, 217 ff., esp. 222–24; Wallace, chap. 5, "Are the Brains of Males and Females Different?"

73. The patchwork pair-bond relationship, though based on our ancient consortships, flew in the face of the much more usual jungle time pattern of promiscuity for both males and females.

74. Warren Farrell, *Why Men Are the Way They Are*, index under Fantasies; Glantz and Pearce, chap. 6, "On Gender," esp. 96–98, chap. 7, "The Reproductive Strategy of the Female," and chap. 9, "The Reproductive Strategy of the Male"; Symons, chap. 7, "The Desire for Sexual Variety."

75. Fisher, *Anatomy of Love*, index under !Kung Bushmen—adultery of.

76. Fisher, ibid., index under Jealousy, and 167–69; Symons, index under Sexual Jealousy—underpinning marriage.

77. Fisher, *Anatomy of Love*, index under Four-Year Itch, and 153–54.

78. Klein, GROWTH OF THE CRANIUM: *Australopithecus*—430–520 cc (p. 148); *Homo habilis*—510–750 cc, 2.5-2 mya, rapid expansion toward development of *Homo erectus* (p. 156); *Homo erectus*—brain increased from 850–900 cc to 1,000 cc, from 1.8 mya to 500,000 ya (p. 192); ARCHAIC *Homo sapiens*—1,000 cc to modern size between 500,000 ya to 130,000 ya (p. 224).

79. Campbell, 48, 54, 288–90; Corballis, 137–67, 235–38; Desmond, en toto; Howells, 45–46, 94–96, 118, 161.

80. Campbell, esp. 285–307.

81. Both the cause and the result of feeling superior to animals who seem to be able to modulate their drives for aggression and sexuality less well, and who seem to have less self-awareness than we do. I maintain that the attitude of disparaging the animal is comprehensive, and includes both the outer and the inner animals. If this attitude follows the psychological mechanism of projection, which it seems to me it does, we can both love and dislike our own inner animal indirectly by loving and disliking animals in the outer world. The fact that people generally prefer pets to wild animals indicates a similar attitude toward their own animal natures: they can afford to love *themselves* as long as *they're* "domesticated"; but they fear their own wildness. I might add, these attitudes apply equally to our feelings about the animal core of our partners.

82. De Waal, *Peacemaking Among Primates*, 183–86.

83. This is part of the principle of sexual selection mentioned earlier. See notes 16, 23, 24, 25, 26, 27, 28, 29, this chapter.

84. See note 29, this chapter.

85. See note 14, chap. 2, the present work. See also Moore and Gillette, *The King Within*, index under Mothers.

86. Campbell, 291; David Gilmore, *Manhood in the Making: Cultural Concepts of Masculinity*, 101, 103–4; In fact, we were both choosing each other for brains, among other things. Noel Korn and Fred Thompson, eds., *Human Evolution: Readings in Physical Anthropology*, 108–9; Wallace, 83; Morris, *Intimate Behavior*, 64; also see notes 16, 23, 24, 26, 27, 40, 57, 58, 63, 71, 72, 83, this chapter.

87. John Hurrell Crook, "Sexual Selection in Primates," esp. 274, in Campbell; Fisher, *Anatomy of Love*, 22; Morris, *Intimate Behavior*, 73, 99–101; Morris, *The Naked Ape*, chap. 7, "Comfort." Also see note 29, this chapter.

88. Fisher, *Anatomy of Love*, chap. 11, "Women, Men, and Power," esp. 218–19. Also see note 70, this chapter.

89. This is because women are generally less promiscuous than men, and much less driven by the desire for sexual variety, a desire that can easily lead to the formation of new pair-bonds. See notes 32, 33, 74, this chapter. Also see note 29. It is certain that men selected women who would be more or less sexually faithful. It could be that their selection of relatively childlike females—with childlike dependency needs—reinforced ancestral females' sexual loyalty.

90. Glantz and Pearce, 168–69; Symons, 228.

91. Shame and guilt seem to operate as reactions to moralistic aggression in many primate species. Aberrant behavior in group members is punished in chimpanzee societies by both males and females. The main enforcer in primate infancy is the mother. The primary enforcer for the overall community is the alpha male. See De Waal, *Chimpanzee Politics*, 124–25; Fisher, *Anatomy of Love*, 255–56; Goodall, *Through a Window*, 35–36. Also see Desmond, index under Self-awareness, and compare with Lewis, chap. 1–3.

92. Farrell, index under Marriage and Options.

93. Passive-aggressive behaviors are usually the result of a person's fear of expressing his or her aggressive feelings directly. See Moore and Gillette, *The Warrior Within: Accessing the Knight in the Male Psyche*, esp. chap. 7, "The Masochist: A Dishonest Warrior."

94. This pressure is easing somewhat because more women are working. However, many men are still the primary and even sole breadwinners for their families.

95. Depriving men of avenues for exercising their instinctual desires to protect and provide for women and children is enormously frustrating, especially to their savanna time primate patterns. Human males need to be able to compete for their place in the hierarchy—for their share of status and wealth—ultimately, females and access to their own practical immortality. Depriving men of opportunities to do this, through classism, racism, and other discriminatory systems of emotional and economic violence leads all

too often to violent acting out behavior on the part of the deprived. I can't help but note the vast numbers of young black males who fill our prisons. See Storr, *Human Destructiveness*, 10, 21.

96. Farrell, en toto, but esp. 228–29, 235–36, 360–63; index under Success and ego-fragility, Success Objects, Violence, women and men, Sexism, new.

97. The literature on codependency and its many manifestations is vast. See John Bradshaw's discussion of the relationship between codependency and shame in his *Healing the Shame That Binds You*, esp. 14.

98. Klein, 35 ff., 344, 397; Korn and Thompson, 50, 89, 102, 120–22, 395.

99. Fisher, *Anatomy of Love*, 284–85, 288–91; Symons, index under Marriage—as entailing economic cooperation, as entailing rights and duties.

100. Fisher, *Anatomy of Love*, 278–79, 284–85, 288–91. Also see her index under Monogamy—economic factors in, and Monogamy, permanent.

101. See chap. 8, the present work. The connection between our evolutionary heritage as a neotenous species and the emphasis on inner child work in current psychology occurred to me unexpectedly. Actually, psychologists have known for a long time that part of what many people seek in a mate is a substitute parent, and that we often turn our relationships into "repetition compulsion" reenactments of our early childhood patterns of relating to our parents and other caregivers, and siblings. Recognizing this and doing something about it—together—is the whole thrust of Harville Hendrix's Imago Therapy Work. See his *Getting the Love You Want: A Guide for Couples*.

102. Fisher, *Anatomy of Love*, 288–91.

103. It may be, as some commentators have suggested, that neurosis is an ever-present danger for an intelligent animal, almost as if the combination of neuronal complexity and the need and capacity for learned behavioral responses to social and other environmental factors were a setup for things to go wrong. I subscribe to this theory—that complexity, and flexibility of response—along with the need to acquire many behaviors through learning—open up increased opportunities for major perceptual mistakes and inappropriate behavioral responses. In terms of neurotic behavior in nonhuman primates specifically, see Desmond, 228; Morris and Morris, 169, 215–18, 222—on Harlow's experiments with rhesus monkeys. Also see Goodall, *Through a Window*, index under Passion, and Pom—face-dabbing, and chap. 10, "War."

104. See Norman O. Brown, *Life Against Death: The Psychoanalytic Meaning of History*, en toto (bibliography); and Herbert Marcuse, *Eros and Civilization: A Philosophical Inquiry into Freud*, en toto (bibliography).

105. Lonnie Barbach, *For Each Other: Sharing Sexual Intimacy*, index under Sexual Dysfunction, and Sexual Interest—lack of, boredom and, stored anger and, loss of, emotional trauma, relationship problems, sporadic desire; Lynn Rosellini, "Sexual Desire."

106. Sagan and Druyan, 375; note 104, this chapter. Also see Robert Moore and Douglas Gillette, *The Lover Within: Accessing the Lover in the*

Male Psyche, 139–40, and relevant notes, and 172. In addition, see Patricia Edmonds, "Pope's Hit List of Sins Is Likely to Fall on Deaf Ears," *USA Today,* October 1, 1993; Jeffrey L. Sheler, et al., "The Gospel on Sex," *U.S. News and World Report,* June 10, 1991.

107. See notes 104 and 106, above. Catholicism emphasizes the virginity ideal, while Protestantism encourages workaholism. These religious ideals, both with ancient pre-Christian roots, have thoroughly permeated our secular societies. They may even be, as Freud suggested, the bases for civilization itself.

108. If we accept Anthony Storr's understanding of the aggression-to-violence continuum (Storr, *Human Destructiveness,* 8, 10, 12, 13, 21) and put this together with the recognition that many men are profoundly sexually frustrated (Kramer and Dunaway, 7; Glantz and Pearce, chap. 9, "The Reproductive Strategy of the Male," and chap. 10, "Men on the Contemporary Scene"), we have a plausible explanation for at least *some male* violence. Also see Sagan and Druyan, 187.

109. It's a psychological truth that what we don't face about ourselves, and integrate into our conscious personalities, we will be forced (by ourselves) to face in the external world in an unintegrated—i.e., raw—form.

110. See note 43, this chapter.

111. See chapter 7, "War between the Sexes."

112. What those who shame usually fail to realize is that their victims will eventually be unable to accept further abuse. Inevitably, the victims of shaming will retaliate. I think it's possible that the higher incidence of rape and the actions of the Spur Posse, for example, *may* be extreme examples of male outrage at the attempted disempowerment of men *as* men. A measured male response is yet to emerge. Although the men's movement is now defunct in terms of large, public events, a part of its agenda, as expressed in weekly and monthly gatherings of men all over this country and in Europe was learning to cope with the radical feminist attack on men and maleness, per se. Organizations such as The Society of Free Men and the Men's Wellness Network are growing manifestations not only of male dissatisfaction with traditional forms of the oppression of men but also, in part, expressions of growing male outrage at radical feminist attacks. I believe that men in general are slow to confront female abusers because of biological and cultural factors which have favored their protector and provider roles. But if present trends continue, we can expect a massive, and much less reasonable, male backlash against the radical feminists.

113. Ardrey, *The Hunting Hypothesis,* 108.

4. Real Time: The Past in Our Relationship Present

1. This loss of motivation in our relationships fits with what we know about the stages of love. See Fisher, *Anatomy of Love,* 52–58; Hendrix, *Getting the Love You Want,* 68; also see note 6, chap. 1, the present work.

2. Goodall, *Through a Window,* chap. 11, "Sons and Mothers," esp. 118; Sagan and Druyan, 291.

3. Many men report feeling at a disadvantage vis-à-vis women in terms of sharing their feelings. Not only do many men have more difficulty in verbalizing what they feel; they may also be *unaware* of their emotions. Even when men *know* what they're feeling, they are often afraid to share freely with women. Glantz and Pearce write: "Most therapists today believe in fostering communication. And most therapists deplore the fact that men are so often less communicative than their female partners want them to be. Some degree of caution is necessary here. There may be good reasons why men don't communicate their feelings. One is that some of their feelings (e.g., desire for other women) would be unacceptable to their partners. Another is that certain negative feelings (e.g., fear, low self-confidence) might frighten their partners and/or cause them to lose the respect of other men." (Glantz and Pearce, 166); also see notes 12 and 14, chap. 2, and note 88, chap. 3, the present work.

4. See notes 59, 65, 66, 67, 68, 69, 70, 71, chap. 3, the present work.

5. See note 9, chap. 1, and notes 10, 13, 51, 71, chap. 3, the present work.

6. This is relative, though. There is a fair amount of play with infants and juveniles on the part of males, and males are frequently involved in exercising disciplinary or "containment" functions for the group as a whole, including females. It's also true that we *do* have the bonobo-like tendency for closer male emotional interactions with females (Frans De Waal, "Behavioral Contrasts between Bonobo and Chimpanzee," and Frances J. White, "Social Organization of Pygmy Chimpanzees," in Heltne and Marquardt.)

7. Fisher, *Anatomy of Love,* index under Serial Monogamy; Glantz and Pearce, chap. 9, "The Reproductive Strategy of the Male," esp. 151–52; Symons, index under Monogamy: as unnatural; note 77, chap. 3, the present work; JEALOUSY: note 76, chap. 3, the present work.

8. See notes 67, 68, 69, 70, chap. 3, the present work.

5. Predictable Passions: The Forms, Stages, and Chemistry of Love

1. Fisher, *Anatomy of Love,* 42.

2. Sagan and Druyan, op. cit., pp., 160–162, 290, 463—Note 6.

3. Fisher, *Anatomy of Love,* 41.

4. Sagan and Druyan, 224.

5. Ibid., 212—note 18; 224–25. Also see Paul Gray, "What Is Love?" *Time,* February 15, 1993.

6. Christensen, 3–4; Moir and Jessel, 106–7; Symons, index under Sexual Arousal—by nudes, by the sight of genitals, by visual stimuli.

7. Glantz and Pearce, 166–68; also see notes 23, 24, 86, chap. 3, the present work.

8. Christensen, en toto, but note 4–5; Moir and Jessel, 106–7; Symons, index under Sexual Arousal—by touch.

9. Fisher, *Anatomy of Love,* 314—note 12, and index under Conversation, and in courtship; Judith Sills, *A Fine Romance: The Passage of Courtship from Meeting to Marriage,* 105–7, 125–27; Symons, index under Copulation as a Female Service, and Female Choice; note 17, below, this chapter. The current emphasis in the dating scene on becoming "friends" first is not only a reasonable precaution in the age of AIDS; it also fits the female mate selection agenda.

10. Moir and Jessel, 18, 42–49; Springer and Deutsch, 223–24; Wallace, 101, 111, 112–14. Also see notes 44, 51, 58, 65, 71, 72, chap. 3, the present work. For an alternative explanation of men's visual orientation in terms of their sexual arousal, and their less personal sexual interest, see "The Mating Game" by William Allman, *U.S. News and World Report,* July 19, 1993.

11. It may have been absolutely essential that ancestral mothers be able to detect the slightest stirrings of their infants as they carried them close to their bodies, and that they be able to quiet them instantly and effectively. The savanna environment was filled with predators, and there were no trees to climb to escape them.

Most researchers link the relative hairlessness of modern women to increased capacity for sexual arousal and/or to ancestral men's selection of mates who showed greater paedomorphic characteristics. These interfacing explanations are both probably right. But some researchers also believe women's hairlessness and greater skin sensitivity may be related to the savanna-predator scenario as well. See Fisher, *Anatomy of Love,* 314—note 13; Fisher, *The Sex Contract,* 144–45; Moir and Jessel, 18, 55; Morris, *Intimate Behavior,* 16–30.

12. Fisher, *Anatomy of Love,* chap. 10, "Why Can't a Man Be More Like a Woman?"; Storr, *Human Aggression,* chap. 7, "Aggression in the Relationship between the Sexes"; Symons, chap. 7, "The Desire for Sexual Variety," and chap. 8, "Copulation as a Female Service." Also see notes 44, 51, 58, 65, 71, 72, chap. 3, the present work.

13. If we bracket the pathological expressions of male sexual predation, it is still true that because of men's largely testosterone-driven "hunter" and "penetrator" propensity in the mating process, and because of their generally more urgent sexual desire, there is some justification for viewing even normal men as "sexual predators." There is also some justification in viewing women—because of their generally lower sexual drive and their more "receptive" mating role—as "withholding." See Roy Schenk, *Thoughts of Dr. Schenk on Sex and Gender,* 26–31, 34–38, 48–53, 74–76, 96–98, 107–10; and Symons, chap. 8, "Copulation as a Female Service."

14. Theodor Reik, *Of Love and Lust,* part 1: chap. 2, "Origin and Nature of Love," esp. 63ff., and chap. 3, "The Widening Circle."

15. Hendrix, *Getting the Love You Want,* 41–53; Reik, chaps. 2 and 3. See esp. 49 ff.

16. Hendrix, op. cit., chap. 3, "Your Imago," and chap. 4, "Romantic Love," esp. 49 ff.; Reik, chaps. 2 and 3, esp. 42 ff.

17. Fisher, *Anatomy of Love*, 20, 24–25; Lorenz, 104; Symons, chap. 8, "Copulation as a Female Service"—also p. 24, and index under Female Choice—and chap. 6, "Sexual Choice," esp. 166, 180; Wilson, 125.

18. Glantz and Pearce, chap. 7, "The Reproductive Strategy of the Female," and chap. 9, "The Reproductive Strategy of the Male"; note 74, chap. 3, the present work.

19. Symons, chap. 8, "Copulation as a Female Service," esp. 271–73.

20. Fisher, *Anatomy of Love*, 52–55; Hendrix, *Getting the Love You Want*, 40–41. Also compare Reik, chaps. 2 and 3.

21. Fisher, *Anatomy of Love*, 52–55; Hendrix, op. cit., 40–41.

22. The literature on the courtship rituals of animals is vast. See Campbell, index under Courtship; Fisher, *Anatomy of Love*, index under Courtship (compared with human courtship practices); Lorenz, chap. 11, "The Bond"; Sagan and Druyan, index under Courtship.

23. The literature on the innate nature of human courtship practices is likewise extensive. See Fisher, *Anatomy of Love*, chap. 2, "Infatuation"; Morris, *Intimate Behavior*, chap. 2, "Invitations to Sexual Intimacy."

24. Fisher, *Anatomy of Love*, 47, 90; Symons, 254–61. For the relationship between male gift giving and the ancient practice of supplying women with meat, see notes 9, 65, 68, 69, 70, 71, chap. 3, the present work. For male gift giving in exchange for sex among chimpanzees and bonobos, see De Waal, *Peacemaking Among Primates*, 206–11. Also see note 62, chap. 3, the present work. Concealed ovulation could have allowed females to trade sex for resources on an ongoing basis.

25. While it is common for men in many cultures both to supply the food *and* cook for their prospective mates during the courtship process (Fisher, *Anatomy of Love*, 34–35), in children's "playing house" games, the boys will bring home the "meat" and the girls will "cook" it for them (Fisher, ibid., 267–68). And among the Mehinaku of central Brazil, on the wedding night, the new husband brings home a large catch of fish, and his bride cooks a meal (Fisher, ibid., 269).

26. Reik, chaps. 2 and 3; Sills, 142–44.

27. Hendrix, *Getting the Love You Want*, chap. 5, "The Power Struggle"; Sills, index under Conflict, and Negotiation Phase.

28. Sills, index under Plateau Phase, Stalemate, Testing Love, Trust.

29. Because men's desire for sexual variety is generally stronger than women's, on this point men have more to lose by marrying, and will often express more deeply ambivalent feelings about it when the prospect looms. See Farrell, *Why Men Are the Way They Are*, index under Fantasies; Sills, 156–59 ff., 208, and index under Fear—of commitment, of entrapment, of intimacy; Symons, 241.

30. Sills, 142–44, 154–55, 160, 165–68, 209, and index under Negotiating Phase.

31. Hendrix, op. cit., chap. 5, "The Power Struggle," esp. 56–65; Reik, chap. 2, esp. 42 ff.

32. Hendrix, op. cit., 199–200.

33. AESTHETIC APPRECIATION: Morris and Morris, 250–54. Perhaps male appreciation of female estrus-swollen buttocks and female appreciation of male physique applies here as well. SEXUAL ATTRACTION: This is obvious. RO-MANCE: Consortships; see note 14, chap. 3, the present work. PARENT-CHILD: note 49, chap. 3, the present work. CHILD-PARENT: Goodall, *Through a Window,* chaps. 4 and 11. FRIENDSHIP: see note 11, chap. 1, and note 10, chap. 3, the present work. AGAPE: This includes the selfless actions of mothers throwing themselves in harm's way to protect their children, and alpha males risking their lives to protect their communities. See Goodall, *In the Shadow of Man,* 73–74; MacKinnon, 85; Wallace, chap. 8, "The Myth of Altruism"; Wilson, chap. 7, "Altruism."

34. Fisher, *Anatomy of Love,* 56–58; Paul Gray, "What Is Love?"

35. Hendrix, op. cit., chap. 3, "Your Imago," and chap. 4, "Romantic Love"; Reik, chaps. 2 and 3.

36. Campbell, 292, 307–8, 347–48. Lorenz, in *On Aggression,* writes: "Since this relation of the misceability of the three great drives is different in the two sexes, a male can only pair with an awe-inspired and therefore submissive female, and a female only with an awe-inspiring and therefore dominant male. Thus the behavior mechanism just described guarantees the pairing of two individuals of opposite sex. In many variations, and modified by different ritualizations, this process of sex recognition and pair formation plays an important part in very many vertebrates right up to man" (Lorenz, 104). Also see note 14, chap. 2, and note 49, chap. 3, the present work. The fact that the incest taboo against mothers and sons mating is stronger is because, in Lorenz's terms, a mother is not "awe-inspired" by her son. Also, primate mothers *know* who their children are, and the mother-child bond is the most ancient and most powerful relationship among primates. Most primate males do *not* know who their daughters are, and fathering as meaningful paternal investment—except in a few species, distantly related to human beings—is a very late primate development.

37. The literature on animal hunger and satiety, and security and stimulation needs, is vast. See Lorenz, chap. 3, "What Is Aggression Good For?" and chap. 4, "The Spontaneity of Aggression," esp. 53–56; Morris, *The Naked Ape,* chap. 4, "Exploration."

38. Fisher, *Anatomy of Love,* 53–55; Hendrix, *Keeping the Love You Find: A Guide for Singles,* 40–47; note 37, above, this chapter.

39. See note 6, chap. 2, the present work. One proof of this is the high rate of adultery for both men and women (note 4, chap. 2, the present work).

40. Moir and Jessel, 86–87. For an interesting comparison of older human relationships and those of the distantly but ancestrally related lemurs, see Russell, 116–17.

6. The Same Species—Just Barely

1. Moir and Jessel, en toto, but especially chap. 3, "Sex in the Brain"; Wallace, chap. 5, "Are the Brains of Men and Women Different?"; note 72, chap. 3, the present work; notes 46, 47, 48, 49, 52, 56–66, below, this chapter.

2. Goodall, *Through a Window,* chap. 4, "Mothers and Daughters," and chap. 11, "Sons and Mothers"; note 9, chap. 1, and note 10, chap. 3, the present work.

3. Fisher, *Anatomy of Love,* 199; MacKinnon, 212; note 11, chap. 1, note 2, chap. 4, note 2, above, this chapter, the present work.

4. Our neocortexes have evolved, in part, as neuronal extensions of our more ancient limbic systems. While our limbic systems, or old mammalian brains, mediate many of the instinctual behaviors common to all mammals, others are what ethologists term "species-typical" or "species-characteristic." These species-typical behaviors have to do with the ways we organize ourselves in groups, the ways we feel about and care for our young, display other forms of affection, and exhibit aggression, to name a few. Our neocortical intelligence is a refinement and, in some cases, an amplification of the instinctual patterns of our limbic systems. Our particular form of human intelligence, therefore, is an outgrowth of and "commentary" upon both generalized mammalian, characteristically *primate,* and specifically *pongid* instinctual patterns. Therefore, our ways of being "intelligent"—that is, our ways of perceiving, feeling and thinking about the world, and acting on it— are only partly generalized mammalian.

5. Anthropologists have noted that our evolution on the savannas is marked less by bipedalism (for which we may have been preadapted toward the end of our jungle time) and more by the growth of our neocortexes. They have found a rapid increase in the size of our ancestors' brains from later *Homo erectus* to fully modern humans (500,000 years ago—from 1,000 cc to 1,350+); Klein, 349; note 75, chap. 3, the present work.

6. Corballis, 41; Klein, 344.

7. Corballis, 65–67; Klein, chap. 5, "Early *Homo sapiens,*" esp. 261.

8. Robin Fox, "Alliance and Constraint: Sexual Selection in the Evolution of Human Kinship Systems," esp. 289–93, 300–301, also 307 ff. and 323, in Campbell; Fisher, *The Sex Contract,* "Who's Who."

9. Klein, 344, 356–97.

10. Corballis, 152–62, 163–65; Klein, index under Speech.

11. Corballis, 39, 185–86.

12. Ibid., 161–63.

13. See note 8, above, this chapter.

14. Paul D. MacLean, *The Triune Brain in Evolution: Role in Paleocerebral Functions.* Many authors refer to MacLean's work, among them John Bradshaw, Helen Fisher, Kalman Glantz and John Pearce, Erich Harth, Harville Hendrix, Detler Ploog, Carl Sagan and Ann Druyan, and Anthony

Stevens—to mention only a few of those on whose work I've based many of my own understandings. MacLean's critics believe his R-complex and limbic system are not relatively unchanged from former evolutionary epochs, but have instead become fully integrated into the human brain. I think the bulk of the evidence is in MacLean's favor.

15. Fisher, *Anatomy of Love*, 56; MacLean, chap. 17, "The Limbic System in Historical Perspective"; Sagan and Druyan, 371–72.

16. Desmond, 116 ff., and chap. 6, "Cries and Whispers"; Sagan and Druyan, 275, 278, 400–402.

17. MacLean, 133, 341–42, 356, 373; Wallace, 108–9.

18. MacLean, 142–47, 189, 228, 236–39, 241.

19. Ibid., 103–5, 109 ff., 119 ff, 125–26, 129 ff., 140, 148.

20. This is a common understanding of many schools of psychology. Many people attempt to be self-sacrificial and giving to others as a substitute for affirming themselves. Self-affirmation can be a risky thing, but the alternative almost always pushes us into passive-aggressive behavior and barely repressed resentments. Resentments pile up and eventually undermine our feelings of goodwill and love for the other person. The animal part of each of us absolutely insists that his or her basic needs be met to a significant degree.

21. Freud recognized the importance of working to free and then channel the "Id." Alfred Adler helped his patients acknowledge their aggressive impulses and then channel them into "fellow feeling." Heinz Kohut devised a treatment program based on reconstructing the primal self, both through affiliative and adversarial "self-object" relationships. Alice Miller saw that the inner child must be freed to express himself or herself to an accepting and boundary-setting adult. And John Bradshaw has highlighted the importance of unshaming our real feelings and desires.

22. Judah Goldin, ed. and trans., *The Living Talmud*, 69.

23. Fisher, *Anatomy of Love*, 43, 52–53, 56, 173; MacLean, 264–65; Sagan and Druyan, 371–72.

24. Fisher, *Anatomy of Love*, 52–53.

25. See note 38, chap. 5, and notes 23, 24, this chapter, the present work.

26. Fisher, *Anatomy of Love*, 52–55, 172; Springer and Deutsch, 135–39, 206ff.; notes 23, 24, above, this chapter. Also, compare Theodore Millon's *Disorders of Personality: DSM-III: Axis II*, chap. 12, "Borderline Personality: The Unstable Pattern."

27. MacLean, chap. 21, "Participation of Thalamocingulate Division in Family-Related Behavior"; Moore and Gillette, *The King Within*, appendix B.

28. MacLean, 251–52.

29. Ibid., 314, 338, 354, 362, 375; Moore and Gillette, *The King Within*, appendix B.

30. Lorenz, chap. 3, "What Aggression Is Good For"; Storr, *Human Destructiveness*, chap. 1, "The Nature of Human Aggression"; Ernest Wolf, *Treating the Self: Elements of Clinical Self-Psychology*, 55, 56, 67, 185.

31. Fisher, *Anatomy of Love,* 286–87; MacLean, 340; Sagan and Druyan, index under Testosterone—and dominance hierarchies; Wallace, 107–11.

32. MacLean, 342, 345, 349, 351, 354, 375; Moore and Gillette, *The King Within,* appendix B.

33. Fisher, *Anatomy of Love,* 317—note 30; MacLean, 359, 370; Moir and Jessel, 116, 119, 192–93.

34. MacLean, 389 ff.; Moore and Gillette, *The King Within,* appendix B.

35. Interestingly, there is evidence that at least some dinosaurs cared for their young. Birds, probably the dinosaurs' direct descendants, also show "love" in this way. See MacLean, 16, 556ff., 559, 562.

36. Orangutans, for the most part, do not live in communities. They are solitary individuals for ecological reasons. See MacKinnon, 119.

37. MacLean, 556 ff., 559, 562. As a species-typical response illustrating the principle of "inclusive fitness," see Moore and Gillette, *The Lover Within,* 98–99; Symons, 6–7; Wallace, chap. 8, "The Myth of Altruism"; Wilson, chap. 7, "Altruism."

38. See note 16, above, this chapter.

39. John Hurrell Crook, "Sexual Selection, Dimorphism, and the Social Organization of Primates," in Campbell. Compare with Robin Fox, "Alliance and Constraint: Sexual Selection in the Evolution of Human Kinship Systems," in Campbell; Corballis, 66–67, and index under Brain Size—in hominid evolution; Heltne and Marquardt, 377; Howells, 94–96, 230; MacLean, chap. 28, "Neocortex, with Special Reference to the Frontal Granular Cortex," esp. 532 ff.

40. Erich Harth, *Windows on the Mind: Reflections on the Physical Basis of Consciousness,* 66–67; MacLean, 266, 578–79; Wallace, 110.

41. Campbell, 306; Wallace, 105–8.

42. See notes 20, 21, above, this chapter. Also, see Robert Moore and Douglas Gillette, *The Warrior Within,* part 3, "The Uninitiated Warrior: Malfunctions and Shadow Forms." Compare Theodor Reik's brilliant discussion of masochistic behavior in his *Of Love and Lust,* part 2, "Masochism in Modern Man."

43. Researchers know that fear and despondency lower the level of testosterone in the male, particularly if that fear and despondency are generated by a hostile and shaming "other." The neocortex itself often operates as a hostile and shaming "other" toward the limbic system—our animal self. This is Freud's "super-ego," which includes the so-called parental introjects with their "shoulds" and "shouldn'ts." It seems reasonable to believe that the frequently shaming neocortex can similarly lower testosterone levels in the human male. A similar situation may apply to PEA levels. If the neocortex deprives the animal self/limbic system of its expression of powerful emotion (which is one of its evolved roles), including aggressive self-affirmation and sexuality, the result is often listlessness, malaise, and boredom. We know that low levels of PEA are often associated with boredom (and depression). So perhaps shaming messages from the neocortex to the limbic system actually can cause PEA deprivation. See Fisher, *Anatomy of Love,* 172; Stevens, 262–67; notes 23, 24, 25, above, this chapter.

44. Moore and Gillette, *The Lover Within,* index under Agape; Anders Nygren, *Agape and Eros,* in toto.

45. This neocortical arrogance shows up in all the spiritual traditions in which doctrines such as "mind over matter," "the spiritual man versus the carnal man," and "transcendence" appear.

46. Fisher, *Anatomy of Love,* 43, 317—note 30; MacLean, 340; Moir and Jessel, chap. 5, "The Brains Come of Age"; Springer and Deutsch, 218–25; Anthony Stevens, *Archetypes: A Natural History of the Self,* 184; Sagan and Druyan, 205, 216; Wallace, 107–11.

47. Moir and Jessel, 23 ff., 38; Wallace, 116–17.

48. Moir and Jessel, 69 ff.

49. Ibid., 69.

50. Ibid., index under Childhood Differences; Wallace, 100–102.

51. Moir and Jessel, 86, 181.

52. Ibid., 195–96; Desmond, 257.

53. Moir and Jessel, 46–47.

54. Ibid., 15–16, 39–41, 45, 95.

55. Fisher, *Anatomy of Love,* 193–94; Moir and Jessel, 18, 42–47.

56. Moir and Jessel, 18, 179.

57. Ibid., 18, 55, 100.

58. Ibid., 18. The pattern of male emotional "detachment" in terms of social connectedness with females as well as in terms of sexual arousal and expression would fit with the greater male visual orientation (stimulation at a distance), relative insensitivity to physical pain, and more compartmentalized brain.

59. Ibid., 46–48.

60. Ibid., 48. Also see note 62, below, this chapter.

61. Ibid., chap. 3, "Sex in the Brain," chap. 4, "Childhood Differences," chap. 6, "The Ability Gap," and pp. 43–44, 46, 48, 90, 96, 100–101, 180–181; Wallace, 112–13.

62. Fisher, *Anatomy of Love,* chap. 10, "Why Can't a Man Be More Like a Woman?" esp. 197–98; Moir and Jessel, chaps. 3, 4, and 5—note esp. p. 48.

63. Moir and Jessel, 17, 94–98.

64. Fisher, *Anatomy of Love,* index under Testosterone; Moir and Jessel, 79–82, index under Aggression; Sagan and Druyan, 223, index under Aggression—testosterone levels and—EMOTIONAL INDEPENDENCE: This fits with men's greater competitiveness for status and wealth, and ultimately females, as well as with their related risk-taking behaviors; Moir and Jessel, 79–82, index under Aggression.

65. Estrogen increases a woman's level of alertness. She notices the details of the world around her through heightened sensory awareness. This would seem to contradict the notion of estrogen as a natural tranquilizer. However, anxiety may block our noticing of details and lower our awareness, whereas synthetic tranquilizers may have the opposite effect; a greater sense of well-being may enhance our perceptivity. See Fisher, *Anatomy of Love,* chap. 11, "Women, Men, and Power," and 192, 194, 204; Moir and Jessel, 17, 71–73, 78ff., 96.

66. MacLean, 322–25; Sagan and Druyan, 222–23, 228, 230.

67. Many primate females have what primatologists call "auntie" systems in which child-rearing is shared within the female coalitions.

68. De Waal, *Peacemaking Among Primates,* 55–57; Fisher, *Anatomy of Love,* 196–97; Heltne and Marquardt, 75, 81.

69. The literature on the extent to which primate societies are based on "culture," that is, the passing on of various forms of knowledge, is extensive. Jane Goodall, Frans De Waal, and many other primatologists have written extensively about this feature of primate life. See De Waal, *Peacemaking Among Primates,* 226–27; Heltne and Marquardt, 10; Sagan and Druyan, index under Culture—animal, chimp.

70. Fisher, *Anatomy of Love,* 335—note 31; Morris, *The Naked Ape,* 21, 34–35; Wallace, 83; Wilson, 126–27. See also American Museum of Natural History, *The First Humans: Human Origins and History to 10,000 B.C.,* 22–23.

71. Springer and Deutsch, 223–24; note 10, chap. 5, notes 53, 54, 56, above, this chapter, the present work.

72. Fisher, *Anatomy of Love,* 195–96; notes 61, 63, above, this chapter. One advantage of the compartmentalized neocortex of ancestral males was that it could enhance concentration by muting the interference of feelings. As modern athletes often report, they perform better when they can block their feelings and concentrate on mental-physical *skill.*

73. Grasping the whole picture taps into our intuitive capacities and augments our ability to foresee outcomes and strategize in an instantaneous way. See notes 53, 54, above, this chapter.

74. Fisher, *Anatomy of Love,* 198; note 11, chap. 5, notes 55, 57, 60, 62, above, this chapter.

75. As psychologists who specialize in codependency note, the codependent person must be able to anticipate and adapt to the mood changes and behaviors of the dominant partner in order to avoid provoking the more powerful individual's wrath. The codependent person is motivated by his or her fear of abandonment, perhaps even fear for his or her physical safety. See Natalie Shainess, *Sweet Suffering: Woman as Victim.* Also, see notes 67–71, chap. 3, the present work (on ancestral women's economic, hence emotional, dependency on ancestral men).

76. Douglas Gillette, "Men and Intimacy," *Wingspan: Journal of the Male Spirit,* summer 1990; Glantz and Pearce, 158; Lorenz, 123–25; Eleanor Emmons Maccoby and Carol Nagy Jacklin, *The Psychology of Sex Differences,* vol. 1/text, 239; MacLean, 171; note 20, chap. 3, the present work.

77. This inhibition on the part of men to harm females is not just a cultural teaching; the cultural teaching—"Don't hit a woman"—is a reenforcement of the underlying biological program. See note 76, above, this chapter.

78. Men's self-sacrifice—in terms of working at jobs they dislike and which offer them no personal gratification, as well as their participation in warfare (ultimately to protect and extend their and their mates' gene pools), have been hallmarks of our species since jungle times. See Sagan and Druyan, 285.

79. See note 24, chap. 3, the present work.

80. This is evident not only from the extensive social welfare systems, which essentially male governments have instituted, but also in the lives of the many individual men who volunteer their time and energy to social organizations and causes—from Nation of Islam community patrols to Rotary clubs, from mentor programs to coaching. See Gilmore, 229 ff.

81. Moir and Jessel, 179.

82. Glantz and Pearce, chap. 7, "The Reproductive Strategy of the Female," and chap. 9, "The Reproductive Strategy of the Male." Willard Harley, Jr., *His Needs, Her Needs: Building an Affair-proof Marriage*, en toto, but see p. 10. Also see notes 32, 33, chap. 3, the present work.

83. This is almost certainly related to the male reliance on visual cues for sexual arousal. Visual stimuli are not personal, and they are stimuli at a distance. See Christensen, in toto, but especially 2–7, 27 ff.; Farrell, *Why Men Are the Way They Are*, index under Fantasies; Glantz and Pearce, 168–70; Symons, chap. 7, "The Desire for Sexual Variety." Moir and Jessel, 106, 132–35, 137. Compare Kramer and Dunaway, 8–10. Also, see notes 58, 63, above, this chapter.

84. Glantz and Pearce, chap. 7, "The Reproductive Strategy of the Female," chap. 8, "Women on the Contemporary Scene"; Symons, 220–23, 246–50. Also, see notes 50, 60, 62, 74, above, this chapter.

85. See note 83, above, this chapter.

86. See note 83, above, this chapter.

7. War Between the Sexes

1. Fisher, *Anatomy of Love,* 196–97, note 28 on 197; R. L. McNeely and Gloria Robinson-Simpson, "The Truth About Domestic Violence: A Falsely Framed Issue," *Social Work,* November-December 1987; Storr, *Human Aggression,* 65–69, 71–76; Storr, *Human Destructiveness,* chap. 1, "The Nature of Human Destructiveness," esp. 7–8, 10–14, 20, 23; note 68, chap. 6, the present work. Compare to Wilson's seven trajectories of aggression—Wilson, 101–2.

2. Storr, *Human Destructiveness,* chap. 1, "The Nature of Human Aggression," esp. 7–8, 10–14, 20, 23.

3. Lorenz, chap. 3, "What Aggression Is Good For"; Storr, *Human Destructiveness,* chap. 1, "The Nature of Human Aggression," esp. 12, 14, 16–17, 22–23.

4. Wilson, 101–2.

5. Fisher, *Anatomy of Love,* chap. 11, "Women, Men, and Power," esp. 216–17, 219–24, and 284–87; Moir and Jessel, 95–98; 157ff.; Sagan and Druyan, 223, 230, 237, 298, index under Dominance Hierarchies; note 10, chap. 3, notes 46, 64, chap. 6, the present work.

6. Goodall, *Through a Window,* 112, 116–18.

7. Fisher, *Anatomy of Love,* chap. 1, "Courting"; Glantz and Pearce, 103–4; Katchadourian, 51; Maccoby and Jacklin (vol. 1), 259 ff.; Storr, *Human Destructiveness,* 65–66, 70–71, 92, 95. See notes 12, 14, chap. 2, notes 8, 11, this chapter, the present work.

8. Lorenz, 103–4, 123–25, 128; Storr, *Human Aggression,* chap. 7, "Aggression in the Relation Between the Sexes," esp. 68–69; note 14, chap. 2.

9. Lorenz, 103–4; Storr, *Human Aggression,* chap. 7, "Aggression in the Relation Between the Sexes," esp. 68–69.

10. Many of my male counselees report that when they have become physically violent in their relationships they've first experienced what for them was an intolerable feeling of frustration. When I've encouraged them to sort out the emotional components of this frustration they've usually defined it as a deep feeling of shame. Shame is far more destructive not only of our self-concepts but, more importantly, of our basic sense of safety and well-being than most of us realize. The reason for this is that shame triggers our fear of death. (See chap. 9, the present work.) Symons, 276–85; notes 1, 2, 5, 6, 7, 8, above, this chapter.

11. Farrell, *Why Men Are the Way They Are,* 268–69; Gilmore, 26–29; Moore and Gillette, *The King Within,* 21, 143–45, 203, 204–205, 280–82, note on 309, note on 312; notes 12, 14, chap. 2, notes 6, 7, 8, above, this chapter.

12. Human males, like nearly all primate males, are made for exercising a powerful protector role in their communities. Nature has crafted them to "go physical," even to the point of risking their own lives for those in their care—especially females and young. This specialized evolution of primate males shows up both in their physiques and in their psychological wiring—in the structures of their brains and in their hormonal systems. See notes 29, 31, 46, 58, 64, 66, 70, 72, 76, 78, chap. 6, the present work. Also see note 10, chap. 5, notes 2, 5, chap. 4, notes 10, 65, 70, 71, 72, 95, chap. 3, the present work.

13. Men may "snap" for a number of different reasons—frustration with their work situations (oppressive and shaming bosses, inordinate stress, basic dissatisfaction, and so on), anxiety about their financial situations, and conflicts with their partners. It pays a female partner to recognize that man is wired differently in his limbic system (perhaps in his neocortex as well) and that he has between ten and twenty times the aggression-inducing testosterone. This means that he will react to inordinate stress differently from the

way she does. While, as we've seen, primate males, including humans, experience strong instinctual inhibitions against harming females and young (in fact, they are wired to *protect* them), under certain circumstances—those that sufficiently frustrate their needs for aggressive self-affirmation and sexual expression, and which ultimately feel like shaming—the rage that nature has crafted to mobilize them against feelings of powerlessness may override these instinctual inhibitions. Then human males, like their chimpanzee counterparts, may go into "display" behavior. As we've noted, when this occurs, females and young may be at risk if they get in the way. In addition, if a significant part of the stress a man is experiencing is coming from his interactions with his partner, his primate self may "read" her as a challenging male. Since he is wired to attack challenging males, she may find herself in physical jeopardy.

See Farrell, op. cit., 76; Douglas Gillette, "Men and Intimacy," *Wingspan;* Symons, 283; note 14, chap. 2, notes 8, 9, above, this chapter. Also see Campbell, 273–75; notes 10, 11, above, this chapter.

14. While women's need to feel secure about their partners' ability to be good financial providers is a natural inheritance from our savanna time, a number of my female counselees have expressed a level of desperation about this need that has approached what seems to me to be pathological proportions, even if their partners are making a good living. When male partners have been unemployed or underemployed, these women have reported feelings of paralyzing rage and escalating patterns of verbal and emotional attacks against their partners.

15. Many, if not most, human females, like their nonhuman primate counterparts, need to feel that their partners can "frame" them—emotionally hold them in a benevolent yet firm protecting male "energy field." This need can degenerate into violent emotionality if it is significantly frustrated. The sources of the frustration can be several. For one thing, their male partners *may not be* sufficiently masculine in this respect (see Storr, *Human Aggression,* 70–75). The woman senses this and may try to provoke a "framing" response from her partner. For another thing, her childhood wounding may cause her to have feelings of hostility toward her parents, perhaps her father, and/or men in general. She may be unable to experience herself as "subdominant" in a feminine way (see Storr, ibid., 70–75; notes 8, 9, above, this chapter, and note 14, chap. 2). In this case, she will express her own "masculine" aggressiveness, appear to the animal self of her partner as a challenging male, and escalate the conflict to dangerous levels. If this occurs, it's certainly not that she is seeking to be abused, although some women may (see Reik, part 2, "Masochism in Modern Man"). Rather, it is probable that her need to feel "framed" and protected—taking this bizarre twist—has overridden her rational faculties. She has now paradoxically put herself in a position to feel that her male partner *can* go physical to "protect" her, although in an emotionally desperate way, *and,* at the same time, to feel threatened by him. His momentary rageful "display" behavior has almost certainly come out of his underly-

ing sense of impotence. The woman knows this; and the entire exercise has been both futile and dysfunctional. In addition, it is likely to have caused her partner to feel guilty and shameful, thereby deepening his sense of inadequacy.

See the Ape Empowerment Exercise in chap. 10, the present work. Also see note 14, chap. 2, notes 8, 9, 10, 11, above, this chapter. In addition, see notes 21, 29, 67, 68, 69, 70, 71, 72, chap. 3, the present work.

16. McNeely and Robinson-Simpson; Storr, *Human Destructiveness,* 55–57. Also see notes 1, 2, above, this chapter.

17. Ibid.

18. Robert I. Levy, *Tahitians: Mind and Experience in the Society Islands,* 186, 283, 330, 467, 497; Stevens, *Archetypes,* 212, 233; Stevens, *The Roots of War: A Jungian Perspective,* 15 ff., 30–31, 130–31, 167; see esp. chap. 1, "War and Peace," and chap. 2, "Warlike and Peaceful Behavior."

19. Betty Roszak and Theodore Roszak, eds., *Masculine/Feminine: Readings in Sexual Mythology and the Liberation of Women,* 4.

20. Symons, 262.

21. David Gates, "White Male Paranoia," *Newsweek,* March 29, 1993.

22. Lance Morrow, "Men: Are They Really That Bad?" *Time,* February 14, 1994. See also Susan Brownmiller, *Against Our Will: Men, Women and Rape,* esp. 13–17.

23. This may manifest in many different ways, from the exercise of *personal* power in the lives of individual couples to sweeping cultural and institutional dynamics. Some of women's oppressive power over the lives of men shows up in direct ways, but at other times its expression is indirect. Men are taught, for example, to take the most dangerous and unrewarding jobs and to give their lives in work and war for women. Women, on the other hand, generally do not work in dangerous professions, are not drafted into military service, and when they do enter the service, they are not obligated to do combat duty; they are seldom homeless, imprisoned, held hostage (the same length of time as men), made homeless, or executed (when compared with men) (Warren Farrell, "Glass Cellars, Death Professions . . . ," *Transitions: Newsletter of the National Coalition of Free Men,* January/February 1994; they have more per capita wealth as a whole group than men—Farrell, *The Myth of Male Power: Why Men Are the Disposable Sex.* New York: Simon and Schuster, 1993. En toto, but especially Parts I and II, 32–33, 48; spend most of the money—*Ibid.,* 33–34; and they outlive men by a growing margin—Farrell, "Death Professions." Also see Farrell, *Why Men Are the Way They Are,* 8–14, index under Marriage and Options, War, Violence; Fisher, *Anatomy of Love,* chapter 11, "Women, Men, and Power"; Schenk, chap. 4, "Socialization," chap. 6, "Female Moral Superiority," chap. 9, "Women's Power," chap. 19, "Sex as Commodity"; Storr, *Human Aggression,* chap. 7, "Aggression in the Relation Between the Sexes"; Symons, chap. 6, "Sexual Choice," chap. 8, "Copulation as a Female Service." Also see notes 24, 25, below, this chapter.

24. Farrell, *Why Men Are The Way They Are*, 225, 232, 234, 360–63. It is certainly true that I learned it was my duty to risk my life for "my country" from women, mostly my female grade school teachers. Translated, "my country" means women and children. Ultimately, what *this* means is protecting the gene pool—those individuals who have been defined as "kin." One may protect the gene pool by protecting and even expanding the resource base that keeps the gene pool thriving.

I'll never forget the day I learned my draft number—number 76—while I was still in college. I went to a close female friend—a fellow student—and expressed my fear and dismay. She responded by telling me it was my duty to protect her from the communists. I was shocked and deeply hurt. I told her, "I'm not afraid of the communists. If you're so afraid, why don't *you* go and protect *me?*" Her callous disregard for me—for my life itself—was the first wake-up call I was able to "hear" about women's complicity in warfare.

25. If women are generally more predisposed than men by their primary reproductive strategy to embrace the lifelong sexually exclusive monogamy ideal as the best means for achieving their practical immortality, and if they feel that their primary reproductive strategy is threatened by men's (which, in fact, entails multiple sexual partners), then they are likely to use whatever psychological weapons they can to force men to conform as much as possible to their reproductive agenda. The most effective weapon at hand is shaming, or as biologists and anthropologists call it, "moralistic aggression." Since the human neocortex may have evolved in part to respond especially well to moralistic aggression (Robin Fox, "Alliance and Constraint: Sexual Selection in the Evolution of Human Kinship Systems," in Campbell), and since human males, like their chimpanzee and bonobo counterparts, are particularly vulnerable to the moralistic aggression of their mothers (see note 12, chap. 2, notes 87, 88, chap. 3, the present work), women are apt to use this psychological weapon to good effect—in the context of marriage.

See Wilson's reflections on moralistic aggression (Wilson, 162). He writes: ". . . human altruism is shaped by powerful emotional controls. . . . Moral aggression is most intensely expressed in the enforcement of reciprocation. The cheat, . . . and the traitor are objects of universal hatred. Honor and loyalty are reinforced by the stiffest codes. . . . The rules are the symmetrical counterparts to the canalized development of territory." His reflections are done in a different context than marriage. However, the conceptual framework, and many of the specific terms he uses, seem to me to fit men's predicament, vis-à-vis women's moralistic aggression in the context of marriage exactly. Women believe men should be "reciprocal" in marriage by being as little motivated to "cheat" and become "traitors" to their relationships as many women are, and they use the concepts of "honor" and "loyalty" to enforce their particular idea of "reciprocity" according to "stiff codes"—usually upheld by courts of law (for example when it comes to child custody disputes). Women, like men, view their marriage as "territory" over which they exercise exclusive sexual rights. In fact, because men's primary reproductive strategy is to inseminate as many women as possible, pledging their "loyalty" and "honor" to the primarily female "territory" of marriage is an act of "altruism" for many men.

The situation is actually more complicated than this, of course, since many women also "cheat" and are "disloyal" to the "territory" of their marriages, and men are moved to attempt to "reciprocate" (even at the expense of their sexual enthusiasm), not only because of women's "moral" pressure but also because men's secondary sexual strategy is monogamous commitment, even if not for a lifetime. Because marriage promises the fulfillment of men's secondary reproductive strategy (as well as because of their vulnerability to the emotional power of their internalized mothers), men are likely to be at least temporarily persuaded by women's moralistic aggression in this, and other, respects. It pays both men and women to frankly acknowledge the fierce determination on the part of their *im*personal reproductive instincts to achieve their own practical immortality.

See Farrell, *Why Men Are the Way They Are,* index under Fantasies, Marriage and Options; Moir and Jessel, 139; notes 27, 28, 29, 32, 36, 40, 43, 44, 46, below, this chapter; Schenk, chap. 6, "Female Moral Superiority," chap. 9, "Women's Power," chap. 19, "Sex as Commodity."

26. Diamond, 69–70, 94–97; Fisher, *Anatomy of Love,* 79–80, 282–83; Symons, 131, 138–41.

27. Symons, 211.

28. Diamond, 94; Glantz and Pearce, 132, 150; Symons, 208–13; Wallace, 277–79.

29. The Coolidge Effect is the expression of the male's primary sexual strategy and is reflected in men's fantasies about multiple sexual partners as well as in their generally increasing boredom with their marriage partners over a period of time. For a fascinating firsthand anthropological account of the Coolidge Effect operating in an alien culture, see Robert I. Levy's *Tahitians: Mind and Experience in the Society Islands,* 125. See Symons, chap. 7, "The Desire for Sexual Variety"; notes 27, 28, above, this chapter.

30. Diamond, 76–77; Goodall, *In the Shadow of Man,* 79, 180–82 (except with their mothers, 183), index under Sexual Behavior; Goodall, *Through a Window,* index under Chimpanzees—sexual behavior; Sagan and Druyan, 195–96, index under Sexual Behavior.

31. Christensen, 3–10; Diamond, 93–94; Farrell, *Why Men Are the Way They Are,* 18–20; Glantz and Pearce, 94–95, 217; Moir and Jessel, 105–12, esp. 107; Phyllis Taylor Pianka, *How to Write Romances,* 6; Symons, chap. 7, "The Desire for Sexual Variety," 241.

32. Diamond, 93–94; Farrell, op. cit., chap. 2, "What Women Want: The Message the Man Hears," 102–6, index under Fantasies; Fisher, *Anatomy of Love,* 89; Symons, chap. 7, "The Desire for Sexual Variety," 158–62, 219ff., 232 ff.

33. See note 4, chap. 2, the present work.

34. See note 4, chap. 2, the present work.

Notes / *315*

35. Jerry Adler, "Sex in the Snoring '90s," *Newsweek,* April 26, 1993.
36. Campbell, 251; Wilson, 124–25; Sagan and Druyan, 149, 199, 237, 309–10. Sagan and Druyan write, on 149: "Because females and males are physiologically different, they sometimes pursue different strategies, each to propagate its own hereditary line; and these strategies, while of course not wholly incompatible, introduce a certain element of conflict in the relations between the sexes." The ultimate physiological difference is the different natures, numbers, and behaviors of our reproductive cells—the egg and sperm. See Storr, *Human Aggression,* 69; Symons, 22. Also see notes 37, 38, below, this chapter.
37. See Fritjof Capra, *The Tao of Physics,* in toto; David Loye, *The Sphinx and the Rainbow: Brain, Mind, and Future Vision,* en toto.
38. James Gleick, *Chaos,* en toto.
39. Sagan and Druyan, 309—note 13.
40. Diamond, 88–89ff.; Fisher, *Anatomy of Love,* 178. Symons, chap. 5, "Reproductive Competition"; chap. 6, "Sexual Choice"; chap. 7, "The Desire for Sexual Variety," esp. 222–23. In the present work: note 1, introduction; note 3, chap. 1; notes 6, 14, 15, 32, 33, 74, 77, 106, 108, chap. 3; notes 6, 13, 17, 19, 29, 39, chap. 5; notes 33, 46, 64, 65, 70, 72, 75, 82, 83, 84, 85, chap. 6. Also see notes 8, 9, 25, 27, 28, 29, 31, 32, 36, 41, this chapter.
41. The frequent ambivalence expressed in a woman's initial No response reflects, in part, her more cautious reproductive strategy. She needs to make as certain as she can that: (*a*) this potential mate is offering the best genetic mix she can get at the time; and (*b*) that this potential mate is likely to stick around to help with child-rearing. The unconscious (or conscious) anxiety this decision-making process entails for a woman resonates with more personal concerns about love and compatibility. This can be expressed in the hostility/idealization dynamic that Theodor Reik illuminates (Reik, part 1: "A Psychologist Looks at Love.") For a comparison with chimpanzee behavior, see Goodall, *Through a Window,* 93–94. Also see Lorenz, 104, 166–69; Symons, chap. 6, "Sexual Choice," chap. 8, "Copulation as a Female Service"; Wilson, 125. Also see note 17, chap. 4, the present work. Of course, No *can,* and often *does* mean No; but frequently neither the woman nor the man can tell for sure.
42. Many of my male and female counselees report feeling romantically and sexually rejected as a deeply shaming experience. Frequently, men bear the brunt of initial sexual rejection, whereas women often experience getting romantically "dumped" further into the relationship. See Farrell, *Why Men Are the Way They Are,* xxix, 13, 76; Storr, *Human Aggression,* 77.
43. Based on all the evidence we've looked at up to this point, both in the text of the present work, and in the notes, it seems reasonable to conclude that men's primary fantasy—for multiple sexual partners (with sex for its own sake—without romantic attachment)—is coming more from their jungle time primate patterns, and women's primary fantasy—for romantic love and economic support for the options (ultimately, child-rearing) they may wish to

pursue—comes more out of their savanna time pair-bonding primate patterns. See Farrell, op. cit., index under Fantasies; Fisher, *Anatomy of Love,* 89; Fisher, *The Sex Contract,* "The Sex Contract"; Harley, 10 ff.; notes 44, 45, 46, 47, below, this chapter.

44. See notes 30, 31, 36, 40, above, this chapter.

45. See note 25, above, this chapter. Men do want love, companionship, and long-term emotional security as well. They are also at least as jealous as women, perhaps more so. (See Symons, index under Sexual Jealousy.) See Farrell, op. cit., 18–20, index under Fantasies; Harley, 10ff.; Symons, 228.

46. Farrell, op. cit., 19 ff., 55 ff., 60 ff.; Fisher, *Anatomy of Love,* 89, 91, 104 ff.; Fisher, *The Sex Contract,* "The Sex Contract"; Harley, 10 ff.; Kramer and Dunaway, chap. 1, "The Eternal Struggle"; Symons, index under Marriage.

47. Farrell, 53ff., index under Fantasies—secondary; Harley, en toto, but esp. 10 ff.

48. Fisher, *Anatomy of Love,* 66 ff., 90, 93–94, 311; Symons, 143, 150–51, 211, 223 ff., index under Prostitution; Wilson, 125–26.

49. The centers for aggression and sexuality lie very close to each other, both in the R-complex and in the limbic system (note 17, chap. 6, the present work). Add to this the fact that rape is mostly a crime of disempowered males and it becomes clear that there is no simple way to separate the aggressive from the sexual component of rape. See Fisher, *Anatomy of Love,* 122, 330—note 17; Sagan and Druyan, 313–14, 370, 459—note 20; Symons, 276–85, index under Rape. Also, see notes 1, 2, 7, 8, 9, 10, 11, 13, above, this chapter.

50. There are many ways of structuring romantic plots in order to achieve this end and conform to this theme, including plots that end with the disappointment of love or the heroine's self-sacrifice for a nobler ideal. And, of course, some romantic novels today emphasize the *heroine's* need to "see the light." But, in my view, it all finally amounts to the same thing—the man's adoring commitment, regardless of the ins and outs of the heroine's internal process or the external forces she must contend with. See Pianka, 6, 10–11, 83–85.

51. Farrell, *Why Men Are the Way They Are,* index under Cinderella, Fantasies, Romance Novels; notes 32, 46, above, this chapter.

52. Farrell, op. cit., 49–53, 254, chap. 7, "The New Sexism," index under Cinderella, Fantasies, *Ms.* magazine—and advertisements.

53. The clash is worse for men because of the greater urgency of their sexual drive. See Glantz and Pearce, 165–70; note 25, above, this chapter.

54. A number of the men in my support/therapy groups have expressed this sensation of a physical ache when they see a woman they're attracted to who is unavailable to them either because she's married (or in a committed relationship), or because *they* are. To their genes, every time this happens it's a reproductive opportunity gone by, and there's the hint of genetic death about it. See Glantz and Pearce, 168–69.

55. Symons, index under Marriage, esp.—as entailing economic cooperation; as entailing rights and duties; as not founded on sexuality; child-rearing and.

56. Campbell, 113ff., 298, 305–6, 308; Diamond, 79–80; Symons, 132, 138–41, 153, 203–4, 256–57.

57. Farrell, op. cit., 102–3, index under Marriage and Options; note 25, above, this chapter. Levy, 193, 196–97; Moir and Jessel, 139.

58. Notes 31, 36, 40, 43, 44, 48, 54, above, this chapter.

59. Writing down our thoughts and feelings does several things. It helps us clarify them. It helps us honor them (and the unconscious forces and agendas that are expressing them). It helps us objectify them by externalizing them. And it helps us remember them. All of these things are important for engaging in the process of self-knowledge, self-acceptance, and integration of the psyche.

60. "Transference" of our childhood feelings about our parents onto our present relationship partners through the dynamic of "repetition compulsion" is a common experience. Harville Hendrix has built an entire couple counseling theory and practice around this powerful tendency in the lives of many relationship partners (Hendrix, *Getting the Love You Want,* en toto, especially chaps. 3, 4, 5). See John Beahrs's *Unity and Multiplicity: Multilevel Consciousness of Self in Hypnosis,* en toto, but esp. chap. 5, "Dissociative Disorder—Severe, Common, Treatable," chap. 6, "Treatment of Dissociative Disorder," and chap. 7, "Working with Persecutors"—for a discussion of hostile and destructive inner "voices."

8. Childlike and Childish: Why We Don't "Act Our Age"

1. Bradshaw's PBS appearances have led the way, but the ground had already been prepared by Alice Miller, Transactional Analysis, and Primal Scream Therapy.

2. The literature and references to our neotenous nature are vast. See, for example: Campbell, 251, 301, 353ff.; Corballis, 69, 70–71; Desmond, 16, 160; De Waal, *Peacemaking Among Primates,* 251–52; Fisher, *Anatomy of Love,* 181n, 339–40; Fisher, *The Sex Contract,* 97–98; Suehisa Kuroda, "Developmental Retardation and Behavioral Characteristics of Pygmy Chimpanzees," esp. 184, 192, in Heltne and Marquardt; MacKinnon, 106; Morris, *The Naked Ape,* 32–34.

3. Campbell, 301; Corballis, 70–71; De Waal, *Peacemaking Among Primates,* 252; Fisher, *Anatomy of Love,* 339–40; Morris, *Men and Apes,* chap. 7, "Intelligent Apes."

4. Again, the literature, both about humans and about nonhuman primates, is vast. See, for example: Bruno Bettelheim, *Freud and Man's Soul,* 13; John Bradshaw, *Homecoming: Reclaiming and Championing Your Inner Child,* en toto, but esp. 41–43, 70 ff., 125–26; Ronald Lee and J. Colby Martin, *Psychotherapy After Kohut: A Textbook of Self Psychology,* 79, index under Idealized Parental Imago; Miller, *The Drama of the Gifted Child,* en

toto, but esp. 25, index under Idealization Image Formation, Mother; Miller, *For You Own Good: Hidden Cruelty in Child-Rearing and the Roots of Violence,* en toto; Miller, *Thou Shalt Not Be Aware: Society's Betrayal of the Child,* en toto; Moore and Gillette, *The King Within,* 204, 230, 309—note, index under Mothers; Loren Pedersen, *Dark Hearts: The Unconscious Forces That Shape Men's Lives,* index under Mother: anima and—Mother: terrible—Mother: complex—Mother-Son Bond, love and—Mother Worship, castration and; Lillian Rubin, *Intimate Strangers: Men and Women Together,* index under Motherhood. Also, compare De Waal, *Peacemaking Among Primates,* 42; Goodall, *Through a Window,* 32–33.

5. Lee and Martin, 79, index under Idealized Parent Imago; Miller, *The Drama of the Gifted Child,* index under Introject, Introjection; Moore and Gillette, *The King Within,* 204, 230, 309—note.

6. The bonobo, of course, is an example of this that is very close to our own evolutionary line. Probably the most famous case of neoteny in other species is the axolotl (a salamander). Morris, the *Naked Ape,* 32.

7. SELECTION FOR EARLIER AND EARLIER BIRTHS DUE TO BIPEDALISM: Morris, *The Naked Ape,* 3; Fisher, *Anatomy of Love,* 339–40. SELECTION FOR CREATIVITY: Fisher, *Anatomy of Love,* 339–340. The present work, notes 57, 75, 80, 86, chap. 3; notes 5, 6, 7, 8, 10, 11, chap. 6. SELECTION FOR MUTUAL DEPENDENCY: Fisher, *Anatomy of Love,* 180–81; Fisher, *The Sex Contract,* 96–98; notes 29, 87, chap. 3, the present work. SELECTION FOR SEXUAL SENSITIVITY: Campbell, 249, 251, 254, 273; Fisher, *Anatomy of Love,* 180–81; Fisher, *The Sex Contract,* 98; Morris, *Intimate Behavior,* 35–36, 72–74, 80, 99–102; Morris, *The Naked Ape,* 51, 52–53.

8. Campbell, 301; Fisher, *Anatomy of Love,* 339–40.

9. Corballis, 70–71; Desmond, 160; De Waal, *Peacemaking Among Primates,* 251–52; Fisher, *Anatomy of Love,* 339–40; Fisher, *The Sex Contract,* 97–98; Heltne and Marquardt, 192; Morris, *The Naked Ape,* 33–34.

10. Corballis, 70; Desmond, 160; Fisher, *Anatomy of Love,* 181—note 16, 339–40; Heltne and Marquardt, 192.

11. Corballis, 70.

12. Corballis, 70; Fisher, *Anatomy of Love,* 339.

13. MacKinnon, 108.

14. De Waal, *Peacemaking Among Primates,* 201; Fisher, *Anatomy of Love,* 181–82; Fisher, *The Sex Contract,* 95.

15. Fisher, *Anatomy of Love,* 187–88; Fisher, *The Sex Contract,* 35, 95, 98; notes 27, 28, chap. 3, the present work.

16. See note 28, chap. 3, the present work.

17. See note 28, chap. 3, the present work.

18. See note 28, chap. 3, the present work.

19. Campbell, 251; Fisher, *The Sex Contract,* 96–97. The present work: notes 29, 69, 70, 71, chap. 3; notes 65, 78, 84, chap. 6; notes 9, 14, 15, 32, 50, 51, chap. 7; 2, 7, 9, 10, 12, 14, above, this chapter.

20. See note 62, chap. 3, the present work.

21. See notes 2, 3, 9, above, this chapter.

22. De Waal, *Peacemaking Among Primates,* 22, 199; Fisher, *Anatomy of Love,* 265–330; Goodall, *In the Shadow of Man,* 171, 188, 244, 247; Heltne and Marquardt, 109–10, 166; Morris, *Intimate Behavior,* 99, 101–2; Morris, *The Naked Ape,* 80.

23. De Waal, *Peacemaking Among Primates,* 11–12, index under Eye Contact, Hand Gestures; Goodall, *In the Shadow of Man,* 244, 247–48; Morris, *Intimate Behavior,* 75; Morris, *The Naked Ape,* 162 ff.

24. See note 23, above, this chapter.

25. De Waal, *Peacemaking Among Primates,* 224, index under Grins; Fisher, *Anatomy of Love,* index under Smiles; Heltne and Marquardt, 155–56. Compare Konrad Lorenz's analysis of the dog's "smile," Lorenz, 96–98, also 178.

26. Depending on how far we draw back our lips when we smile—whether or not we expose our canine teeth—our smiles can also express a mixture of nervousness, fear, and hostility. See Fisher, *Anatomy of Love,* index under Smiles, esp. 23–24, 137; Lorenz, 96–98; Sagan and Druyan, 297.

27. De Waal, *Peacemaking Among Primates,* 224.

28. Campbell, 273–74; Lorenz, 134–36; Morris, *Intimate Behavior,* 36; notes 23, 24, 25, above, this chapter.

29. Often, pretending an emotion opposite to the one we're feeling—as long as we don't repress the primary affect—acts as a control on this basic feeling. In this way, anger can be channeled into aggressive self-affirmation and can be kept from splitting off into rage. Of course, if we repress, in this instance, our anger, and are unaware of it, eventually we will experience the opposite effect; the bottled-up and denied feeling will often explode in a way that is beyond our conscious control. See note 30, below, this chapter.

30. Lorenz, 173 ff., 211, 219; Reik, part 1, "A Psychologist Looks at Love," chap. 2, "Origin and Nature of Love," esp. 63, 66, chap. 3, "The Widening Circle," esp. 132, 149.

31. If our own larger, more empathic and impulse-regulating brains are a neotenous feature which, in part, amplify mental and emotional characteristics of immature primates, including their reconciling behaviors, then it follows that our capacity for greater affiliation and cooperation is augmented by our neoteny. See Campbell, 285 ff.; De Waal, *Peacemaking Among Primates,* chap. 5, "Bonobos," esp. 220–21, 206, chap. 6, "Humans"; Heltne and Marquardt, 171–73, 192, 376–77.

32. Robin Fox, "Alliance and Constraint: Sexual Selection in the Evolution of Human Kinship Systems," en toto, but esp. 285–307, in Campbell; MacLean, chap. 28, "Neocortex, with Special Reference to the Frontal Granular Cortex"; note 39, chap. 6, the present work.

33. This is conjecture on my part. To my knowledge, researchers do not know enough about the human limbic system as yet to definitely conclude that *any* of the human behaviors which appear to depart from the species-characteristic behaviors of the other apes are anything more than cultural in origin. However, if any of our typical patterns—for example, our mixed reproductive strategies—are encoded in our limbic systems (which I believe they almost certainly are), then we would have to conclude that at least the second layer of our primate patterns has been structured into our essentially chimpanzee limbic systems. See note 27, chap. 6, the present work.

34. The increased sexuality in bonobos has been linked to infantile behavioral patterns, including food begging, food sharing, and submissive behaviors designed to reduce group tensions. See De Waal, *Peacemaking Among Primates,* index under Food Sharing, Sexual Behavior—as alternative to hostility; Heltne and Marquardt, 164–71, 181.

35. De Waal, *Peacemaking Among Primates,* 206–13. Compare Lorenz, 135.

36. De Waal, *Peacemaking Among Primates,* 29, 206–13, 226; Goodall, *In the Shadow of Man,* 34, 82, 127; Goodall, *Through a Window,* 212.

37. Note 33, chap. 3, the present work.

38. Perhaps especially women who, because of fetal exposure to higher than usual levels of androgens, have masculinized brains. See Christensen, 4–7; Moir and Jessel, 25, 29–32, 92ff.

39. Bettelheim, 53–64; Gérard Lauzun, *Sigmund Freud: The Man and His Theories,* 97–98, 118, 126, 152.

40. Carl Jung, *Aion: Researches into the Phenomenology of the Self,* 31, 195.

41. Moore and Gillette, *The King Within,* 25.

42. ALICE MILLER: See note 4, above, this chapter. KAREN HORNEY: Feminine Psychology, index under Childhood. JEAN PIAGET: Dorothy Singer and Tracey Revenson, A Piaget Primer: How a Child Thinks, en toto. NORMAN O. BROWN: Brown, en toto, but esp. chap. 3, "Sexuality and Childhood."

43. Most of the major psychologies assume that the basic cause of neurosis in human beings is what could be called "overcontrol" of our instincts for aggression and sexuality. We need to be able to reaffirm these primal instincts and, at the same time, learn to control them in an appropriate way—not too much and not too little. This, in fact, is the basic thrust of the present work. As Alice Miller and Anthony Storr, among many others, have pointed out, violence, including violent criminality, is frequently the result—not of *under*control, but of *over*control of aggressive and sexual impulses. See Miller's *For Your Own Good;* Storr's *Human Destructiveness.*

44. Desmond, 38–40, 79–84, 93, 254; MacKinnon, 87; Morris and Morris, chap. 7, "Intelligent Apes"; notes 2, 3, above, this chapter.

45. Joshua Cooper Ramo and Debra Rosenberg, "The Puzzle of Genius," *Newsweek,* June 28, 1993.

46. Fisher, *Anatomy of Love,* 339—note 18; MacKinnon, 87–88.

47. Morris and Morris, 250.

48. Ibid., 225–26.

49. De Waal, *Peacemaking Among Primates,* 195–200.

50. Ibid., 200; Heltne and Marquardt, 162–63.

51. MacKinnon, 90.

52. Ibid., 90.

53. Morris and Morris, 252–54.

54. Corballis, 120–21; Desmond, 86–87.

55. Corballis, index under Language, Apes—communication in; Desmond, chap. 2, "Do Ape Words Make Sense?", chap. 4, "A Metalinguistic Leap," chap. 5, "Stretching Between Worlds," esp. 116–17.

56. Desmond, 80–83.

57. Corballis, 70–71; Fisher, *Anatomy of Love,* 230–31; Sagan, *The Dragons of Eden,* 197.

58. Miller, *The Drama of the Gifted Child,* viii–ix, 30, 32, 84, 101.

59. Miller, ibid., 32ff., index under Mother.

60. Stevens, *Archetypes: A Natural History of the Self,* 87–88.

61. Morris, *Intimate Behavior,* 19–20, 101; Morris and Morris, 214.

62. Human beings turn literal behaviors into metaphors on a regular basis. See, for example, Storr, *Human Destructiveness,* 13.

63. Goodall, *In the Shadow of Man,* 147–48; Miller, *The Drama of the Gifted Child,* en toto; Morris, *Intimate Behavior,* 19–20. Also, compare J. F. Eisenberg and Dillon, 148ff.

64. Morris and Morris, 215–18.

65. Barbara Dockar-Drysdale, *The Provision of Primary Experience: Winnicottian Work With Children,* 46–47.

66. Goodall, *In the Shadow of Man,* 168.

67. Ibid., 167.

68. Ibid., 167, 181–82; Goodall, *Through a Window,* 35–38.

69. Goodall, *In the Shadow of Man,* 167, 181–82; Goodall, *Through a Window,* 35–38.

70. Miller, *The Drama of the Gifted Child,* 16, 32, 35; Moore and Gillette, *The King Within,* 129, 152, 301n.

71. Goodall, *In the Shadow of Man,* 148–50, 157; Goodall, *Through a Window,* 33–36, index under Passion.

72. This is the basic contract set up between a narcissistically wounded mother and her child. The mother forces the child to fill her narcissistic needs and uses shame (ultimately, the threat of psychological if not physical death) as her weapon of enforcement. See Miller, *The Dream of the Gifted Child,* en toto, but esp. 34 ff.

73. Goodall, *In the Shadow of Man,* 236–37; Goodall, *Through a Window,* 122. Also see note 71, above, this chapter.

74. Hendrix, *Getting the Love You Want,* 18–19.

75. Alice Miller herself has been criticized by some radical feminists for putting so much responsibility on mothers for the future psychological well-being of their children. Miller, *The Drama of the Gifted Child,* 4.

76. Miller, ibid., 108–13.

77. Though of course there is much overlapping in the way chimpanzee mothers relate to their sons and daughters—because of their different devel-

opmental tasks—mothers implement different strategies in their child-rearing practices, depending on the gender of their children. Basically, they *teach* their daughters (who learn mostly through imitation) and they *encourage* and *fight for* their sons (who need their backing, but who *learn* from the adult *males*). Goodall, *In the Shadow of Man,* 177–80; Goodall, *Through a Window,* chap. 4, "Mothers and Daughters," chap. 11, "Sons and Mothers." See esp. 112, 116, 118.

78. Goodall, *Through a Window,* 112, 118.

79. Goodall, *In the Shadow of Man,* 176–79, chap. 10, "The Hierarchy"; Goodall, *Through a Window,* chap. 5, "Figan's Rise," chap. 6, "Power," esp. 116–17.

80. Goodall, *Through a Window,* 112–14, 116–17.

81. Ibid., index under Prof.

82. Heltne and Marquardt, 19. Eugene Linden, "Bonobos: Chimpanzees with a Difference." *National Geographic.* It seems to be true that even in the relatively matriarchal society of bonobos alpha males still exercise many dominance functions, thus conceivably enhancing their mother's status, or at least helping to maintain it. At the same time, when a powerful female falls in status she takes her alpha male son with her.

83. Heltne and Marquardt, 191–92; Goodall, *In the Shadow of Man,* 174–75; Goodall, *Through a Window,* 116–17.

84. Heltne and Marquardt, 191.

85. Ibid., 190.

86. Ibid., 191.

87. Human females tend to do this too, but it has different consequences: it may not affect their sexual interest in their partners, whereas when *men* re-create the mother-son pattern in their adult relationships it does affect their sexual interest in their partners. For a general discussion of this manifestation of the "repetition compulsion," see Miller, *The Drama of the Gifted Child;* Miller, *For Your Own Good;* Hendrix, *Getting the Love You Want,* en toto, but esp. part 1, "The Unconscious Marriage."

88. Diamond, chap. 5, "How We Pick Our Mates and Sex Partners," esp. 106–08; Eisenberg and Dillon, chap. 4, "Attraction, Affiliation, and Attachment"; Herant Katchadourian, 64–75.

89. Campbell, 126ff.; Diamond, 101–2; Hendrix, *Getting the Love You Want,* esp. part 1, "The Unconscious Marriage."

90. Diamond, 106–7.

91. Ibid., 107.

92. Fisher, *Anatomy of Love,* 26–27, 132, 251–52; Goodall, *In the Shadow of Man,* 182–83; Katchadourian, 70–75.

93. See note 36, chap. 5, the present work.

94. I've counseled a number of couples in which it was clear that this was the case. We can all evoke latent qualities in each other, and *shape* each other's reaction patterns and characteristic ways of feeling and behaving.

Jung talked about "psychic infection" in a somewhat different context. I think the concept applies here as well, in that we can "infect" each other with the dynamics of our childhood dramas and thereby change the whole tenor of our present relationships. We all know, on a less intense basis, that we often feel different about ourselves and behave in different ways depending upon what particular friends or associates we're with at any given time.

95. Glantz and Pearce, 170 ff.

96. The virtually universal occurrence of the Coolidge Effect and the "madonna/whore" split in men from many different cultures, and the way they both tend to propel men either to philander and/or to leave their present partners, argues for a biological basis for both of them, and suggests that they're both manifestations of the power of the male mixed reproductive strategy.

97. Farai Chideya, "Endangered Family," Newsweek, August 30, 1993; Guy Corneau, Absent Fathers, Lost Sons: The Search for Masculine Identity, en toto, but esp. 31–34; Nancy Gibbs, "Bringing Up Father"; Gilmore, 26–29; Gilbert Herdt, Rituals of Manhood: Male Initiation in Papua New Guinea, index under Gender Identity, Initiations—rites of, Mother/Son Separation; Michele Ingrassia, et al., "Daughters of Murphy Brown"; Moore and Gillette, King, Warrior, Magician, Lover: Rediscovering the Archetypes of the Mature Masculine, chap. 1, "The Crisis in Masculine Ritual Process"; Moore and Gillette, The King Within, 143–46. For a related discussion of the ongoing power of chimpanzee mothers over the lives of their adult sons and the need for these sons to break with their mothers, see De Waal, Peacemaking Among Primates, 42; Goodall, In the Shadow of Man, 177; Goodall, Through a Window, 42, 118.

98. Gibbs, op. cit. See also Linda Schierse Leonard, The Wounded Woman: Healing the Father-Daughter Relationship.

99. De Waal, Peacemaking Among Primates, 39–43, index under Reconciliation.

100. In fact, Harville Hendrix says this is the primary ingredient in mate selection in the first place. He also advocates staying with our partners, almost no matter what, until both of us have healed our own and each other's wounds. Actually, he advocates staying together forever. While agreeing with him that this is an important factor in mate selection, especially for people who have not been able to work through many of their childhood wounds, I part company with Hendrix's mandating of lifelong, sexually exclusive partnership—no matter what. Human beings are extremely complex creatures, with many needs other than having their childhood needs met. Compare Stevens, Archetypes, 145.

101. Hendrix, Keeping the Love You Find, 211–12, 213–14.

102. From my perspective, and from my experience with counselees and in my own life, the more completely a man or woman has worked through his or her childhood wounds, and the patterns of dysfunctional relationship "im-

printed" upon him or her in the context of early childhood, the freer that man or woman is to find a partner who may more fully meet his or her adult needs. See Hendrix, op. cit., part 1: "The Unconscious Marriage."

9. Shame: Our Ultimate Weapon

1. Shame deepens every "negative" feeling because it carries with it the primate instinctual fear of the hostile gaze (in traditional cultures, the "evil eye"). The *internalized* hostile gaze can paralyze us even when there is no one else around. Ultimately, the intention of the "evil eye"—both external and internalized—is our death. See notes 3, 4, 5, 10, 12, 20, 34, below, this chapter.

2. Robert Karen, "Shame."

3. Lewis, chap. 2, "Our Emotional Lives," esp. 30–31.

4. Heltne and Marquardt, 156; MacKinnon, 114; Morris, *The Naked Ape*, 161, 163ff.; Sagan and Druyan, 295–96; S. Zuckerman, *The Social Life of Monkeys and Apes*, 294.

5. De Waal, *Peacemaking Among Primates*, 254; De Waal, *Chimpanzee Politics*, 113; Goodall, *In the Shadow of Man*, 266; Lewis, 22–25; Morris and Morris, 238; Morris, *The Naked Ape*, 163 ff.; Sagan and Druyan, 189; note 4, above, this chapter.

6. Campbell, 285–307 (Fox uses the terms "guilt" and "conscious" and "unconscious inhibitions."); John Bradshaw, *Healing the Shame That Binds You*, 5–9; Karen, op. cit.; Lewis, 34–35.

7. Karen, op. cit.

8. In a sense, our aggressive self-affirmation is what biologists call "proximate causation," or a proximate mechanism, whose goal it is to effect an ultimate goal. From the biological point of view, the ultimate goal ("ultimate cause") of our aggressive self-affirmation, like everything else about us, is our genetic survival through our offspring. This ultimate cause demands our aggressive self-affirmation on the deep instinctual level in order to implement our reproductive strategies, whose purpose *is* to achieve our practical immortality.

9. "Playing dead" is a form of flight reaction when literal flight is not possible: the turtle withdraws into its shell, the opossum goes limp, and so on. We human beings can do the same thing on a psychological level, allowing ourselves to become listless and depressed. See Lorenz, 95ff.; Morris, *The Naked Ape*, chap. 5, "Fighting," esp. 153ff.

10. Beahrs, index under Persecutor Alter-personalities.

11. The idea here is that the *real* suffering is too painful to bear, so the person creates a symbolic or false pain that can be consciously endured. See Jolande Jacobi, *Complex, Archetype, Symbol in the Psychology of C. G. Jung*, 18; Joel Kovel, *A Complete Guide to Therapy: From Psychoanalysis to Behavior Modification*, 19 ff., 139 ff.; Miller, *The Drama of the Gifted Child*, en toto.

12. The most destructive impulses behind moralistic aggression come from the woundedness—ultimately, the original shaming—of the aggressor,

whatever their stated motives may be. Campbell, 285–307; De Waal, *Peace-making Among Primates*, 3, 69; Miller, *For Your Own Good*, "Poisonous Pedagogy"; Storr, *Human Aggression*, 102. Also see William Allman, "The Evolution of Aggression," *U.S. News and World Report*, May 11, 1992.

13. Eric Hoffer, *The True Believer*, en toto, but esp. part 1, "The Appeal of Mass Movements," and part 2, "The Potential Converts"; Miller, *For Your Own Good*, "Adolf Hitler's Childhood: From Hidden to Manifest Horror"; Andrew Bard Schmookler, *Out of Weakness: Healing the Wounds That Drive Us to War*, 101–4, 135, 277–81.

14. Moralistic aggression (as expressed both within the community and vis-à-vis "outsiders") seems to be rooted in an animal's need for territory and status—in other words, resources, ultimately the resources he or she needs to achieve his/her practical immortality. The intensity and direction of the expression of territoriality and status-seeking at the expense of others depend, in part, on which other animals are regarded as "kin." The definition of kin, certainly in human beings, can be expanded or contracted—expanded to include *all* human beings or contracted to include only one's immediate family. Animals, like human beings on a much more complex ideational level, include as kin those who look and behave like themselves. See Ardrey, *The Territorial Imperative*, en toto; Ardrey, *African Genesis*, en toto; Ardrey, *The Social Contract*, en toto; Eisenberg and Dillon, 196; Lorenz, chap. 3, "What Aggression Is Good For."

15. De Waal, *Peacemaking Among Primates*, 42—Compare his observations of this behavior in monkeys, 15, 234–35; De Waal, *Chimpanzee Politics*, 56–59, 138–39, 186; De Waal, *Peacemaking Among Primates*, 212.

16. De Waal, *Peacemaking Among Primates*, 15; Goodall, *In the Shadow of Man*, 266; Goodall, *Through a Window*, 56, 60; MacKinnon, 79. Compare Zuckerman's observations of monkey behavior, Zuckerman, 228–29.

17. This may include the aggression-neutralizing act of crouching and "presenting." See notes 4, 5, 16, above, this chapter.

18. We can deduce this from the fact that nonhuman primate mothers have enormous power to shape the emotional lives of their children—both male and female (see note 14, chap. 2, notes 49, 50, 85, 87, 88, 101, chap. 3, note 77, chap. 6, note 11, chap. 7, see, in the present work, notes 4, 59, 60, 63, 64, 66, 67, 68, 69, 70, 71, 73, 75, 77, 81, 83, 84, 85, 86, 88, 90, chap. 8; notes 12, 15, above, this chapter) and from the fact that both men and women today are seeking "mother" in their intimate relationships with each other (see notes 87, 88, 94, 100, 101, 102, chap. 8). See also note 25, below, this chapter, notes 4, 5, below, chap. 11, the present work.

19. Campbell, 287–309.

20. Ardrey, *The Social Contract*, 141 ff., 166–70; John Hurrell Crook, "Sexual Selection, Dimorphism, and Social Organization in the Primates," 254–72, in Campbell; and Robin Fox, "Alliance and Constraint: Sexual Selection in the Evolution of Human Kinship Systems," 288–91, 300, 305, 308, in Campbell; Sigmund Freud, *Totem and Taboo*, 141.

21. Herbert May and Bruce Metzger, *The Oxford Annotated Bible: Revised Standard Edition,* Matthew 22:13.

22. Freud, *Totem and Taboo,* 141–61.

23. I realize this is a rather dramatic statement; but when I analyze the various myths of God's wrath (His aggression) and his "copulation," albeit "spiritual," with Mary (His sexuality) in light of Freud's psychological interpretations, this is what I come up with.

24. Stevens, *The Two-Million-Year-Old Self,* frontispiece quote from C. G. Jung's *Psychological Reflections.*

25. Miller, *The Drama of the Gifted Child,* 9–14, index under Introject, Introjection; notes 59, 60, 63, 64, chap. 8, note 18, above, this chapter.

26. De Waal, *Peacemaking Among Primates,* 200–206; Goodall, *In the Shadow of Man,* index under Sexual Behavior—in adolescent females, in adolescent males, in infants, in juvenile males.

27. Miller, *The Drama of the Gifted Child,* 14–26.

28. Hendrix, *Getting the Love You Want,* 19–21, 26–27.

29. Ibid., chap. 3, "Your Imago," esp. 30–38.

30. Carl Jung believed this drive came from the primordially whole Self. Alice Miller and others talk about the need to rediscover the "true self" in order to live "an authentic emotional life" (Miller, *The Drama of the Gifted Child,* 14ff.). This is the same core part of each of us, and the same process, that I'm describing as the "primate self" and the drive to reclaim our "authentic" instincts for aggressive self-affirmation and sexuality. I mean "authentic" not just in terms of our authentic *personal* selves but also in the sense of our authentic species-characteristic primate patterns for expressing these basic drives.

31. Christensen, 148; Lewis, 11; Miller, *For Your Own Good,* en toto, but esp. "Adolf Hitler's Childhood: From Hidden to Manifest Horror," and "Jurgen Bartsch: A Life Seen in Retrospect"; Stevens, *The Two-Million-Year-Old Self,* 119; Storr, *Human Destructiveness,* chap. 1, "The Nature of Human Aggression," esp. 10–17; Symons, 283.

32. Although the concept that some women may experience "penis envy" is currently out of fashion, I think there may be some truth to the idea that both genders may envy characteristic aptitudes and abilities of the other. For example, some women who seek to enter the male hierarchies of political and economic power, may be unconsciously envious—not necessarily of the literal penis—but of phallic power, focused ambition, and drive—all "masculine" qualities to a significant degree: the male brain—even in the limbic system—is wired for these things, and fueled by testosterone (and other androgens?), which most men have between ten and twenty times more of than most women. At the same time, theorists and social commentators have also observed that *men* have built civilizations out of their sense of deficit vis-à-vis women's capacity to bear children. While I don't want to push the concepts of "penis envy" or "womb envy" very far, I do think such now officially discarded notions may yet prove fruitful in illuminating some dark corners of

our instinctually based gender conflicts. The fact is, as an enormous amount of current research has shown, men and women *do* have overlapping but different abilities and enthusiasms—as genders. See Fisher, *Anatomy of Love*, chap. 10, "Why Can't A Man Be More Like A Woman?", chap. 11, "Women, Men, and Power"; Lewis, 11; Moir and Jessel, en toto, but esp. chap. 6, "The Ability Gap." Pool, *Eve's Rib* en toto.

33. Individual male counselees as well as many of the men in my groups, and in workshops around the country, frequently report feeling intimidated—and hence, shamed—by women's generally greater language skills, including their capacity to express what they feel, especially in the heat of an argument. Many of these men say they feel "outgunned," "castrated," "like a little boy," and so on. See Fisher, *Anatomy of Love*, 191–92; Moir and Jessel, 17, 42–47, 65, 84–85.

34. A case in point is the practice of genocide, which has a long history. The Nazis publicly *shamed* Jews, Gypsies, and others before they implemented the *final* shame—genetic death. See Miller, *For Your Own Good*, "The War of Annihilation Against the Self." Also see Lewis, 2. The wish to die is an expression of the internalized parents' wish to kill us.

10. Reclaiming Our Primal Roots

1. Fisher, *Anatomy of Love*, 104–7, 325—note 18, 326—note 38.

2. Storr, *Human Aggression*, 76.

3. Bradshaw, *Healing the Shame That Binds You*, 54.

4. The ultimate effect of the unisex idea is to eliminate heterosexual sexuality. Whatever the stated goals—for example, ending "discrimination" and achieving equality through *sameness* (actually pseudomasculinity and pseudofemininity), the effect of eliminating the biopsychological differences between the genders is to reduce the "cues" that stimulate us to mate with each other. I think the underlying motivation for this whole program—to the extent that it is something more than an attempt on the part of homosexual men and women, and/or truly androgynous persons to impose their ways of being sexual on the heterosexual majority—is an *anti-sexual* attitude. An anti-sexual attitude has deep roots in our historical past. Asceticism, distrust of the animal passions, and exhortations to achieve celibacy (through self-mutilation and/or "spiritual" discipline) have expressed themselves as a major theme in a number of spiritual traditions, especially Christianity. In its most virulent form, the attack against the "carnal man" manifested in the Christian tradition as the Manichaean heresy. However, this Christian ascetic bent seems to be derived, in part, from older Gnostic and Hellenistic sources, which, in turn, may have Persian Zoroastrian antecedents. Whatever the historical progression of this sexual pathology in human affairs, its ultimate source is shaming. The reason for this shaming of our sexuality is twofold: (1) the primate males' need to control the sexual impulses of the younger males in order to keep the choicest females for themselves; and (2) both genders' attempts to minimize the threat they feel about the other's different and mixed reproductive strategies.

5. Beahrs, index under Multiple Personality.

6. Ibid., en toto, but note esp. 36.

7. Wallace, en toto, but see esp. chap. 2, "The Reproductive Imperative— Or Why You *Really* Love Your Children"; Wilson, en toto, but see esp. chap. 1, "Dilemma," chap. 2, "Heredity," chap. 3, "Development."

11. Reclaiming Our Aggression and Sexuality

1. Aaron R. Kipnis, *Knights Without Armor: A Practical Guide for Men in Quest of Masculine Soul,* 194; Marsha Sinetar, *Do What You Love, the Money Will Follow: Discovering Your Right Livelihood,* 9.

2. Diamond, 184; Fisher, *Anatomy of Love,* 267.

3. ABC *World News Tonight* with Peter Jennings, March 18, 1994.

4. Hendrix, *Getting the Love You Want,* 14–16; Lee and Martin, index under Merger Transference.

5. Hendrix, op. cit., chap. 3, "Your Imago."

6. See note 28, chap. 9, the present work.

7. Eugene Gendlin, *Focusing,* chap. 11, "The Listening Manual"; Hendrix, op. cit., 121–24, 216–17, 227–28.

8. Shere Hite, *The Hite Report* (female sexuality), masturbation, esp. 73–75. In addition to Shere Hite's statistical survey and her respondents' testimonies, it seems to me that common sense also argues for this understanding of the role of masturbation in freeing ourselves to experience sexual pleasure without shame.

9. That is, sex manuals and broader-scope "how-to" books. One of my favorites is Elaine Kittredge's *Masterpiece Sex: The Art of Sexual Discovery.*

10. In the present work, see note 14, chap. 2; notes 85, 87, 88, chap. 3; note 3, chap. 4; notes 17, 31, 46, 64, 65, chap. 6; notes 5, 6, 7, 8, 9, 11, 15, 36, 40, 49, chap. 7; notes 69, 78, 87, 98, chap. 8; notes 18, 31, chap. 9; notes 2, 3, chap. 10.

11. Glantz and Pearce, 166–70.

12. Hendrix, op. cit., 130–31.

13. One of my colleagues, Don Jones, has adapted Edward Edinger's discussion (and diagram) about the gradual separation of the ego from the Self (within a Jungian framework) to help couples picture the direction in which their relationships often need to grow.

Whether our relationships express a parent-child, a lost or disowned self, or a cross-gender type of "merger fantasy" pattern (diagrams *a, b,* and *c,* respectively), the goal is for both partners to pull out of the merger and stand on their own two feet (diagram *d*). Then their appropriate male and female energies create a charged psychological space around them. Instead of "containing" each other—as a parent would a child, or as in projection (when we make the other person carry elements of our own unlived lives and unexpressed male or female characteristics)—the energy field we set up between us and around us contains us both. *The relationship* is the container—not the people involved.

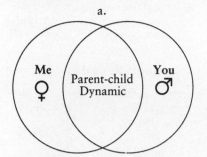

a.

Parent-Child Merger

We're both each other's parents *and* children.

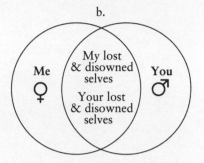

b.

Lost and Disowned Self Merger

I make you "contain" and carry my lost and disowned selves, and you make me carry yours.

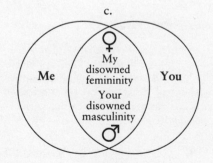

c.

Cross-Gender Merger

I'll live out your masculine characteristics, and you live out my feminine qualities

d.

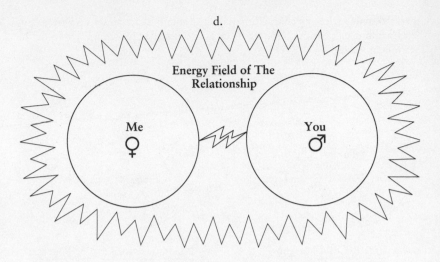

The Adult Relationship

I am me, and you are you. We each express our own masculine and feminine energies. The *relationship* is our container. We can still play parent-child roles with each other to some extent (an inevitable ingredient in lasting love), but this is no longer the major focus of our relationship. We have achieved a "passionate partnership."

12. "Resolving" Our Hot Issues

1. In the early industrialized economies, men left the "campsite" to "hunt" in the factories and at the office, while women stayed at the "campsite" to raise the children, often with the help of "auntie" systems. They also "gathered" as they shopped for food and other necessities, and cooked the meals. These patterns are not the product of our agricultural/civilization era, but, rather, our hunter-gatherer savanna time. See notes 69, 70, 71, 72, chap. 3, note 3, chap. 6.

2. Moir and Jessel, 141 ff.; in the present work, notes 44, 45, 49, 63, 68, 69, chap. 3; note 6, chap. 4; 79, 80, chap. 6.

3. Gibbs, "Bringing Up Father," *Time*, June 28, 1993.

4. See notes 69, 70, 71, 72, chap. 3; note 3, chap. 6.

5. See, in the present work, notes 10, 37, 40, 57, 58, 59, 80, chap. 3; notes 19, 20, chap. 9.

6. Moir and Jessel write: "Better . . . to welcome and exploit the complementary differences between men and women. Women should contribute their specific female gifts rather than waste their energies in the pursuit of a sort of surrogate masculinity. . . . The best argument for the acknowledgment of differences is that doing so would probably make us happier. The appreci-

ation, for instance, that sex has different origins, motives, and significance in the context of the male and female brains, that marriage is profoundly unnatural to the biology of the male, might make us better and more considerate husbands and wives. The understanding that the roles of father and mother are not interchangeable might make us better parents." (Moir and Jessel, 7.) I concur.

7. See notes 47, 48, chap. 3, the present work.
8. See note 46, chap. 3, the present work.
9. Fisher, *Anatomy of Love,* 156–60, 303–4.
10. Farai Chideya et al., "Endangered Family." They quote an African proverb: "It takes a whole village to raise a child." Also, see Fisher, *Anatomy of Love,* 156–60, and Stevens, *The Two-Million-Year-Old Self,* 119.

SELECTED BIBLIOGRAPHY

✳

Adler, Jerry. "Sex in the Snoring '90s." *Newsweek,* April 26, 1993.

Akins, Faren R., Gillian S. Mace, John W. Hubbard, Dianna L. Akins. *Behavioral Development of Nonhuman Primates: An Abstracted Bibliography.* New York: IFI/Plenum, Plenum Publishing Corp., 1980.

Allman, William F. "The Evolution of Aggression." *U.S. News and World Report,* May 11, 1992.

————. "The Mating Game." *U.S. News and World Report,* July 19, 1993.

American Museum of Natural History, eds. *The First Humans: Human Origins and History to 10,000 B.C.* San Francisco: HarperSanFrancisco, 1993.

Ansbacher, Heinz L., and Rowena R. Ansbacher. *The Individual Psychology of Alfred Adler.* New York: Harper & Row, 1964.

Ardrey, Robert. *African Genesis: A Personal Investigation into the Animal Origins and Nature of Man.* New York: Dell, 1963.

————. *The Hunting Hypothesis: A Personal Conclusion Concerning the Evolutionary Nature of Man.* New York: Atheneum, 1976.

————. *The Social Contract: A Personal Inquiry into the Evolutionary Sources of Order and Disorder.* New York: Dell, 1971.

Ashbrook, James B. *The Human Mind and the Mind of God: The Theological Promise in Brain Research.* New York: University Press of America, 1984.

Baber, Asa. *Naked at Gender Gap: A Man's View of the War Between the Sexes.* Secaucus, N.J.: Carol Publishing Group, A Birch Lane Press Book, 1992.

Barbach, Lonnie. *For Each Other: Sharing Sexual Intimacy.* New York: Penguin Books, U.S.A., 1984.

Baxandall, Lee, ed. *Sex-Pol: Essays, 1929–1934: Wilhelm Reich.* New York: Vintage Books, 1972.

* Beahrs, John O. *Unity and Multiplicity: Multilevel Consciousness of Self in Hypnosis, Psychiatric Disorder, and Mental Health.* New York: Brunner/Mazel, 1982.

Begley, Sharon. "The Flintstone Diagnosis." *Newsweek,* May 10, 1993.

————. "The Puzzle of Genius." *Newsweek,* June 28, 1993.

Bettelheim, Bruno. *Freud and Man's Soul.* New York: Alfred A. Knopf, 1983.

*—Active Imagination Dialogue Techniques
+—Active Listening Techniques
x—Inner Child Workbooks

Bourne, Geoffrey H. *Primate Odyssey*. New York: G. P. Putnam's Sons, 1974.

Bowlby, John. *Separation: Anxiety and Anger*. New York: Basic Books, 1973.

x Bradshaw, John. *Bradshaw On: Healing the Shame That Binds You*. Deerfield Beach, Fla., Health Communications, Inc., 1988.

*x ———. *Homecoming: Reclaiming and Championing Your Inner Child*. New York: Bantam Books, 1990.

Branden, Nathaniel, and Devers Branden. *What Love Asks of Us: Solutions to the Challenge of Making Love Work*. New York: Bantam Books, 1983.

Brown, Norman O. *Life Against Death: The Psychoanalytical Meaning of History*. Middletown, Conn.: Wesleyan University Press, 1959.

Brownmiller, Susan. *Against Our Will: Men, Women and Rape*. New York: Fawcett Columbine, 1975; Ballantine, 1993.

Buck, William. *Ramayana*. Berkeley: University of California Press, 1976.

Campbell, Bernard, ed. *Sexual Selection and the Descent of Man 1871–1971*. Chicago: Aldine Publishing Company, 1972.

Capra, Fritjof. *The Tao of Physics*. Boulder: Shambhala, 1975.

Cavalli-Sforza, L. Luca, Paolo Menozzi and Alberto Piazza. *The History and Geography of Human Genes*. Princeton: Princeton University Press, 1994.

Cheney, Dorothy L., and Robert M. Seyfarth. *How Monkeys See the World*. Chicago: University of Chicago Press, 1990.

Chideya, Farai et al. "Endangered Family." *Newsweek*, August 30, 1993.

Christensen, F. M. *Pornography: The Other Side*. New York: Praeger, 1990.

Corballis, Michael C. *The Lopsided Ape: Evolution of the Generative Mind*. New York: Oxford University Press, 1991.

Corneau, Guy. *Absent Fathers, Lost Sons: The Search for Masculine Identity*. Boston: Shambhala, 1991.

Crook, John Hurrell. "Sexual Selection, Dimorphism, and Social Organization in the Primates." In *Sexual Selection and the Descent of Man: 1871–1971*. Chicago: Aldine Publishing Company, 1972.

Desmond, Adrian J. *The Ape's Reflection*. New York: The Dial Press/James Wade, 1979.

De Rougemont, Denis. *Love in the Western World*. New York: Harper/Colophon Books, 1974.

Diamond, Jared. *The Third Chimpanzee: The Evolution and Future of the Human Animal*. New York: HarperCollins, 1992.

De Waal, Frans. *Chimpanzee Politics: Power and Sex Among Apes*. New York: Harper & Row, 1982.

———. *Peacemaking Among Primates*. Cambridge: Harvard University Press, 1989.

Dibell, Ansen. *Plot: How to Build Short Stories and Novels, etc.* Cincinnati: Writer's Digest Books, 1988.

Dockar-Drysdale, Barbara. *The Provision of Primary Experience: Winnicottian Work With Children*. Northdale, N.J.: J. Aronson, 1991.

Edinger, Edward F. *Ego and Archetype: Individuation and the Religious Function of the Psyche*. Baltimore: Penguin Books, 1972.

Edmonds, Patricia. "Pope's Hit List of Sins Is Likely to Fall on Deaf Ears." *USA Today,* October 1, 1993.

Eisenberg, J. F., and Wilton S. Dillon, eds. *Man and Beast: Comparative Social Behavior.* Washington, D.C.: Smithsonian Institution Press, 1971.

Eisler, Riane. *The Chalice and the Blade: Our History, Our Future.* San Francisco: Harper & Row, 1987.

Erikson, Erik H. *Insight and Responsibility: Lectures on the Ethical Implications of Psychoanalytic Insight.* New York: W. W. Norton, 1964.

Fagan, Brian M. *The Journey from Eden: The Peopling of Our World.* New York: Thames & Hudson, 1990.

Falk, Kathryn. *How to Write a Romance and Get It Published.* New York: New American Library/Signet, 1990.

Farrell, Warren. "Glass Cellars, Death Professions, and Slightly Different Options." *Transitions: Newsletter of the National Coalition of Free Men,* January/February 1994.

———. *The Myth of Male Power.* New York: Simon & Schuster, 1993.

———. *Why Men Are the Way They Are.* New York: McGraw-Hill, 1986; Berkley Books, 1988.

Fast, Irene. *Gender Identity: A Differentiation Model.* Hillsdale, N.J.: Analytic Press, 1984.

Fisher, Helen. *Anatomy of Love: The Natural History of Monogamy, Adultery, and Divorce.* New York: W. W. Norton, 1992.

———. *The Sex Contract: The Evolution of Human Behavior.* New York: Quill, 1983.

Fossey, Dian. *Gorillas in the Mist.* Boston: Houghton Mifflin, 1983.

Freud, Sigmund. *The Interpretation of Dreams.* Translated by James Strachey. New York: Avon Books, First Discus Printing, March, 1965.

———. *Totem and Taboo.* Translated by James Strachey. New York: W. W. Norton, Copyright, 1950, by Routledge and Kegan Paul Ltd.

Gates, David. "White Male Paranoia." *Newsweek,* March 29, 1993.

+* Gendlin, Eugene T. *Focusing.* New York: Everest House, 1978.

Gibbs, Nancy R. "Bringing Up Father." *Time,* June 28, 1993.

———. "How Should We Teach Our Children About Sex?" *Time,* May 24, 1993.

Gillette, Douglas. "Manhood in the Making" (book review). *Wingspan: Journal of the Male Spirit,* April–June 1991.

———. "Men and Intimacy." *Wingspan: Journal of the Male Spirit,* summer 1990.

Gilmore, David D. *Manhood in the Making: Cultural Concepts of Masculinity.* New Haven: Yale University Press, 1990.

Glantz, Kalman, and John K. Pearce. *Exiles From Eden: Psychotherapy From an Evolutionary Perspective.* New York: W. W. Norton, 1989.

Glasser, William. *Reality Therapy: A New Approach to Psychiatry.* New York: Harper & Row/Perennial Library, 1965.

Gleick, James. *Chaos: Making a New Science.* New York: Viking Penguin, 1987.

Goldin, Judah, ed. and trans. *The Living Talmud.* New York: New American Library, 1957.

Goodall, Jane. *In the Shadow of Man.* Boston: Houghton Mifflin, 1971.

———. *Through a Window: My Thirty Years with the Chimpanzees of Gombe.* Boston: Houghton Mifflin, 1990.

Gorman, Christine. "Sizing Up the Sexes." *Time,* January 20, 1992.

———. "The Race to Map Our Genes." *Time,* February 8, 1993.

+ Gray, John. *Men Are From Mars, Women Are From Venus: A Practical Guide for Improving Communication and Getting What You Want in Your Relationships.* New York: HarperCollins, 1992.

Gray, Paul. "What Is Love?" *Time,* February 15, 1993.

Halpern, Howard. *How to Break Your Addiction to a Person.* New York: Bantam Books, published in association with McGraw-Hill, 1983.

* Hannah, Barbara. *Encounters with the Soul: Active Imagination as Developed by C. G. Jung.* Boston: Sigo Press, 1981.

Harley, Willard F., Jr. *His Needs, Her Needs: Building an Affair-proof Marriage.* Tarrytown, N.Y.: Fleming H. Revell, 1986.

Harth, Erich. *Windows on the Mind: Reflections on the Physical Basis of Consciousness.* New York: Quill, 1983.

Heltne, Paul G., and Linda A. Marquardt, eds. *Understanding Chimpanzees.* Cambridge: Harvard University Press in cooperation with The Chicago Academy of Sciences, 1989.

+x Hendrix, Harville. *Getting the Love You Want: A Guide for Couples.* New York: Henry Holt, 1988.

*+x ———. *Keeping the Love You Find: A Guide for Singles.* New York: a division of Simon & Schuster/Pocket Books, 1992.

Herdt, Gilbert H. *Rituals of Manhood: Male Initiation in Papua New Guinea.* Berkeley: University of California Press, 1982.

Hite, Shere. *The Hite Report: A Nationwide Study of Female Sexuality.* New York: Dell, 1976, 1981.

Hoffer, Eric. *The True Believer: Thoughts on the Nature of Mass Movements.* New York: Harper & Row/Perennial Library, 1951.

Hornblower, Margot. "The Skin Trade." *Time,* June 21, 1993.

Horney, Karen. *Feminine Psychology.* Edited by Harold Kelman. New York: W. W. Norton/The Norton Library, 1967.

———. *The Neurotic Personality of Our Time.* New York: W. W. Norton, 1937.

Howells, William. *Getting Here: The Story of Human Evolution.* Washington, D.C.: The Compass Press, 1993.

Ingrassia, Michele et al. "Daughters of Murphy Brown." *Newsweek,* August 2, 1993.

Jacobi, Jolande. *Complex, Archetype, Symbol in the Psychology of C. G. Jung.* Princeton: Princeton University Press, Bollingen Series 57, 1959.

x Janov, Arthur. *The Primal Scream: Primal Therapy: The Cure for Neurosis.* New York: G. P. Putnam's Sons, 1970.

Jaynes, Julian. *The Origin of Consciousness in the Breakdown of the Bicameral Mind.* Boston: Houghton Mifflin, 1976.

Jung, Carl. *Aion: Researches into the Phenomenology of the Self.* Translated by R. F. C. Hull. Bollingen Series 20: The Collected Works of C. G. Jung, vol. 9, part 2. Princeton: Princeton University Press, 1959.

Karen, Robert. "Shame." *The Atlantic Monthly,* February 1992.

Katchadourian, Herant A., ed. *Human Sexuality: A Comparative Developmental Perspective.* Berkeley: University of California Press, 1979.

Kingma, Daphne Rose. *The Men We Never Knew: Women's Role in the Evolution of Gender.* Berkeley: Conari Press, 1993.

Kipnis, Aaron. *Knights Without Armor: A Practical Guide for Men in Quest of Masculine Soul.* Los Angeles: Jeremy P. Tarcher, 1991.

Kipnis, Aaron, and Elizabeth Herron. *Gender War, Gender Peace: The Quest for Love and Justice Between Women and Men.* New York: William Morrow, 1994.

Kittredge, Elaine. *Masterpiece Sex: The Art of Sexual Discovery.* Chicago: Optext, 1994.

Klein, Richard G. *The Human Career: Human Biological and Cultural Origins.* Chicago: University of Chicago Press, 1989.

Korn, Noel, and Fred Thompson, eds. *Human Evolution: Readings in Physical Anthropology.* New York: Holt, Rinehart & Winston, 1967.

Kovel, Joel. *A Complete Guide to Therapy: From Psychoanalysis to Behavior Modification.* New York: Pantheon Books, 1976.

Kramer, Jonathan, and Diane Dunaway. *Why Men Don't Get Enough Sex and Women Don't Get Enough Love.* New York: Simon & Schuster/Pocket Books, 1991.

Lauzun, Gérard. *Sigmund Freud: The Man and His Theories.* Paris: Savants de Monde Entier, Pierre Seghers, 1962.

Lee, Ronald R., and J. Colby Martin. *Psychotherapy After Kohut: A Textbook of Self Psychology.* Hillsdale, N.J.: The Analytic Press, 1991.

Lemonick, Michael D. "How Man Began." *Time,* March 14, 1994.

x Leonard, Linda Schierse. *The Wounded Woman: Healing the Father-Daughter Relationship.* Boulder: Shambhala, 1983.

Levy, Robert I. *Tahitians: Mind and Experience in the Society Islands.* Chicago: University of Chicago Press, 1973.

Lewis, Michael. *Shame: The Exposed Self.* New York: Macmillan/The Free Press, 1992.

Linden, Eugene. "Bonobos: Chimpanzees with a Difference." *National Geographic* 181, no. 3 (March 1992).

Lorenz, Konrad. *On Aggression.* San Diego: Harcourt Brace Jovanovich.

Loye, David. *The Sphinx and the Rainbow: Brain, Mind, and Future Vision.* Boulder: Shambhala/New Science Library, 1983.

Maccoby, Eleanor Emmons, and Carol Nagy Jacklin. *The Psychology of Sex Differences,* vol. 1/Text. Stanford, Calif.: Stanford University Press, 1974.
———. *The Psychology of Sex Differences,* vol. 2/Annotated Bibliography. Stanford, Calif.: Stanford University Press, 1974.
MacKinnon, John. *The Ape Within Us.* New York: Holt, Rinehart & Winston, 1978.
MacLean, Paul D. *The Triune Brain in Evolution: Role in Paleocerebral Functions.* New York: Plenum Press, 1990.
McNeely, R. L., and Gloria Robinson-Simpson. "The Truth About Domestic Violence." *Social Work,* November-December 1987.
Marcuse, Herbert. *Eros and Civilization: A Philosophical Inquiry into Freud.* Boston: Beacon Press, 1955.
May, Herbert G., and Bruce M. Metzger. *The Oxford Annotated Bible: The Holy Bible,* Revised Standard Version. New York: Oxford University Press, 1962.
May, Rollo. *Love and Will.* New York: W. W. Norton, 1969.
x Miller, Alice. *The Drama of the Gifted Child: How Narcissistic Parents Form and Deform the Emotional Lives of Their Talented Children.* New York: Basic Books, 1981. Originally published in German as *Das Drama des Begabten Kindes.* Frankfurt am Main: Suhrkamp, 1979.
x ———. *For Your Own Good: Hidden Cruelty in Child-Rearing and the Roots of Violence.* New York: Farrar Straus & Giroux, 1984. Originally published in German as *Am Anfang war Erziehung.* Frankfurt am Main: Suhrkamp, 1980.
x ———. *Thou Shalt Not Be Aware: Society's Betrayal of the Child.* New York: Farrar Straus & Giroux, 1984. Originally published in German as *Du sollst nicht merken.* Frankfurt am Main: Suhrkamp, 1981.
Millon, Theodore. *Disorders of Personality: DSM-III: Axis II.* New York: John Wiley, 1981.
Moir, Anne, and David Jessel. *Brain Sex: The Real Difference Between Men and Women.* New York: Carol Publishing Group/A Lyle Stuart Book, 1991.
* Moore, Robert, and Douglas Gillette. *The King Within: Accessing the King in the Male Psyche.* New York: William Morrow, 1992.
* ———. *The Warrior Within: Accessing the Knight in the Male Psyche.* New York: William Morrow, 1992.
* ———. *The Magician Within: Accessing the Shaman in the Male Psyche.* New York: William Morrow, 1993.
* ———. *The Lover Within: Accessing the Lover in the Male Psyche.* New York: William Morrow, 1993.
———. *King, Warrior, Magician, Lover: Rediscovering the Archetypes of the Mature Masculine.* San Francisco: HarperSanFrancisco, 1990.
Morgan, Elaine. *The Descent of Woman.* New York: Stein & Day, 1972.
Morris, Desmond. *Intimate Behavior.* New York: Random House, 1971.

————. *The Naked Ape: A Zoologist's Study of the Human Animal.* New York: McGraw-Hill, 1967.

Morris, Ramona, and Desmond Morris. *Men and Apes.* New York: A Bantam Book/published in association with McGraw-Hill, 1968.

Myers, David G. *The Pursuit of Happiness.* New York: William Morrow, 1992.

New York Times News Service. "Sperm Cells May Detect the Scent of Fertile Egg." *Chicago Tribune,* February 2, 1992.

Nimmons, David. "Sex and the Brain," *Discover,* March 1994.

Nygren, Anders. *Agape and Eros.* Translated from Swedish by Philip S. Watson. Philadelphia: Westminster Press, 1953.

Oatley, Keith. *Brain Mechanisms and Mind.* New York: Dutton, 1972.

O'Conner, Dagmar. *How to Make Love to the Same Person for the Rest of Your Life.* New York: Bantam Books, published in association with Doubleday, 1986.

————. *How to Put the Love Back into Making Love.* New York: Bantam Books, published in association with Doubleday, 1990.

Peck, M. Scott. *The Road Less Traveled: A New Psychology of Love, Traditional Values and Spiritual Growth.* New York: Simon & Schuster/A Touchstone Book, 1978.

Pedersen, Loren E. *Dark Hearts: The Unconscious Forces That Shape Men's Lives.* Boston: Shambhala, 1991.

Penney, Alexandra. *How to Make Love to a Man.* New York: Dell, 1981.

Peterson, Dale, and Jane Goodall. *Visions of Caliban: On Chimpanzees and People.* Boston: Houghton Mifflin, 1993.

Pianka, Phyllis Taylor. *How to Write Romances.* Cincinnati: Writer's Digest Books, 1988.

Pool, Robert. *Eve's Rib: The Biological Roots of Sex Differences.* New York: Crown Publishers, Inc., 1994.

Prochiantz, Alain. *How the Brain Evolved.* New York: McGraw-Hill. Originally published in French as *La Construction du cerveau,* Paris: Hachette, 1989.

Ramo, Joshua Cooper and Debra Rosenberg. "The Puzzle of Genius," *Newsweek,* June 28, 1993.

Rasmussen, D. Tab, ed. *The Origin and Evolution of Humans and Humanness.* Boston: Jones & Bartlett, 1993.

Reichel-Dolmatoff, Gerardo. *Amazonian Cosmos: The Sexual and Religious Symbolism of the Tukano Indians.* Chicago: University of Chicago Press, 1971.

Reik, Theodor. *Of Love and Lust: On the Psychoanalysis of Romantic and Sexual Emotions.* New York: Jason Aronson, 1974.

Restak, Richard M. *The Brain.* Toronto: Bantam Books, 1984.

Rosellini, Lynn. "Sexual Desire." *U.S. News and World Report,* July 6, 1992.

Rosenberg, Debra et al. "Sexual Correctness: Has It Gone Too Far?" *Newsweek,* October 25, 1993.

Roszak, Betty, and Theodore Roszak, eds. *Masculine/Feminine: Readings in Sexual Mythology and the Liberation of Women.* New York: Harper & Row/Harper Colophon Books, 1969.

Rubin, Lillian B. *Intimate Strangers: Men and Women Together.* New York: Harper & Row/Perennial Library, 1983.

Russell, Robert Jay. *The Lemur's Legacy: The Evolution of Power, Sex, and Love.* New York: G. P. Putnam's Sons, A Jeremy P. Tarcher/Putnam Book, 1993.

Sagan, Carl. *The Dragons of Eden: Speculations on the Evolution of Human Intelligence.* New York: Ballantine Books, 1978.

Sagan, Carl, and Ann Druyan. *Shadows of Forgotten Ancestors: A Search for Who We Are.* New York: Random House, 1992.

Schenk, Roy U. *Thoughts of Dr. Schenk on Sex and Gender.* Madison: Bioenergetic Press, 1991.

Schmookler, Andrew Bard. *Out of Weakness: Healing the Wounds That Drive Us to War.* Toronto: Bantam Books, 1988.

Shainess, Natalie. *Sweet Suffering: Woman as Victim.* New York: Simon & Schuster/Pocket Books, 1984.

Shapiro, David. *Neurotic Styles.* New York: Basic Books, 1965.

Sheler, Jeffrey L., Joanne M. Schraf, and Gary Cohen. "The Gospel on Sex." *U.S. News and World Report,* June 10, 1991.

Sills, Judith. *A Fine Romance: The Passage of Courtship from Meeting to Marriage.* New York: Ballantine Books, published in association with St. Martin's Press, 1987.

Sinetar, Marsha. *Do What You Love, the Money Will Follow: Discovering Your Right Livelihood.* New York: Dell, 1987.

Singer, Dorothy G., and Tracey A. Revenson. *A Piaget Primer: How a Child Thinks.* New York: New American Library, 1978.

Springer, Sally P., and Georg Deutsch. *Left Brain, Right Brain.* New York: W. H. Freeman, 1989.

Stevens, Anthony. *Archetypes: A Natural History of the Self.* New York: Quill, 1983.

———. *The Roots of War: A Jungian Perspective.* New York: Paragon House, 1989.

———. *The Two-Million-Year-Old Self.* College Station: Texas A&M University Press, 1993.

Storr, Anthony. *Human Aggression.* New York: Bantam Books, 1970.

———. *Human Destructiveness.* New York: Grove Weidenfeld, 1991.

———. *The Integrity of the Personality.* New York: Ballantine Books. Originally published in Great Britain by William Heinemann Medical Books Ltd. in 1960.

Sullivan, Barbara. "The Victim Trap." *Chicago Tribune,* October 14, 1993.

Symons, Donald. *The Evolution of Human Sexuality.* New York: Oxford University Press, 1979.

+ Tannen, Deborah. *You Just Don't Understand: Women and Men in Conversation.* New York: William Morrow, 1990.

Tavris, Carol. *The Mismeasure of Woman: Why Women Are Not the Better Sex, the Inferior Sex, or the Opposite Sex.* New York: Simon & Schuster, 1992.

Tinbergen, Nikolaas. *The Study of Instinct.* New York: Clarendon Press, 1989.

Toufexis, Anastasia. "Seeking the Roots of Violence." *Time,* April 19, 1993.

Trinkaus, Erik, and Pat Shipman. *The Neandertals: Changing the Image of Mankind.* New York: Alfred A. Knopf, 1993.

Viscott, David. *How to Live With Another Person.* New York: Simon & Schuster, Pocket Books, 1974.

Von Franz, Marie-Louise. *Projection and Re-collection in Jungian Psychology: Reflections of the Soul.* La Salle, Ill.: Open Court, 1980. Originally published as *Spiegelungen der Seele: Projektion und innere Sammlung,* Kreuz Verlag, Stuttgart, 1978.

Wallace, Robert A. *The Genesis Factor.* New York: William Morrow, in association with Publisher's Inc., 1979.

Webster, Hutton. *Primitive Secret Societies.* New York: Macmillan, 1932.

Wilson, Edward O. *On Human Nature.* Cambridge: Harvard University Press, 1978.

Wolf, Ernest S. *Treating the Self: Elements of Clinical Self-Psychology.* New York: The Guilford Press, 1988.

Woodward, Kenneth L. "The Sins of the Fathers." *Newsweek,* July 12, 1993.

Zuckerman, S. *The Social Life of Monkeys and Apes.* 2d ed. London: Routledge and Kegan Paul, 1932.

INDEX

✳

ABOUT THE AUTHOR

✻

Douglas Gillette, M.A., M.Div., is a graduate of the University of Chicago and Chicago Theological Seminary. He has built community organizations, counseled predelinquent and delinquent teens, served as a pastor in several local churches of the United Church of Christ, and been a leader in the men's movement. He is the coauthor of a five-book series on male psychology, including the best-selling *King, Warrior, Magician, Lover.* He is the cofounder of EarthMen Resources and The Institute for World Spirituality, a not-for-profit organization which facilitates cooperative ventures between the world's religions. He is a counselor in private practice working with individual men and women, couples, and several men's support/therapy groups. He is an internationally known lecturer and workshop leader in the fields of men's issues and gender reconciliation. He has lived in the Near East and traveled widely in Latin America, where he has studied the interface between traditional and modern cultures in the context of gender relations and spirituality. He is also an artist and has shown his paintings widely in Chicago and New York. He currently resides in Chicago.